THEORIES OF MYTH

From Ancient Israel and Greece
to Freud, Jung, Campbell,
and Lévi-Strauss

Series Editor

ROBERT A. SEGAL

University of Lancaster

A GARLAND SERIES

SERIES CONTENTS

VOLUME

4

LITERARY
CRITICISM
AND MYTH

Edited with introductions by

ROBERT A. SEGAL

University of Lancaster

GARLAND PUBLISHING, INC.
New York & London
1996

Library of Congress Cataloging-in-Publication Data

Literary criticism and myth / edited with introductions by Robert A.
Segal.
    p. cm. — (Theories of myth ; 4)
    Includes bibliographical references.
    ISBN 0-8153-2258-5 (alk. paper)
    1. Myth in literature. 2. Criticism.   I. Segal, Robert Alan.
II. Series.
PN56.M94L57   1996
809'.915—dc20
                       95-36269
                       CIP

Printed on acid-free, 250-year-life paper
Manufactured in the United States of America

CONTENTS

SERIES INTRODUCTION

The modern study of myth is already more than a hundred years old and is the work of many disciplines. This six-volume collection of 113 essays brings together both classic and contemporary analyses of myth from the disciplines that have contributed most to its study: psychology, anthropology, folklore, philosophy, religious studies, and literature. Because myth has been analyzed for so long by specialists in so many fields, knowledge of the range of sources and access to them are difficult to secure. The present collection provides a comprehensive and systematic selection of the most important writings on myth.

All of the essays in this collection are theoretical. All are concerned with myth per se, not with a single myth or set of myths. Many of the essays make explicit claims about myth generally. Others use individual myths to make or to test those claims. Most of the essayists are proponents of the theories they employ. Some are critics.

By no means has each of the disciplines considered here developed a single, unified theory of myth. Multiple, competing theories have arisen within disciplines as well as across them. The leading theories from each discipline are represented in the collection.

Theories of myth are never theories of myth alone. Myth always falls under a larger rubric such as the mind, culture, knowledge, religion, ritual, symbolism, and narrative. The rubric reflects the discipline from which the theory is derived. For example, psychological theories see myth as an expression of the mind. Anthropological theories view myth as an instance of culture. Literary theories regard myth as a variety of narrative. Within a discipline, theories differ about the nature of myth because they differ about the nature of the rubric involved. At the same time, theorists qualify as theorists of myth only when they single out myth for the application of the larger rubric. Writings that completely subsume myth under its larger rubric—discussing only religion or symbolism, for example—fail to qualify as writings on myth.

Theories of myth purport to answer one or more of the fundamental questions about myth: what is its origin, what is its function, what is its subject matter? Theories differ, first, in the answers they give to these questions. For most theorists, myth originates and functions to satisfy a need, but that need can be for anything—for example, for food, information, hope, or God. The need can be on the part of individuals or on the part of the community. Similarly, the subject matter, or referent, of myth can be anything. It can be the literal, apparent subject matter—for example, gods or the physical world—or a symbolic one—for example, human beings or society.

Theories differ even more basically in the questions they seek to answer. Few theories claim to answer all three of the major questions about myth. Some theories focus on the origin of myth, others on the function, still others on the subject matter. The answer a theory gives to one question doubtless shapes the answer it gives to another, but most theories concentrate on only one or two of the questions. Writings that merely describe or categorize myths fail to qualify as theories, as do writings that are skeptical of any universal claims about myths.

Still more basically, theories differ in the definition of myth. By some definitions myth can be a sheer belief or conviction—for example, the American "myth" of the frontier or of the self-made man. By other definitions myth must be a story. By some definitions the agents in a story can be humans or even animals. By others the agents must be either gods or extraordinary humans such as heroes. Theories employ definitions that reflect the disciplines from which they come. For example, theories from literature assume myth to be a story. Theories from religious studies assume the agents in myth to be gods or other superhuman figures.

Theorizing about myth is as old as the Presocratics. But only since the development of the social sciences in the last half of the nineteenth century has the theorizing become scientific. Some social scientific theories may find counterparts in earlier ones (see Burton Feldman and Robert D. Richardson's introduction to *The Rise of Modern Mythology* [Bloomington: Indiana University Press, 1972]), but social scientific theorizing still differs in kind from earlier theorizing. Where earlier theorizing was largely speculative and philosophical in nature, social scientific theorizing is far more empirical. The anthropologist John Beattie best sums up the differences, which apply to all of the social sciences and to the study of more than myth:

Thus it was the reports of eighteenth- and nineteenth-century missionaries and travellers in Africa, North America, the Pacific and elsewhere that provided the raw material upon which the first anthropological works, written in the second half of the last century, were based. Before then, of course, there had been plenty of conjecturing about human institutions and their origins; to say nothing of earlier times, in the eighteenth century Hume, Adam Smith and Ferguson in Britain, and Montesquieu, Condorcet and others on the Continent, had written about primitive institutions. But although their speculations were often brilliant, these thinkers were not empirical scientists; their conclusions were not based on any kind of evidence which could be tested; rather, they were for the most part implicit in their own cultures. They were really philosophers and historians of Europe, not anthropologists. (*Other Cultures* [New York: Free Press, 1964], 5–6)

By no means do all of the theories represented in this collection come from the social sciences. But even theories from philosophy, religious studies, and literature reflect strongly the impact of these fields.

The first four volumes in this collection are organized by disciplines. The selections in each volume typify the nature of the theorizing in the discipline. By far the most influential psychological theories of myth have been Freudian and Jungian. Anthropological theories have proved both more numerous and more disparate, with no one theory dominating the field. Folklorists have been particularly concerned with distinguishing myth from other verbal genres. Many theories of myth from philosophy and especially from religious studies grow out of attempts to decipher the classics and the Bible. Literary critics have understandably been preoccupied with both the similarities and the differences between myth and literature.

The final two volumes of the collection are grouped by theories rather than by disciplines. While the number of essays written on any major theory would readily fill a volume, the number written on the myth-ritualist theory and more recently on structuralism has been so large as to necessitate individual volumes about them. The burgeoning of writing on these theories stems in part from the array of disciplines that have adopted the theories. The myth-ritualist theory originated in the fields of classics and biblical studies but soon spread to the study of myth everywhere and, even more, to the study of secular literature. As a theory of myth, structuralism began in anthropology but has since been incorporated by many other fields.

Space does not permit inclusion in this collection of any essays that survey the field of theories of myth. Some useful surveys in

English are the following:

Campbell, Joseph. "The Historical Development of Mythology," *Daedalus* 88 (Spring 1959): 234–54.

Cohen, Percy S. "Theories of Myth," *Man*, n.s., 4 (September 1969): 337–53.

Dorson, Richard M. "Theories of Myth and the Folklorist," *Daedalus* 88 (Spring 1959): 280–90.

———. "Current Folklore Theories," *Current Anthropology* 4 (February 1963): 93–112.

Eliade, Mircea. "Myth," *Encyclopaedia Britannica*, 14th ed. (1970), vol. 15, 1132–40.

———. "Myth in the Nineteenth and Twentieth Centuries," in *Dictionary of the History of Ideas*, ed. Philip P. Wiener (New York: Scribner, 1973–74), vol. 3, 307–18.

Farnell, L. R. "The Value and the Methods of Mythologic Study," *Proceedings of the British Academy* (1919–20): 37–51.

Fischer, J. L. "The Sociopsychological Analysis of Folktales," *Current Anthropology* 4 (June 1963): 235–73, 292–95.

Georges, Robert A. "Prologue" to *Studies on Mythology*, ed. Georges (Homewood, IL: Dorsey, 1968), 1–14.

Halpern, Ben. "'Myth' and 'Ideology' in Modern Usage," *History and Theory* 1 (1961): 129–49.

Herskovits, Melville J. and Frances S. *Dahomean Narrative* (Evanston, IL: Northwestern University Press, 1958), 80–122.

Kaines, J. "The Interpretation of Mythology," *Anthropologia* 1 (1873–75): 465–75.

Kluckhohn, Clyde. "Recurrent Themes in Myths and Mythmaking," *Daedalus* 88 (Spring 1959): 268–79.

Larson, Gerald James. "Introduction: The Study of Mythology and Comparative Mythology," in *Myth in Indo-European Antiquity*, ed. Larson (Berkeley: University of California Press, 1974), 1–16.

MacIntyre, Alasdair. "Myth," *Encyclopedia of Philosophy* (1968), vol. 5, 434–37.

Maranda, Elli Köngäs. "Five Interpretations of a Melanesian Myth," *Journal of American Folklore* 86 (January-March 1973): 3–13.

Patterson, John L. "Mythology and Its Interpretation," *Poet Lore* 37 (Winter 1926): 607–15.

Puhvel, Jaan. *Comparative Mythology* (Baltimore: Johns Hopkins University Press, 1987), 7–20.

Reinach, Solomon. "The Growth of Mythological Study," *Quarterly Review* 215 (October 1911): 423–41.

Rogerson, J. W. "Slippery Words: V. Myth," *Expository Times* 90 (October 1978): 10–14.

Segal, Robert A. "In Defense of Mythology: The History of Modern Theories of Myth," *Annals of Scholarship* 1 (Winter 1980): 3–49.

Simon, Ulrich. "A Key to All Mythologies?" *Church Quarterly Review* 117 (1956): 251–61.

INTRODUCTION

The relationship between myth and literature is the central issue for the essays in this volume. Some of the essays emphasize the similarities between myth and literature; others stress the differences. The origin of literature out of myth, the appropriation of myth by literature, and the transformation of myth by literature are among the topics considered. Some of the essays apply to literature theories of myth from psychology, anthropology, folklore, and religious studies. Other essays criticize either the applicability of those theories to literature or the theories themselves. A few essays introduce additional factors like history in evaluating the nexus between myth and literature.

Literary critics are particularly attentive to the plot of myth. Myth for them is above all a story, whatever its subject. How myth tells its story, not just what the meaning of the story is, is their special concern.

Literary Criticism and Myth

CULTURAL ANTHROPOLOGY AND CONTEMPORARY LITERARY CRITICISM*

HASKELL M. BLOCK

Roger Fry put the matter somewhat delicately when he wrote, "we have the possibility of infinitely diverse reactions to a work of art." The variety of principles and methods in contemporary literary criticism is perhaps not infinite, but we hear very little said about criticism as a common discipline following fixed and immutable laws. Over the gate to our critics' Paradise one may read "FAY CE QUE VOULDRAS," freely translated as "Anything Goes!" We have not method but methods, for criticism today is considered as limitless, as all embracing, as art itself. Long ago Alexander Pope could equate "Those Rules of old discovered, not devis'd" with "Nature," but we have since left off talking about "the critic's laws." To be sure, the subject-matter of criticism may be works of art, but the critic's principles and methods are more likely to be derived from history and biography, sociology and psychology, science and religion, philosophy and philology, and much besides. I say nothing of permutations and combinations, but it should not shock us when T. S. Eliot declares that even Shakespeare's laundry bills should not be too casually dismissed, "in the possibility that some genius will appear who will know of a use to which to put them."[1] I do not share Mr. Eliot's optimism, but it is at least understandable. The expansion of the boundaries of art, the attempt by writers to enlarge the magnitude of their work, to pack more and more into the printed page, has been accompanied by a parallel development in literary criticism. Today our critic is a would-be *uomo universale*, aiming at the total interpretation of the work of art and employing whatever means may serve to provide illumination.

The role of cultural anthropology in contemporary literary criticism is of special significance, not merely because of the ways in which critical values have been affected, but because anthropology provides an index to many of the preoccupations of the great creative thinkers of our time. The literary critic ought not to be thought of as a bleak and huddled figure in a darkened room, perpetually whispering to himself. He cannot help being moved by the stir and jostling of ideas around him, by attempts in every area of experience to interpret and evaluate human activity. Thus it is important for the critic to know that investigations into the thought and action of so-called primitive peoples have shed not a little light on their descendants, that myth and ritual are not exclusively pre-historic phenomena. Out of an understanding of human behavior in times past we have come to know a good deal more about ourselves. And new interpretations of customs and beliefs have led to new ways of looking at literature. One has only to glance at an issue of any of our leading critical journals to see how boldly anthropological concepts and techniques have in-

* Presented at the annual meeting of the American Society for Aesthetics at the State University of Iowa, Iowa City, Iowa, November 9, 1951.

[1] T. S. Eliot, "The Function of Criticism," *Selected Essays*, Faber and Faber, London, 1934, p. 33.

2

vaded literary criticism. I said invaded, not engulfed, for "Literature tills its crops in many fields," and our literary anthropologists are not strong enough to rule the land. But they have made headway to this extent, that with innumerable critics, committed or not to any particular point of view, the use of anthropological methods has come to be taken for granted.

The way in which this development took place has been explored in some detail by Messrs. Chase, Hyman, Frye, and others, and I have neither the time nor the desire to retrace well worn paths in so brief a survey.[2] Vico, Herder, Renan and Nietzsche have all been honored as progenitors. For my part, I find Renan's notion of philology as "la science des produits de l'esprit humain" particularly applicable to present-day critical trends. Renan conceived of philology as the vast synthesizing discipline, to embrace not only history, poetry, and philosophy, but also primitive mythology, ancient cults, comparative religion, and the ways in which all these subjects constitute part of the heritage of mankind.[3] It may have been easy to make grandiose prophecies in 1848, but it is clear, I think, that since then, for good or ill, literary study has come at least part of the way toward fulfilling Renan's expectations. In the twentieth century the work of the so-called Cambridge School of Classical Anthropology has been especially influential. The meticulous and fascinating investigations of Sir James Frazer into almost every area of primitive rite were followed by the studies of Jane Harrison, F. M. Cornford, A. B. Cook, and Gilbert Murray, all applying the findings of comparative anthropology to the origins of Greek drama.[4] These scholars showed conclusively that Greek drama developed out of ancient ritual and that expressions of ritual are preserved in the structure, characterization, theme, and even incidental details of many of the Greek plays which have come down to us. Nor has Frazer's influence been limited to the study of Hellenic literature. As early as 1903 Sir Edmund Chambers demonstrated the enormous relevance of *The Golden Bough* in helping us to understand medieval English drama. Jessie Weston's researches, culminating in *From Ritual to Romance* (1920), applied Frazer's methods to the legend of the Grail. More recently, in the same tradition, we have had Lord Raglan's provocative inquiry into the supposed historicity of heroic narrative (*The Hero*, 1936) and Miss E. M. Butler's investigation of patterns of heroic legend (*The Myth of the Magus*, 1948). All of this work has had fruitful implications, not only for anthropology and the social studies, but for much of the literary criticism of our time.

Now I am well aware that we cannot identify cultural anthropology with

[2] For background material I am especially indebted to Richard Chase, *Quest for Myth*, Louisiana State University Press, Baton Rouge, 1949; Stanley Edgar Hyman, *The Armed Vision*, Knopf, N. Y., 1948, pp. 134–137; Northrop Frye, "The Archetypes of Literature," *Kenyon Review*, XIII (1951), 92–110; Francis Fergusson, *The Idea of a Theater*, Princeton University Press, Princeton, 1949, pp. 26ff.; and Helen Adolf, "The Essence and Origin of Tragedy," *The Journal of Aesthetics and Art Criticism*, X (1951), 112–125.

[3] Ernest Renan, *L'Avenir de la Science, Œuvres complètes*, t. III, Calmann-Lévy, Paris, 1949, pp. 839ff.

[4] For bibliographical details, see Stanley Edgar Hyman, "Myth, Ritual and Nonsense," *Kenyon Review*, XI (1949), 463–466. Cf. John J. Gross, "After Frazer: the Ritualistic Approach to Myth," *The Western Humanities Review*, V (1951), 379–391.

the Cambridge school. All the same, I do not share the attitude of our American anthropologists who decry Frazer's separation of ritual from its cultural constituent and sneer at literary critics who take his work seriously.[5] Of course, I know that the present-day anthropologist is not interested in ancient Greek drama or in aught else that smacks of the Classical tradition, and that a trip to Melanesia is held in much greater esteem than an understanding of Frazer's work.[6] What matters for us is not the inadequacy of the assumptions of Frazer and his followers so much as the ways in which their findings have affected literature and literary interpretation. To a large extent, literary critics have been compelled to recognize the value of anthropology in criticism because of the sheer inclusiveness of modern literature. Contemporary writers have cast a wide net indeed, and anyone familiar with the writings of Eliot, Yeats, Joyce, Mann, Lawrence, to list only a few, will understand at once how far reaching the effect of Frazer's work has been. I do not mean that Frazer and his successors have always exerted their influence apart from parallel developments in psychology, language, or social thought, but T. S. Eliot did not understate the case when he said, in 1924, that *The Golden Bough* is a work of no less importance than the writings of Freud and perhaps of greater permanence. Frazer, Eliot declared, "has extended the consciousness of the human mind into as dark and backward an abysm of time as has yet been explored." And Eliot went on to predict that the work of Frazer and other anthropologists "will not fail to have a profound effect upon the literature of the future."[7]

Indeed, by 1924 this effect was already apparent. Two years earlier critics were confounded by the publication of Joyce's *Ulysses* and Eliot's *The Wasteland*. I need not refer you to the notes which, I take it, serve to make Eliot's work the longest poem in the English language. The important point for us is that critical attention perforce was directed to the use of anthropological methods and materials in literature. Eliot himself summarized the new tendency in his review of *Ulysses:* "In using the myth, in manipulating a continuous parallel between contemporaneity and antiquity, Mr. Joyce is pursuing a method which others must pursue after him. They will not be imitators, any more than the scientist who uses the discoveries of an Einstein in pursuing his own, independent, further investigations. It is simply a way of controlling, of ordering, of giving a shape and a significance to the immense panorama of futility and anarchy which is contemporary history."[8] Whether or not we agree with Eliot's emphasis on the Homeric sub-structure in *Ulysses*, his horo-

[5] For this controversy, see Stanley Edgar Hyman, "Dissent on a Dictionary," *Kenyon Review*, XII (1950), 721–730 and "Communications: Mr. Hyman and the Dictionary," *loc. cit.*, XIII (1951), 315–322.

[6] It is interesting to note that the Macmillan Company has recently announced a complete reissue of Frazer's *The Golden Bough* for the spring of 1952.

[7] T. S. Eliot, "A prediction in regard to three English authors . . .," *Vanity Fair*, XXI (February, 1924), 29. Also see T. S. Eliot, "Euripides and Gilbert Murray," *Arts and Letters*, III (1920), 38.

[8] T. S. Eliot, "Ulysses, Order, and Myth," in S. Givens (ed.), *James Joyce: Two Decades of Criticism*, Vanguard Press, N. Y., 1948, p. 201. This essay first appeared in *The Dial* for November, 1923.

scope was remarkably accurate. Let me call to your attention D. H. Lawrence's *Plumed Serpent* (1926). Now I would not "kidnap" Lawrence for the anthropologists. It is true that he pondered long over Tylor, Frazer, Harrison, and Murray, but as W. Y. Tindall points out, he also drew generously on Freud and Frobenius, Blavatsky and Pryse, Oriental mysticism and Aztec mythology, all part of his effort to bring life into direct contact with the elemental powers of the universe.[9] This qualification made, there can be no doubt of the value of anthropology in helping us understand Lawrence's novel. Quetzalcoatl, the plumed serpent, is very much in the traditional pattern of Frazer's dying god, whose death is the fount of human spiritual revival. There are other examples of the conscious use of anthropology in literature. Among the richest are Edith Sitwell's *Gold Coast Customs* (1929), a savage celebration of the primitive and at the same time, a denunciation of contemporary civilization, clearly part of the "Wasteland" tradition, and Joyce's *Finnegans Wake* (1939), a mythical representation of the universal processes of creation, death, and re-creation. The researches of Campbell and others have but partially disclosed the remarkable extent to which Joyce pillaged the folklore, mythology, and fable of all cultures.[10] The road to an understanding of such writers as Eliot, Lawrence, Sitwell, or Joyce is a tortuous one, but of this much we can be sure: in many instances, the structure of their works, the development of primary themes, the significance of even the most recondite allusions, all can be clarified to some extent by anthropological reference. Such analysis, let me add, often goes far beyond source hunting or philological exegesis; it drives at the central meaning of the work.

What, we may now ask, are the dominant assumptions of this new critical approach? First of all, it is almost a commonplace among a respectable number of critics that literature—or indeed any art—cannot be understood and appreciated as an isolated expression, cannot be limited to the working out of a pattern within the framework imposed by an art form, but rather must be viewed as part of the totality of human experience. Thus the simple separation of form and content, intrinsic and extrinsic values, or the like, falls away even for purposes of analysis—indeed, especially for such purposes. From this central assumption it is but one further step to assert that literature is part of a social situation and that literary works must be approached primarily as modes of collective belief and action. Myth and ritual, then, become essential qualities of literary expression. We have already seen examples which would support such a view, but the anthropological critic is not concerned merely with deliberate reference. Let me quote Colin Still, whose interpretation of mythical patterns in *The Tempest* is of seminal importance for modern practical criti-

[9] W. Y. Tindall, *D. H. Lawrence and Susan His Cow*, Columbia University Press, N. Y., 1939, pp. 97–98.

[10] Cf. Joseph Campbell, "Finnegan the Wake," in S. Givens, *op. cit.*, pp. 368–389; William Troy, "Notes on Finnegans Wake," *ibid.*, pp. 302–318. C. L. Barber makes some brief but stimulating comments on ritual patterns in *Ulysses* in "The Saturnalian Pattern in Shakespeare's Comedy," *The Sewanee Review*, LIX (1951), 611, n. 9. Also see Edward Duncan, "Unsubstantial Father: A Study of the *Hamlet* Symbolism in Joyce's *Ulysses*," *University of Toronto Quarterly*, XIX (1950), 139.

5

cism: " . . . genuine imaginative art is the result of an unconscious process whereby expression is given to perceptions of which the artist may or may not be conscious."[11] Thus we can see that any element or collocation of elements in a work may be considered an expression of recurring symbols basic in human experience, hence common to primitive and modern cultures.[12] It is for this reason that Northrop Frye recently declared that *The Golden Bough* is primarily a study in literary criticism.[13] Through it, Frye would insist, we can arrive at an understanding of the essential patterns—the archetypal images— of human experience, which must necessarily find expression in constant representational symbols.

I have stated the position as concisely as I can, without showing how particular modifications have affected individual practices. The disagreements in anthropology itself between the comparative, historical, and functional schools, the intrusion of Freudian and Jungian terminology, the ink that has been spilt over the relation of myth to ritual, these things need not concern us here.[14] The disputes among anthropologically minded critics should not blind us to the more important fact that they have the same enemies and, within a spacious framework indeed, the same objectives.

In what practical ways has anthropology entered into literary interpretation? Let me begin with a simple illustration: the use of folklore in the elucidation of difficult passages. In the epilogue to *As You Like It* Rosalind declares, somewhat enigmatically for the modern reader: "If it be true that good wine needs no bush, 'tis true that a good play needs no epilogue. Yet to good wine they do use good bushes, and good plays prove the better by the help of good epilogues." The proverb of the wine and the bush refers to the vintner's practice of placing a tuft of ivy on the door of his shop, originally in order to curry favor with the wine god.[15] Similar instances abound in early English literature, and I have no doubt that folklore can do a good deal more than it has in helping us to understand the writings of semi-literate peoples or in illuminating that shadowy no-man's-land between folk tradition and conscious art.[16] Whatever

[11] Colin Still, *The Timeless Theme*, Ivor Nicholson and Watson, London, 1936, p. 7.

[12] Cf. Philip Wheelwright, "Notes on Mythopoeia," *The Sewanee Review*, LIX (1951), 574–592.

[13] Northrop Frye, *op. cit.*, 106. For an excellent illustration of Frye's method, cf. his explanation of catharsis as the imaginative analogue of the sacrifice ritual, in "The Argument of Comedy," *English Institute Essays, 1948*, Columbia University Press, N. Y., 1949, p. 64. Also see "A Conspectus of Dramatic Genres," *Kenyon Review*, XIII (1951), 543–562. These essays are of primary importance in contemporary criticism, not as a flat application of any particular discipline, but as an attempt to systematize all literary interpretation. It is evident that Frye owes a great deal to cultural anthropologists as well as to the psychology of C. G. Jung.

[14] Cf. the Communications of E. W. Voegelin and M. J. Herskovits, in *Kenyon Review*, XIII (1951), 315–320. Also see John J. Gross, *op. cit.*, pp. 379ff.; David Bidney, "The Concept of Myth and the Problem of Psychocultural Evolution," *American Anthropologist*, LII (1950), 16–26.

[15] *As You Like It*, ed. G. L. Kittredge, Ginn and Co., Boston, 1939, p. 189.

[16] See Archer Taylor, "Folklore and the Student of Literature," *The Pacific Spectator*, II (1948), 216–223; Frank Goodwyn, "A Proposed Terminology for Clarifying the Relationship between Folklore and Literature," *Southern Folklore Quarterly*, XIV (1950), 143–149.

objections one may have to Robert Graves' *The White Goddess*, there is no doubt that medieval Welsh and Celtic poetry owe much to primitive representations of "the birth, life, death and resurrection of the God of the Waxing Year."[17] Similarly, the early English Mummers' plays, in celebration of St. George, present vestiges of creation myths and fertility rites: the conqueror of dragon and Turk was also renowned for his ability to cure barrenness among women.[18] It must be admitted, however, that in dealing with early folk drama we are on somewhat shaky ground; even the most careful investigators have had to rely heavily on analogy and conjecture.

I cannot pause to examine the study of anthropological material merely as part of the sources of a work.[19] This is matter for scholarship; the materials of art can come from any area of human experience. More important is the conception of drama as ritual.[20] Here the classical illustration is Sophocles' *Œdipus Rex*,[21] but an equally good example would be Euripides' *Bacchae*, a mythical projection of fertility rite wherein a human sacrifice serves as the source of generative power, of group purification. In *The Bacchae* Pentheus, ruler of Thebes, attempts to observe the worship of Dionysus by spying on the Bacchants from a tree top. They discover him and, maddened with fury, uproot the tree, seize Pentheus, and tear his body to pieces. Bather, Murray, Dodd, and Thomson have shown that even seemingly insignificant details of the action point to the preservation of ancient ceremonial traditions.[22] Like Œdipus, Pentheus is both king and scapegoat, the incarnation of the dying god. The power of ancient ritual is all the more impressive when we realize that in Euripides' day the deeper and more savage practices of Dionysiac worship had long been eliminated.[23]

We are only beginning to understand the importance of ritual in more recent drama. Francis Fergusson's discussion of *Hamlet* in his brilliant *Idea of a Theater* demonstrates convincingly that a primary concern of Shakespeare's play is the welfare of the community, expressed in Hamlet's attempts to purify the state, to destroy the rottenness in Denmark. In this sense, the drama is not purely one of individual introspection. The stages of the development of the action are mirrored constantly in scenes of civic, military, or religious rituals. These ritual scenes, Fergusson declares, are all "ceremonious invocations of the well-being of society, and secular or religious devices for securing it."[24] At the same

[17] Robert Graves, *The White Goddess*, Creative Age Press, N. Y., 1948, p. 10.

[18] E. K. Chambers, *The English Folk-Play*, The Clarendon Press, Oxford, 1933, pp. 170ff.

[19] A representative example is Elizabeth Drew's analysis of "The Wasteland" in *T. S. Eliot: The Design of His Poetry*, Charles Scribner's Sons, N. Y., 1949, pp. 68–90, a study written largely from the viewpoint of Jungian psychology.

[20] Fundamental for this conception is Jane Harrison, *Ancient Art and Ritual*, Henry Holt and Co., N. Y., 1913.

[21] Cf. the illuminating discussion of *Œdipus Rex* in Francis Fergusson, *op. cit.*, pp. 13–41.

[22] A. G. Bather, "The Problem of the Bacchae," *Journal of Hellenic Studies*, XIV (1894), 244–263; Gilbert Murray, *Euripides and His Age*, Henry Holt and Co., N. Y., 1913, pp. 118–119; E. R. Dodd, "Maenadism in the Bacchae," *Harvard Theological Review*, XXXIII (1940), 155–176; George Thomson, *Aeschylus and Athens*, International Publishers, N. Y., 1950, pp. 139–142.

[23] E. R. Dodd, *op. cit.*, p. 168.

[24] Francis Fergusson, *op. cit.*, pp. 114ff.

time, Fergusson points out that *Hamlet* is improvisation as well as rite, and much of the latter part of the play, from the players' scene on, is parody of ritual. One must not press analogies too hard, but it should be clear that Fergusson is insisting that the Elizabethan stage served a communal function resembling that of the theater of Sophocles and that this function adds an important dimension to Shakespeare's dramas. Similarly, in the case of *Macbeth*, it would not be difficult to show that the dénouement represents the purgation of evil and the triumph of the divine cosmic order. The green leaves of the branches of Birnam Wood symbolize the rebirth of the powers of goodness, the re-establishment of the health of the "body politic."[25]

This view of drama as ritual does not deny the presence of conscious art, the role of artistic handling, of individual modification. Euripides and Shakespeare are no less poets for having ordered their material in accordance with ancient ritual, whether they did so deliberately or not, and there is still every reason to inquire why their plays continue to move us as they do. Yet we gain in understanding if we see how the formal elements of drama are at least sometimes arranged in conformity with a traditional rhythm of tragic action. I have no doubt that our insight into Greek and Elizabethan drama has been deepened by the application of anthropological methods.

When we come to the examination of more recent literature we are likely to discover vestiges of ancient ritual rather than direct expressions. Civilization has its price, not the least of which is the extinction of mystery and the impoverishment of wonder. Nietzsche was acutely aware of the rootlessness and isolation of modern man: "And now the myth-less man remains eternally hungering among all the bygones, and digs and grubs for roots, though he have to dig for them even among the remotest antiquities. The stupendous historical exigency of the unsatisfied modern culture, the gathering around one of countless other cultures, the consuming desire for knowledge—what does all this point to, if not to the loss of myth, the loss of the mythical home, the mythical source?"[26] Nietzsche's *Birth of Tragedy* (1872) is above all an attempt to re-establish a living relationship between myth and poetry, and it is this same attempt that animates much of contemporary criticism. For through an awareness of myth we can perhaps recapture the spirit of the now forgotten rites which lent passion and purpose to the most ordinary experiences of our forbearers. An understanding of myth has come to be a central concern of a large body of twentieth century thought.

There is no doubt that Myth is one of the most muddled and abused concepts in our critical vocabulary. It has been defined as a lie, a popular delusion, as mystical fantasy, as primitive science, as a record of historical fact, a symbol of philosophical truth, a reflection of unconscious motivations, indeed, any

[25] Cf. Roy Walker, *The Time Is Free: A Study of Macbeth*, Andrew Dakers, Ltd., London, 1949, pp. 194–195. For the structural significance of ritual in Shakespeare's comedies, see C. L. Barber, *op. cit.*, 593–611.

[26] Friedrich Nietzsche, *The Birth of Tragedy* (tr. Haussmann), T. N. Foulis, Edinburgh, 1910, p. 175.

unconscious assumption.[27] It is all very confusing and the anthropologists can offer little help. Myth has been feasted on for so long by the psychologist and the historian, the sociologist and the literary critic, that the anthropologist can do little more than pick at the bones. It was with much irritation but, I suspect, even more restraint, that Malinowski insisted that myth, if it is to have any meaning at all, cannot be divorced from its social function;[28] and it is no surprise to come across a sociological essay entitled *"Robinson Crusoe as a Myth"* in a quarterly dedicated to literary criticism.[29] Clearly, what matters in such an inquiry is not Defoe's novel but the use which society made of it. Richard Chase and those who agree with him that "Myth is literature" might not accept this notion of the term, but they offer no way out.[30] It is perhaps an important feature of our modern mythomania that its converts are willfully obscure. When any of them sets about defining his terms and clarifying his assumptions, we must be grateful.

We have not yet reached the point where we talk about the myth of the critic—though I do not doubt we will be there shortly—but we hear a good deal about the myth of the artist: Blake's myth, Joyce's myth, Kafka's myth, as though myth somehow existed apart from any social belief or collective function. Worse yet is the gratuitous use of primitive ritual as a source of mythical identification. William Troy is a sensitive reader of modern fiction, yet in his study, "Stendhal: In Quest of Henri Beyle," he tries to convert the author into the ceremonial scapegoat-hero through an easy identification with Julien Sorel.[31] Pressed into such purposes, anthropological analogues can serve only as themes and motifs—*Stoffgeschichte*—and ultimately break down into speculative biography. For further illustration, examine some of the recent critical studies of Melville and you will discover a full catalogue of initiation rites, fertility cults, myths, and ceremonies of every description, all too often finding support only in the mind of the critic.[32] It is especially disquieting to find Stanley Edgar Hyman, who knows as much about the subject of this paper as anyone, declare with aplomb that problems of action and motivation in Conrad's plots can be solved by the application "of such ancient tribal rituals as initiation, fertility, the totemic feast, purification, and expiation ceremonies, the killing of the god-king, etc."[33] Compare Hyman's bewildering picture of

[27] For some of these definitions, consult Robert Heilman, "The Lear World," *English Institute Essays, 1948*, Columbia University Press, N. Y., 1949, pp. 32–33; "Symposium on Myth," *Chimera*, IV (Spring, 1946); Stanley Edgar Hyman, "Myth, Ritual, and Nonsense," *loc. cit.*, 455–475.

[28] B. Malinowski, *Myth in Primitive Psychology*, W. W. Norton, N. Y., 1926, pp. 18–19.

[29] Ian Watt, "Robinson Crusoe as a Myth," *Essays in Criticism*, I (1951), 95–119.

[30] It should be noted that Mr. Chase has altered his position somewhat. Cf. "Myth Revisited," *Partisan Review*, XVII (1950), 885–891, in which he argues that myth is not all literature but a special kind of literature, hence subject to a separate mode of analysis.

[31] William Troy, "Stendhal: In Quest of Henri Beyle," *Partisan Review* IX (1942), 1–22.

[32] Cf. Charles Olson, *Call Me Ishmael*, Reynal and Hitchcock, N. Y., 1947; Richard Chase, *Herman Melville*, Macmillan, N. Y., 1949; Newton Arvin, *Herman Melville*, William Sloane Associates, N. Y., 1950, pp. 182–193.

[33] Stanley Edgar Hyman, "The Critic as Narcissus," *Accent*, VIII (1948), 187–191.

the ideal critic in the final chapter of *The Armed Vision* with this simplified reduction of Conrad's works. Too often, anthropological criticism has substituted the discovery of analogies for the examination of artistic structures. In this way, literature becomes for the critic little more than it is for the anthropologist: an artifact—an index of cultural behavior.

Some critics have gone far enough in their thinking to distinguish between mythical and non-mythical values in literature. Such a distinction does not depend on antique sources, primitive allusions, or the like. When operative as a controlling principle, as part of the organic unity of a work, mythical patterns are at the core of aesthetic experience and cannot be neglected by criticism. I should add at once, however, that to explain such patterns as unconscious metaphors is to abandon all concern with the origin, structure, and function of art.

It should be clear that a good deal of literary anthropology takes no account of the uniqueness of individual works of art, or indeed, of the fact that the value of a work of art transcends its documentary function. The mere presence of anthropological material in a novel, play, or poem does not help us differentiate between masterpieces and drivel. Anthropological methods may convince us that the cow that jumped over the moon was a totem, but they cannot tell us how to distinguish poetry from fact. We may conclude that the use of anthropological concepts can contribute to an enlargement of artistic experience only in combination with an approach grounded in the aesthetic value of a work of art. The critic who feels that in anthropology he has found the key to the interpretation of literature will soon discover the loneliness of a darkened corridor. Apart from any specific conditions which may affect critical judgment, methodology is never enough. No method or combination of methods can mean anything in the hands of those who are insensitive or indifferent to art. These qualifications made, let us welcome the new approach but let us not cease to demand modesty and lucidity, as well as "that glimpse of truth" for which we may have forgotten to ask.

KENNETH BURKE

Myth, Poetry and Philosophy

I.   General nature of combat myth; general nature of difference between problem of origins as viewed folkloristically and as viewed in terms of Poetics.

II.   Main themes of the combat myth—and preparatory account of how the various clauses should be "derived" in terms of Poetics.

III.   How principle of negative is translated into terms of rival temporal purposes; and how "Eros" and "Thanatos" serve as mythic terms for purpose.

IV.   Dialectic of Love and Death, with combat myth as "cause" (*aition*) that serves as sanction for the Order with which it is associated.

V.   Contrast between folkloristic and "entelechial" ways of viewing variations on a theme.

VI.   Different implications in statements that at first glance seem alike.

VII.   Intrinsic tests of combat myth's "perfection" as a story are not identical with its "perfection" as *aition;* thus there are two different sets of questions to be answered.

VIII.   Our very stress upon the "use" of the combat myth now enables us to go back and theoretically prescind this element. Since the combat myth contains the designs of both tragedy and comedy, the problem of these species is introduced.

IX.   Summary: on combat myth, tragedy, and comedy viewed entelechially.

X.   Dialectics of monotheism and polytheism, the "perfection" in which problems of generalization concerning the combat myth would culminate.

I

THOUGH *mythos* originally meant but "word" (being the Homeric equivalent for *logos*), the important consideration for present purposes is that it came to mean a tale, story, fable, a *narrative* form. Such expansion (from a word that meant word to a word that meant a tale composed of many words) is like the step whereby the title of the play *Hamlet* becomes expanded into all the words and simulated actions, characters, and situations of which that play is composed. The title is in effect an "essence." And in the narrative expansion that comprises the drama, the "essence" that is named in the title acquires in effect a kind of "existential definition." It is the relation I had in mind when writing these lines, that are perhaps too "ideological" as judged by current imagistic canons but that at least serve to sum up my point:

Any may we have neither the mania of the One
Nor the delirium of the Many—
But both the Union and the Diversity—
The Title and the manifold details that arise
As that Title is restated
In the narrative of History

Not forgetting that the Title represents the story's Sequence,
And that the Sequence represents the Power entitled.[1]

Here "History" is but a more "cosmic" word for "story," a usage in line with the analogy between books and the "Book of Nature." What we have called the "existential definition" would be the expansion of the title in terms of *poetry;* a discussion of the theoretic principles involved in its construction would be an expansion in terms of *poetics.*

In an essay entitled "The First Three Chapters of Genesis" (still unpublished in its entirety, though the gist of it appeared in *Daedalus,* Autumn 1958), I try to show how the "creation myth" of those opening chapters was a way of propounding "principles of governance," by translation into terms of narrative rather than as they might be formulated in philosophy, metaphysics, or theology. The problem, involving the relation between terms for "logical priority" and terms for "temporal priority," concerns ways of shuttling between the two kinds. In my *Grammar of Motives,* the translation of logical principles into terms of temporal "firsts" is called the "the temporizing of essence"; for when the narrative style makes a statement about essence, it does so in quasi-historical terms (terms referring to the "primordial" or "prehistoric").

While revising my poetics I came upon a recent work of quite stupendous scholarship (*Python, A Study of Delphic Myth and Its Origins,* by Joseph Fontenrose, University of California Press, 1959), concerned with the origins and transformations of what it calls the "combat myth." The investigation is so admirably thorough it even points beyond itself; essentially folkloristic in its approach, it impinges upon problems of poetics. Consider, for instance, this closing paragraph of the book proper:

"So we may look upon the whole combat in all its forms as the conflict between Eros and Thanatos. It is that opposition between life instincts and death instincts that Freud was the first to formulate, albeit tentatively, as the central principle of all living organisms from the beginning; though it was seen dimly and expressed in dramatic or metaphysical terms by poets and philosophers before him. But in life the two kinds of instincts, though opposed, are always mingled. Thus do the fantasies of myth disguise the fundamental truths of the human spirit." (p. 474)

Unfortunately, we cannot stop here and merely appreciate the book's great skill in tracking down "versions" and "variants" of the "combat myth." Instead, we must use it somewhat tendentiously, and even in a supererogatory way. For though the author accomplished a plenty, yet in effect we are asking him to do still more, and to concern himself with a problem that is ours rather than his.

Accordingly, I must admonish that my points of difference with the book do not imply criticisms of it as such. Our reservations derive mainly from the fact that we would use its material for an "ulterior" purpose, making central what the author considers but peripherally, somewhat as a final afterthought: the relation between myth's "fantasies" and "fundamental truths" (a relation which we would further shift into a concern with the difference between myth's narrative modes of statement and what Coleridge would have called the style of the "philosopheme").

Taking as its point of departure the myth of the combat between Apollo and Python, the book inquires into the origins of all such "combat myths" in Greek literature. It seeks for "origins" in the sense of the probable place or places from which the myth spread, the probable ways in which the spreading occurred, the

12

various transformations involved, etc. In the course of its speculating, it outlines two main types of the myth. The later type concerns a struggle between an "older" god and a "new" god, with the new god triumphing and founding a cult; but this is said to be derived from an earlier type, concerning a struggle between dragon and sky god, with the sky god triumphing.

As we shall see, the two types are more complicated than this first statement of their nature would suggest. But for the moment the important thing to note is that, in the course of discussing these types, the author reduces each of them to a paradigm. And as soon as he has done so, he has provided material for speculating on "origins" in a quite different sense. We can now ask about "origins" in the sense of the logic implicit in the forms of these paradigms. The study of the "combat myth's" emergence in history would be "folkloristic" or "anthropological." The study of the motives involved in such paradigms (the principles of the myths' structure as progressive forms having beginning, middle, and end) would belong to Poetics.

Also in the course of his study the author considers another problem of origins. He offers good reasons for doubting that the "combat myths" which are associated with particular cults ordinarily derive from the rituals associated with those same cults, though he grants that there can be considerable "interpenetration" between myth and ritual. By and large, however, he would incline to infer that the "combat myth" begins in legends of struggle that may themselves have developed originally out of men's literal experiences with hunt, war, and the like. And he assumes that the "combat myth" thus arose independently of cults, but was adopted by them because it lent itself particularly well to use as an *aition* for a cult, a mythic explanation for the cult's origins and services. Thus, in its final development, a myth is said to be a traditional story having beginning, middle, and end, and purporting "to tell of the occasion on which some religious institution, a cult or certain of its rites and festivals, had its beginning." (p. 3)

II

The main "themes of the combat myth" are given as follows on pages 9 to 11 (all told, including the sub-divisions, forty-three are listed, though of course no particular version or variant is likely to embody the whole lot):

1) The Enemy was of divine origin.
2) The Enemy had a distinctive habitation.
3) The Enemy had extraordinary appearances and properties.
4) The Enemy was vicious and greedy.
5) The Enemy conspired against heaven.
6) A divine Champion appeared to face him.
7) The Champion fought the Enemy.
8) The Champion nearly lost the battle.
9) The Enemy was finally destroyed, after being outwitted, deceived, or bewitched.
10) The Champion disposed of the Enemy and celebrated his victory. (In connection with this last stage, after being "purified of blood pollution," the Champion "instituted cult, ritual, festival, and built a temple for himself.")

A glance at this list, from the standpoint of Poetics, suggests a problem of "derivation" quite different from an attempt to retrace the myth's probable development and diffusion through history. Consider, for instance, theme 7, which along with 8 concerns the stages of the actual combat. Subdivision 7C is: "The other gods were panicstricken: they appeased the Enemy or fled." Much later in the book, on that subject the author writes: "The gods are afraid and take to flight. ... in this way the champion god's bravery is emphasised." (p. 250) Here obviously, the author is concerned with a kind of "origin" that has nothing to do with the spread of a theme from Mesopotamia, Egypt, or wherever. Clause 7C concerns a function within the story as such, a dramatic device for building up the character of the champion. From the standpoint of Poetics, then, the question becomes: Regardless of where the "combat myth" came from, and how many transformations it may have undergone, to what extent can we derive its form from the logic of that form? In other words: To what extent does the paradigm give us, not some "first" story from which the many versions and variants were derived, but rather a "perfect" form towards which such a story would "naturally" gravitate? And could we so define its nature that such an "entelechy" would seem natural? In brief, Poetics would ask: In order to be a "perfect combat myth," what form "ought" the story have?

Scattered through the book there are numerous observations that can be used to this end. Here is one, for instance, with regard to the earlier of the two myth types: "The hero-gods of the displaced peoples tended to become cast in the role of dragon or brigand." (p. 424) One can readily see why such a development could take place without the need of a previous example to borrow from. For a variant of this response takes place after every successful revolution, which views the losers from the standpoint of the winners. We do not need a prototype to account for it, but can explain it dialectically by the fact that, when one orientation is replaced by another, the first is "naturally" viewed in terms of its successor.

However, when noting that such adjectives as "insolent" (hybristês), "violent" (bíaios), "lawless" (ánomos) and "impious" (asebés) are applied to various forms of the enemy character, the author seems to consider this overlap as the sign of a common historical origin. Yet whether or not such epithets indicate a myth in common, should we not note that their application to an enemy of the cult's particular deity would be wholly "natural" and would need no historical strand in common, just as atrocity stories "naturally" arise in war time, without necessarily having some particular past atrocity story to start from (the atrocity of war itself being enough to make sure that the human mind will gravitate towards the imagining of the "perfect" atrocity story)?

Looking again at the author's ten major themes, and seeking to "prophesy them after the event" in terms of Poetics, we can see many good purely "internal" reasons for the paradigm. For instance, as regards the first clause, concerning the Enemy's divine origin: Unless the Champion fights someone his own size, it's not a "perfect" combat. Hence, the "natural" tendency here would be for the Enemy to be of divine origin, like the figure he is opposing. The sub-clauses deal with particular ways of amplifying this detail, by giving the Enemy parents or companions appropriate to such a role. (Another way of stating the case would be: The most "perfect" combat would be "heroic" in scale; and in a polytheistic age the most "heroic" scale would involve a conflict between gods.)

Clause 2, regarding the Enemy's "distinctive habitation" (usually in places where monsters and demons dwell), represents an appropriate scene-agent ratio, the principle of artistic consistency whereby characters are given their proper settings.[2]

Clause 3, regarding the Enemy's "extraordinary appearance and properties," builds him up as an enemy. Clause 1 built him up as a worth-while enemy; clause 3 builds him up as an enemy in the sense that our sympathies should be turned against him. The sub-clauses here list various ways in which he can be physically repugnant.

Clause 4 deals with the Enemy's repugnance morally. To this end he is shown as being the kind of vicious, lecherous, greedy character and doing the kind of atrocious things that would make you glad to be rid of him.

Clause 5, regarding the Enemy's conspiring "against heaven," in a desire to rule the world, is the "perfection" of the charges levelled against him. Here the enemy becomes as *complete* as he can be, in his role as a repugnant power. (In this sense his ambition is the "ultimate conclusion" of the traits considered in Clause 4.)

Clause 6 introduces the Champion (a young "weather god or sky god"). For the time being, I doubt whether we have the grounds for fully "prophesying" why the Champion "should be" this particular kind of god. We must be content with a purely "tautological" explanation. If the myth is used as *aition* for a cult devoted to a sky god, then by the same token the most perfect hero would be that sky god himself, including whatever attributes were associated with such a god in that particular culture, regardless of what a story of combat may have been in its origins. But this also brings up a problem which is best considered in connection with Clause 7.

First of all, obviously, Clause 7 is a response to the principle of *enargeia*. If there is to be a combat, it must be fought before our very eyes—otherwise the story-teller has not lived up to the obligations of his trade. Tautologically stated: If a combat myth, then certainly a combat. Hence also, under this head, we consider the various kinds of force and fraud available to combat as so conceived (including the resources of magic as defined by the modes of priestcraft then current).

Later, we shall consider other reasons why there should be a "combat myth" at all. For the moment, taking it as "the given," we observe that if there is to be a combat, there must be at least two combatants (Clause 7 thus pointing back to Clauses 6 and 1). But there might be a kind of combat with only one combatant who vanquished himself, though at present we don't have enough material for the adequate treatment of that possibility. Meanwhile, any athletic contest or war is sufficient evidence that, so far as drama and narrative are concerned, a combat to be "perfect" in form needs at least two combatants. Even in solitaire, one plays against "the Jack." The book also refers to many ways in which the two sides can be amplified by the addition of allies.

Clause 8, in which the Champion nearly loses the battle, lends itself as beautifully to Poetics as though the primitive narrators of the "combat myth" had read Aristotle on the dramatic value of plots complicated by reversal ("peripety"). Obviously, a story about someone who simply goes out and wins is much less effective (hence less perfect) than a story about someone who nearly loses, then wins at the last moment as the result of a new development. Also, because of certain ambiguities regarding death and immortality among the gods the period of near-defeat can even be carried to the "perfect" point where the Champion is slain and lamented, as per five sub-clauses which the author lists under 8.

Clause 9 marks the victory of our hero, by rival use of force and fraud (including, of course, magic). For in one sense the "combat myth" is misnamed. It is really a "victory myth." It isn't just the story of a fight; it is the story of a radical triumph (with qualifications still to be considered).

Clause 10 completes the form by detailing the final triumphant celebration of the Champion and those loyal to his cause. It attains its last touches of perfection in the author's sub-clauses 10C and 10D, regarding the Champion's purging of blood-guilt and his setting up of institutions devoted to his worship (the myth's *telos* thus coming to a head in its priestly use as sanction for the institutions associated with it). Thoughts on this last point suggest that we might even want to give the combat myth some such revised name as the "inaugural agon," having in mind its way of merging a mythic account of "origins" with a theory of *sanctions* for a given order of priestly governance.

III

So far, it must be admitted, our comments on the author's ten-clause paradigm, as viewed from the standpoint of Poetics, have been superficial, being intended merely to suggest the general slant. We shall now try to dig beneath the surface. For our point of departure, let's select this good formulation, from among the sixteen "important observations and discoveries" which the author lists by way of conclusion on pages 465 through 466: "The combat-myth is a myth of beginnings, a tale of conflict between order and disorder, chaos and cosmos."

We should begin by noting that, considered simply as terms, the members of these pairs imply each other. Though both types of the combat myth, in their simplicity, proceed *from* disorder *to* order, there is no such progression in the relation between the terms themselves, considered as logical opposites (or "polar" terms). We can say with equal justice either that "order" implies "disorder" or that "disorder" implies "order"—and the same will be found true of "chaos" and "cosmos," insofar as they stand opposed.

We would derive this state of affairs not from such *historical* "origins" or "firsts" as men's primitive battles with nature, wild beasts, and one another, but from the nature of that peculiarly linguistic marvel, the *negative*. The negative as such offers a basis for a tendency to think in terms of antitheses (yes-no, good-evil, true-false, right-wrong, order-disorder, cosmos-chaos, success-failure, presence-absence, pleasure-pain, clean-unclean, life-death, love-hate—or, recombining these last two sets, Eros-Thanatos). *

---

* However, one must guard against the temptation to interpret such groupings too symmetrically, with all the "good" on the "positive" side and all the "evil" viewed as "negative." Consider, for instance, the theological pair, "finite-infinite," where the Grammatically negative term is immeasurably the superior (whereby ingenious dialectical operations are employed to show that the finite is "really" the negative, and vice versa). Or consider the fact that freedom is the *destruction* of bondage, purification the *elimination* of guilt, redemption the *cancelling* of debt, etc. One great fatality overhanging the Freudian nomenclature in this regard is that Freud approaches the negative from a *biological* emphasis rather than as an intrinsically *linguistic* phenomenon—hence the tendency towards an over-symmetrical equating of "positive" with "life" and "negative" with "death." Yet surely, it is not a "death-instinct," but a "love of life," that makes us seek for ways of *negating* our distresses. There is nothing essentially deathy about zero or the minus sign in mathematics. Such negatives are purely a resource of symbol-systems (though they can come to take on psychological associations extrinsic to their nature as sheerly technical signs and functions, and such associations may for some people be of a deathy sort). Killing ceases to be equatable with sheer negativity as soon as one thinks of "negating the negation," thereby piling on still more negativity, as with Donne's challenge, "Death, thou shalt die!"

Hence, were one to ask, "Why the combat myth?" while having such considerations in mind, our specifically "logological" answer would be: Insofar as negatives imply their opposites (as "disorder" implies "order"), the opposition between them is in effect "timeless." In themselves, as "polar" terms, they have no progression or priority, but merely imply each other. *When translated into terms of mythic narrative,* however, *such opposition can become a quasi-temporal "combat" between the two terms,* with the corresponding possibility that one of the terms can be pictured as "vanquishing" the other. Or they can be thought of as alternatively uppermost, in periodic or cyclic succession (an arrangement that comes closer to retaining the notion of their mutual involvement in each other, even while distinguishing between them and giving each a measure of predominance). Similarly, the pattern can be further modulated by the thought of an *interregnum,* with one of the terms not an out-and-out victor but a temporary *interrex,* eventually to be replaced by the other.

Note, also, that once you have translated the logical principle of antithesis into terms of narrative combat, by the same token you have set the conditions for a *purposive* development. Thus, for instance, the principle of disorder can be pictured as *aiming to win* over the principle of order, and vice versa, so that the purely directionless way in which polar terms imply each other can be replaced by schemes intensely teleological, as with "quest-myths" recounting the earnest effort to attain some greatly desired object or destination, a category wide enough to include all mythic narratives insofar as such narratives involve action and all action implies purpose.

Python does not deal with the "quest-myth" as such. But when the author finally arrives at his reduction to Eros and Thanatos, he is really doing in his way what the proponents of the "quest-myth" are doing in theirs: By such a trend towards "mono-myth," the motives for narrative development are in effect reduced to dramatic synonyms for "purpose." This is made obvious by the very term, "quest-myth." And it should be clear enough in the case of Eros, the basic meaning of which is "desire for" (whereat we also readily realize the strong teleological ingredient in such Freudian concepts as "wish-fulfillment" and "purposive forgetting").

To show that Thanatos is similarly but a dramatic synonym for purpose, we must be a bit more roundabout, but not much. First, we recall the two meanings of "end," as cessation or aim. The two merge in the sense that the fulfilment of an aim and the completion of a development are characterizable as the "death" of that aim or development, once you permit yourself to describe the process in so dramatic a term. The attaining of any given end marks the "death" of such efforts as went with the attaining of it.

"Death" also figures in another sense. For besides the "killing" of a desire by its *attainment,* there is also the *frustrating* of a desire. Here again, permitting ourselves a dramatic vocabulary, we could introduce the Thanatos theme, since any frustrating of a desire can be treated as a species of "mortification."

Thus in two opposite ways a *purpose* can undergo *transformations* which, if stated in terms of Love and Death, could be called modes of "dying." And insofar as the sheer Grammar of such semi-mythic language is concerned, reduction to terms of Eros and Thanatos is in effect reduction to the three categories: purpose, fulfilment of purpose, frustration of purpose. In this sense, the terms are intrinsically as "mono-mythic" as reduction to the "quest." And insofar as they are

17

reductions to the one category of "purpose," they are necessarily insufficient; for obviously there are other loci of motives. [3]

IV

However, though semi-mythic when applied to action generally, the terms can be literal when applied specifically to the biological realm of sexual desire and to the presence or absence of life in an organism. And this literal reference adds plausibility to their universalistic usage. But obviously, their "universalistic" usage (as terms for aspects of purpose) quickly takes us beyond any possible restriction to natural conditions alone, as when we are told that Eros helped Zeus conquer "by putting into Typhon's soul a readiness to be charmed by Kadmos' music," or when we recall that in the combat myth the divine contestants both "die" and are "immortal."

Not only does polytheism provide a style of expression whereby the terms for gods can duplicate the vocabulary of human psychology (as a desire can be attributed to a god of desire, a fear to a god of fear, etc.); it also allows for a further complication whereby the gods themselves can be treated sometimes as having purely personal motives and sometimes as having motives which were induced in them by other gods (as a god might directly be said to experience a desire, or the desire might be said to have been aroused in him by the action of Eros). Hence note that, when Desire itself becomes a god, a frustrated desire can become in principle "immortal," to the extent that it *persists,* in however gnarled or imperfect or imprisoned a form. That is, insofar as a desire can be "killed" by its *fulfilment,* in failing to be fulfilled it can "live on."

In this sense, the ambiguous relation between death and immortality in the combat myth can be seen to be a perfect narrative translation for the underlying polarity of the antithetic principles (expressed in terms of warring principals). Insofar as one term excludes the other, if we had to state this logical relation in terms of a mythic combat, we could properly say that one term "slays" the other. Yet insofar as the term timelessly implies its opposite, we could say that the "slain" term remains "immortal," and though vanquished, is ever ready to make a come-back if the opportunity offers, like Typhon fuming beneath Aetna. For insofar as narrative involves *action* and action implies *purpose,* the relation between the terms would remain one of purposive combat.

The underlying dialectic of the Love-Death pair is further complicated by the fact that they are not directly antithetical in the way that order-disorder and cosmos-chaos are. Strictly, the antithesis of Love would be Hate, and the antithesis of Death would be Life. By crossing the pairs, we get the invitation to equate Hate with Death (Styx meant the "hateful") and Love with Life. But as viewed in terms of death, there are at least two major incentives to equate Love *with* Death rather than treating them as contestants. Physiologically, the sense of release through sexual orgasm can be likened to a pleasurable form of dying (an association frequently found in poetry). Sociologically, there is the fact that the lovers' immersion in a common identity implies the "death" of whatever separate identities they may have outside the circle of their mutual engrossment. It is a way of "transcending" ordinary "mortal" concerns, a kind of claim to "immortality" (though the principles of dialectic are so inexorable that such "im-mortality" can be but a species of "mortality," so far as the experience of mortals is concerned). As regards the vagaries of poetic catharsis, the love-death equation has the further advantage that, while symbolizing sexual union, it can also symbolize "punishment" for such union, thereby merging guilt, gratification, and redemption.

Thus, when following Professor Fontenrose's purely folkloristic efforts to derive the "Venusberg theme" from earlier stories of a trip to the underworld of the dead, we should keep in mind also such sheerly "entelechial" concerns as the above. As a principle of operatic "perfection," the Wagnerian theme of the *Liebestod* is to be derived not from an original version of the "combat myth," but from the implications of the Wagnerian canon. Poetics would study it not as a derivation, but as a kind of culmination, an entelechy that is implicit in *Tannhäuser*, but that attains its full narrative expression in *Tristan*, since it is the theme on which the opera closes. The plot of *Tristan* might be viewed as the "perfect paradigm" for a "myth" so equating Eros and Thanatos that any "combat" between them becomes transformed into a species of "concerted action." (We say "concerted," having in mind that the Latin verb *concerto* meant to strive, rival, dispute, and that such connotations are present in the idea of a musical *concerto,* which involves a kind of "contest" between the orchestra and the solo instrument.)

To sum up the steps already taken: First, we considered the combat myth purely as a narrative way of handling "polar" opposition, a response to the genius of the negative. Next, when the author ended on Freud's Eros-Thanatos pair, we noted that, besides their bearing upon love, hate, life, and death as ultimate terms of combat, they functioned as somewhat dramatized synonyms for aspects of *purpose.*

This point about purpose is particularly important because, as the author of *Python* repeatedly makes clear, the combat myth comes to a head in its use as *aition.* Here is its *purpose,* its function as a story to account for the cult or services associated with it. In this regard, the author calls it a myth of "origins," whereupon we would add the important reminder that such an account of "origins" is also a way of establishing *sanctions.* Its narrative stating how things *were* in the past thereby substantiates the principles of governance to which the faithful *should be* vowed in the present.

V

Such an "entelechial" perspective ("deriving" the many versions and variants not from some one story that may have originally been going the rounds, but rather from poetic and rhetorical principles that would attain their perfect embodiment in Fontenrose's paradigms) would locate the "principles" of a form not in temporally past moments that a form develops *from,* but in possibilities of perfection which reside in the form as such and *towards* which all sorts of stories might gravitate. Similarly, as considered from the entelechial point of view, the "principles" of Greek tragedy would be sought not in the incunabula of tragedy, but in *late* developments, such "perfect" tragedies as those of Aeschylus of Sophocles, in line with Aristotle's statement, in Chapter IV of the Poetics [4]: "After going through many stages" in its gradual evolution, tragedy "stopped when it had found its natural form." *

---

* The tendency to treat of motivational *principles* ("beginnings") in terms of the primordial past is central to the method of myth (which expresses essence temporally, in terms of narrative). To end by borrowing Freud's highly imaginative Eros-Thanatos pair comes close to explaining a myth by a myth. Freud's great stress upon the "primal" and the "infantile" naturally favors the placement of psychological principles in terms of the temporally prior, as when he seeks for the fundamental source of man's guilt in a hypothetical act of patricide committed by our prehistoric

But note that, even as regards the "entelechial" perspective itself, we have come upon two sources of motives. Besides the combat myth's way of translating contraries and contradictories into narrative terms of combat (involving a search for a corresponding perfection of *dramatis personae* and plot), there is the aetiological use of myth for a somewhat "propagandistic" purpose, to account for the "origins" of the cult with which the myth has become identified. The matter of such "origins" brings up further considerations, which we shall deal with next.

First, there is one problem that plagues us at every stage of this inquiry. The author of *Python* encounters it in his way when, having equated sea and death, he seeks to answer a critic's objection "that sea and death do not belong to the same level of concept." In reply he observes that by the use of personification mythic thinking does frequently place "concepts of different levels . . . on the same level." (p. 142) Also, he notes that folklorists generally interpret the sea as "realm of death."

Insofar as myth is poetic, it naturally expresses its ideas in terms of imagery and personification. Thus, the *idea* of death will be replaced by the imagery of a realm in which the dead reside and which can be duplicated in terms of a supernatural power presiding over this realm. Hence, whatever details may be used in the amplifying of the idea, they are necessarily somewhat extrinsic to the idea as such. If for instance, the realm of death is equated with the sea, there is also the fact that the sea, *qua* sea, is not a realm of death. In fact, it may be gloriously fertile with life. Or if the idea of death is equated, say, with absence, we recognize that absence *qua* absence is not identical with death. For instance, a person may be absent from some gathering not because he is dead, but because he is having a good time elsewhere.

Now, reversing the matter, suppose that you come upon the theme of a god's absence. Are you to treat it categorically as a surrogate for the theme of his death? Or can it sometimes refer simply to absence *qua* absence, without any reference to death? For instance, if at some point in a story the exigencies of the plot require that a certain character be absent, any sufficient reason might serve. If he is said to have gone on a trip, must this necessarily be interpreted as a disguised variation on the theme of a trip to the dead? In *Python* there are references to such absence on pages 381 through 382. Here the god's absence is interpreted as sign of his death, though it was certainly a highly qualified form of death, since it had to do with months during which Apollo spent the winter in "the northern paradise of the Hyperboreans" (p. 345), a form of "death" not unlike that of healthy tourists who, during the bleak northern winter, sun-bathe and water-ski in the tropics.

The entelechial perspective suggests a third possibility. Here would be the steps: (1) In a narrative, the theme of "absence" may be a motive in its own right, a narrator's convenience in accounting for a development that could not have taken place so "naturally" had the absent character been present. (2) The theme of

ancestors (a quasi-scientific analogue of the notion that man's guilt results from the "first" sin committed by the "first" man against the foremost authority, as narrated in the opening chapters of Genesis). In another paper, still in progress, when tentatively working out a scheme for trying to trace exactly how Freud's terminology as a whole is implicit in his equating of "repression" and the "unconscious" (a formula that is as fertile in implications as was Spinoza's *Deus sive Natura* or Berkeley's *"esse* is *percipi"*), I have proposed as Freud's stylistic rule number one the instruction to reduce every motive, insofar as seems possible or plausible, to terms of some remote past, either infantile or primordial or both. Thus, dream and neurosis are treated as perfect instances of such survival; and even processes of "condensation" and "displacement" are viewed rather in terms of their manifestations in dreams, neurosis, and primitive myth than as the utilization of resources "natural" to mature symbol-systems as well.

absence might be variously motivated (two obvious possibilities being either that the absent person had gone on a trip or that he was dead). (3) For a heroic combat myth, the most "perfect" explanation would be one which equated absence-on-a-trip with absence-through-death, hence arriving at absence-on-a-trip-to-the-world-of-the-dead.

Thus instead of treating the theme of absence as a variation on the theme of death, we should treat each as designed to solve a problem within the story, a problem that was solved by the theme of absence as such. However, once the narrator starts accounting for the absence, entelechial pressures attract him towards terms for death as the "most thorough" explanation. Such an entelechial view of the situation would not require us to assume that the theme of absence stood for the theme of a journey to the realm of the dead. Far from a situation whereby the theme of absence as such indicates the theme of death, it could indicate merely that the given version was not so "thorough" in accounting for the absence as it would have been had the explanation been in terms of death. Indeed, lack of "thoroughness" in this regard can often result from the fact that the narrative is being "thorough" in quite different ways, to quite different ends. Such considerations would figure particularly if, in the examination of myths from many lands, every reference to a stage in which a god is absent were interpreted as a disguised, fragmentary variation on the theme of his death.

Similarly, one man might write a story about gambling for money, and another about gambling for one's life. There is no reason to assume that the story about gambling for money is a mere variation on the theme of gambling for one's life (though both stories may be studied as variations on the theme of gambling, with its motivational range from symbolic self-abuse to the *beau geste* of "aristocratic" adventurousness). But we could say that, *caeteris paribus,* the theme of gambling for one's life is more "thorough" than the theme of gambling for money; and certainly the theme of losing one's life at gambling would be heroically more thorough than the theme of winning money. Yet to say as much is to suggest a further ironic possibility: The hero wins a fortune in gambling for money; but this very success leads ironically to events that culminate in his downfall and death, and that would not have "transpired" had he lost.

Or a woman dreaming of being jilted by her lover, might punningly dream so in terms of an incident that involved his dropping a garment of hers. Or the dream might be of an incident in which she was about to fall over a cliff, her lover was rescuing her, then he too began to slip, and to save himself he let her go—whereat she awoke in terror, after the plunge to her certain death had begun. Both versions would be on the theme of her being "dropped." But the milder version would not be a surrogate for the more drastic one. Each of the two variations on the same theme could arise without necessary reference to the other. But one would be more "complete," so far as tests of tragic fulfilment are concerned.

In all such cases, *caeteris paribus,* we might expect an entelechial pressure in the direction of the more drastic version, as regards the motives of a "perfect paradigm."

VI

In an excellent introductory summary of the variations which a theme may undergo (pp. 7-8), the author makes two kinds of observations which might at first glance seem the same; yet when viewed from the standpoint of our "entelechial" concern they can be shown to have quite different implications.

21

Here is an example of a statement that can mislead: "A striking feature of one variant may be reduced in another to something less striking, or it may be disguised. Death may be changed to wound, sleep, defeat, exile, disappearance." (p. 8) In the light of our analysis, would we not be justified in saying that the author himself here spontaneously exemplifies, without proper safeguards, the entelechial principle of tragedy, in taking the most drastic member of his series as the essence of the lot? His statement, if uncriticized, becomes an invitation to see a disguised reference to death in every mention of a contestant's wound, sleep, defeat, exile, or disappearance. By such a rule, Thanatos is bound to turn up just about everywhere, universalistically joining with its partner, Eros, to encompass the whole field.

Here, on the other hand, is an example of a statement which seems to avoid such an invitation to error: "The mode of combat may change from one variant to another. One kind of punishment or deception may be replaced by another." (p. 7) The statement is so generalized that no one example is offered as basic, with others treated as departures from it. All examples would be equally valid, so far as their inclusion under this head is concerned, though we might next proceed to show why one particular example was more "perfect" for a particular context.

The statement that "There may be expansion or doubling of themes, persons, episodes" can be somewhat misleading. (p. 8) For though it is often more "perfect" to have a principle summed up in the role of an individual contestant, a work like *The Iliad,* or stories of "titanomachies," "theomachies," and "gigantomachies" indicate that in many narratives a principle of opposition as such can be properly represented by assigning several contestants to one side, a consideration that also applies specifically to the combat myth, since both Enemy and Champion can have allies (including defectors from the opposition).

The statement that "A deed may become merely the attempt to do it" would require the addition of the words "and *vice versa*"; otherwise the assumption is that deed is primary and attempt is derivative. In the next paragraph, this corrective is actually introduced, when the author notes that "deeds or traits may be transferred from one character to another . . . even from champion to enemy and *vice versa.*" (p. 8)

Insofar as the author's summary here is to be taken merely as a convenience for the reader, there is no particular reason why it should have been written any more exactingly than it is. As regards the test of sheer preparatory serviceability, the outline is wholly adequate, and we are straining at gnats if we seem to be asking that it be legalistically holeproof. Our point is simply that, though there is no particular need for having those clauses any more accurate than they are, they happen to be of two sorts whereas at first they all seem to be of one sort. And insofar as we distinguish between them, we can make clear the distinction we are after, regarding the relation between themes and variations as viewed from the standpoint of Poetics.

You might put the matter thus: Christian theologians treat figures in the Old Testament as "types of Christ." Another approach might be to pick such a figure in the Old Testament, and to treat Christ and Christian martyrs, and all similar Old Testament figures as variations on this theme. A third way would be to treat both Christ and all such characters in the Old Testament or later as examples of a more generalized category, such as: The principle of sacrifice, exemplified in various roles that embody this principle with varying degrees of "perfection."

Here would be the "entelechial" approach. Clauses ending "and *vice versa*" would allow for it, whereas it would not be accommodated by clauses that imply the temporal priority of one among the lot, with the others treated as variants (derivatives) of this ancestral term.

Professor Fontenrose's use of thematic paradigms is like the first view insofar as the paradigms are a kind of ideal summing-up. It would be like the second, insofar as certain early figures were taken to be the probable thematic originals and all others were treated as variants of these. It is strongly influenced by the *pressures* of the third; but the folkloristic stress upon temporal priority keeps the entelechial aspect of the paradigms from attaining its full rationale, and makes it look as though the "variants" were descended from ideal prototypes which came *first in time*, whereas actually the paradigms are prototypes only in the sense that they possess the "perfection" of over-all generalizations or schematizations.

VII

If the combat myth were nothing but a story of combat, designed to appeal simply as a story in keeping with the aesthetic canons of Art for Art's Sake, the study of its paradigm from the entelechial point of view would require only such considerations of internal symmetry. But a cult is a system of *governance*. Thus its moral authority is a direct or indirect means of influencing the dispositions and habits of the believers. And insofar as the myth of "origins" serves as a precedent on which to base this authority, it must be designed not merely to account for "origins," but also to account for them in ways that provide *sanctions* for the given order. This aetiological factor complicates the entelechial perspective by so localizing the tests of a myth's "perfection" that a version which would best sanction one authority would need revision if applied to the sanctioning of a different authority.

Thus, whereas the mythic translation of opposition into terms of a contest allows ideas like order and disorder, cosmos and chaos to be represented by personified contestants that can triumph over each other or succeed each other, there still remains the fact that any system of order implies corresponding kinds of disorder. This persistence of the logical opposites despite the possibilities of mythic victory can be best handled in these two ways: (1) By a myth according to which, though one of the contestants has been vanquished (or, in the most thorough terms, "slain"), he still somehow survives (like Typhon buried by Zeus beneath Sicily and fuming through Aetna), with the constant threat that he may again rise in revolt. (2) By a myth according to which the vanquished principle does periodically take over, to reign for a season, and to be periodically replaced again by the opposing principle. (Obviously, the resources of dialectic being what they are, under certain conditions such *opposition* can be translated into terms more like *cooperation*, with both powers or principles being necessary to make a world, whereby the principle of "disorder" becomes in its way a species of order, too. Even the Kingdom of Darkness is not just rebellion against Light, but has its own modes of organization.)

The design of human combat itself would seem to provide the basic imagery for the first of these versions, according to which one side conquers but can never remain wholly sure of his victory. And obviously, the periodicity of the seasons provides the basic image for the second version, which translates the principle of opposition into terms of cyclical succession. The second primarily concerns us now, since the paradigm calls for the victory of a sky god or weather god, and seasonal change is most readily associated with such a power.

There is one notable difference between rituals designed to influence irregular phenomena (like magic for ending drought in a season normally rainy) and rituals designed for influencing regular phenomena (like magic for "causing" the return of spring at a time when spring is normally due): The second kind of rite can possess a measure of "infallibility" not possible to the first. And insofar as a priesthood can associate its rites with the orderly production of inevitable processes, it has optimum conditions for establishing its authority. For what system of priestly magic could possibly be more authoritative than one which had such obvious pragmatic sanction, in that its services proved "successful" year after year?

Too great a stress upon primitive magic as "bad science" (a faulty method of *coercing nature*) can deflect our attention from its efficacy as "good rhetoric" (an authoritative method of *persuading people*). No one could say with certainty whether magic began with the attempt to influence the irregularities of nature or in a "poetic" responsiveness to nature's regular cycle of transformations. But one can say with certainty that, insofar as a cult could associate its rites with the lore of the calendar, it had the best basis for establishing the authority of those rites, since it could then work out ritual ways of "bringing about the inevitable." Thus, whatever may have been the beginnings of magic, its rites attained a certain "perfection" when identified with the seasons. And in this sense, with the translation of polar opposition (order-disorder, cosmos-chaos, rule-misrule) into terms of powers whose jurisdiction fluctuated with the seasons, the combat myth was brought to a state of "aetiological perfection."

We now can see clearly the two kinds of "perfection" that the "entelechial" perspective must deal with, in the case of the "combat myth." There is its perfection simply as a story that translates polar opposition into terms of narrative. And there is its perfection as an instrument in the establishing of a cult's authority. For this second kind, we have suggested, there is the added factor of identification with seasonal regularities. But obviously, in taking responsibility for seasonal *regularities*, the magician also had to take responsibility for the correcting of seasonal *irregularities*. It has often been pointed out that there was an irrefutable explanation within the system itself whenever such rites failed, since any failure could be ascribed to counter-magic. But that would not be a "perfect" answer, since it would tend to impugn the power of the cult's own magic, by implying that there could be stronger rival powers.

The "perfect" answer involved merely a further extension of a principle already present in both contestants of the myth: the principle of *victimage*. The Champion's period of suffering was in the cause of order. And *a fortiori* the Enemy had also participated as a victim in the contest, so that his suffering was a major contribution to the maintenance of order. This principle could be further extended, not simply to the use of human sacrifice as a way of appeasing offended powers, but also to the notion of the "hidden imposthume," the undetected offender *within* the tribe, the problematical source of moral or ritual uncleanness still to be located by the experts (as with Sophocles' Oedipus). The "perfect" answer, in this sense, may not always have been resorted to. But it was there. And it really did involve an "abscess" hidden *within* the tribe—for our ideas of the *threats* to order arise from our ideas of order itself, guilt thus being intrinsic to the system (the very means of purgation reënforcing the sense of uncleanness, as the flying of flags in Tibet to *drive away* evil spirits reënforces the sense of their *presence*).

For a complete discussion of "teleological perfection," we should have to know a great deal about the particular "interests" which a given cult favored, though sometimes such proclivities may be inferred from the nature of the version itself, as when the relation between Apollo and Dionysos was presented rather in terms of alternate rule than rivalry. (A similar development seems to have occurred in early Christianity, when a threatened doctrinal rivalry between followers of Christ and followers of John the Baptist became transformed into the account of the Baptist as the Savior's forerunner.) This problem is further complicated by the fact that, though religious institutions contribute to governance, thereby using religion as a means of "social control," they are sounder when the identification between priest-hood and secular administration is not too close, as then they can better survive shifts in secular authority.

In general, for a wholly accurate account of the "teleological perfection" which a given version of a myth might have, while making such latitudinarian allowances for its relations to secular authority we should have to know a great deal not only about the local conditions of a given cult through the various stages of its history, but also about its relation to different economic systems (hunting, agriculture, trade, etc.), and to such social distinctions as patrilineal-matrilineal and patrician-plebeian (with the apparent merging of popular and aristocratic trends in the forms of Greek tragedy). Though the subject is not discussed systematically, there is material for such speculation scattered through the book. For instance: "It is possible that political changes in the Delphic state brought with them correspond-ing changes in the slant of the Charila myth, so that the heroine was transformed from demoness to a humble girl of the people." (p. 460)

This issue adds complication atop complication because of the fact that, although we tend to view religions as systems of internally generated doctrines, they are often *polar* terms, being best defined at a given time in history by some other doctrine they are *against*, though if they last long enough, they may be shaped by a changing series of such opponents, even to the extent of incorporating many of the oppo-nents' principles.

VIII

Insofar as the nature of the combat myth as *aition* involved a discussion of uses to which the myth was put in different historical situations, it could not be described purely in terms of Poetics. The discussion would require considerations which modern anthropology would analyze in terms of ritual and magic, but which in the categories of classical education would fall under "rhetoric." [5]

However, by the very fact of having so greatly stressed the problem of the myth's specific "propagandistic" utility, we are in a position to go back and ask what kind of form the myth is seen to have, if this complication is dropped out of account (theoretically prescinded).

Considered as sheer design, the combat myth comprises two modes of plot that are related to each other as obverse and reverse, concave and convex. The contesting principles (or principals) of the combat are so related that the gains of one are the losses of the other. If we next add the "entelechial" notion that a combat, to be dramatically perfect, requires a peripety, the complementary designs are seen to be so formed that one contestant meets with increasing success until there is a reversal

25

of fortune and he fails, while by the same token the opponent meets with increasing failure until the same reversal of fortune brings success.

There are two major ways of distinguishing between comedy and tragedy: (1) Tragic characters are said to be "better" than ordinary people, comic characters "worse"; (2) Comedy has a plot that builds towards a "happy" ending, tragedy towards an "unhappy" ending. Each in its way involves the entelechial principle. But for the moment we are concerned with the more obvious case, the test by endings (an "entelechial" consideration because endings, like entelechies, are culminative, formal fulfilments).

The mere combat pattern as such is most directly illustrated by an athletic contest in which there is no need to have the two sides so distinguished that the one is "virtuous" and the other "villainous," one for "cosmos" and the other for "chaos," etc. (though partisan sympathies can make for an equivalent response among the spectators). Judged as sheer form, the most "perfect" game would be one in which at the last minute the losing side breaks through and wins ("complex plot" with "peripety"). Since one side's gain would be the other side's loss, the pattern thus contains simultaneously the designs of both tragedy and comedy (as tested by the outcome).

However, in a well-formed work, the ending is not something that can merely be tacked on (as though the poet were to write his drama without reference to its ending, and at the last minute tossed up a coin to decide whether he'd have his hero end in anguish like Sophocles' *Oedipus Rex* or end up with a banquet and two girls like Dicaeopolis in Aristophanes' *Acharnians*). To be perfect, an ending must be perfectly prepared for. And such preparation when most thorough involves not merely the curve of the plot but the choice of appropriate characters. For if the action is to be tragic, the characters must be of a sort that is appropriate to tragic action.

The question of tragedy and comedy thus shifts from considerations of outcome to considerations of dramatis personae. Although, simply as regards the test of endings, the outcome of an athletic contest would be in principle "comic" for the victors and "tragic" for the losers, the test of dramatis personae suggests that in principle both sides are "tragic." For they are "better" than most people (in the sense that, in their role as athletes, they represent a skill which people ordinarily do not possess). Thus in this technical sense they would meet the requirements of Aristotle's formula. Insofar as he performs properly, each player has his peculiar way of being "serious" (*spoudaios*).

The analogue of a "comic" game would be one in which, instead of directing all their efforts earnestly, the players complicated things by clowning. In this technical sense they would be "worse" even than ordinary people who took the game seriously.

In Chapter XIV of the Poetics, the word that Aristotle uses, when giving his total recipe for a tragic character, is *chrestos*. Though it is usually translated as "good," we might well remember that its primary meaning is goodness in the sense of usefulness, serviceability. Particularly in view of the fact that the Greek idea of service has the same range of pragmatic and ritualistic connotations as in English, we submit that the notion of a tragic character's "goodness" might best be approached through a hypothetical example of this sort:

Think of a funeral service. Think next of an usher officiating at that service. Insofar as he performed his function properly, he would contribute to the austerities of the occasion by being "better" than he ordinarily was. He would accept the responsibilities of his tragic role, and act accordingly. Only the most discreet kinds of bodily expression would be permitted, nothing more "purgative" than a barely audible clearing of the throat. Even if he smiled, it would be a wan smile, a sad smile, by all means not a carefree beaming smile. (On the contrary as regards bodily purgative imagery in Aristophanic comedy: just as a comic character was ornamented with a large stylized phallus, so in a state of comic fright he might befoul himself, such manners obviously being "worse" than those of ordinary people.) Similarly, despite the low rating placed on a slave in Greek culture, the character of a slave could be introduced into tragedy. But those aspects of the role must be stressed which "live up to" the solemnities of the occasion.

The striking difference between the low status of women in Athenian society (except for an occasional famous courtesan like Aspasia) and the tremendous roles assigned to them in tragedy is a perfect instance of the way in which tragic figures could be called "better" than the ordinary, even though many of Euripides' women were "better" in quite horrifying ways, thereby providing the plot for Aristophanes' comedy, the *Thesmophoriazusae*, built around the theme of Athenian women who organize against Euripides in indignation at his slandering of their sex (a comic situation that is at its best when Mnesilochus, who undertakes the defense of the playwright, makes things still worse by reciting the many evil things that Euripides might with justice have said about women but left unsaid).

Again, by the test of "better" and "worse," what would you do with a character like Iago? Is he to be called "better" than ordinary people? Or must he be denied a "tragic" character, despite the fact that, had he been any less enterprising in villainy than he was, the whole tragedy would have collapsed? He is a tragic character, since he contributes so well to the tragic roles of Othello and Desdemona. But he is "less tragic" than they. For no wholly tragic character can be loathed, and Iago is loathed except insofar as a critic might feel sorry for an inventive soul who so thoroughly took upon himself the playwright's serious job of keeping the tragedy in motion, a sturdy role for which we must always give the Devil his due.

The tragic "flaw" or "error of judgment" (*hamartia*) is matched by what we might call the comic "blotch" (*hamartema*, a word incidentally that in the New Testament came to mean "sin"). Comic characters are "worse" than ordinary people in the sense that caricatures of public figures look "worse" than if simply "life-like." Such picturesque disfigurement and distortion also applies to characters with whom we are meant to be in sympathy, though the kinds of over-emphasis will differ. Thus the political cartoonist might exaggerate a large mouth by picturing it as disproportionately still larger, but he could still choose between giving this "comic blotch" a grin or a leer.

To the test by endings and the test by character we might add the related test by response. Tragedy naturally attains its culmination in tears, comedy in laughter. But there are complications such as the *comédie larmoyante* (which may be seasoned with incidental tearful "endings," such as an episode depicting the pitiful death of some pathetic secondary character). And the Shakespearean theatre allows for the "perfect" possibility of a double-plot in which a sympathetically unhappy ending for heroic characters is interwoven with a vindictively unhappy ending for similarly "serious" villainous characters, along with an out-and-out happy ending for some comic characters, and a measure of minor vengeance for their comic enemies. The tearfulness would relate predominantly to the tragic set, the laughter to the comic set. Yet there could be incidental crossing of the borders, too. (I say that the canons of the Shakespearean theatre would allow for this as a "perfect possibility." But I do not think of any play that fully embodies such a range.)

As regards the test by endings alone, the design of Christ's sacrifice combines tragedy and comedy. For whereas the death of Christ on the Cross is in itself a tragic ending, Christ's resurrection and return to Heaven sets the pattern for a "divine comedy." As with the combat myth, the hero goes through a stage in which he "dies" and is lamented, followed by a stage of rebirth and celebration. The idea of Christ-Jesus as God-man allowed for a greater dissociation between the idea of the Christian Champion's "death" (as a man) and his "immortality" (as a divine Person).

As regards the test by character and response, though the Christian agon was weak in comedy, this defect was remedied somewhat in the semi-secular Miracle Plays that re-enacted Biblical stories. (Cf. the stock comic character of Noah's wife as a scold, and the devices whereby actors who were assigned the role of devils made their hard lot bearable by giving such devils the character of comic imps and pranksters.)

By progressing from Hell through Purgatory to Paradise, Dante gives his epic the design of a happy ending, particularly since the poet's pilgrimage is presented as a kind of object-lesson intended for his salvation. However, behind this "temporal" unfolding there remains the fact that Hell is not merely a stage along the way but as long-lasting as Paradise. Thus, though the epic *ends* on the theme of Paradise, one-third of it is concerned with characters whose sufferings are *unending*. In this sense it is one hell of an idea of comedy, though technically the way out of the difficulty would probably be along these lines: (1) Tragedy involves pity; (2) according to Aristotle we feel pity only for suffering that is undeserved; (3) the eternal hellish suffering of the damned is said to be a "just" punishment; (4) hence, in the last analysis, it should not awaken pity—and, according to Saint Thomas, does not arouse the pity of the saints in Heaven; (5) however, being a mere mortal, in some circles of Hell Dante does feel pity; but mostly his attitude is one of fascinated fear and repugnance; and sometimes he is moved by *vindictive* satisfaction, an attitude that the saints would not share; (6) Aristotle also says that we feel pity for people like ourselves—and Dante's sudden feelings of pity concern sufferers with whose temptations he most readily identifies himself.

IX

When Fontenrose says (p. 22) that "Often in the following chapters the name Python will be used merely as a convenient designation for Apollo's opponent without regard to sex or species," and (p. 70) "I shall henceforth use the term *dragon* broadly to mean any kind of monster or animal or mixed shape," we confront in another way the kind of problem we encountered when asking whether the terms "Eros" and "Thanatos" might be interpreted as mythical equivalents for the concept of "purpose." (We noted that the word "quest," stressed by some literary folklorists, could be similarly analyzed. And we might also have noted that in philosophic writings the word "good" is similarly analyzable, as per the definition at the beginning of the *Nichomachean Ethics*: "The Good is that at which all things aim." [6])

We dealt with a similar problem when considering the author's use of "Enemy" and "Champion" in his paradigm for the final type of combat myth with which he is concerned. We contended that they might be shown to imply in turn a principle of sheerly logical opposition (as with "polar" terms), for which they provide a quasi-narrative equivalent.

But now we might also supply an intermediate step, along these lines:

If we wanted to stress purely narrative opposition but in terms that would be as highly generalized as possible without losing the idea of sheerly logical opposition, we might designate the contestant principles simply as Negative and Positive. In doing so, however, we should immediately confront the fact that there would be no basis for deciding which of the opposing principles should be called Positive and which Negative. This situation is made apparent in a succinct footnote (*Python*, p. 240) where the author says that he applies the term "rebel gods" to the "older generation of gods" which the "victory-destined younger gods" displace. He also notes here that in the Hesiodic Titanomachy, "the younger gods are those who revolt." And we might add: In a sense it is always the younger gods who revolt, as with the Champion who goes forth to end the tyrannical reign of the Enemy; but the displaced gods are the rebels because, once the new order has become the norm, the old order stands for the corresponding principle of disorder which constantly threatens to regain control and can even be said to reign periodically (but not permanently, thanks to the efficacy of the cultic rites with which the myth is associated).

Considering the pattern as sheer design, all we can say is that either side negates the other. But despite the traditional associating of law and order, and despite the fact that law is essentially negative (a structure of thou-shalt-not's), there is also the traditional tendency to associate the Negative with "bad" and the Positive with "good." So we might arbitrarily use the Negative as the mark of the Enemy, though the idea of the Enemy should be replaced in turn by some such designation as "the principle not to be favored," while we replace the Champion with "the principle to be favored."

Building from there, we should next ask how things should be if both sides were perfect examples of their kind. The answer to this question would give us our first step from sheer pattern to mythic particularization: Both sides should be "gods." We have now translated our Negative and Positive into terms of *body*, though a kind of body which also shades off into ideas of the *disembodied*.

Next should follow the ways of "amplifying" the two principles, as when the Unfavored Principle is placed in terms of a habitat deemed unfavorable, a set of details which introduce many terms for body (as with descriptions connecting the Unfavored Principle with some forbidding place where monsters and demons are traditionally thought to dwell). Association with a set of similarly unfavored physical traits (such as a monstrous form) would carry the process of amplification further in terms that myth traditionally associated with the physically repulsive. The principle would now have been given still more body. Yet however monstrous, and however identified with super-human or non-human powers, this principle, to be narratively "perfect," must be a *person*. Hence, amplification in terms of moral traits (powers and habits) upon which men look most strongly with disfavor. And this unfavored character must cap the climax by association with a purpose that is the most thoroughly (or "perfectly") disfavored. This should be his ambition for total tyranny, absolute misrule.

29

If the narrative structure is to be as neat in its internal adjustments as possible, this culminating purpose on the part of the Unfavored Principle (or Principal) must serve as motive for the action of the rival Positive Favored Principle (endowed with correspondingly favored background, physical and moral powers and habits, all culminating in the intention to undo the Negative Principle's culminating intention).

The two principles must come to terms—and the most fitting way to do so narratively is in terms of a contest. In some respects, a sheerly physical combat is not "perfect" for all conditions, as we realize when we come to the agons of tragedy and comedy. But we are here concerned with principles, or *"firsts,"*—and terms for physical combat are prior in our imagination (as in our experience) to terms for moral combat. (Recall that, behind the account of rule and misrule in the opening chapters of Genesis, there lies the account of Lucifer's rebellion; and though the tragedies deal with moral scruples, they generally come to a focus in the imagery of physical violence.)

The combat, in turn, must be amplified by appropriate details, centering in accounts of force and fraud (the only resources of combat) which also attain their proper supernatural completion in terms of magic. This combat, to be perfect as a plot, must undergo a peripety whereby the Positive principle is first defeated, then successful. Given the nature of the contestants, the defeat can be expressed in the most thorough terms possible: The Positive principle can actually be said to "die" (a proper juncture for lamentations on the part of those who favor the vanquished principle). For "death" under such conditions is not incongruous with "immortality" (and the two taken together make a perfect narrative equivalent for the underlying Paradox of the Negative whereby polar terms both exclude each other and necessarily require each other).

When, by the use of similar resources (force and fraud aided by such magic as was deemed "natural" to the gods) the Reversal in the narrative occurs and the Positive principle ultimately prevails, conditions are set for the appropriate aftermath: cleansing of guilt, celebration of victory, and (when the myth is "put to use" as an *aition*) inaugurating of rites (rites rationalized in accordance with the principle-of-principles whereby the Positive still goes on implying its corresponding Negative).

We should now add that, when the myth is given body by translation into descriptive details, not all the details are explainable solely in terms of their identification with one or the other of the contestant principles. Many will be "neutral." Indeed, the contestants can "come to terms" only insofar as they have grounds of altercation in common. Thus, a battlefield or a banquet hall will merit some details in its own right. So, in our search for explanations in terms of perfection, we must also keep in mind the pressures that keep the contest from becoming too simply itself, and that call for an underlying neutrality of details designed to help the narrative look real. This ambiguity is true of all characters in fiction. Some things they do because of their specific roles; but they do other things simply because they are "people."

Up to this point, the design is not unambiguously describable as either tragedy or comedy. The ambiguity prevails all the more in that under the conditions of polytheism, as Professor Fontenrose reminds us (p. 425): "The enemy, although and precisely because he is fearful, always receives cult: there can be no doubt about the worship of most dragons and demons that have been mentioned in these pages." So, particularly when you get to comparing fragmentary versions of myths that have come down through many sources, the symmetry becomes impaired, even to the extent that favored and unfavored traits can change sides; and only in the theoretically perfect paradigm towards which the myths were gravitating would the symmetry be as unerring as here suggested. For various reasons, mortal narratives will "fall" from such a state of Paradisiac innocence.

For one thing, as becomes apparent when you turn from thoughts of the combat myth to speculations about tragedy and comedy (a field with which Professor Fontenrose is not concerned at all and which we have introduced into the discussion purely for reasons of our own), the principles of perfection shaping the combat myth are found to differ intrinsically from those shaping tragedy and comedy, though there are also overlaps, quite as Aristotle recognized overlaps between the principles of drama and epic despite the considerable differences between these poetic species. Though, as we have tried to show, the design of the combat myth has the makings of both tragic and comic plots, we need but think of a clown like Aristophanes' Dicaeopolis to realize that here much different entelechial principles are operating.

As regards test by endings, the themes of banqueting and celebration at the end of comedy are closer to the combat myth than tragedy is. As regards test by character, tragedy is the closer. But the main point is that, whereas the combat myth is not to be viewed simply as incipient tragedy or incipient comedy but as a form responding to potentialities of its own, so either the "drastic" preferences which tragedy cultivates or the comic poet's emphases should be taken as final only with regard to one particular poetic species. Along with both the heroics of tragedy and the extremes of the comic blotch, there must be rules for many kinds of understatement to which they are closed, and which work further refinements on the distribution, nature, and proportions of favorable, unfavorable, and neutral terms in the given work. While admiring the drastic aims of a Dostoevsky, we turn with relief to a Chekhov, whose modes of exasperation range from the hilarious to the moody, but who consistently aims to avoid the very effects that Dostoevsky aims to produce. Aristophanic burlesque was replaced by Menander's sentimental comedy of errors, an elaborate adding of tangle to tangle until all came out benevolently at the end. The picturesque assortment of rogues in Ben Jonson is a different world (representing different "perfections") from the prim, subdued comedy of Jane Austen. Tartuffe is a kind of "comedy" built around a kind of villain close to melodrama (not a butt of derision but almost an Iago in the scope of his viciousness). And so on.

Our point is: One might undertake to show how each such art is derivative, as a development out of some previous art, or prophetic, as a forerunner of something that developed out of it. But from the standpoint of *Poetics*, the rules of "derivation" are of an essentially different sort. Each species has aims intrinsic to itself. Aristotle's *Poetics* remains remarkable because he makes this problem clear by so exemplarily solving it in the case he is discussing.

Should criticism, then, but try to do the same job on all other species? Beyond doubt, it would be a worthy cause. For in the effort critics would correct the current catch-as-catch-can procedures which might be pardoned as a concession to human weakness, but which are usually put forward as something to be *desired*. The attempt to codify principles, as Professor Fontenrose has codified his views on the combat myth, would be a notable step forward, but one for which I find slight

31

reason to have hopes, literary criticism being the haphazard pursuit it now generally is and is expected to be.

However, in my zeal I should not be too thorough. For it is true that much tentativeness is now called for. The problem of man as the symbol-using animal is *not* a subject to be treated as *settled*. And the risk in the "entelechial" approach is that it may manoeuver us into too great love for the "finishedness" of such a method.

But beyond all procedures and observations there looms the vexingly unsettled question, "Just what does it mean, to be the symbol-using animal?"

Close to the essence of this animal is the problem of the negative, of words for nothing, minus, thou-shalt-not, hence the yes-and-no of "polar" terms which, since man is an organism living in time whereas logical relations as such are timeless, can provide mythic-narrative equivalents for non-temporal aspects of symbolism (equivalents which, if pursued persistently enough, are found to track back upon themselves, thus ultimately denying the very progression whereby they seemed to progress).

But along with the problem of the "slain" principle's "immortal" survival (involving the guilt-laden paradox whereby each new law implies new crimes, each rule its corresponding misrule), there is the further logological fact that the "cosmos" of every clear definition fades into a "chaos" of implications, making a "chaos of clear ideas" that lead from one to another in an endless circle, and are best symbolized by the mythic design of the serpent Uroboros with his own tail in his mouth (I started to say "like a dictionary"!). The thought of such "formless-ness," such a Daedalian maze, lurking behind the paradigms leads to considerations on which we shall end this essay.

X

When discussing ways in which at Delphi Dionysos merged with Python, Fontenrose observes (p. 380): "It may be true that both alike are derived from an ancient Mediterranean deity who assumed a different name and complexion in every region, perhaps in every village, and that the cult and name of Dionysos spread out from its native land and absorbed many of the cults that had worshipped the ancient god under other names."

The conjecture but carries one step farther the author's decision (already quoted) to use the name Python "merely as a convenient designation for Apollo's opponent without regard to sex or species." And it involves fascinating possibilities with regard to the hazy relationship between polytheism and monotheism. For in effect it is suggesting a development whereby one god split into many.

As regards the sheer dialectics of the case, is monotheism as monotheistic as we usually take it to be, and polytheism as polytheistic? Are Jewish Yahweh, Islam's Allah, the Johannine logos, and the Roman Deus Dominus all the "same God" under different names? Or, within Christianity, is there no difference between the God of a devout Catholic and the God of Jehovah's Witnesses, no difference between the benign God of a Unitarian and a severe, Calvinistic God who condemns many wretched mortals to hellish suffering eternally? Or if the idea of "one" God spreads over many areas, and if that "one" God is necessarily conceived within the terms peculiar to each particular area, is this situation to be viewed as no different from, say, the choice of *Baum* or *arbre*, depending upon whether you would speak of trees to a German or a Frenchman?

The history of Mediterranean paganism is the history of gods whose attributes variously overlap upon one another, variously merging and dividing like language itself, with its many modes of "condensation" and "displacement" (modes of transformation not at all confined to the symbolism of myth, dream, and neurosis, but also present in symbol-systems at their most mature stage of development). The polytheistic nomenclature provided resources whereby any motive, habit, habitat, natural power, institution, or means of livelihood could by linguistic abstraction become a "god." Often the process was hardly more than the effect we get by capitalizing a word, writing "Thunder" instead of "thunder," plus mythic personifying of such abstractions. Where we might go from "finance" to "Finance," polytheism could readily go a step further, to the personal god, Plutus. In brief, polytheism could easily designate as gods many motives which monotheism would tend rather to define "a-theistically," yet monotheistic theologians are wont to warn that men "make gods" of many such "godless" things, a proclivity which we might at least call "moral polytheism," as distinct from an out-and-out ontological variety.

On the other hand, the polytheistic personifying of motives made possible a kind of duplication that in turn pointed in the direction of monotheism. For if a desire could be either just that, or the action of a god of Desire, here was a situation whereby the gods were profoundly implicated in one another, since every personal motive experienced by them could also be treated as the action of whatever god was most directly associated with that motive (a situation whereby in effect two gods would be one). Conversely, one god becomes two when the Homeric epithet for Ares, "Warlike" (*enyalios*) is treated by later authors as a separate person, a subaltern of Ares.

Also, obviously, where a combat myth figured, along with the fact that all gods had to be propitiated, there were further incentives for traits to overlap. Before we ever get to the ultimate problem of polar terms, there is the comparatively superficial fact that ambiguities and shifts of allegiance could confuse the allocation of favored and unfavored attributes. Hence, when all the versions and variants of a myth are collated, from sources that did not all represent the same attitude towards a given combat, Champion and Enemy are found to overlap, with corresponding confusion as regards the "perfect" distinction between "favored" and "unfavored" contestant.

Hellenistic imperialism itself also provided a step towards the "monotheizing of polytheism" in that it tended to treat all gods simply as regional motives, each of which could be represented by its appropriate temple in the capital city. Such convergence of outlying deities provided a visual incentive for the sort of thinking that could culminate in the idea of a temple to "The Unknown God." And this idea in turn could culminate in Paul's assurance to the Greeks that he represented precisely that God, the *Deus absconditus* of nascent Christian *trinitarian* monotheism.

But above all, *note this sheerly linguistic fact*: Whatever else gods are or are not, they are *terms*. And as terms their nature is such that, when you put all the gods together, you get a group with one over-all trait in common: Each of the many gods is divine, godly. Thus all the polytheistic nouns merge into one common monotheistic adjective.

So far as Greek was concerned, this adjective in turn could be transformed into a neuter noun, "the divine" (*to theíon*). The same word, astoundingly enough, also

33

meant brimstone—and the related verb, *theióō,* meant: to smoke with brimstone, to fumigate, hence to purify, to hallow. This range of meanings seems spontaneously to bring dragon and champion together!

But note one further significant fact about a word for the "divine." However generalized the idea of any particular god may be (as a term for powers or motives), the idea of the "divine" is still more highly generalized, since all words for particular deities could be classed under this one head. But central to our theory of words is our concern with the mythic tendency to state logical priority in terms of the temporally prior, to define principles in terms of the primordial. Following this pattern, the "mythic" way to say that the one principle of the divine is logically prior to particular examples of it would be to say that monotheism "came first" and was broken down into polytheism, when the unitary principle of godhead got different names (and eventually different attributes) in different places.

Thus, as seen from the logological point of view, you can "begin with" either monotheism or polytheism, depending upon whether you would stress the element of "the divine" that all gods have in common, or the theological differences that characterize people and peoples who supposedly worship the same God.

We are not here discussing a question of theology as such. For present purposes, our concern is with the turn from *mythos* to *logos* (both of them originally words for "word")—and thus from mythology to logology. We are trying to show how, as the approach through *mythology* led to over-all generalizations in mythic terms of Love and Death, so an approach through *logology* leads to overall generalizations in dialectical terms of composition and division, as shaped by the role of the negative and its translation into quasi-temporal terms of narrative combat. The problems of generalization underlying the author's paradigms, his reduction to Eros and Thanatos, his generalized use of the term "Python," and his thoughts on a unitary principle of godhead possibly underlying the names for many gods, thus are seen to reach their peculiar kind of "perfection" in speculations on the shifting relation between polytheism and monotheism.

The book we have been considering (and using as our point of departure!) is so thorough, it admirably helps us to confront these issues. Thus, in closing, we would again admonish that we have been attempting to *use* the book, not to argue with it. If peace is ever to be attained in this world, it will be attained through an educational system that can systematically study the principles underlying precisely the ways whereby man, the symbol-using animal, makes his peculiar contributions to the "combat myth," in all its variations.

NOTES

[1] Quoted from "Dialectician's Prayer," reprinted in my *Book of Moments* (Hermes Publications, Los Altos, California, 1955), p. 41.

[2] On scene-agent ratio see my *Grammar of Motives* (New York, 1945), pp. 7 ff.

[3] In my *Grammar of Motives* I reduce such loci to five: act, scene, agent, agency, and purpose.

[4] Chapter IV, Section 15.

[5] At various places in my *Rhetoric of Motives* (New York, 1950), I have aimed to show how the "Hierarchal" motive figures in the sense of mystery.

[6] Chapter I, Section I.

3.

The Hero and the God

THE standard path of the mythological adventure of the hero is a magnification of the formula represented in the rites of passage: *separation—initiation—return:* which might be named the nuclear unit of the monomyth.[35]

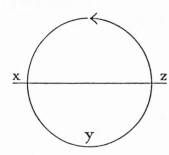

A hero ventures forth from the world of common day into a region of supernatural wonder: fabulous forces are there encountered and a decisive victory is won: the hero comes back from this mysterious adventure with the power to bestow boons on his fellow man.

Prometheus ascended to the heavens, stole fire from the gods, and descended. Jason sailed through the Clashing Rocks into a sea of marvels, circumvented the dragon that guarded the Golden Fleece, and returned with the fleece and the power to wrest his rightful throne from a usurper. Aeneas went down into the underworld, crossed the dreadful river of the dead, threw a sop to the three-headed watchdog Cerberus, and conversed, at last, with the shade of his dead father. All things were unfolded to

[35] The word *monomyth* is from James Joyce, *Finnegans Wake* (New York: Viking Press, Inc., 1939), p. 581.

30

him: the destiny of souls, the destiny of Rome, which he was about to found, "and in what wise he might avoid or endure every burden." [36] He returned through the ivory gate to his work in the world.

A majestic representation of the difficulties of the hero-task, and of its sublime import when it is profoundly conceived and solemnly undertaken, is presented in the traditional legend of the Great Struggle of the Buddha. The young prince Gautama Sakyamuni set forth secretly from his father's palace on the princely steed Kanthaka, passed miraculously through the guarded gate, rode through the night attended by the torches of four times sixty thousand divinities, lightly hurdled a majestic river eleven hundred and twenty-eight cubits wide, and then with a single sword-stroke sheared his own royal locks—whereupon the remaining hair, two finger-breadths in length, curled to the right and lay close to his head. Assuming the garments of a monk, he moved as a beggar through the world, and during these years of apparently aimless wandering acquired and transcended the eight stages of meditation. He retired to a hermitage, bent his powers six more years to the great struggle, carried austerity to the uttermost, and collapsed in seeming death, but presently recovered. Then he returned to the less rigorous life of the ascetic wanderer.

One day he sat beneath a tree, contemplating the eastern quarter of the world, and the tree was illuminated with his radiance. A young girl named Sujata came and presented milk-rice to him in a golden bowl, and when he tossed the empty bowl into a river it floated upstream. This was the signal that the moment of his triumph was at hand. He arose and proceeded along a road which the gods had decked and which was eleven hundred and twenty-eight cubits wide. The snakes and birds and the divinities of the woods and fields did him homage with flowers and celestial perfumes, heavenly choirs poured forth music, the ten thousand worlds were filled with perfumes, garlands, harmonies, and

[36] Virgil, *Aeneid*, VI, 892.

31

shouts of acclaim; for he was on his way to the great Tree of Enlightenment, the Bo Tree, under which he was to redeem the universe. He placed himself, with a firm resolve, beneath the Bo Tree, on the Immovable Spot, and straightway was approached by Kama-Mara, the god of love and death.

The dangerous god appeared mounted on an elephant and carrying weapons in his thousand hands. He was surrounded by his army, which extended twelve leagues before him, twelve to the right, twelve to the left, and in the rear as far as to the confines of the world; it was nine leagues high. The protecting deities of the universe took flight, but the Future Buddha remained unmoved beneath the Tree. And the god then assailed him, seeking to break his concentration.

Whirlwind, rocks, thunder and flame, smoking weapons with keen edges, burning coals, hot ashes, boiling mud, blistering sands and fourfold darkness, the Antagonist hurled against the Savior, but the missiles were all transformed into celestial flowers and ointments by the power of Gautama's ten perfections. Mara then deployed his daughters, Desire, Pining, and Lust, surrounded by voluptuous attendants, but the mind of the Great Being was not distracted. The god finally challenged his right to be sitting on the Immovable Spot, flung his razor-sharp discus angrily, and bid the towering host of the army to let fly at him with mountain crags. But the Future Buddha only moved his hand to touch the ground with his fingertips, and thus bid the goddess Earth bear witness to his right to be sitting where he was. She did so with a hundred, a thousand, a hundred thousand roars, so that the elephant of the Antagonist fell upon its knees in obeisance to the Future Buddha. The army was immediately dispersed, and the gods of all the worlds scattered garlands.

Having won that preliminary victory before sunset, the conqueror acquired in the first watch of the night knowledge of his previous existences, in the second watch the divine eye of omniscient vision, and in the last watch understanding of the chain

32

of causation. He experienced perfect enlightenment at the break of day.[37]

Then for seven days Gautama—now the Buddha, the Enlightened—sat motionless in bliss; for seven days he stood apart and regarded the spot on which he had received enlightenment; for seven days he paced between the place of the sitting and the place of the standing; for seven days he abode in a pavilion furnished by the gods and reviewed the whole doctrine of causality and release; for seven days he sat beneath the tree where the girl Sujata had brought him milk-rice in a golden bowl, and there meditated on the doctrine of the sweetness of Nirvana; he removed to another tree and a great storm raged for seven days, but the King of Serpents emerged from the roots and protected the Buddha with his expanded hood; finally, the Buddha sat for seven days beneath a fourth tree enjoying still the sweetness of liberation. Then he doubted whether his message could be communicated, and he thought to retain the wisdom for himself; but the god Brahma descended from the zenith to implore that he should become the teacher of gods and men. The Buddha was thus persuaded to proclaim the path.[38] And he went back into

[37] This is the most important single moment in Oriental mythology, a counterpart of the Crucifixion of the West. The Buddha beneath the Tree of Enlightenment (the Bo Tree) and Christ on Holy Rood (the Tree of Redemption) are analogous figures, incorporating an archetypal World Savior, World Tree motif, which is of immemorial antiquity. Many other variants of the theme will be found among the episodes to come. The Immovable Spot and Mount Calvary are images of the World Navel, or World Axis (see p. 40, *infra*).

The calling of the Earth to witness is represented in traditional Buddhist art by images of the Buddha, sitting in the classic Buddha posture, with the right hand resting on the right knee and its fingers lightly touching the ground.

[38] The point is that Buddhahood, Enlightenment, cannot be communicated, but only the *way* to Enlightenment. This doctrine of the incommunicability of the Truth which is beyond names and forms is basic to the great Oriental, as well as to the Platonic, traditions. Whereas the truths of science are communicable, being demonstrable hypotheses rationally founded on

33

the cities of men where he moved among the citizens of the world, bestowing the inestimable boon of the knowledge of the Way.[39]

The Old Testament records a comparable deed in its legend of Moses, who, in the third month of the departure of Israel out of the land of Egypt, came with his people into the wilderness of Sinai; and there Israel pitched their tents over against the mountain. And Moses went up to God, and the Lord called unto him from the mountain. The Lord gave to him the Tables of the Law and commanded Moses to return with these to Israel, the people of the Lord.[40]

Jewish folk legend declares that during the day of the revelation diverse rumblings sounded from Mount Sinai. "Flashes of lightning, accompanied by an ever swelling peal of horns, moved the people with mighty fear and trembling. God bent the heavens, moved the earth, and shook the bounds of the world, so that the depths trembled, and the heavens grew frightened. His splendor passed through the four portals of fire, earthquake, storm, and hail. The kings of the earth trembled in their palaces. The earth herself thought the resurrection of the dead was about to take place, and that she would have to account for the blood of the slain she had absorbed, and for the bodies of the murdered whom she covered. The earth was not calmed until she heard the first words of the Decalogue.

---

observable facts, ritual, mythology, and metaphysics are but guides to the brink of a transcendent illumination, the final step to which must be taken by each in his own silent experience. Hence one of the Sanskrit terms for sage is *mūni*, "the silent one." *Sākyamūni* (one of the titles of Gautama Buddha) means "the silent one or sage *(mūni)* of the Sakya clan." Though he is the founder of a widely taught world religion, the ultimate core of his doctrine remains concealed, necessarily, in silence.

[39] Greatly abridged from *Jataka*, Introduction, i, 58-75 (translated by Henry Clarke Warren, *Buddhism in Translations* (Harvard Oriental Series, 3) Cambridge, Mass.: Harvard University Press, 1896, pp. 56-87), and the *Lalitavistara* as rendered by Ananda K. Coomaraswamy, *Buddha and the Gospel of Buddhism* (New York: G. P. Putnam's Sons, 1916), pp. 24-38.

[40] Exodus, 19:3-5.

34

"The heavens opened and Mount Sinai, freed from the earth, rose into the air, so that its summit towered into the heavens, while a thick cloud covered the sides of it, and touched the feet of the Divine Throne. Accompanying God on one side, appeared twenty-two thousand angels with crowns for the Levites, the only tribe that remained true to God while the rest worshiped the Golden Calf. On the second side were sixty myriads, three thousand five hundred and fifty angels, each bearing a crown of fire for each individual Israelite. Double this number of angels was on the third side; whereas on the fourth side they were simply innumerable. For God did not appear from one direction, but from all simultaneously, which, however, did not prevent His glory from filling the heaven as well as the earth. In spite of these innumerable hosts there was no crowding on Mount Sinai, no mob, there was room for all." [41]

As we soon shall see, whether presented in the vast, almost oceanic images of the Orient, in the vigorous narratives of the Greeks, or in the majestic legends of the Bible, the adventure of the hero normally follows the pattern of the nuclear unit above described: a separation from the world, a penetration to some source of power, and a life-enhancing return. The whole of the Orient has been blessed by the boon brought back by Gautama Buddha—his wonderful teaching of the Good Law—just as the Occident has been by the Decalogue of Moses. The Greeks referred fire, the first support of all human culture, to the world-transcending deed of their Prometheus, and the Romans the founding of their world-supporting city to Aeneas, following his departure from fallen Troy and his visit to the eerie underworld of the dead. Everywhere, no matter what the sphere of interest (whether religious, political, or personal), the really creative acts are represented as those deriving from some sort of dying to the world; and what happens in the interval of the hero's nonentity,

[41] Louis Ginzberg, *The Legends of the Jews* (Philadelphia: The Jewish Publication Society of America, 1911), Vol. III, pp. 90-94.

35

so that he comes back as one reborn, made great and filled with creative power, mankind is also unanimous in declaring. We shall have only to follow, therefore, a multitude of heroic figures through the classic stages of the universal adventure in order to see again what has always been revealed. This will help us to understand not only the meaning of those images for contemporary life, but also the singleness of the human spirit in its aspirations, powers, vicissitudes, and wisdom.

The following pages will present in the form of one composite adventure the tales of a number of the world's symbolic carriers of the destiny of Everyman. The first great stage, that of the *separation* or *departure*, will be shown in Part I, Chapter I, in five subsections: (1) "The Call to Adventure," or the signs of the vocation of the hero; (2) "Refusal of the Call," or the folly of the flight from the god; (3) "Supernatural Aid," the unsuspected assistance that comes to one who has undertaken his proper adventure; (4) "The Crossing of the First Threshold"; and (5) "The Belly of the Whale," or the passage into the realm of night. The stage of *the trials and victories of initiation* will appear in Chapter II in six subsections: (1) "The Road of Trials," or the dangerous aspect of the gods; (2) "The Meeting with the Goddess" *(Magna Mater)*, or the bliss of infancy regained; (3) "Woman as the Temptress," the realization and agony of Oedipus; (4) "Atonement with the Father"; (5) "Apotheosis"; and (6) "The Ultimate Boon."

The return and reintegration with society, which is indispensable to the continuous circulation of spiritual energy into the world, and which, from the standpoint of the community, is the justification of the long retreat, the hero himself may find the most difficult requirement of all. For if he has won through, like the Buddha, to the profound repose of complete enlightenment, there is danger that the bliss of this experience may annihilate all recollection of, interest in, or hope for, the sorrows of the world; or else the problem of making known the way of illumina-

36

tion to people wrapped in economic problems may seem too great to solve. And on the other hand, if the hero, instead of submitting to all of the initiatory tests, has, like Prometheus, simply darted to his goal (by violence, quick device, or luck) and plucked the boon for the world that he intended, then the powers that he has unbalanced may react so sharply that he will be blasted from within and without—crucified, like Prometheus, on the rock of his own violated unconscious. Or if the hero, in the third place, makes his safe and willing return, he may meet with such a blank misunderstanding and disregard from those whom he has come to help that his career will collapse. The third of the following chapters will conclude the discussion of these prospects under six subheadings: (1) "Refusal of the Return," or the world denied; (2) "The Magic Flight," or the escape of Prometheus; (3) "Rescue from Without"; (4) "The Crossing of the Return Threshold," or the return to the world of common day; (5) "Master of the Two Worlds"; and (6) "Freedom to Live," the nature and function of the ultimate boon.[42]

The composite hero of the monomyth is a personage of exceptional gifts. Frequently he is honored by his society, frequently unrecognized or disdained. He and/or the world in which he finds himself suffers from a symbolical deficiency. In fairy tales this may be as slight as the lack of a certain golden ring, whereas in apocalyptic vision the physical and spiritual life of the whole earth can be represented as fallen, or on the point of falling, into ruin.

Typically, the hero of the fairy tale achieves a domestic,

[42] This circular adventure of the hero appears in a negative form in stories of the deluge type, where it is not the hero who goes to the power, but the power that rises against the hero, and again subsides. Deluge stories occur in every quarter of the earth. They form an integral portion of the archetypal myth of the history of the world, and so belong properly to Part II of the present discussion: "The Cosmogonic Cycle." The deluge hero is a symbol of the germinal vitality of man surviving even the worst tides of catastrophe and sin.

37

microcosmic triumph, and the hero of myth a world-historical, macrocosmic triumph. Whereas the former—the youngest or despised child who becomes the master of extraordinary powers —prevails over his personal oppressors, the latter brings back from his adventure the means for the regeneration of his society as a whole. Tribal or local heroes, such as the emperor Huang Ti, Moses, or the Aztec Tezcatlipoca, commit their boons to a single folk; universal heroes—Mohammed, Jesus, Gautama Buddha— bring a message for the entire world.

Whether the hero be ridiculous or sublime, Greek or barbarian, gentile or Jew, his journey varies little in essential plan. Popular tales represent the heroic action as physical; the higher religions show the deed to be moral; nevertheless, there will be found astonishingly little variation in the morphology of the adventure, the character roles involved, the victories gained. If one or another of the basic elements of the archetypal pattern is omitted from a given fairy tale, legend, ritual, or myth, it is bound to be somehow or other implied—and the omission itself can speak volumes for the history and pathology of the example, as we shall presently see.

Part II, "The Cosmogonic Cycle," unrolls the great vision of the creation and destruction of the world which is vouchsafed as revelation to the successful hero. Chapter I, *Emanations*, treats of the coming of the forms of the universe out of the void. Chapter II, *The Virgin Birth*, is a review of the creative and redemptive roles of the female power, first on a cosmic scale as the Mother of the Universe, then again on the human plane as the Mother of the Hero. Chapter III, *Transformations of the Hero*, traces the course of the legendary history of the human race through its typical stages, the hero appearing on the scene in various forms according to the changing needs of the race. And Chapter IV, *Dissolutions*, tells of the foretold end, first of the hero, then of the manifested world.

38

The cosmogonic cycle is presented with astonishing consistency in the sacred writings of all the continents,[43] and it gives to the adventure of the hero a new and interesting turn; for now it appears that the perilous journey was a labor not of attainment but of reattainment, not discovery but rediscovery. The godly powers sought and dangerously won are revealed to have been within the heart of the hero all the time. He is "the king's son" who has come to know who he is and therewith has entered into the exercise of his proper power—"God's son," who has learned to know how much that title means. From this point of view the hero is symbolical of that divine creative and redemptive image which is hidden within us all, only waiting to be known and rendered into life.

"For the One who has become many, remains the One undivided, but each part is all of Christ," we read in the writings of Saint Symeon the younger (949-1022 A.D.). "I saw Him in my house," the saint goes on. "Among all those everyday things He appeared unexpectedly and became unutterably united and merged with me, and leaped over to me without anything in between, as fire to iron, as the light to glass. And He made me like fire and like light. And I became that which I saw before and beheld from afar. I do not know how to relate this miracle to you. . . . I am man by nature, and God by the grace of God." [44]

A comparable vision is described in the apocryphal Gospel of Eve. "I stood on a loftly mountain and saw a gigantic man and another a dwarf; and I heard as it were a voice of thunder, and drew nigh for to hear; and He spake unto me and said: I am thou,

[43] The present volume is not concerned with the historical discussion of this circumstance. That task is reserved for a work now under preparation. The present volume is a comparative, not genetic, study. Its purpose is to show that essential parallels exist in the myths themselves as well as in the interpretations and applications that the sages have announced for them.

[44] Translated by Dom Ansgar Nelson, O.S.B., in *The Soul Afire* (New York: Pantheon Books, 1944), p. 303.

39

and thou art I; and wheresoever thou mayest be I am there. In all am I scattered, and whensoever thou willest, thou gatherest Me; and gathering Me, thou gatherest Thyself." [45]

The two—the hero and his ultimate god, the seeker and the found—are thus understood as the outside and inside of a single, self-mirrored mystery, which is identical with the mystery of the manifest world. The great deed of the supreme hero is to come to the knowledge of this unity in multiplicity and then to make it known.

[45] Quoted by Epiphanius, *Adversus haereses*, xxvi, 3.

40

Myth as Literature

꙾

By RICHARD CHASE

W E CANNOT CONSIDER myth in relation to modern literature for very long without feeling that the term "myth" is too comprehensive to be very usable. I should like to begin, therefore, by trying to limit the meaning of the word, not in an effort to arrive at an absolute definition so much as to suggest a definition useful in literary studies.

We cannot say, then, that any untrue story or idea is a myth. If someone tells us that "the threat of international Russian expansion" is a myth, we know, of course, what he means, whether or not we agree with him. But suppose we phrase it differently. Suppose that instead of "the threat of international Russian expansion" we say "the Red menace." Surely, we feel, however vaguely, that "the Red menace" is *more* mythical than the original phrase. As soon as we perceive this, we feel that the term which tries to describe *both* phrases cannot be very precise. The difference between the two phrases indicates the direction which our definition, as literary scholars, must take. The phrase we intuitively feel to be the more mythical of the two is so because it contains an image (red), because the word "menace" makes us think of something living and terrible, a dragon or a scourge, and because the phrase as a whole is obviously calculated to play strongly upon the passions.

A difference in context and intention may make the same "untrue idea" either more or less mythical. In an economics book the law of supply and demand may be stated flatly and dispassionately as a truth. If we think it is an untruth, we shall do well to call it simply that, and save the term "myth" for the law of supply and demand as it is pictured in a philippic by a member of the National Association of Manufacturers, who translates a barren idea into an image of the All-father or the *élan* of the universe.

As for a story, we cannot suppose that a novelist makes a myth out of the life of Abraham Lincoln simply by changing some of the biographical facts. That would indicate a purely statistical method of defining myth: history becomes myth when a certain number of dates and incidents have been misrepresented.

A second opinion about myth which is only indirectly useful in literary studies belongs primarily to anthropology. I mean the notion that a story or idea understood, admired, or believed by a whole class or a whole society is, *ipso facto,* a myth. A mythical idea, properly so called, *may* be entertained by great numbers of people, may be a cultural image having great normative or aesthetic value. But that is not in itself what makes the idea mythical. The anthropological definition, again, is too broad for students of literature and also, I suspect, for anthropologists. We feel intuitively that the idea of the Empire State building, as it is entertained by millions of Americans, is mythical. But we have to turn from anthropology to psychology to find out why: we have to consider such things as the symbolic value of the building, its color, its shape, its size, and the stories which cluster around it, the number of men killed in its construction, the suicides who leap from the summit—in short to the quality of the emotive response to it. The binomial theorem is understood, admired, and believed by millions of Americans, but that does not make it a mythical idea in the sense that the Empire State building is.

Again, the elusive American idea which we designate by the word "Mom" has the most crucial and pervasive significance in our culture. But before this idea can be properly called mythical, we have at least to notice the different ways in which the idea is presented: differences in the mode of symbolization, differences in context and intention. When the idea of "Mom," which we vaguely feel to be "mythical," appears in art forms, we have something tangible to deal with; we can perhaps determine to what extent and in what ways the idea is mythical. Thus we must look to specific representations of the idea: one of the many movies in which the strong, enduring, wise, and mature woman strokes the worried brow of her regressive, baffled, defeated, and inarticulate lover; or such highly literate novels as Isabel Bolton's *Do I Wake or Sleep* and Robert Penn Warren's *All the King's Men.*

"Mom" is an example of a pervasive cultural image which is also represented mythically in different kinds of literature. My point is that it is this representation which makes it, in varying ways, mythical. The anthropological notion of myth, as I once discovered in a controversy with an eminent lady anthropologist, leaves no place for T. S. Eliot or W. H. Auden. These poets are known only to a few people: therefore their poetry is not mythical. No anthropologist has *said* this as far as I know. But that is the logic of their position. I do not mean for a moment that the study of cultural images may not be relevant to the study of literature. It is highly relevant in the books of Constance Rourke, for example. I speak here only of the study of myth, a more limited and special problem than the study of literature.

A third misleading idea about myth is that any story or poem which invokes or refers to the remote past thereby becomes mythical. This idea is based upon the traditional—but in the light of modern anthropology, highly erroneous—notion of the "mythical age" of man. The implication of this idea is that in the early ages of history all literature, as well as all cognition, was mythical whereas in our own later ages human thought has left the mythical stage and become rational or enlightened, or at least disillusioned. This idea further implies that a modern poem is mythical because it refers to Aphrodite or Prometheus. But these mythical beings, as we know them, are the creatures of highly rational and sophisticated poets whose thinking was not necessarily more or less mythical than that of our poets. The Greek poets did not, of course, make *their* poems mythical by referring to a yet more ancient mythological literature. Aeschylus'

Prometheus is a primitive and original creature who takes his being *from Aeschylus' poems*. So with Shelley's very different Prometheus. Any personage in any poem must earn the right, so to speak, to be called mythical, and he must do this, regardless of his origin, within the poem in which he appears. Henry James's *The Golden Bowl* does not become mythical because one of the characters is named Adam, nor is *The Waste Land* a mythical poem because it mentions Tiresias.

Stated very generally, the fourth and last idea which I wish to question is that myth is philosophy. We can distinguish two aspects of this idea: (1) that myth is a cognitive activity; a proto-scientific or proto-philosophical attempt to understand natural, social, or metaphysical phenomena; and (2) that myth is not only cognitive but has normative value as dogma and is therefore a world view or a way of life.

The idea that myth is a naive mode of explaining the universe has had currency at least since the time of Thales and Pythagoras who, apparently, thought that the old myths contained secrets about the operations of nature. And this has been the common rationalist opinion right down through the Enlightenment philosophers, the "Aryan" philologists, and the Victorian rationalists to such a modern philosopher as Santayana and such a folklorist as Joseph Campbell. This idea has been opposed by two heroes of mythological study, David Hume and Herbert Spencer, and in later times by Dewey. Their perception that myth is not primarily cognitive (I do not say it has *no* cognitive value) has been abundantly supported by the American anthropologists. Professor Ruth Benedict, for example, finds it "ironic that the academic study of folklore should have labored through its course under the incubus of theories explaining seven-headed monsters and magic swords as survivals of primordial conditions, allegories of the sun and moon or of the sex act or etiological philosophizing and have ignored the unconfined role of the human imagination in the creation of mythology"—a clear challenge, certainly, to literary scholars to take up what is in the nature of things their proper study. But as literary scholars we must be aware that the rationalist fallacy often pervades our own thinking. This has been borne in upon me recently in reading current Melville scholarship, the great majority of which presents Melville as a sort of bumbling philosopher who wrote books in order to discuss the nature of the universe and to arrive at something called "the ultimate truth." This attitude represents a serious underestimation of what creative literature—poetry in the larger sense—is and does.

No doubt there are certain senses in which the word "myth" may justifiably be used to signify a world view, a way of life, or a whole intellectual-emotive cultural synthesis: for example, T. S. Eliot's "Christian society" or the agrarian Utopia on which the Southern writers once took their stand. This vision of the Southern writers, at once archaist and futurist, with its pleasing picture of the man of passion and tragic sense living in an organic society and emulating Cicero and Castiglione and Burke, is certainly in some sense of the word a myth. I think, however, that we ought to call it so only in so far as it may be delineated aesthetically. This will keep us from confusing myth with dogma and theology and religion, which are something else again. To say, as many modern writers of various persuasions do, that we need to discover or manufacture a comprehensive societal "myth" before we can hope to have an admirable culture and a fruitful literature is to make two related errors—the error of placing an impossibly heavy burden on one human faculty (for myth alone will not make a Utopia, any more than reason alone) and the error of putting the cart before the horse: myth proceeds from culture and literature, and not vice versa. This is not to say that myth has no normative moral value. It has. Like other modes of art, it sometimes speaks with definitive moral authority. Myth may even be said, as Malinowski points out, to have the efficacy of dogma; but as that excellent writer makes clear in his *Myth in Primitive Psychology,* myth is made *ad hoc* to sanctify cultural and aesthetic phenomena. Myth is fluid and adaptable —less so than the historical process, but more so than dogma.

The opinions about myth which we have been discussing have one thing in common: they are formalist descriptions. I hope I do not sound like a Soviet Commissar if I say that formalist descriptions of myth—if they are nothing else—are misleading: but that would be true only if I were trying to substitute one formalism for another. As Andrew Lang remarked, the attempt to produce formal descriptions of myth has for centuries been "the history of rash, premature, and exclusive theories." That is why some other attitude toward myth is necessary.

In discussing what myth is not, we have been led to suggest what it is: namely, literature. The question of how myth is related to culture, philosophy, or religion is the question of how literature is related to these things; or rather, it is a special aspect of the larger literary question. And it is a special aspect because myth is a special kind of literature; myth is literature functioning in a special way, achieving special modes of expression. The remaining problem in this paper, then, is to suggest what special kind of literature myth is.

Myth is magic literature, literature which achieves the wonderful, uncanny, or brilliant reality of the magical vision of things. Magic is a compulsive technique for controlling experience and creating or resurrecting the sense of reality. It is a mimetic device, at once utilitarian and aesthetic—indeed it is utilitarian *because* it is aesthetic—for summoning that supernatural force the savages call *mana* and compelling it to do one's bidding. Myth, R. R. Marett has said, is *mana* grown picturesque. In the vision of the magician, objects take on the quality of *mana* in exactly the same way in which they take on other qualities: color, size, sound. This fusion of quality and object produces an impression, not of unreality, but of more than usual reality—an aesthetic reality which impresses the magician as uncanny, awful, brilliant, fearful, or beautiful in its motion or its state of repose.

Magic, we see, is not only a compulsive technique but an aesthetic activity. Magic is immediately available to art and art to magic. Myths may be regarded, on the one hand, as the aesthetic exercise which preserves and reaffirms the magic fusion; myths keep the magician's world—and the poet's world—from falling apart. On the other hand, myths are poetic dramatizations of the conflicts and interactions of powers operating within the qualities and objects with which these powers seem to be identical. If these observations are sound, any narrative or poem which reaffirms the dynamism and vibrancy of the world, which fortifies the ego with the impression that there is a magically potent brilliancy or dramatic force in the world, may be called a myth.

Let me suggest certain modes which the mythical vision of things may take in modern literature—with the thought in mind that the method of studying myth in an American or British poet may be, more nearly than we usually think, the same as that of studying myth in a Polynesian or Algonquin or Greek poet. Of the writers I mention—Wordsworth, Auden, and Yeats—the first may seem to be in strange company. But to speak of Wordsworth in connection with these more modern writers is to remind ourselves of those necessities of poetry which are implicit in poetic composition regardless of time and change.

In a paper read before the English Institute in 1941, Lionel Trilling subjected Wordsworth's "Ode: Intimations of Immortality" to a very illuminating analysis. Trilling's point was that in the "Ode" Wordsworth "is talking about something common to us all, the development of the sense of reality." I should like to turn briefly to Wordsworth's "Resolution and Independence" and show that this poem, too, is about the sense of reality. The usual notion about this poem seems to be that Wordsworth, as poets will, has become despondent. He is lonesome and so poor that he must postpone his marriage, and he fears that the poet's lot is to know a measure of "gladness" in his youth and to sink but too soon into "madness." A walk over the moors, however, and an encounter with a noble and resolute old Leech-gatherer restore his self-confidence and his inspiration. But let us look more closely at the poem. Trilling speaks of the passage on pre-existence in the "Ode" as "a very serious conceit . . . intended to give high value to . . . natural experience." There is such a conceit, or myth, in "Resolution and Independence," and it serves just the same purpose.

Wordsworth's poem is not an exercise in Romantic melancholy. As the poet walks out on a beautiful, bright morning, he is, to be sure, oppressed with his worldly condition: his "solitude," his "distress," his "poverty." But I do not think these words indicate the full content of his despondency:

> as it sometimes chanceth, from the might
> Of joy in minds that can no further go,
> As high as we have mounted in delight
> In our dejection do we sink as low;
> To me that morning did it happen so;
> And fears and fancies thick upon me came;
> Dim sadness—and blind thoughts, I knew not,
> nor could name.

Notice that Wordsworth is talking of "minds"; his sadness is "dim"; thoughts are "blind." In a later stanza we hear that he is "perplexed," and in writing about his poem Wordsworth says specifically that what he gains from meeting the Leech-gatherer is "new insight." The sense of the reality of natural experience, which Wordsworth cherishes above all else, suddenly leaves him. When he speaks of "madness" in an ensuing stanza, he is not using a trope. There is nothing sentimental or soft in the word. He means insanity: the abyss opens before him. The two following stanzas demonstrate the dilemma Wordsworth is in:

> Even as these blissful creatures do I fare;
> Far from the world I walk, and from all care;
> But there may come another day to me—
> Solitude, pain of heart, distress, and poverty.
>
> My whole life I have lived in pleasant thought,
> As if life's business were a summer mood;
> As if all needful things would come unsought
> To genial faith, still rich in genial good;
> But how can he expect that others should
> Build for him, sow for him, and at his call
> Love him, who for himself will take no heed at all?

Now, these lines are, to be sure, full of apprehension concerning the poet's worldly estate and full of self-blame. But what is responsible for "the fear that kills," the sudden wave of "fears and fancies," that has come over the poet? Is it not that he perceives a scale of values other than his own and that he suddenly fears that the other scale is the true reality and that if this is so, he is lost in an appalling emptiness? Wordsworth's sense of

reality, the whole foundation of his sanity and produc-
tiveness, is called into question. For the moment a
rival reality presents itself. The word "resolution" in
the title of the poem does not mean anything ethical
like "the determination to carry on." It means, I
think, the resolution of a dilemma, the banishment of
a false reality, the reassertion of a true reality. And the
true reality is reasserted mythically.

The old Leech-gatherer appears to Wordsworth as a
revelation. It is so felicitous a revelation that it seems
to have happened out of the necessity of Wordsworth's
dilemma. The appearance of the old man may be
"a leading from above, a something given." The reason why the Leech-gatherer affects Wordsworth so
strongly is that, as we should say, he has *mana*. He is a
rough-hewn man of flesh and blood, but he is also a
vehicle of natural forces and a visitor from the primeval world ("like a man from some far region sent").
As Malinowski might put it, he is "a primeval,
greater and more relevant reality by which the present life, fates and activities of mankind are determined."

> As a huge stone is sometimes seen to lie
> Couched on the bald top of an eminence;
> Wonder to all who do the same espy,
> By what means it could thither come, and whence;
> So that it seems a thing endued with sense:
> Like a sea-beast crawled forth, that on a shelf
> Of rock or sand reposeth, there to sun itself . . .

I think it important that Wordsworth attributes to
the Leech-gatherer just that sense of the reality of

nature which the poet himself fears that he may have lost. The Leech-gatherer, with his "yet-vivid eyes," is able to "con" the ponds and pools of water "as if he had been reading in a book." And Wordsworth describes the old man's mind as "firm."

Yet the poet does not recover his own sense of natural reality by observing the old man and emulating him. The vision in which the old man appears (for it *is* a vision) is to Wordsworth the essence of reality. The universe acquires vibrancy and vitality; things are set in motion again by the presence of the Leech-gatherer. "Natural experience," which had for a moment become flat and cold, again acquires a "high value."

I mention Auden's poem called "Voltaire at Ferney" partly because it so unpretentious. It is perhaps too easy to confuse myth with size, violence, or flamboyance. The first four stanzas of Auden's poem are somewhat loose and discursive; they are almost light verse. We see Voltaire as an old man returning to his estate. Approaching his estate, he observes an exile making watches; he looks at a hospital being built; an "agent" pauses to tell him that some orchard trees are progressing well. He thinks of his enemies in Paris, who whisper that he is wicked. He muses that, like gardening, the fight against the false and the unfair is always a worthy fight. And he utters the hortatory word "Civilize." The fourth stanza is wry, witty, and final in its judgments: he

never doubted, like D'Alembert, that he would win:
Only Pascal was a great enemy, the rest

Were rats already poisoned; there was much, though, to be
    done,
And only himself to count upon.
Dear Diderot was dull but did his best;
Rousseau, he'd always known, would blubber and give in.

Now a poem like this, so far slack, loose, and discursive, is in danger of "falling apart," of dissipating itself into a kind of vague aura of thought and emotion
which leaves the reader with no total impression. The
last stanza must provide one or more bright and compelling images if a sense of aesthetic fact is to be
achieved—if, in other words, the poet is to recreate the
full emotive intensity of Voltaire's thoughts and to
fuse his own emotions and thoughts into a meaningful
totality. The last stanza runs thus:

So, like a sentinel, he could not sleep. The night was
    full of wrong,
Earthquakes and executions. Soon he would be dead,
And still all over Europe stood the horrible nurses
Itching to boil their children. Only his verses
Perhaps could stop them: He must go on working. Over-
    head
The uncomplaining stars composed their lucid song.

(It has suddenly become night, providing a dramatically ironic situation for the master of Enlightenment.) There are three mythical images in this last
stanza: the sentinel, the horrible nurses, and the stars'
lucid song. In the earlier stanzas, Voltaire, looking
over his estate, watching the progress of civilization,
had been merely Voltaire. Now he acquires the magic
virtue of a superhuman figure, a demigod, an awful
symbol watching over the unruly and disastrous con-

tinent. The horrible nurses who itch to boil their children may stand in Auden's mind for many things. They are, for one thing, ordinary human nurses, who, as a poet knows whether or not he has read Freud, entertain certain sadistic feelings about the children they care for. Again, the horrible nurses are the perpetuators of barbaric stories and superstitious folklore which, as Voltaire notes in one of his writings, they whisper into the ears of children, thereby hindering the cause of civilization and mature rationality. Furthermore, the nurses are themselves creatures of the folklore imagination—the witches of European folktales. Finally, the horrible nurses are the nations of Europe who instead of nursing their children up to the level of civilization conspire to kill them by persecution and war. And so the nurses become awful images of violence and death stirring uneasily in the European night.

The purpose of the magician is to summon the magical powers of the universe into his own control. He does this to enforce reality and signficance upon a chaotic and meaningless world and, by opposing the magical *mana* to forces which threaten him or his vision of things, to promote a dramatic clash the upshot of which is a resolution of forces into a new harmony. Voltaire, looking into the sky and hearing the lucid song of the stars, becomes this magician. For the implication of the poem is that Voltaire will be able, once he has heard this magic song, to enlist its help. He will be able to fuse this celestial song with his own song—that is, he will be able to heighten the reality and efficacy of his own song in opposition to evil. Notice that the myth in Auden's poem is something which the poem itself strives to become and does become. It is not a ready-made construct or system of symbols or body of dogma on which the poem falls back.

The problem of studying mythical poems which make use of specific, well-known mythical figures or stories is essentially the same as studying those which do not. We must study how the poem becomes mythical within itself, out of its own structural and emotive necessity. Yeats's poem called "Among School Children" makes use of the myth of Leda and the Swan, but the appearance of Leda does not, by itself, make Yeats's poem mythical. The poem begins discursively; the first stanza presents details and arranges properties. It also states a problem, for the sixty-year-old smiling public man (that is, Yeats) who walks through the schoolroom watching the nuns and children has a "question" in his mind. The question of the smiling public man may be something rather obscure, like What is this vague presentiment of excitement and significance which I seem to feel? The poet, apart from the public man, also has a problem: How to discover in the given situation the energy and order of a coherent poetic statement. The poet needs an incandescent focus around which to consolidate and realize his disunified, incipient thoughts and his more or less random emotions. In short, he needs a mythical image. It cannot, of course, be *any* mythical image, but one that is legislated by the given situation and the as yet half-unconscious poetic intensity into which it strives to translate itself.

> I dream of a Ledaean body, bent
> Above a sinking fire, a tale that she
> Told of a harsh reproof, or trivial event
> That changed some childish day to tragedy—

Now the Ledaean body probably refers to Yeats's beloved revolutionary, Maud Gonne, whom the poet was in the habit of representing in various mythological guises. She seems to signify in "Among School Children" what Leda signifies in Yeats's sonnet called "Leda and the Swan." The sonnet refers to Leda's ravishment by Zeus and says in effect that Zeus makes Leda into a vessel of magic efficacy: she has "put on" the "power" of Zeus and perhaps his "knowledge" (as the 13th line of the sonnet alleges), just as the primitive magician puts on the power and knowledge of the superhuman forces he invokes. Furthermore, by a kind of sexual-apocalyptic vision, she has been made to symbolize a turning-point in the history of man, an awful revolution:

> A shudder in the loins engenders there
> The broken wall, the burning roof and tower
> And Agamemnon dead.[1]

As Yeats thinks of the Ledaean body, in "Among School Children," "our two natures," as he says, "blend." In other words, the poet has now himself become the magician, for he has fused into the developing process of his poem the mythical force and meaning of Leda, who is, of course, not simply a Greek

[1] See *A Vision*, Bk. V, for the further significance of Leda.

maiden but a complex of images sieved through the soul of Yeats. The invocation of Leda has made the poem possible by bringing the poet the conviction that a "childish day" may be "tragedy"; the uncreated situation presented by the public man in the school-room now becomes significant in such a way that it is available to poetry. Again, the poet looks around at the children, sees in each one a "daughter of the swan," and senses the working of the passions which the myth has inaugurated and directed:

> And thereupon my heart is driven wild:
> She stands before me as a living child.

From there on the poem moves toward its wonderful conclusion out of the necessity of the mood and meaning created by the myth.

I am well aware that to some of my readers my account of myth will seem an impoverishment rather than an enrichment. I have mentioned Dewey. And "Dewey" means a prosaic and arid sensibility, unaware of the further reaches of human experience. I should, however, prefer to call my approach "aesthetic" or "naturalistic" rather than "pragmatic." And I would ask those who do find this "aesthetic" approach an impoverishment if they are not committing a cardinal error of our time: that underestimation and misunderstanding of art which denies it a primary function and efficacy in human thought by making it always dependent on something else, such as theology, dogma, religion, cultural Utopias, the State, economics. Mr. T. S. Eliot, in his famous review of *Ulysses,* wrote that "the mythical method" might make "the modern world possible for art." This implies that myth is something else than art, something anterior to art which operates not within art but upon the world in such a way that art may come into being. It implies that artists should be sociologists or theologians or prophets or pontiffs and that art will somehow issue forth automatically once the proper cultural context has been created. The same idea is expressed by Mr. Mark Schorer, who, writing of Blake, says that "myth is the indispensable substructure of poetry." Modern writers have very consciously striven to create a mythological literature, an attempt which for various reasons we must think admirable and hopeful. And so if I reverse these dicta on myth I do not wish to imply any lack of hope for a mythological literature or any underestimation of its possible grandeur. We ought to question Eliot and Schorer, however, and ask ourselves whether it is not better to say that "the mythical method" *can make art possible for the modern world* and that *poetry is the indispensable substructure of myth.* When we construct our cultural Utopia and man it with priests, pontiffs, commissars, yogis, censors, and the common man let us not forget to include the artist-magician, who has always had such a prominent part in flourishing cultures.

My account of myth is not a complete systematic. It must leave to others the discussion of myth in terms of anthropology or of literary-philosophical structure, or of rhetoric, symbol, or semantic. These disciplines are, of course, necessary. To prove this, we have only to reflect that myth for sophisticated minds must have cultural, philosophical, and symbolic meaning. Obviously we cannot and should not think of Oedipus, Joseph of Egypt, Philoctetes, or Captain Ahab without thinking of their philosophic, symbolic, religious, or political value. The method of studying myth which I have set forth is not comprehensive enough to lead to a completely adequate definition. What I have tried to do is rescue the word "myth" from the far too comprehensive meanings associated with it in current literary criticism. My definition of myth is, then, only the first step. The second step will have to arrive at a definition which is more comprehensive without being more vague or confusing. But this second step, it seems to me, necessarily presupposes the first.

THE MEANINGS OF "MYTH" IN MODERN CRITICISM

WALLACE W. DOUGLAS

ACCORDING to Professor Stallman, contemporary criticism reflects the spiritual disorder and incapacity of the age: its lost traditions, its lost conventions, its lost world order, and its lost belief in religion and myth.[1] This is perhaps an oversimplified description, but it does suggest one preoccupation of one group of critics who happen to be writing at the present time. And in the last term of the series, "myth," it is possible to find meanings which incorporate portions of meaning from all the other terms. Indeed at times "myth" seems to be the most important and inclusive word in modern criticism: a little magazine devoted a whole issue to it, the English Institute spent a meeting on its various aspects, and now critics, using the anthropological connotations of "myth," dignify criticism by extending it to a search for The Myth in the work of poets who have wanted to recreate The Myth. The word is used by critics of many sorts; and, since modern critics constantly deny that they form a single school, it can be expected to have almost as many meanings as critics who use it; as it turns out, the meanings are almost as many as the uses. The word is protean and its fate is procrustean, I would say, if an old-fashioned decorative mythological allusion is still permitted. But behind the many meanings lie the moral presuppositions that sanction some of the aesthetic values of modern critics, and an examination of the meanings and uses of the word "myth" may get at some of these presuppositions, which otherwise are lost in the brilliant linguistic and grammatical insights of modern criticism.

I

Occasionally "myth" can still be found, in its naïve or popular sense, as a synonym for "illusion," "legend," or false propaganda, or in an earlier literary sense of decorative or illustrative material.[2] More often it occurs as a surrogate term for the fact that the characters and the actions of literary works have qualities that make them representative of types or classes or ideas. In one example of this use, the critic may have wanted to make something more of the word, for he also spoke of "myths or fairy tales or dreams, where again the people act under compulsion, toward fatally predetermined ends."[3] Presumably it is this representative quality that another critic refers to when he says: "Words open out into the larger symbolizations on all levels—for example, into archetypal symbol, ritual, and myth."[4] In a slightly more complex use "myth" becomes a heavy synonym for "belief" or sometimes "convention";[5] as when Shakespeare's themes of love, Christianity, and

[1] R. W. Stallman, "The New Critics," in *Critiques and Essays in Criticism*, ed. R. W. Stallman (New York, 1949), pp. 488–90.

[Modern Philology, May, 1953]

[2] S. E. Hyman, "Some Bankrupt Treasuries," *Kenyon Review*, X (Summer, 1948), 496–97, notes a number of such usages. I have noticed a few other examples, which, like his, are drawn from writers not generally associated with the new critics.

[3] Malcolm Cowley, "William Faulkner's Legend of the South," in Allen Tate (ed.), *A Southern Vanguard* (New York, 1947), p. 26.

[4] Cleanth Brooks, "Foreword" in Stallman, *Critiques and Essays*, p. xix.

[5] E. L. Hubler, "Three Shakespearian Myths: Mutability, Plenitude, and Reputation," *English Institute Essays, 1948* (New York, 1949), p. 97. Mr. Hubler's point is that, so far as he can tell, that is all that "myth" really means.

governance are described as "mythic."[6] This meaning very easily acquires connotations of value; for example, when the neutral idea of "belief" is changed into something like "the received forms, the symbolic versions of human wisdom,"[7] or when a myth is described as having "an archetypal meaning quite independent of any individual's conscious exploitation of it,"[8] or when it is made superior to philosophy and likened to "the blush of blood in the face," or when it is said to have a reality that lies far beneath "the words in which it happens to appear."[9]

Thus the spread in usage seems to be from "illusion" through "belief" to "higher truth." But before examining this last area of meaning, in which "myth" becomes a name, so far as I can tell, for revelation, I must mention the special way in which Mr. Hyman, Mr. Frye, and Mr. Fergusson are interested in the concept of myth. They all follow the Cambridge Hellenists in being more interested in the ritual, which, they hold, is explained by the myth, than in the myth itself; and they all accept the comparative method of the Cambridge school. According to Mr. Frye, "a purely structural approach has the same limitations in criticism that it has in biology. In itself it is simply a discrete series of analyses based on the mere

existence of the literary structure, without developing any explanation of how the structure came to be what it was and what its nearest relatives are." Literary criticism, he says, needs a central hypothesis, which can be arrived at inductively from structural analysis by associating data and seeking larger patterns, or deductively by following out the consequences of what he regards as a necessary initial postulate of criticism, the postulate of the unity and total coherence of criticism. "Total literary history moves from the primitive to the sophisticated, and here we glimpse the possibility of seeing literature as a complication of a relatively restricted and simple group of formulas that can be studied in primitive culture. If so, then the search for archetypes is a kind of literary anthropology, concerned with the way that literature is informed by preliterary categories such as ritual, myth and folk tale."[10] These critics differ, however, in the rituals to which they would reduce literary patterns: Mr. Fergusson, whose primary source seems to be in Aristotelian commentary, always finds in works of literature traces of an original dithyrambic ritual; Mr. Frye discovers signs of fertility rites; and Mr. Hyman expects the "monomyth" to be an elaboration of Van Gennep's famous *rites de passage:* "as students of myth we must separate from the world, penetrate to a source of knowledge, and return with whatever power or life-enhancement the truth may contain."[11]

As the quotation from Mr. Hyman suggests, these three critics are ultimately interested in some special knowledge and, in Mr. Hyman's case at least, also in a power, *mana, orenda, virtù,* which they

---

[6] R. B. Heilman, "The Lear World," *English Institute Essays, 1948,* p. 36; Leslie A. Fiedler, "The Defense of the Illusion and the Creation of Myth," *English Institute Essays, 1948,* p. 76.

[7] R. P. Blackmur, "Between Myth and Philosophy: Fragments of W. B. Yeats," *Southern Review,* VII (1942), 408.

[8] Fiedler, p. 76. Mr. Fiedler is talking about the play within the play, in *Hamlet* and in general, which he calls a "technical or structural myth," like the happy ending or the reversal: "a plot configuration or a technical device with an archetypal meaning quite independent of any individual's conscious exploitation of it." It is difficult to see here what other purpose is served by "myth" and "archetypal meaning" than that of allowing the critic to express approval of a convention which most modern audiences would find awkward and "unnatural."

[9] Blackmur, pp. 417–18.

[10] Northrop Frye, "The Archetypes of Literature," *Kenyon Review,* XIII (1951), 95–97, 99.

[11] S. E. Hyman, "Myth, Ritual, and Nonsense," *Kenyon Review,* XI (Summer, 1949), 455. (The connection with Van Gennep is my inference.)

would discover in literature, if I understand their position, by following evolutionary anthropology, especially in its use
of the theory of survivals, and examining
modern works for traces of such things as
"the lost collective rites that enabled the
tribe to function." Thus, though in analyzing works they pay more attention to
structure and form than most modern
critics (and have a more systematic conception of literary forms), in the end they,
too, come around to treating a literary
work as a repository of truth, of racial
memories, or of unconsciously held values;
and to the extent that they do so, they are
connected with the general school of
mythical criticism.

In the simplest of the meanings that associate it with revelation or higher truth,
"myth" is taken as a representation in
fictional form of truths or values that are
sanctioned by general belief: myth "tells
the truth to the extent that people believe
that it tells the truth";[12] it can be called
"the lie as truth."[13] Sometimes in this
view myth seems to be out-and-out ration-
alization created by an individual ("Arnold offered his humanistic theory of
great poetry as effective and saving
myth"[14]), or a special group ("A myth is
the creation of a group which has the need
to believe in it and it is valid only to those
who benefit by it through belonging to the
group . . ."[15]). It may also mean a story
in which historical, scientific, or metaphysical facts, regarded here as "true" but
cold and uninteresting, are endowed with
human values;[16] or it may be a concept or

system of concepts which are regarded as
worthy of belief, "belief" being then defined as "an unquestionable basis for action, a mode of reality in which one
lives."[17] In the most common variant of
this class of meanings, "myth" becomes
the sanctified and dogmatized expression,
not necessarily in the form of literature,
of basic social or class conventions and
values, concepts which may be as inclusive as the "togetherness of the community mind," but which are more likely to
be thought of as, for example, "the modern *daimon* of money" (as embodied somewhat anachronistically, it seems to me, in
Fafnir) or the now sanctified assumptions
of the Enlightenment, the Declaration of
Independence, the French Revolution,
and so forth.[18] In all of these meanings
there are traces of social or psychological
functionalism.

The myth helps [people] in their beliefs. It
satisfies a desire or a need. It answers a riddle.
It gives us a home, so that the universe is no
longer so dizzying, or frightful, or empty.
A society that possesses myths is a healthy
human society. . . . [But myths] will come into
being, as they probably have in the past, only
out of deep and long-continued passion,
crystallized and given shape, perhaps, by some
deeply passionate seer-artist, and slowly
absorbed into a common culture because they
reflect or create profound convictions and
satisfy the impossible ideas of that culture.[19]

For obvious reasons such a functionalist definition cannot be very popular
among critics oppressed by the spiritual
disorder of the age and harried by regret
for lost traditions and conventions; and

[12] Donald A. Stauffer, "The Modern Myth of the
Modern Myth," *English Institute Essays, 1947* (New
York, 1948), p. 23.

[13] Fiedler, p. 78.

[14] Alba H. Warren, *English Poetic Theory, 1825–
1865* (Princeton, 1950), p. 170.

[15] Nicholas Calas, "Myth and Initiation," *Chimera*,
IV (Spring, 1946), 15.

[16] Herman Brock, "The Heritage of Myth in
Literature," *Chimera*, IV, 36.

[17] Heilman, p. 30; cf. Stauffer, p. 26.

[18] "Togetherness of the community mind": Heil-
man, p. 31, citing Wheelwright; "*daimon* of money":
William Troy, "Postlude: Myth, Method, and the
Future," *Chimera*, IV, 82; assumptions of the En-
lightenment, etc.: Erich Kahler, "The Persistence of
Myth," *Chimera*, IV, 7–8.

[19] Stauffer, pp. 23, 24. Cf. Robert Brown, "Film
Myth and the Limits of the Film," *Hudson Review*,
IV (Spring, 1951), 111.

most critics use "myth" to refer to truths that are inexpressible in discursive language, in other words, perhaps, as a synonym for "paraphrasable content," which, in their system of analyzing the relations among the words of a poem, cannot be discussed unless disguised by some mystical name like "myth."

The play virtually says that wisdom and insight must be sought by a denial of the ordinary sense and logic of the world and must be found in the intuitions of the especially gifted mind, the unusual mind, even the disordered mind. Here again, then, we find paradox asserting the Mystery, and the content of the play taking on a strongly mythical case.[20]

"Myth" legitimizes the heresy of paraphrase, in the first place, because it implies a whole series of antitheses that are important in modern criticism. Myth or myths are opposed to facts, to "cataloguable and manageable phenomena," to the logic of ordinary knowledge, to positivism, the empirical, the finite,[21] to the logos,[22] to the intelligence and will,[23] and to the consciousness.[24] "Myth" can be a sanctifying word, in the second place, because its content or form is said to originate in passionate, poetic,[25] or intuitional views of reality; in the unconscious, the dream; in memories of the primordial, the Mystery, the primordial Mystery; in the world of

spirit, of value, of an extra dimension; in the imagination; or in man's now suppressed or denied awareness of his sin. The line here seems to be that "myth" calls attention to the dark places in which this kind of truth originates, and it suggests the paradox and language of multiple reference in which it must be expressed: in fiction and myth "a typical human or folk character or landscape lives in an irrational image, that can only be described but not *explained* or referred back any farther than exactly that specific appearance and experience."[26] Myth being, then, a living embodiment of insights, any discussion of it will be descriptive, not analytical, and the terms of the discussion will be neither manageable words nor cataloguable phenomena, but semipoetic devices to call attention to the structural paradoxes, ironies, or tensions (depending on the critic) which partly suggest the nonrational and hence linguistically indescribable elements of experience which lie behind the myth that is being described. Thus whatever else he may be doing, the mythogogic critic is not at least constructing simplistic moral statements about what the poem says.

It is true that the critics occasionally seem to reduce myths to very simplistic meanings; indeed, one can sometimes come upon almost Renaissance phrasings.

[20] Heilman, p. 43. In this sense "myth" is presumably a virtue word for "substance of literature," and no one would deny that the substance of literature is a proper subject of investigation. But "myth," with its heavy anthropological connotations, adds nothing to the clarity of the extremely complex problem of the relation of substance and paraphrasable content, especially when, as in this passage, it is a paraphrased proposition that is given and then dignified by being called "mythic."

[21] *Ibid.*, pp. 32 (quoting Wheelwright), 41, 45, 50.

[22] *Ibid.*, p. 33; Brock, p. 34.

[23] F. W. Dupee, "Thomas Mann," *Kenyon Review*, XIV (Winter, 1952), 150.

[24] Fiedler, p. 77: "The myth, by definition, cannot be conscious, and the moment we take pains to know it, it is degraded, profaned—the Joseph story in Genesis is mythic, in Thomas Mann an endless, middle-aged joke."

[25] Cf. Myra Reynolds: "Modes of speech, a conception of nature, such that high-wrought emotion might justify it, or that it might be natural and inevitable when the poet's thought was ruled by a living mythology, became mere frigid conventionalities when there was no passion, and when the spirits of stream and wood no longer won even poetic faith" (Myra Reynolds, *The Treatment of Nature in English Poetry from Pope to Wordsworth* [Chicago, 1896], p. 35). Miss Reynolds' position was, of course, much simpler than that of modern critics, and she uses words like "poetic" and "mythology" in a very old-fashioned way. The quotation suggests, however, that a good deal of modern theorizing on this point has only been an elaboration of a standard generalization of the literary histories.

[26] Heilman, pp. 41, 43; Kahler, p. 6; Louise Bogan, "The Secular Hell," *Chimera*, IV, 12, 13.

'Thus one critic speaks of the myth of Penelope's farewell to Icarius: "Such was the Greek genius for embodying eternal truths in stories almost as eternal in their grace." And another critic says that the myths of Prometheus and Epimetheus record the classical "sense of the whole of life which must not be too quickly disturbed for the prosecution of special scientific interests."[27] But more often (and this is the third way in which the concept of "myth" allows critics to talk about the content of a poem) myth is said to contain either the otherwise inexpressible insights or values of the individual or group unconscious or the projections of group or individual felt needs or values. The mythic is "what the French have traditionally called the 'merveilleux,' the lost world of dream and disorder and grotesquerie, without which our possibilities of freedom and power are impoverished."[28] Myth implies a belief in a "penumbral reality," which is both the "psychic extrapolation" of the collective representations of the primitive mind, and a recognition of an otherness that is "radically different [from man], awful, potentially hostile."

Myth implies a prelogical mentality that is not bound by the law of contradiction but operates under the law of participation, according to which "objects and phenomena can be, though in a manner incomprehensible to us, at once themselves and not themselves." The mythic involves insights into the universal, or "commerce between the community and the mysteries," and undertakes a part of the ordering of experience.[29] Myth deals with the "fundamentals of our existence"; it is derived from "the word as the most ancient, the original account of the origins of the world";[30] it also imbeds a "complex of human problems"[31] or carries "one of the archetypes from the collective unconscious of mankind"[32] or "the timeless meaning" of an individual's psychic life.[33] In what must be its widest senses, "myth in its union with logos, comprises the totality of human existence";[34] or, as "the myth," it is "the totality of all visions of truth which are untestable, non-demonstrable, non-empirical, non-logical."[35]

[27] F. L. Lucas, *Literature and Psychology* (London. 1951), p. 65, for Penelope's farewell. and see p. 265 for an interesting example of the influence of Freud and the theory of survivals on the exegesis of myths: Mr. Lucas says that the myth of the castration of Uranus by Cronus is "a survival of primitive folklore. interesting as showing how old in human prehistory is the Oedipus complex." The interpretation of the Promethean myth is from Allen Tate. "To Whom Is the Poet Responsible?" *Hudson Review*, IV (Autumn. 1951), 329.

[28] Isn't this a somewhat extended meaning for the French word? And note the critic's comment on Eliot's notion of a decline in English literature from the perfection of the seventeenth century to the excessive rationalism of the eighteenth and the emotional orgy of the nineteenth centuries: "It is a typical mythical pattern—a Garden, a Fall complete with a tempter, and the promise of a Messiah—much more satisfying to the contemporary sensibility than the 19th Century's manichean melodrama [= bad myth?] of an endless struggle between Classicism and Romanticism; and we are tempted to apply it universally" (Leslie A. Fiedler, "The Critic's Excluded Middle," *Kenyon Review*, XIII [Autumn. 1951], 689. 699).

[29] Philip Wheelwright. "Notes on Mythopoeia," *Sewanee Review*, LIX (Autumn. 1951), 577. 578; Heilman. p. 41, quoting Wheelwright. I recognize that in Wheelwright and Heilman there are traces of Lévy-Bruhl and perhaps Durkheim and Malinowski. Of that more later.

[30] Kahler, pp. 2–3.

[31] Troy. p. 83. The "complex" seems to be part of "The Myth." I assume that a myth has one problem.

[32] Graham Hough. *The Last Romantics* (London. 1949), p. 112.

[33] Francis Fergusson, "The Pilgrim on the Threshold of Purgation," *Hudson Review*, IV (Winter, 1952), 558.

[34] Brock, p. 34.

[35] Heilman, p. 32. And cf. Fiedler, "Archetype and Signature," *Sewanee Review*, LX (Spring, 1952), 261–62: "The word Archetype is the more familiar of my terms; I use it instead of the word 'myth,' which I have employed in the past but which becomes increasingly ambiguous, to mean any of the immemorial patterns of response to the human situation in its most permanent aspects: death, love, the biological family, the relationship with the Unknown, etc., whether those patterns be considered to reside in the Jungian Collective Unconscious or the Platonic World of Ideas. The archetypal belongs to the infra- or metapersonal, to what Freudians call the Id or the Unconscious; that is, it belongs to the Community at its deepest. pre-conscious levels of acceptance."

Perhaps the best way to conclude this description of modern mythogogy is to attempt a summary of the theories of Professor Chase, who is undoubtedly our most sedulous student of myth. He begins by assuming a mythopoeic mind or a mythopoeic psychology,[36] which is superior to, or in its operation more inclusive than, rational or speculative reason. For such a mind, objects are not perceived "as such but as vehicles of efficacious activity analogous to and identifiable with the impersonal powers of the universe projected out of human emotions."[37] He then argues, asserting that "modern anthropologists" are in agreement with him, that primitive man lives in two worlds: the matter-of-fact world of the practical reason and the magico-religious world of the mythopoeic faculty. He argues also that civilized man lives "in the same world as the savages," by which he means not only that our experience is similarly divided but also that "Our deepest experience, needs, and aspirations are the same, as surely as the crucial biological and psychic transitions occur in the life of every human being."[38] Of course, what Mr. Chase wants to do is to validate not only his concept of the double world but also his approval of the mythopoeic descriptions of the magico-religious experience of primitive man, as opposed to that of modern man. So he assumes pan-human needs and aspirations, which he grounds in the biological process of growth; then he can argue that modern man has arbitrarily limited experience to that portion subject to analysis by reason; and there is no health in him.[39]

Following Locke, the thinkers of the Enlightenment were jealous of that small area of experience they had set aside as the province of Reason. To step out of this province, to take myth seriously, seems to the philosopher a piece of folly, to the literary critic a serious breach of decorum, and to the moralist a giving of hostages to the priests. This is in my opinion an attractive attitude, even an eminently decent canon of criticism. Yet it will not do; myth has a habit of being sometimes unattractive or indecent. And the cost of refusing to take it seriously is too. For what was the cost to the Enlightenment of its failure to create an adequately complicated mythology if not the tremendous and destructive intellectual upheavals at the end of the eighteenth century? The terrific forces of the human emotions cannot for long be trifled with. They are not to be controlled and made useful by a too mechanical or indiscriminate repression. (It was no accident, as we suggest in the chapter on psychoanalysis, that the obsessive emotion of the eighteenth century was fear.) But they can be controlled and made useful by the creation of myths. And the first step toward understanding myth is to perceive this truth.[40]

On the basis of his anthropological analysis of myth as defensive projections of man's unconscious, Mr. Chase moves on to a definition of myth as "literature which suffuses the natural with preternatural efficacy (*mana*)."[41] The psycho-

[36] He denies the article of faith that asserts the existence of a mythopoeic age. See his "Myth as Literature," *English Institute Essays, 1947,* p. 6; also "Myth Revisited," *Partisan Review,* XVII (1950), 536.

[37] Richard Chase, *Quest for Myth* (Baton Rouge, 1949), p. 20.

[38] *Ibid.,* p. 78.

[39] Cf. Sapir's comment: "Myths are not isolated formations. They differ characteristically for different times and places largely because they tend to conform to certain typical patterns. To assume that these characteristic differences are directly due to deep-seated differences of psychology of the myth-making people is too naïve for serious consideration. . . . The cultural anthropologist can make nothing of the hypothesis of the racial unconscious nor is he disposed to allow an immediate psychological analysis of the behavior of primitive people in any other sense than that in which such an analysis is allowable for our own culture" (David G. Mandlebaum [ed.], *Selected Writings of Edward Sapir* [Berkeley, 1951], p. 527).

[40] Chase, *Quest,* p. 21.

[41] *Ibid.,* p. 78. He says (p. 79) that he is following Malinowski, though he thinks Malinowski has overlooked the psychological function of myth. What he actually does is to add some of Malinowski's functionalism to a definition he credits to Otfried Müller, namely, that myth is a narrative which unites the real and the ideal or the imaginary. On p. 97 he gives as a

logical function of myth is to fuse the perception of power with the perception of physical qualities.[42] "If these observations are sound, any narrative or poem which reaffirms[43] the dynamism and vibrancy of the world, which fortifies the ego with the impression that there is a magically potent brilliancy or dramatic force in the world, may be called myth."[44] Elsewhere he has said that myth is literature "functioning in a special way, achieving special modes of expression";[45] it is "literature operating in certain more or less definable ways which set it off from other kinds of literature."[46] But also it is a magical tale dealing with critical passages of life,[47] and in several reviews Mr. Chase has written as if myth, rather than being a quality, were a thing contained in literature, a part of the material of literature.[48] Most often, though, Mr. Chase uses the word just about as Longinus used "the sublime," as a means of asserting his approval of various works.

II

In all of this mythogogic theorizing there are a good many parallels to the early Nietzsche of *The Birth of Tragedy:* not only, for example, such notions as that reason cannot explain all of experience, that art deals with the ineffably concrete and particular, and that there is a "primordial contradiction and primordial pain in the heart of the Primal Unity," in itself a sphere "beyond and before all phenomena," but also the general world view —in Nietzsche's case a great melodrama of sin and destruction in which Socrates and Euripides, representing critical intelligence, accomplish the estrangement of man and nature and the subjugation of the latter to practical controls.[49] For Nietzsche, at this stage, myths seem to have been legends revealing or embodying the folk wisdom of the Greeks. "The Greek knew and felt the terror and horror of existence. That he might endure this terror at all, he had to interpose between himself and life the radiant dream-birth of the Olympians."[50] This was the pre-Socratic Greek, who still—a little bit like Mr. Chase's pre-eighteenth-century man —felt a wonder which he expressed in myth, "the concentrated picture of the world, which, as abbreviature of phenomena, cannot dispense with wonder." Like contemporary critics, Nietzsche assumes a modern man essentially different in his modes of thinking and feeling from primitive man: he is "so broken up by the critico-historical spirit of our culture, that he can only make the former existence of myth credible to himself by learned means through intermediary abstrac-

---

full definition: "Myth is an aesthetic device for bringing the imaginary but powerful world of preternatural forces into a manageable collaboration with the objective facts of life in such a way as to excite a sense of reality amenable to both the unconscious passions and the conscious mind." Whether this is merely an expansion of Malinowski's "pragmatic charter of primitive faith and moral wisdom." I am not sure (see Malinowski's *Myth in Primitive Psychology* [New York, 1926], p. 19).

[42] Cf. W. D. Oliver, "Knowledge, Myth, and Action," *Journal of Philosophy*, XLIV (1947), 9: Myth is one of the devices men have used "to lend to their ideals that sort of objective content which would insure their persistence through time and render intelligible man's struggle to realize them." Also Malinowski: Myth "expresses, enhances and codifies belief; it safeguards and enforces morality; it vouches for the efficiency of ritual and contains practical rules for the guidance of man" (p. 19).

[43] But reaffirms how? By statement? In its form?

[44] Chase, *English Institute Essays*, p. 11.

[45] *Ibid.*, p. 10.

[46] Chase, *Partisan Review*, XVII, 885.

[47] *Ibid.*, p. 890. I assume that the reference to "critical passages of life" means that Mr. Chase is adding Van Gennep to his anthropological supporters.

[48] Cf. his review of Professor Howard's *Melville*, in *Nation*, CLXXIV (1952), 255; "A Poet's Economy," *Hopkins Review*, V (Fall, 1951), 37; and "Sense and Sensibility," *Kenyon Review*, XIII (Autumn, 1951), 688.

[49] Friedrich Nietzsche, *The Birth of Tragedy* in *The Philosophy of Nietzsche* (New York, 1927), p. 979; cf. also pp. 951, 954–55, 993.

[50] *Ibid.*, p. 962.

tions." Without myth, any culture loses a "healthy creative power"; myth gives meaning to the foundations of the state and to the life of the individual.

On the other hand, let us now think of the abstract man unguided by myth, the abstract education, the abstract morality, the abstract justice, the abstract state: let us picture to ourselves the lawless roving of the artistic imagination, unchecked by native myth: let us imagine a culture which has no fixed and sacred primitive seat, but is doomed to exhaust all its possibilities, and to nourish itself wretchedly on all other cultures—there we have the Present, the result of Socratism, which is bent on the destruction of myth.[51]

Nietzsche, again like contemporary critics, assumes an eternal conflict between what he calls the theoretic and the tragic world views. The dialectical desire for knowledge destroys man's power to receive myth, which is "a unique type of universality and truth towering into the infinite."[52] It

substitutes for a metaphysical comfort an earthly consonance, in fact a *deus ex machina* of its own, the god of machines and crucibles, that is, the powers of the forces of nature recognized and employed in the services of the higher egoism; it believes that it can correct the world by knowledge, guide life by science, and actually confine the individual within a limited sphere of solvable problems, from which he can cheerfully say to life, "I desire thee: it is worth while to know thee."

In a tragic culture,

wisdom takes the place of science as the highest end, wisdom which uninfluenced by the seductive distractions of the sciences, turns with unmoved eye to a comprehensive view of the world, and seeks to conceive therein, with sympathetic feelings of love, the eternal suffering as its own.[53]

III

I am not trying to establish *The Birth of Tragedy* as a source for contemporary

mythogogic criticism. Instead I want to use it to suggest how, since 1871, such romantic speculation has been extended, strengthened, freshened, and provided with an apparently firm empirical foundation by evidence borrowed from psychology and anthropology, especially from the theorizing about the primitive mind, so-called. Of all anthropological theories, those of Lévy-Bruhl must have been the most persuasive to the critics who have sought to define "myth" in such a way as to provide themselves with "real" and extra-literary reasons for approving the various doctrines that from time to time they want to discover in literature. Whatever its intention, the effect of Lévy-Bruhl's work is to create a primitive mind, which, because it does not know the law of contradiction but only the "law" of participation, lives in a special and vitalizing relationship with the totality of nature. And in many places he seems to say that the primitive mind is richer and more complex than the civilized mind because it does not recognize any separation between images or ideas of objects and the emotions evoked by them; because it does not differentiate powers and qualities from things; because it does not have any concept of universal or abstraction; and because it does not operate according to conventional categories of causation or of abstract reasoning.[54] To critics who pre-

[51] *Ibid.*, p. 1045. (The actual antecedent of "It" is the cheerful, "senile, unproductive love of existence" of the "Alexandrian" mind; but I assume this is equivalent to Socratism, the dialectical desire for knowledge and so forth.) The quotation about the tragic culture is on p. 1049. I should note that Nietzsche constantly refined and clarified the ideas of this early work.

[54] But in later works Lévy-Bruhl clarified his terminology; cf. the preface in *L'Expérience mystique et les symboles chez les primitifs* (Paris, 1938), p. 2, where he distinguishes between literal and conventional senses of *primitifs*. In the former sense, he says, the word implies that the men so designated are closer to "la condition humaine originelle" than modern man and represent in the contemporary world the characteristics of our remotest ancestors. "C'est

[51] *Ibid.*, pp. 1077, 1078.   [52] *Ibid.*, p. 1042.

suppose an exhaustion of language and culture due either to a disruption of some primal connection between man and nature or to a dissociation of thought and emotion in men, the attractions of this concept are obvious, especially if the characteristics of contemporary primitive minds are used as evidence from which to infer the existence and characteristics of a general primitive mind comparable, in relation to the mental development of man, to the primitive horde in its relation to the social development of man. Furthermore, there would seem to be involved in this speculation the idea of some great and total shift in the human way of thinking, a shift in which man's participation with and feeling of the greater forces of nature (expressed by the idea of *mana* or in animistic religions; concepts of great importance in nineteenth-century anthropology and in modern mythogogic criticism) were destroyed by the effects of the discovery of practical logic and physical causes: the postulation of such a change would be valuable to the antiscientism of modern criticism.[55]

Behind these oddly assorted ideas, and holding them together to the extent that they can be held together, lie the assumptions of the Cambridge Hellenists, in whose work modern critics have found a most attractive idea, that of the ritual (i.e., religious, nonpractical, nonscientific) origin of literary forms. The first assumption is that there is a uniform pattern of cultural evolution,[56] all societies passing through the same stages from a hypothetical primitive horde to the differentiated classes of a mature civilization. The stages of this evolution can be described by comparative study of the cultural forms in contemporary "primitive" societies, especially of the unintegrated forms, which are assumed to be survivals of earlier stages. The second assumption, derived from the first and controlling the literary theories of the critics, is that phenomena of civilized societies have the same basic values (functionally or symbolically) as apparently parallel phenomena in primitive societies, either those now existing or others the nature of which is determined by speculation on the evidence of monuments of quite mature civilizations; and that ultimate causes and true origins[57] of contemporary phenomena can be determined by this backward tracing of the evolutionary pattern. The Cambridge school, of course, was most interested in establishing the ritual origin of Greek literary forms, and they stuck pretty close to the evidence of Greek monuments, drawing on the world-wide comparisons of

---

là une vue de l'esprit, liée à l'hypothèse évolutionniste, mais que l'on serait bien embarrassé de confirmer par des faits." In the conventional sense, which is the one in which he uses the word, *primitifs* means only "savages," people neither more nor less primitive than civilized man, but whose institutions may be regarded as either lower or less advanced than ours.

[55] These are probably the most important of the theories of cultural anthropology that have been used by modern critics, though occasionally one suspects traces of ideas like Malinowski's functionalism, and like Durkheim's that religious entities represent a divinization of society and that the powers of nature are projections of human emotions. Perhaps Tylor and Marett are ultimate sources, but Durkheim, as introduced by Jane Harrison, and Lévy-Bruhl seem the most likely proximate sources. And certainly this whole series of ideas would have had considerably less impact, were it not for the theories of Freud and Jung, especially the latter's notions about racial memories, which provide a kind of channel for the transmission of those poor remains of primitive virtue which man still enjoys.

[56] Lord Raglan comments: "Belief in the unity of myth and ritual is what we now call Fundamentalism." It could just as well be said that "belief in a pan-human evolution is what we now call Fundamentalism," and to go on with Lord Raglan, "a Fundamentalist is a person to whom the historic fact is of no importance" (Lord Raglan, *The Hero* [London, 1936], pp. 760–61).

[57] The question of the origin of a myth as an organized literary form is a different one, of course, from the question of the origin of or psychoanalytic meaning of its component parts. As a literary structure a myth is generally a synthesis of various elements with independent developments and affiliations (see Sapir, pp. 525, 528).

scholars like Frazer only for confirmation. Contemporary literary critics have paid more attention to the confirmatory footnotes than to the body of the evidence. For them Br'er Rabbit "means" the same as an animal hero in a totemic culture, both being embodied in "animal stories." For them the shooting of an albatross by a presumably medieval sailor "meant" to an eighteenth-century audience and "means" to a modern high-school student or sophisticated literary critic precisely what the real event or its fictional[58] representation would "mean" to a member of an albatross clan or totemic group, if any; or at least to a member of a totemically organized society—all killings of all animals, wherever, whenever, or however accomplished, sharing some or all of the characteristics of a violation of totemic taboo.[59] This persistence of meaning is explained either by the theory of the survival of cultural forms or—perhaps in most cases it is *and*—some variant of the Jungian theory of racial memories, itself based, of course, on the theory of survivals.[60] On the basis of these assumptions, critics are prepared to argue that the literature of Western civilization can be understood and evaluated by establishing its connection with, or similarity to, the religious rituals and the literature of an assumed world-wide primitive society

[58] Apparently the concept of "fiction" is not universal; the Ojibwa, for example, are said to lack it entirely. Hence there would be no possible comparison between generalizations based on their sacred stories and any based on those of a people recognizing "fiction." In each case the significance of the genesis, transmission, and content would be quite different (see A. I. Hallowell, "Myth, Culture, and Personality," *American Anthropologist*, XLIX [1947], 547).

[59] "No folktale is generic..It is always the tale of one particular people with one particular livelihood and social organization and religion" (Ruth Benedict, *Zuni Mythology* [New York, 1935], p. xiii).

[60] "Myths may or may not have been motivated by certain unconscious psychic trends, but it is difficult to understand how they could indefinitely keep their significance as symbols of these trends" (Sapir, p. 527).

and primitive mind, the last being the important idea, since it is assumed that the primitive or unspecialized mind has a greater contact with, a more complete view of, total reality than the modern mind.

None of these ideas helps much in discovering the formal literary characteristics of a myth; and, in general, "myth" seems to be less an analytical than a polemical term, calling attention rather to a critic's mood or moral attitude than to observed facts in the work under discussion. And this moral attitude is roughly similar among all critics who use the concept of "myth," in spite of variations and contradictions among their different descriptions of myth. It presupposes a radical dualism in man's experience. On the one hand is a material world, in which atoms blindly run, unaffected by man's needs and aspirations. This is the workaday world of ordinary logic. It is defined by scientific laws and described by abstractions. It is a world of facts, of things seen as members of classes rather than in their ineluctable reality, of phenomena treated as cataloguable and manageable. On the other hand is a magico-spiritual world, which is either the projection of man's needs and aspirations or the natural world viewed as a totality in which there are certain areas (the emotional, the ethical) so complex as not to be susceptible of scientific analysis, even though they possess a substantive reality similar to that of any natural fact. This is the world of emotion, value, and quality. It is a world of unique moments, of things seen as individuals. It is a world of felt truths, unverifiable, but none the less absolute. It is indefinable and can only be described by poetry.

It is not clear how the mind is related to these "worlds," though, on the whole, the critics seem to assume a parallel dualism of mind and matter. At any rate, they talk as if the mind had two functions or faculties, the speculative reason and the mythopoeic imagination,[61] which correspond to the "world" of fact and the "world" of nonfact. This is the important assumption, for on it are grounded the moral attitudes that are the ultimate subjects of modern criticism. This view of the mind validates the critics' dramatization of modern history as a constant and furious struggle between these two aspects of mind, or more often between two kinds of mind, the predominantly rational and the predominantly mythopoeic. It also prepares for a whole series of antitheses, both

moral and "critical": tradition and disorder, poetry and science, symbol and statement, convention and originality, the particular and the abstraction, metaphysical poetry and Platonic poetry, aristocratic order and democratic chaos, intension and extension, texture and structure, myth and logos—the list is infinite. The concepts of myth and of the mythopoeic mind and the anthropological evidence supporting them constitute a "pragmatic charter" for the beliefs, cravings, social attitudes, and standards of the critics. The word "myth" itself, whether used to refer to the assumed insights of primitive literature or to the content of modern literature, simply calls attention to the complex of ideas constituting this charter; it is, in other words, a sign by which critics can indicate their approval of the doctrine they find in whatever work they happen to be exploring. Somewhere in the background there is, perhaps, a valid literary problem: that of accounting for the continuing interest shown by men in the great classical works. And farther in the background may be the philosophical problem that was at least suggested by Hazlitt's dictum: "wherever there is a sense of beauty, or power, or harmony, as in the motion of a wave of the sea, in the growth of a flower . . . *there* is poetry, in its birth." But, with the problem formulated as it is and with the discussion carried on as it is, the result has been to turn attention away from literature as literature and to import into criticism confusing terms and concepts drawn from a social science that is itself so insight-ridden as to be peculiarly agreeable to critics who in other contexts seem to feel that the sin without name is that of committing a social science.

NORTHWESTERN UNIVERSITY

[61] "For language does not belong exclusively to the realm of myth: it bears within itself, from its very beginning, another power, the power of logic. How this power gradually waxes great, and breaks its way by means of language, we cannot undertake to set forth here. But in the course of that evolution, words are reduced more and more to the status of conceptual signs. And this process of separation and liberation is paralleled by another: art, like language, is originally bound up entirely with myth. Myth, language and art begin as a concrete, undivided unity, which is only gradually resolved into a triad of independent modes of spiritual creativity. Consequently, the same mythic animation and hypostatization which is bestowed upon the words of human speech is originally accorded to *images*, to every kind of artistic representation.

"In the end, what is left of the concrete sense and feeling content it once possessed is little more than a bare skeleton. But there is one intellectual realm in which the word not only preserves its original creative power, but is ever renewing it; in which it undergoes a sort of constant palingenesis, at once a sensuous and spiritual reincarnation. This regeneration is achieved as language becomes an avenue of artistic expression. . . . Among all types and forms of poetry, the lyric is the one which most clearly mirrors this ideal development. For lyric poetry is not only rooted in mythic motives as its beginning, but keeps its connection with myth even in its highest and purest products. The greatest lyric poets, for instance Hölderlin or Keats, are men in whom the mythic power of insight breaks forth again in its full intensity and objectifying power. . . . What poetry expresses is neither the mythic word-picture of gods and daemons, nor the logical truth of abstract determinations and relations. The world of poetry stands apart from both, as a world of illusion and fantasy—but it is just in this mode of illusion that the realm of pure feeling can find utterance" (Ernst Cassirer, *Language and Myth* [New York, 1946], pp. 97–99).

Lillian Feder

MYTH, POETRY, AND CRITICAL THEORY

In the last three decades, critical approaches to the function of myth in poetry have generally been influenced and sometimes determined by nonliterary findings, a development natural enough, since myth is by no means a purely literary structure. Anyone who has investigated recent studies of the role of myth in literature must surely react with some conflict—an appreciation of the perspective and insight provided by such fields as anthropology and psychology, and a certain bewilderment and perhaps resentment at the contradictory definitions and conclusions that seem to emerge from the use of such sources. The situation is, of course, complicated by the intellectual and psychological predispositions of critics. A less obvious but more serious problem is that many commentators either avoid or oversimplify the implications of the very backgrounds of myth that they acknowledge: its primordial beginnings, its relation to ritual, its roots in both the psychic and the social structures it originally reflected and served. The critic who writes on myth in literature must first decide—at least to his own satisfaction—what myth is, and this he cannot do by merely accepting a handy scheme of archetypes and forcing every literary work as well as every mythical allusion or symbol to fit its grand patterns.

Myth is both more complicated and less sophisticated than such schemes would allow. Its aesthetic functions can best be determined by acknowledging its unique characteristics, for these persist not only in literature but in all the arts. I have elsewhere defined myth in some detail;[1] here I only briefly outline what I consider its essential features, which appear in an enormous variety of adaptations.

Myths must be regarded as both historical and perennial structures. Emerging no doubt from dream and fantasy, myths express in symbolic form unconscious mental processes that characterized the stages of human phylogenetic development in which they were created. That the drives and impulses of such stages persist, even as human beings have further developed individually and collectively in relation to environmental and social changes, need, I think, no longer be proven. Each human being's dreams and myths are his own evidence. Myth, not only in its early stages but continually, has also had a social function. Although I do not believe that the ultimate qualification of a myth is its identifiable ritual origin, there is little doubt that the connection of myth with ritual is often inextricable. Such rituals remind us of the earliest functions of religion in binding together individuals in a social unit.

The narrative structure of myth depicts an inner compulsion to control through symbolic means what is fearful and challenging within the self and the universe. The conflict between the human desire for omnipotence and the recognition of limitation is portrayed in endless tales of the involvement of heroes with gods and goddesses. In violating social prohibitions through incest, parricide, infanticide, and cannibalism, mythical figures symbolically express the efforts of human beings to test and come to terms with their own nature and the conditions of human life. Essentially the distortions of mythical narrative convey a perennial struggle between inner demand and external necessity, and in this respect myth is heuristic. Its action is ritualistic, ceremonial, or compulsive. The characters of myth, their action, and motives are inseparable; as one, they are the symbolic means by which unconscious drives are at once expressed, acknowledged, and thus controlled in relation to environmental limitations and social demands.

In its evolution as a literary device, myth has never totally lost its connection with its primordial and ancient roots, except in conventional allusions to "the tuneful Nine" or Phoebus or in other such circumlocutions, which serve a purely literary function. The literary scholar, however, must acknowledge that even in their earliest appearance in extant poetry and drama mythical figures and narratives have already been adapted to new social and aesthetic purposes. The gods of Homer may retain primitive attributes, but Zeus at least often behaves like a Mycenaean overlord. Certainly both Greek and Roman myths concerned with the origins of tribes and cities reflect conscious efforts to adapt primitive materials to later religious and political ends. Myth in literature is thus encrusted with centuries of accumulated adaptations. Nietzsche, for example, in nineteenth-century Germany still rages against Euripides' fifth-century B.C. interpretation of a primordial deity. In so doing, Nietzsche not only reflects his own time and place but resurrects something of the primitive nature of Dionysos.

Although one cannot follow the historical course of every myth one encounters in literature, nor is such a procedure always necessary, one must surely be aware that if, for example, a poem such as Allen Tate's "Aeneas at Washington" is based on a Roman foundation myth, the twentieth-century American poet is imitating in literature a process of constructing a national identity on a mythical and legendary basis that served important political functions in Rome of the second century B.C.[2] The approach to myth in literature is thus complicated by the history of myth itself, and by the special capacity of this structure to retain something of its fundamental character through centuries of adaptation to both general and individual expression. Myths are used in literature in three major ways: mythical narratives and figures are the overt base on which plot and character are created; or they are submerged beneath the surface of realistic characters and action; or new mythical structures are invented that have a remarkable resemblance to traditional ones.

I have no wish to add to the already excessive number of evaluations of Northrop Frye's contribution to archetypal criticism, but since it still seems necessary to estimate the validity of such an approach to poetry, certain central issues in his work must be considered. Whereas Frye's *Anatomy of Criticism* and other works on archetypes have greatly influenced those critics of English literature who know little about classical, Oriental, or other mythologies, they have had practically no effect on scholars and critics who have investigated the origins and functions of myth in ancient societies in relation to their literary adaptations. Yet few critics have revealed more precisely the particular function of actual myths in poetry than Frye has—in the work of Blake, Spenser, and others. Furthermore, while rejecting Frye's equation of literary art with myth, one can certainly accept his sensitive adaptation of Freud's work on the relation of myth to dream and of both to the origins of poetry.

But Frye, of course, is chiefly known for his monomyth concocted out of Jungian archetypes and the ritual theory of myth of the Cambridge anthropologists, which became popular in the 1940s. In speculating on the function of myth and ritual in ancient and primitive societies, Frye goes no further than do Frazer and his literary followers. In abstracting a single all-encompassing myth out of the rich and varied body of actual myths, moreover, Frye ignores mythical narratives and ritual practices that do not serve his hypothetical scheme. Furthermore, as W.K. Wimsatt has pointed out, there are basic errors, such as the hypothetical "four seasons," in the foundation and "coordinating principle"[3] of Frye's structure, and there are contradictions within the critical scheme itself.[4]

None of this would matter very much if Frye's archetypal scheme could accomplish what he intends: "To show how all literary genres are derived from the quest-myth," a "derivation" that is "logical . . . within the science of criticism," and if it could elucidate the structure and contents of literature on the basis of what Frye calls "the central myth of art" that "must be the vision of the end of social effort, the innocent world of fulfilled desires, the free human society."[5] But much of literature, even that based on actual myths, eludes or adjusts only peripherally to this neat pattern.

The fact is that the most fruitful aspects of Frye's scheme are those that grow out of the familiar attributes of the gods and heroic figures and the narrative contents of traditional myths. His discussion of Venus in Spenser's *The Faerie Queene,* for example, as a representative of "the whole order of nature, in its higher human as well as its lower physical aspect,"[6] strikes us immediately as valid because it calls to mind functions of Aphrodite or Venus adapted from ancient myths by writers as different from each other as Homer, Virgil, and Lucretius. When Frye applies his archetypes of the scapegoat, the dying god, or the leviathan to literary works in which their myths are latent or overt, his insights are often profound. When, however, one tries to categorize actual literature within the four mythoi of comedy, romance, tragedy, and irony as "four aspects of a central unifying myth,"[7] one must finally reject this scheme on the basis of one's own experience of myth and the very genres and modes that Frye abstracts from it. Frye's work has served an important function in revealing some of the complicated ways in which actual or latent myths and rituals exist within literature, but his hypothetical monomyth has sometimes obscured the very territory he has been instrumental in opening to exploration.

The essential limitation of the monomyth results from the fact that it is a critical construct that, in imitating a mythical one, simplifies it, imposing anachronistic literary determinants ostensibly for the purpose of releasing "primitive" ways of thinking and feeling. This Frye freely admits, yet he seems also to insist that the roots of his system lie deep in myth itself. Thus Frye both disclaims the "historical" validity of his scheme and continually demands a response to the remnants of the "primitive" elements of myth, indeed to the revitalization of these within his own hypothetical construction. Discussing *The Golden Bough* "from the point of view of literary criticism," Frye insists: "It does. not matter two pins to the literary critic whether such a ritual had any historical existence or not." He goes on to say, however: "It is very probable that Frazer's hypothetical ritual would have many and striking analogies to actual rituals, and collecting such analogies is part of his argument."[8] One can hardly object to such use of analogies in the effort to discover the origins and early nature of a structure so ancient and continuous as myth, especially when they are tested in relation to whatever more precise evidence is available. The question that arises for the critic who believes that evidence of origins is important is: what purpose will such analogies serve? When such analogies are adapted to suit the requirements of a critical scheme employed as an imaginary source of all mythical prototypes and all literary genres, they serve not to elucidate the evolving functions of myth in art but to create an alternate pseudomyth, the distortions of which do not, as in actual myths, function as vehicles of disclosure.

In an essay on Wallace Stevens, generally brilliant in its penetration of what Frye calls "the processes of poetic thought at work,"[9] he at times seems to force the body of Stevens's poetry to the requirements of his own scheme. "In the poems of the winter vision," he says, "the solar hero and the green queen become increasingly identified with the father and mother of a Freudian imago."[10] A parenthetical reference to page 439 of *The Collected Poems of Wallace Stevens* (1954) at the end of this sentence refers to the poem "Imago." Of course, Frye has been discussing Stevens's later poetry in this section of his essay, and "Imago" is but one example, but it seems to me that this poem, like others to which he refers, resists Frye's neat categorization.

As the editors of the *Standard Edition* of Freud's works point out, "The term 'imago' was not often used by Freud, especially in his later writing."[11] Freud uses the term once as a parenthetical explanation in a consideration of "new objects," which are "chosen on the model (imago) of the infantile ones" (11:181). Elsewhere, referring to the "father-imago" as one of the "prototypes" within a patient's mind, he says that he is using "the apt term

introduced by Jung" (12:100). Freud is here discussing the nature
of transference in psychoanalysis, and a bit later in the same essay
he deals with the "regressive course" of this process, which "has
revived the subject's infantile imagos" (12:102). Stevens admired
Freud for having "given the irrational a legitimacy that it never
had before,"[12] and certainly the awareness of the ever-recurrent,
ever-vital past that permeates his poetry is related to Freud's discoveries of the multilayered territories of the archaic and the personal past in the unconscious mind, portions of which are disclosed obliquely in dream, fantasy, myth, and art. Furthermore, as
Frye and other critics have indicated,[13] certain mythical structures
in Stevens's poetry reveal the influence of Jung's work on archetypes, particularly his concept of the anima. But it is not the
"Freudian imago" or the Jungian either that Stevens describes in
"Imago"; it is his own conception of the imagination's capacity,
*"in a leaden time and in a world that does not move for the
weight of its own heaviness,"*[14] to disclose the essence of reality
by means of its unique processes of transformation:

> Who can pick up the weight of Britain,
> Who can move the German load
> Or say to the French here is France again?
> Imago. Imago. Imago.[15]

The solidity of the earth's very presence and the heaviness of its
long history challenge the unsubstantial imagination, whose very
limits are its instruments of conquest. For "Medium man" or man
as "medium" between the inner and external worlds, without
magic but only through the "motions in the mind and heart,"
forms new territories within created out of both realms. It is the
"motions" of the mind that assure the continuity of history, that
move the "weight" of the actual earth with

> Something returning from a deeper quarter,
> A glacier running through delirium,

lifting "this heavy rock," and forming not a "father-imago" but a
conception of a "land" that can *"Move lightly through the air
again,"* more extensive than any actual one and containing all
lands and the buried histories of those who inhabited them. The
imago contains and reveals what Stevens elsewhere says is the
nature of poetry itself: "the movement of a self in the rock."[16]
   Although the "imago" Stevens creates in this poem is not a
myth, the very process of its formation, which he here explores,

enters into the creation of myth, and it is the mythical process rather than myth itself with which Stevens is mainly concerned. Whereas one can only agree with Frye's view that "the father and mother" of Stevens's later poems "in turn expand into a continuous life throughout time of which we form our unitary realizations,"[17] there is no justification for regarding these as myths. They are archetypes, which "the sense of the archaic"[18] that exists within continually recreates out of the material of daily reality. The mere fact that a poet "sees individual and class as metaphorically identical" does not result in his working "with *myths*," as Frye suggests.[19] Stevens's creation and use of archetypal presences and scenes are extremely important elements of his poetry, but not as a pervasive mythical structure. Moreover, when Stevens occasionally employs traditional myths or alludes to them, and even when he creates his own, his purpose is essentially to discover their unique revelations of what he calls the "human" or the "real."

Like many modern poets, Stevens explores the nature of myth in the very process of adapting or creating it. In two apparently contradictory passages about the muse in one of the essays of *The Necessary Angel,* a collection that he describes as his "contributions to the theory of poetry," he provides an essential clue to the philosophical and psychological basis of many of the myths he uses in his poems. Considering "poetic truth" as rooted in factual reality, he declares:

> No longer do I believe that there is a mystic muse, sister of the Minotaur. This is another of the monsters I had for nurse, whom I have wasted. I am myself a part of what is real, and it is my own speech and the strength of it, this only that I hear or ever shall. (p. 60)

Although he never entirely abandons this position, and it can be said that his critical stance is rooted in it, he does modify it as he goes on to recognize that fact is "as extensible as it is ambiguous." His observation that "absolute fact includes everything that the imagination includes" leaves no place for "the false conception of the imagination as some incalculable *vates* within us" (pp. 60–61), but it opens the way for an acceptance of the very muse he has ostensibly rejected. For if, as he says, "Poetry is the imagination of life," depicting a world within of our "own thoughts" and our "own feelings," which are our only connection with perceived reality, the myth that portrays our imaginative synthesis of the "geography" of actuality with our own being—a synthesis achieved only symbolically—is our riddle and our persona, our vehicle of truth:

Inexplicable sister of the Minotaur, enigma and mask, although I am part of what is real, hear me and recognize me as part of the unreal. I am the truth but the truth of that imagination of life in which with unfamiliar motion and manner you guide me in those exchanges of speech in which your words are mine, mine yours. (pp. 65–67)

In his poetry, Stevens seldom uses traditional myth. "The death of one god is the death of all," he says in the first poem of "Notes Toward a Supreme Fiction," and he goes on to declare: "Phoebus is dead." Yet in this poem, as in many others, Stevens probes for the origin of myth itself:

> There was a muddy centre before we breathed.
> There was a myth before the myth began,
> Venerable and articulate and complete. (p. 383)

In the poems of "Notes Toward a Supreme Fiction," Stevens is chiefly concerned with the "abstract" or conceptual basis of myth. The Fiction, as R.P. Blackmur says, "must be an abstract idea of *being*, which when fleshed or blooded in nature or in thought, will absorb all the meanings we discover. That is to say, it must be archetypal, and a source, an initiator of myth and sense, and also a reference or judgment for myth and sense."[20] The "Supreme Fiction" is thus not a myth but an archetype, a symbolic construct of the essential materials of reality—places, presences, relationships—which both incorporates and objectifies human perception and response and can therefore adapt to changing "geographies" and various inner transformations. Such fictions are intrinsic to the myths Stevens evokes and invents in his poems as he seeks the "muddy centre" out of which life springs and to which it returns; for this he has said is ultimately the source of myth itself.

The myths that Stevens invents in *Owl's Clover* have been discussed with great subtlety by Helen Vendler, who points out that even his "mythical satire on myth" in this work ends in lines "too close to approving passages in Stevens ... to be dismissed as a continuing satire on the angels"[21] of "The Greenest Continent."[22] This is Africa, which, he says, "No god rules" (*OP*, p. 55). What Vendler sees, however, as an expression of Stevens's "divided feelings" toward the angels who are powerless against the menace of Africa and yet return to "their tabernacles" to

> . . . contemplate time's golden paladin
> And purpose, to hear the wild bee drone, to feel
> The ecstasy of sense in a sensuous air (*OP*, p. 56)

is a revelation of the ambiguous qualities of myth itself. Incapable of combating the realities of violence and death undisguised in the greenest continent, myth nevertheless, even in the figures of these powerless angels, exerts a form of control—a primitive insistence on the heroic and the purposeful in the very face of the severest limits.

All the myths of *Owl's Clover* incorporate its last one, Ananke or Necessity, which Stevens calls "the common god" (*OP*, p. 59). He is their qualification and by him they are finally defined. Stevens's Ananke seems to have been influenced by Freud's several references to this ancient concept, always capitalized either in Greek or transliterated, and sometimes a personification or a mythicized being. In one place Freud defines Ananke as "the reality of the universe" (16:430), and in another as "the exigencies of reality" (21:139). In his best-known adaptation of this concept Ananke is one of the parents—Eros being the other—"of human civilization" (21:101).

Ananke in *Owl's Clover* is also a principle of reality; his mythicized form as "the common god" or "the final god" only exposes the nature of godhood:

> He sees but not by sight.
> He does not hear by sound. His spirit knows
> Each look and each necessitous cry, as a god
> Knows, knowing that he does not care, and knows,
> Knowing and meaning that he cannot care. (*OP*, p. 59)

Ananke, as the hidden forces within external nature, which includes man, emerges from the human mind in devious forms that would seem to deny his unseeing, uncaring essence. In that mind Ananke sees "the angel" and the other myths that enact the human struggle with his limits, but Ananke himself is incorporated into the very wish for omnipotence that ultimately contains and reveals its origin in human mortality: he is

> Lord without any deviation, lord
> And origin and resplendent end of law,
> Sultan of African sultans, starless crown. (*OP*, p. 60)

In ceremony and ritual honoring lords and gods, it is Ananke who is finally paid tribute.

Ananke named or unnamed is the motivating force behind most of the myths Stevens invents in his poetry. One feels its presence especially in "The Owl in the Sarcophagus," in which Stevens consciously creates what he calls "the mythology of modern death." It is a poem that itself portrays and exposes the process of myth-making. Here Stevens's mythical figures and narrative enact an acceptance of mortality by a mind that has abandoned belief in eternity or any life after death. But death, the ultimate reality, can be apprehended only indirectly, through myths whose very distortions indicate the process of their creation. Thus death takes "two forms of thought," which are "high sleep" and "high peace," mythical "brothers" who attend the dying. These are accompanied by "a third form, she that says / Goodby in the darkness."

Stevens goes on to describe these forms, which "are visible to the eye that needs, / Needs out of the whole necessity of sight." Ananke motivates the creation of these forms and lies within the very contradictions of their nature and conduct. Sleep as "ultimate intellect" is the elemental existence of mind, which includes its end. Peace is both "brilliant" and "hollow"; he has been "formed / Out of our lives to keep us in our death." Both sleep and peace are gentle and destructive, ultimate goals and "nothingness." As mediator between them and the dying, the third figure "is the mother of us all." As "earthly mother and the mother of / The dead," she embodies the contradictory forces of creation and destruction, life and death, which dwell within us and define our being, and therefore "she was a self that knew, an inner thing." This essential inner self holds "men closely with discovery." As "speed discovers," as "invisible change discovers what is changed," the mind of man, without conscious awareness, discovers the reality of his own extinction through the myths he creates out of his own being, out of a "desire that is the will" to confront the conditions of his existence. The very power of creation within him produces "beings of the mind," which, ironically, are his one means of acknowledging the inevitability—indeed the necessity—of death.

In his essays and poetry, Stevens's essential concern with both archetype and myth is not their illustration of the patterns or contents of seasonal ritual. To him they are constructs that both portray and disclose processes of mind, especially those that unite the inner world of the imagination with the demands and limits of reality. Critical theory regarding the use of myth in twentieth-century poetry must include poets' own explorations of the nature of myth even as they employ it, for Stevens is by no means the only modern poet who is continually preoccupied with the conflicts and discoveries revealed in its symbolic structure. After further consideration of critical approaches to myth, I shall return briefly to other investigations within poetry itself, since these, I believe, provide a standard for evaluating any theory of the function of myth in poetry.

One critic, Elizabeth Sewell, illustrates her conviction that it is in poetry that the structure of myth is most evident by including in her theoretical study *The Orphic Voice* a series of what she calls her "Working Poems," which convey through myth some of her major ideas on its nature and functions. Actually the poems repeat in brief the theory that the rest of her book develops: "For the last 400 years, with the coming of what one might call the modern age, poetry has been struggling to evolve and perfect the inclusive mythology on which language works and all thought in words is carried on, and . . . this type of thinking is the only adequate instrument for thinking about change, process, organisms, and life." Orpheus, she explains, "is poetry thinking about itself."[23]

Sewell's theory of myth is even more inclusive than Frye's. If she limits her literary field to poetry, she extends the province of myth in other respects, suggesting that "language and mind, poetry and biology meet and bear on one another in the figure of Orpheus" (p. 5). Logic, mathematics, and biology, like poetry, fall within her conception of discovery as "a mythological situation in which the mind unites with a figure of its own devising as a means toward understanding the world" (p. 20). Essentially her aim is to reunite poetry and science by revealing that both result from similar thought processes that can be defined as mythical. Sewell's view of myth as an "activity" of mind expressed by language encompasses an enormous area of thought and expression: "All striving and learning is mythologizing; and language is the mythology of thought and action, a system of working figures made manifest" (p. 28). It seems fair to say that she regards all conceptual thought and its products as mythical.

Paradoxically, this apparent broadening of the province of myth results in severe limitations in her interpretations of the actual functions of mythical narrative. Thus, while she regrets the failure of contemporary investigations "in the natural history of thinking" to employ the fields of "biology, poetry, psychology, and anthropology" in "a common front" (p. 334), she herself underestimates the importance of both psychology and anthropology in the study of myth. She objects to the extensive use of Freudian and Jungian psychology in contemporary literary discussion of myths and to the influence of Frazer's *The Golden Bough*. While one could hardly approve of the simplistic distortions of Freudian psychology in certain approaches to mythical figures as real persons—not to say patients—it is shortsighted to ignore the extremely important contributions of Freud, Jung, and Frazer to modern investigations of myth as a clue to individual and social expression.

Sewell praises Freud as "a true mythological thinker who had to work at inventing his myths of interpretation for his subject matter," but concludes that he "was hampered by not recognizing that this was the nature of his task, myth and poetry being unacceptable in this era as scientific method" (p. 334). She obviously has not read Freud very carefully. Although by no standards except her own can Freud be considered a "mythological thinker," Freud was probably the first conscious explorer of myth as a self-revealing scientific instrument. In fact, Freud refers to his own use of "scientific myth" (18:135) and to "our mythological theory of instincts" (22:212). "Instincts," he says, "are mythical entities, magnificent in their indefiniteness" (22:95). It was Freud's interpretation, use, and invention of myths as clues to the unconscious mind that opened the way not only to a broader critical understanding of the role of myth in poetry but to poets' own explorations of the ancient figures and narratives they evoked and revitalized.

Sewell's evaluation of Frazer's *The Golden Bough* as a work that "insulates itself from poetry" (p. 335) is surprisingly insensitive. Actually, Frazer's approach to myth and rite is often more literary than scientific. Certainly his capacity to recreate the emotional intensity of the participants in ritual observance and to reveal the importance of myth and rite as keys to social behavior have had an enormous effect on modern poets. John Vickery's comment on *The Golden Bough*, "In literature alone it touches nearly everything, from the most significant to the most ephemeral works,"[24] can hardly be questioned by the reader of twentieth-century poetry and fiction. Sewell's underestimation of the contributions of Freud and Frazer to the study of myth results essentially from her unwillingness to view myth as separable from poetry or poetry as separable in any respect from the processes of conceptual thought.

Perhaps the chief limitation of Sewell's method is that, in rejecting psychoanalytic findings of the unconscious roots of myth, she oversimplifies the many levels of "the activity of mind and language" (p. 57) that enter into the process of creation or discovery.

Her salutary effort to reveal the inextricable connection between imaginative and scientific discovery is impeded by her failure to acknowledge that, while both imaginative and rational conception can make use of mythical constructions, they do not themselves necessarily emerge from either mythical or mythopoeic processes. In distinguishing between these last two modes of thought and discourse, Toshihikio Izutsu offers definitions of both that are valuable to those engaged in the study of myth. "The mythical or mythological level of discourse," he says, is one in which

> words are used in such a way that they disclose all the prehistoric memories and associations that lie dormant in them. Fantastic images are thereby called forth out of the deepest recesses of the mind. The primordial images thus evoked from the forgotten past of humanity tend to conglomerate into a more or less coherent narrative form and bring into being the various myths.

Izutsu describes the shaman as "the man who is endowed with a special ability to conjure up primordial images of this sort out of the semantic storehouse of language." The difference between the mythical level of discourse described above and the mythopoeic is that, whereas the former involves merely an "imaginary transcendence" of empirical reality, the latter expresses actual transcendence—as recorded in the poetry of the shamans Izutsu discusses, the immediate experience of "an ecstatic oblivion of ego in the midst of a primordial purity of Being."[25] In the light of these definitions, it seems clear that although myth, as scientific, philosophical, or literary construct, can portray attitudes and evoke feelings that emerge from a mythopoeic level of consciousness, one can hardly assume that scientific discovery and aesthetic creation must depend upon the use of such unconscious experience.

In objecting to the obvious fallacy that logical and imaginative thinking are sharply separated, Sewell oversimplifies the whole problem, making no differentiation between conscious and unconscious processes, and thus insisting that "all thinking is of the same kind" (pp. 19–20). Surely one cannot believe that the mental processes involved in solving a mathematical problem are exactly the same as those which produce the "atemporal and aspatial dimension" of the mythopoeic level of consciousness.[26] Yeats's description of the "one moment of creation" as "the moment when we are both asleep and awake" and his revelations of his use of his unconscious mind in states of self-induced trance[27] elucidate his own creative processes, but they do not necessarily disclose those of all poets or even the "one" way in which his own mind operated. One of the most remarkable functions of myth in Yeats and other poets is its very capacity to mediate between and thus convey various levels of consciousness and thought.

Although Sewell's "inclusive mythology" is unconvincing, her demonstration of the significance of Orpheus in Renaissance and later literature is often illuminating, as is her perception of the method of approaching reality that the mythical figure and narrative themselves provide. On occasion, however, one wishes she had not ignored the "historical" Orpheus, especially when, as she herself admits, the poet she is considering (in this case Erasmus Darwin) refers to the "founder of a cult" (p. 174). Still, in tracing the poetic adaptations of Orpheus or Orphism as expressions of man's engagement with the world, she elucidates both the mythical evocations and the literary works in which they appear. In her discussion of Goethe's "Urworte: Orphisch," for example, she indicates the means by which the myth is used to reveal "a mind passionately interested in the dynamics of life, in the individual organism, in nature at large, in human beings and in his own thinking and feeling and acting self" (p. 274).

Orpheus has been studied extensively by contemporary critics of poetry as representative of the mind and feelings of the poet himself. "He is the figure, the myth entrusted with the burden of poetry and myth," says Walter A. Strauss in *Descent and Return: the Orphic Theme in Modern Literature*. Concentrating primarily on Continental writers from 1900 to 1925, Strauss examines many adaptations of the myth that depict the "poet-as-thinker." As such, Orpheus "journeys down to the depths of the pysche," to death itself, and finally emerges as a "reconciler of opposites," who creates a poetic fusion of the Dionysian and the Apollonian.[28]

In his brief but suggestive conclusion, Strauss indicates the chief changes in attitudes toward the Orpheus myth in the years since 1925. He points out that even in the "quest... for a total integration of all the contraries," which is the theme of Nikos Kazantzakis's *The Odyssey: A Modern Sequel*, Orpheus "is reduced" to a rather trivial follower of the hero Odysseus.[29] If the "harmonizing" Orpheus does persist among some writers, there is also a widespread rejection of the Orphic ideal, a disbelief in reconciliation, in fact, an insistence on discontinuity.[30]

Since the 1920s, Odysseus has been a more prevalent and more challenging mythical presence in literature than Orpheus. Of course, Odysseus or Ulysses appears in every century of Western literature in a variety of interpretations. But it is in the twentieth century and increasingly in fairly recent poetry that this figure, whose resourcefulness, enormous desire for knowledge, and vast experience no doubt reflect his multiple origins in myth, folk tale, and history, has been employed to represent essential qualities of the mythical symbol itself.[31] In many modern and contemporary poems, Odysseus, like the Orpheus of earlier periods, is depicted as a thinker, but he applies his knowledge and his fabled resourcefulness not to convey the nature of the poet or of poetry, but to explore his own myth as he probes the many meanings of his voyages and adventures.

The development of an increasingly analytic approach to the Odysseus myth within poetry itself is not, of course, unbroken. Still, it can be said that poetic adaptations of this myth in the twentieth century illustrate a general tendency that has already been mentioned in connection with the poetry of Wallace Stevens: the effort by the poet to abstract the mythical process from myth itself, to follow its distortions of reality to the hidden levels of consciousness and experience of the self in relation to natural and social phenomena that they ultimately disclose.

As early as 1911, the Greek poet C.P. Cavafy, in his poem "Ithaca," interprets the journey of Odysseus, "full of adventures, full of things to learn," as taking place in a generalized mind.[32] The quality of the journey is determined by those who undertake it. The savagery that the traditional Odysseus encounters can be avoided: "The Laestrygonians and the Cyclopes and fierce Poseidon you will not meet, unless you carry them in your heart, unless your heart sets them in your path." The poet, as instructor, interprets the myth as a guide to the delights and the "stores of knowledge" to be gathered in a lifetime. But these are to be obtained only at the cost of ultimate disillusion. Ithaca, the goal, has motivated the journey, but "she has nothing more to offer." The "wisdom" and "experience" acquired in encountering reality inevitably destroy the idealized fantasy: "You will have already realized what these Ithacas mean."

Cavafy's interpretation of the myth pits the real experience of life against its imagined goal. Twenty years later, George Seferis, beginning with a glance at Joachim du Bellay's sonnet on Ulysses and echoing his first line, "Fortunate he who's made the voyage of Odysseus," sees the journey as a paradigm for the pain and loss that life exacts.[33] Yet these are redeemed by "the shade of Odysseus" whom the poet summons as a companion to make the voyage and his sense of exile more acceptable. Odysseus provides comfort by his effort to free the modern voyager from the superhuman challenges of his myth:

> It's as if he wants to expel from among us the superhuman
> one-eyed Cyclops, the Sirens who make you forget
> with their song, Scylla and Charybdis:
> so many complex monsters that prevent us from remembering
> that he too was a man struggling in the world with
> soul and body.

and by remaining an example of a heroic encounter with memories and loneliness. Within the mind of the poet, the mythical Odysseus, "as though he were my father / or certain old sailors of my childhood," symbolizes the resourcefulness and endurance demanded by any conquest of reality in the face of "the waveless blue sea in the heart of winter."

The most explicit analysis in poetry of Odysseus as the symbolic interpreter of experience is, not unexpectedly, Wallace Stevens's "The Sail of Ulysses."[34] Introducing him as *"symbol of the seeker,"* who *"read his own mind,"* Stevens records Ulysses' soliloquy as he proceeds on his journey, the goal of which is "knowledge." Ulysses, as symbol, his voyage, and all that he learns are one, for his myth depicts "the thinker / Thinking gold thoughts in a golden mind." His voyage is a quest for the meaning of symbol itself:

> Each man
> Is an approach to the vigilance
> In which the litter of truths becomes
> A whole, the day on which the last star
> Has been counted, the genealogy
> Of gods and men destroyed, the right
> To know established as the right to be.
> The ancient symbols will be nothing then.
> We shall have gone beyond the symbols
> To that which they symbolized, away
> From the rumors of the speech-full domes,
> To the chatter that is then the true legend,
> Like glitter ascended into fire.

Going "beyond the symbols," Ulysses asks: "What is the shape of the sibyl?" Answering his own question, he rejects the traditional image of holiness and power, the "gorgeous symbol," and seeks instead "the sibyl of the self," the creature of "poverty" and "need." Within the self, the sibyl is "a blind thing fumbling for its form." It is a "dream too poor, too destitute / To be remembered." Returning the myth of the sibyl to its origins in the dream's distorted expression of deprival and wish, Ulysses, like all of Stevens's mythical figures, confronts Ananke: "Need names on its breath / Categories of bleak necessity," which, once named, produce "another plane" of knowledge, releasing the symbol from its origins within us, freeing the mind to recognize its own creations: the sibyl is "an inhuman of our features," as is Ulysses himself.

Many modern poets interpret Odysseus' encounters with supernatural beings as a confrontation with the self. W.D. Snodgrass's "μῆτις . . . οὐ τις"[35] suggests the syncretic elements of his myth, as the cunning that distinguishes him as a hero is contrasted with the implications of the name Noman that he assumes to trick the Cyclops. Unable to "silence" his "defiant / Mind," Odysseus carries away with him the guilt of blinding the Cyclops: "I had escaped, by trickery, as no man." Ithaca, when he returns, is "No Man's land," where "all seem stone blind." Finally, it is the "dead blind guide," the Cyclops, the shepherd who had tended his flock, who leads Odysseus to

> Still waters that will never wash my hand,
> To kneel by my old face and know my name.

In a phrase that reminds one of the biblical psalmist, the Cyclops is described as the blinded victim who guides the hero to self-knowledge. The punishment that Odysseus received from Poseidon as a result of proudly shouting his identity to the Cyclops, as he sailed away from his island, is here internalized. Disguised in Ithaca, unknown to others, Odysseus has learned how he won his well-known epithet, and thus he resumes his name. This reestablishment of his sense of self has none of the proud assertiveness of the Odysseus persona of Ezra Pound's *Pisan Cantos,* who, in despair, also sees himself as "ΟῪ ΤΙΣ / ΟῪ ΤΙΣ / I am noman, my name is noman," but whose identity as the omnipotent Odysseus is soon resumed, apparently unqualified by temporary dissociations.[36] "Odysseus / the name of my family," replies this persona in answer to his own question: "ΟῪ ΤΙΣ: ΟῪ ΤΙΣ?" whereas the heroic name Odysseus never appears in Snodgrass's poem, perhaps because its speaker knows that his identity will forever include his role as Noman and his remembrance of the victim who became his guide.

W.S. Merwin's poem "Odysseus" is also concerned with self-knowledge; this is acquired throughout his many voyages to "the islands / Each with its woman," which he recognizes as always "the same."[37] "The knowledge of all that he betrayed" does not bring an end to his quest, for the very betrayal of his myth of varied and fabulous encounters defines his real experience. In recent poems by Yannis Ritsos and Joseph Brodsky, Odysseus is a myth to be exposed within the minds of Penelope and Telemachus. Ritsos's "Penelope's Despair" describes the disparity between the idealized figure in the mind of the woman "waiting and dreaming" and the "wretched stranger / soaked in blood" who returns.[38] Penelope recognizes her husband easily, for the traditional "signs" are "clear," but her voice saying "welcome" seems to be "someone else's." It is the voice of a woman who realizes that she must relinquish a self defined by the dreams and fantasies she now abandons in "her final endurance" of the limitations of her husband's nature and her own.

In Brodsky's "Odysseus to Telemachus," it is Odysseus who expresses weariness and confusion, recalling his years at Troy and his many voyages.[39] Writing to Telemachus, whom he hardly remembers, about a war that is only a vague memory and journeys filled with tedium, of his disgust and his suffering, he finds consolation in the fact that, separated from him for so long, Telemachus is "quite safe from Oedipal passions," and thus can have "dreams" that "are blameless." His address to his son suggests an effort to free him from any influence of the mythicized father and from a mythical concept of heroism that the hero's experience has revealed as a painful illusion.

One of the most striking features of modern poetic explorations of the myths of Odysseus, Dionysos, Agamemnon, and other mythical figures is that, in interpreting them, and the legendary materials they have gathered, as symbolic expressions of psychological need, conflict, and discovery, the poet, in Stevens's terms, reveals the movement of the ancient world in which myth and rite served essential social functions to a realm within the mind of twentieth-century man. This inner territory is depicted by Radcliffe Squires in his recent "A Sequence of Poems" as a series of gardens tended by Medusa, Hecate, Ariadne, and Maia.[40] Juxtaposed with these symbolic sites of inner choices is external reality, "The Garden of the World." The "you" addressed in these poems is suspended, in the garden of Medusa, between the desire to behold Medusa "in the dark mirror you will find / Has grown in the palm of your hand" and the option "to forget the mirror and / See what the face really looks like." Within the garden of Hecate, the observer recognizes imagined lovers as "dead and brittle vines"; in the garden of Ariadne, he finds that

> the priapus at the gate
> Has lost aspect and seems no more
> Than a milestone; . . .

Even those who have lived long under the sway of these mythical realms discover within them the evidence of their dissolution. As the quester, "cold and wet," moves toward the cave of Maia, the nymph herself bars his admission:

> "You cannot enter," she says. "It has been
> Too long. I am nothing now, though I am back
> Of everything. I am not here, though I
> Am behind what is here. Go now and forget
> Me. Or, if you think of me at all, think
> Of me as the white violet crushed beneath
> Your instep. Its will gathers to lift you."

Ejected from the mythical gardens, consigned to the garden of the world, where "the botanist" has replaced the goddesses, "you" must accept your aloneness in and alienation from a natural world without purpose or concern with human affairs. The myths have revealed idealized love and friendship for the "glacial" fantasies they are; the keepers of the mythical gardens have disclosed the frailty beneath their promises of omnipotence. If one still feels their power, it is in "a lust that will almost / Kill you," in the sound of an ancient "laughter" within, exulting in savagery.

> Here, at this point, where the gate dissolves,
> And you are neither within nor without,

the mythical realms, with their threats and comforts, recur as stages of the self, as of mankind, never quite recoverable and never entirely lost. In their explorations of these ambiguous territories, Squires and the other poets I have discussed provide the surest clues to the nature and function of myth in modern poetry.

Notes

---

1. *Ancient Myth in Modern Poetry* (Princeton, 1971).
2. For a brief and excellent discussion of this process, see Walter Donlan, "The

Foundation Legends of Rome: An Example of Dynamic Process," *The Classical World* 64, no. 4 (December 1970):109–14.

3. Northrop Frye, *Fables of Identity: Studies in Poetic Mythology* (New York, 1963), p. 9.

4. W.K. Wimsatt, "Northrop Frye: Criticism as Myth," *Northrop Frye in Modern Criticism: Selected Papers from the English Institute*, ed. Murray Krieger (New York, 1966).

5. *Fables of Identity*, pp. 17–18.

6. Ibid., p. 80.

7. Frye, *Anatomy of Criticism* (Princeton, 1957), p. 192.

8. Ibid., p. 109.

9. "The Realistic Oriole: A Study of Wallace Stevens," *Fables of Identity*, p. 239.

10. Ibid., p. 246.

11. *The Standard Edition of the Complete Psychological Works of Sigmund Freud*, trans. from the German under the general editorship of James Strachey in collaboration with Anna Freud (London, 1966–74), 19:168. References to Freud's work are to this edition.

12. Wallace Stevens, *Opus Posthumous*, ed. Samuel French Morse (New York, 1966), p. 219.

13. See Frank Doggett, *Stevens' Poetry of Thought* (Baltimore, 1966), esp. p. 39.

14. Wallace Stevens, *The Necessary Angel: Essays on Reality and the Imagination* (New York, 1951), p. 63.

15. Unless otherwise indicated, all quotations from Stevens's poetry are from the *The Collected Poems of Wallace Stevens* (New York, 1954). Page numbers are given for passages quoted from longer poems.

16. *The Necessary Angel*, p. viii.

17. "The Realistic Oriole," p. 246.

18. Wallace Stevens, "Things of August," *Collected Poems*.

19. "The Realistic Oriole," p. 249.

20. "Wallace Stevens: An Abstraction Blooded," *Form and Value in Modern Poetry* (New York, 1957), p. 214.

21. *On Extended Wings: Wallace Stevens' Longer Poems* (Cambridge, Mass., 1969), pp. 79–97 and 95–96.

22. *Owl's Clover*, in *Opus Posthumous*, hereafter referred to in the text as *OP*.

23. *The Orphic Voice: Poetry and Natural History* (New Haven, 1960), p. 47.

24. *The Literary Impact of The Golden Bough* (Princeton, 1973), p. 3.

25. "The Archetypal Image of Chaos in Chuang Tzǔ: The Problem of the Mythopoeic Level of Discourse," *Yearbook of Comparative Criticism*, vol. 4, *Anagogic Qualities of Literature*, ed. Joseph Strelka (University Park, Pa., 1971), pp. 271–76.

26. Ibid., p. 270.

27. "The Symbolism of Poetry," *Essays and Introductions* (New York, 1961), pp. 159–60; and *Per Amica Silentia Lunae* (London, 1918), pp. 47–49.

28. Cambridge, Mass., 1971, pp. 17–18.

29. Ibid., pp. 248–49.

30. Ibid., pp. 269–71.

31. See Denys Page, *The Homeric Odyssey* (London, 1955); and W.B. Stanford, *The Ulysses Theme*, 2d ed. (New York, 1968), pp. 8–11.

32. Trans. Constantine A. Trypanis, *The Penguin Book of Greek Verse* (Harmondsworth, Middlesex, 1971).

33. "Upon a Foreign Verse," *George Seferis, Collected Poems, 1924–1955,* trans. Edmund Keeley (Princeton, 1967).
34. "The Sail of Ulysses," *Opus Posthumous.*
35. *Heart's Needle* (New York, 1972).
36. *The Cantos (1–95)* (New York, 1956), Canto 74.
37. *The Drunk in the Furnace* (New York, 1960).
38. *Gestures and Other Poems, 1968–70,* trans. from the Greek by Nikos Stangos (London, 1971).
39. Trans. from the Russian by George L. Kline, *New York Review of Books,* 5 April 1973.
40. *Sewanee Review* 80, no. 3 (Summer 1975).

VII. by Northrop Frye—

THE ARCHETYPES OF LITERATURE

EVERY ORGANIZED body of knowledge can be
learned progressively; and experience shows that there
is also something progressive about the learning of literature.
Our opening sentence has already got us into a semantic
difficulty. Physics is an organized body of knowledge about
nature, and a student of it says that he is learning physics,
not that he is learning nature. Art, like nature, is the subject
of a systematic study, and has to be distinguished from the
study itself, which is criticism. It is therefore impossible to
"learn literature": one learns about it in a certain way, but
what one learns, transitively, is the criticism of literature.
Similarly, the difficulty often felt in "teaching literature"
arises from the fact that it cannot be done: the criticism of

literature is all that can be directly taught. So while no one expects literature itself to behave like a science, there is surely no reason why criticism, as a systematic and organized study, should not be, at least partly, a science. Not a "pure" or "exact" science, perhaps, but these phrases form part of a 19th Century cosmology which is no longer with us. Criticism deals with the arts and may well be something of an art itself, but it does not follow that it must be unsystematic. If it is to be related to the sciences too, it does not follow that it must be deprived of the graces of culture.

Certainly criticism as we find it in learned journals and scholarly monographs has every characteristic of a science. Evidence is examined scientifically; previous authorities are used scientifically; fields are investigated scientifically; texts are edited scientifically. Prosody is scientific in structure; so is phonetics; so is philology. And yet in studying this kind of critical science the student becomes aware of a centrifugal movement carrying him away from literature. He finds that literature is the central division of the "humanities," flanked on one side by history and on the other by philosophy. Criticism so far ranks only as a subdivision of literature; and hence, for the systematic mental organization of the subject, the student has to turn to the conceptual framework of the historian for events, and to that of the philosopher for ideas. Even the more centrally placed critical sciences, such as textual editing, seem to be part of a "background" that recedes into history or some other non-literary field. The thought suggests itself that the ancillary critical disciplines may be related to a central expanding pattern of systematic comprehension which has not yet been established, but which, if it were established, would prevent them from being centrifugal. If such a pattern exists, then criticism would be to art what philosophy is to wisdom and history to action.

Most of the central area of criticism is at present, and doubtless always will be, the area of commentary. But the commentators have little sense, unlike the researchers, of being contained within some sort of scientific discipline: they are chiefly engaged, in the words of the gospel hymn, in brightening the corner where they are. If we attempt to get a more comprehensive idea of what criticism is about, we find ourselves wandering over quaking bogs of generalities, judicious pronouncements of value, reflective comments, perorations to works of research, and other consequences of taking the large view. But this part of the critical field is so full of pseudo-propositions, sonorous nonsense that contains no truth and no falsehood, that it obviously exists only because criticism, like nature, prefers a waste space to an empty one.

The term "pseudo-proposition" may imply some sort of logical positivist attitude on my own part. But I would not confuse the significant proposition with the factual one; nor should I consider it advisable to muddle the study of literature with a schizophrenic dichotomy between subjective-emotional and objective-descriptive aspects of meaning, considering that in order to produce any literary meaning at all one has to ignore this dichotomy. I say only that the principles by which one can distinguish a significant from a meaningless statement in criticism are not clearly defined. Our first step, therefore, is to recognize and get rid of meaningless criticism: that is, talking about literature in a way that cannot help to build up a systematic structure of knowledge. Casual value-judgments belong not to criticism but to the history of taste, and reflect, at best, only the social and psychological compulsions which prompted their utterance. All judgments in which the values are not based on literary experience but are sentimental or derived from religious or political prejudice may be regarded as casual. Sentimental judgments are usually based either on nonexistent categories or antitheses ("Shakespeare studied life, Milton books") or on a visceral reaction to the writer's personality. The literary chit-chat which makes the reputations of poets boom and crash in an imaginary stock exchange is pseudo-criticism. That wealthy investor Mr. Eliot, after dumping Milton on the market, is now buying him again; Donne has probably reached his peak and will begin to taper off; Tennyson may be in for a slight flutter but the Shelley stocks are still bearish. This sort of thing cannot be part of any systematic study, for a systematic study can only progress: whatever dithers or vacillates or reacts is merely leisure-class conversation.

We next meet a more serious group of critics who say: the foreground of criticism is the impact of literature on the reader. Let us, then, keep the study of literature centripetal, and base the learning process on a structural analysis of the literary work itself. The texture of any great work of art is complex and ambiguous, and in unravelling the complexities we may take in as much history and philosophy as we please, if the subject of our study remains at the center. If it does not, we may find that in our anxiety to write about literature we have forgotten how to read it.

The only weakness in this approach is that it is conceived primarily as the antithesis of centrifugal or "background" criticism, and so lands us in a somewhat unreal dilemma, like the conflict of internal and external relations in philosophy. Antitheses are usually resolved, not by picking one side and refuting the other, or by making eclectic choices between them, but by trying to get past the antithetical way of stating the problem. It is right that the first effort of critical apprehension should take the form of a rhetorical or structural analysis of a work of art. But a purely structural approach has the same limitation in criticism that it has in biology. In itself it is simply a discrete series of analyses based on the mere existence of the literary structure, without developing any explanation of how the structure came to be what it was and what its nearest relatives are. Structural analysis brings rhetoric back to criticism, but we need a new poetics as well, and the attempt to construct a new poetics out of rhetoric alone can hardly avoid a mere complication of rhetorical terms into a sterile jargon. I suggest that what is at present missing from literary criticism is a co-ordinating principle, a central hypothesis which, like the theory of evolution in biology, will see the phenomena it deals with as parts of a whole. Such a principle, though it would retain the centripetal perspective of structural analysis, would try to give the same perspective to other kinds of criticism too.

The first postulate of this hypothesis is the same as that of any science: the assumption of total coherence. The assumption refers to the science, not to what it deals with. A belief in an order of nature is an inference from the intelligibility of the natural sciences; and if the natural sciences ever completely demonstrated the order of nature they would presumably exhaust their subject. Criticism, as a science, is totally intelligible; literature, as the subject of a science, is, so far as we know, an inexhaustible source of new critical discoveries, and would be even if new works of literature ceased to be written. If so, then the search for a limiting principle in literature in order to discourage the development of criticism is mistaken. The assertion that the critic should not look for more in a poem than the poet may safely be assumed to have been conscious of putting there is a common form of what may be called the fallacy of premature teleology. It corresponds to the assertion that a natural phenomenon is as it is because Providence in its inscrutable wisdom made it so.

Simple as the assumption appears, it takes a long time for a science to discover that it is in fact a totally intelligible body of knowledge. Until it makes this discovery it has not been born as an individual science, but remains an embryo within the body of some other subject. The birth of physics from "natural philosophy" and of sociology from "moral philosophy" will illustrate the process. It is also very approximately true that the modern sciences have developed in the order of their closeness to mathematics. Thus physics and astronomy assumed their modern form in the Renaissance, chemistry in the 18th Century, biology in the 19th, and the social sciences in the 20th. If systematic criticism, then, is developing only in our day, the fact is at least not an anachronism.

We are now looking for classifying principles lying in an area between two points that we have fixed. The first of these is the preliminary effort of criticism, the structural analysis of the work of art. The second is the assumption that there is such a subject as criticism, and that it makes, or could make, complete sense. We may next proceed inductively from structural analysis, associating the data we collect and trying to see larger patterns in them. Or we may proceed deductively, with the consequences that follow from postulating the unity of criticism. It is clear, of course, that neither procedure will work indefinitely without correction from the other. Pure induction will get us lost in haphazard guessing; pure deduction will lead to inflexible and over-simplified pigeon-holing. Let us now attempt a few tentative steps in each direction, beginning with the inductive one.

II

The unity of a work of art, the basis of structural analysis, has not been produced solely by the unconditioned will of the artist, for the artist is only its efficient cause: it has form, and consequently a formal cause. The fact that revision is possible, that the poet makes changes not because he likes them better but because they are better, means that poems, like poets, are born and not made. The poet's task is to deliver the poem in as uninjured a state as possible, and if the poem is alive, it is equally anxious to be rid of him, and screams to be cut loose from his private memories and associations, his desire for self-expression, and all the other navel-strings and feeding tubes of his ego. The critic takes

over where the poet leaves off, and criticism can hardly do
without a kind of literary psychology connecting the poet
with the poem. Part of this may be a psychological study
of the poet, though this is useful chiefly in analysing the
failures in his expression, the things in him which are still
attached to his work. More important is the fact that every
poet has his private mythology, his own spectroscopic band
or peculiar formation of symbols, of much of which he is
quite unconscious. In works with characters of their own,
such as dramas and novels, the same psychological analysis
may be extended to the interplay of characters, though of
course literary psychology would analyse the behavior of
such characters only in relation to literary convention.

There is still before us the problem of the formal
cause of the poem, a problem deeply involved with the
question of genres. We cannot say much about genres, for
criticism does not know much about them. A good many
critical efforts to grapple with such words as "novel" or
"epic" are chiefly interesting as examples of the psychology
of rumor. Two conceptions of the genre, however, are
obviously fallacious, and as they are opposite extremes, the
truth must lie somewhere between them. One is the pseudo-
Platonic conception of genres as existing prior to and independently of creation, which confuses them with mere
conventions of form like the sonnet. The other is that
pseudo-biological conception of them as evolving species
which turns up in so many surveys of the "development"
of this or that form.

We next inquire for the origin of the genre, and turn
first of all to the social conditions and cultural demands
which produced it—in other words to the material cause
of the work of art. This leads us into literary history, which
differs from ordinary history in that its containing categories,
"Gothic," "Baroque," "Romantic," and the like are cultural
categories, of little use to the ordinary historian. Most literary history does not get as far as these categories, but

even so we know more about it than about most kinds of critical scholarship. The historian treats literature and philosophy historically; the philosopher treats history and literature philosophically; and the so-called "history of ideas" approach marks the beginning of an attempt to treat history and philosophy from the point of view of an autonomous criticism.

But still we feel that there is something missing. We say that every poet has his own peculiar formation of images. But when so many poets use so many of the same images, surely there are much bigger critical problems involved than biographical ones. As Mr. Auden's brilliant essay *The Enchafèd Flood* shows, an important symbol like the sea cannot remain within the poetry of Shelley or Keats or Coleridge: it is bound to expand over many poets into an archetypal symbol of literature. And if the genre has a historical origin, why does the genre of drama emerge from medieval religion in a way so strikingly similar to the way it emerged from Greek religion centuries before? This is a problem of structure rather than origin, and suggests that there may be archetypes of genres as well as of images.

It is clear that criticism cannot be systematic unless there is a quality in literature which enables it to be so, an order of words corresponding to the order of nature in the natural sciences. An archetype should be not only a unifying category of criticism, but itself a part of a total form, and it leads us at once to the question of what sort of total form criticism can see in literature. Our survey of critical techniques has taken us as far as literary history. Total literary history moves from the primitive to the sophisticated, and here we glimpse the possibility of seeing literature as a complication of a relatively restricted and simple group of formulas that can be studied in primitive culture. If so, then the search for archetypes is a kind of literary anthropology, concerned with the way that literature is informed by pre-literary categories such as ritual,

myth and folk tale. We next realize that the relation between these categories and literature is by no means purely
one of descent, as we find them reappearing in the greatest
classics—in fact there seems to be a general tendency on the
part of great classics to revert to them. This coincides with
a feeling that we have all had: that the study of mediocre
works of art, however energetic, obstinately remains a random and peripheral form of critical experience, whereas
the profound masterpiece seems to draw us to a point at
which we can see an enormous number of converging patterns of significance. Here we begin to wonder if we cannot see literature, not only as complicating itself in time,
but as spread out in conceptual space from some unseen
center.

This inductive movement towards the archetype is a
process of backing up, as it were, from structural analysis,
as we back up from a painting if we want to see composition
instead of brushwork. In the foreground of the grave-digger
scene in *Hamlet*, for instance, is an intricate verbal texture,
ranging from the puns of the first clown to the *danse
macabre* of the Yorick soliloquy, which we study in the
printed text. One step back, and we are in the Wilson
Knight and Spurgeon group of critics, listening to the
steady rain of images of corruption and decay. Here too,
as the sense of the place of this scene in the whole play
begins to dawn on us, we are in the network of psychological
relationships which were the main interest of Bradley. But
after all, we say, we are forgetting the genre: *Hamlet* is a
play, and an Elizabethan play. So we take another step
back into the Stoll and Shaw group and see the scene con-
ventionally as part of its dramatic context. One step more,
and we can begin to glimpse the archetype of the scene, as
the hero's *Liebestod* and first unequivocal declaration of
his love, his struggle with Laertes and the sealing of his own
fate, and the sudden sobering of his mood that marks the
transition to the final scene, all take shape around a leap

into and return from the grave that has so weirdly yawned open on the stage.

At each stage of understanding this scene we are dependent on a certain kind of scholarly organization. We need first an editor to clean up the text for us, then the rhetorician and philologist, then the literary psychologist. We cannot study the genre without the help of the literary social historian, the literary philosopher and the student of the "history of ideas," and for the archetype we need a literary anthropologist. But now that we have got our central pattern of criticism established, all these interests are seen as converging on literary criticism instead of receding from it into psychology and history and the rest. In particular, the literary anthropologist who chases the source of the Hamlet legend from the pre-Shakespeare play to Saxo, and from Saxo to nature-myths, is not running away from Shakespeare: he is drawing closer to the archetypal form which Shakespeare recreated. A minor result of our new perspective is that contradictions among critics, and assertions that this and not that critical approach is the right one, show a remarkable tendency to dissolve into unreality. Let us now see what we can get from the deductive end.

III

Some arts move in time, like music; others are presented in space, like painting. In both cases the organizing principle is recurrence, which is called rhythm when it is temporal and pattern when it is spatial. Thus we speak of the rhythm of music and the pattern of painting; but later, to show off our sophistication, we may begin to speak of the rhythm of painting and the pattern of music. In other words, all arts may be conceived both temporally and spatially. The score of a musical composition may be studied all at once; a picture may be seen as the track of an intricate dance of the eye. Literature seems to be intermediate between music and painting: its words form rhythms which approach a musical sequence of sounds at one of its boundaries, and form patterns which approach the hieroglyphic or pictorial image at the other. The attempts to get as near to these boundaries as possible form the main body of what is called experimental writing. We may call the rhythm of literature the narrative, and the pattern, the simultaneous mental grasp of the verbal structure, the meaning or significance. We hear or listen to a narrative, but when we grasp a writer's total pattern we "see" what he means.

The criticism of literature is much more hampered by the representational fallacy than even the criticism of painting. That is why we are apt to think of narrative as a sequential representation of events in an outside "life," and of meaning as a reflection of some external "idea." Properly used as critical terms, an author's narrative is his linear movement; his meaning is the integrity of his completed form. Similarly an image is not merely a verbal replica of an external object, but any unit of a verbal structure seen as part of a total pattern or rhythm. Even the letters an author spells his words with form part of his imagery, though only in special cases (such as alliteration) would they call for critical notice. Narrative and meaning thus become respectively, to borrow musical terms, the melodic and harmonic contexts of the imagery.

Rhythm, or recurrent movement, is deeply founded on the natural cycle, and everything in nature that we think of as having some analogy with works of art, like the flower or the bird's song, grows out of a profound synchronization between an organism and the rhythms of its environment, especially that of the solar year. With animals some expressions of synchronization, like the mating dances of birds, could almost be called rituals. But in human life a ritual seems to be something of a voluntary effort (hence the magical element in it) to recapture a lost rapport with the

natural cycle. A farmer must harvest his crop at a certain
time of year, but because this is involuntary, harvesting itself is not precisely a ritual. It is the deliberate expression
of a will to synchronize human and natural energies at that
time which produces the harvest songs, harvest sacrifices
and harvest folk customs that we call rituals. In ritual, then,
we may find the origin of narrative, a ritual being a temporal
sequence of acts in which the conscious meaning or significance is latent: it can be seen by an observer, but is
largely concealed from the participators themselves. The
pull of ritual is toward pure narrative, which, if there could
be such a thing, would be automatic and unconscious repetition. We should notice too the regular tendency of ritual
to become encyclopedic. All the important recurrences in
nature, the day, the phases of the moon, the seasons and
solstices of the year, the crises of existence from birth to
death, get rituals attached to them, and most of the higher
religions are equipped with a definitive total body of rituals
suggestive, if we may put it so, of the entire range of potentially significant actions in human life.

Patterns of imagery, on the other hand, or fragments
of significance, are oracular in origin, and derive from the
epiphanic moment, the flash of instantaneous comprehension
with no direct reference to time, the importance of which
is indicated by Cassirer in *Myth and Language*. By the time
we get them, in the form of proverbs, riddles, command-
ments and etiological folk tales, there is already a considerable element of narrative in them. They too are encyclopedic in tendency, building up a total structure of significance, or doctrine, from random and empiric fragments.
And just as pure narrative would be unconscious act, so pure
significance would be an incommunicable state of consciousness, for communication begins by constructing narrative.

The myth is the central informing power that gives
archetypal significance to the ritual and archetypal narrative to the oracle. Hence the myth *is* the archetype, though

it might be convenient to say myth only when referring to narrative, and archetype when speaking of significance. In the solar cycle of the day, the seasonal cycle of the year, and the organic cycle of human life, there is a single pattern of significance, out of which myth constructs a central narrative around a figure who is partly the sun, partly vegetative fertility and partly a god or archetypal human being. The crucial importance of this myth has been forced on literary critics by Jung and Frazer in particular, but the several books now available on it are not always systematic in their approach, for which reason I supply the following table of its phases:

1.

The dawn, spring and birth phase. Myths of the birth of the hero, of revival and resurrection, of creation and (because the four phases are a cycle) of the defeat of the powers of darkness, winter and death. Subordinate characters: the father and the mother. The archetype of romance and of most dithyrambic and rhapsodic poetry.

2.

The zenith, summer, and marriage or triumph phase. Myths of apotheosis, of the sacred marriage, and of entering into Paradise. Subordinate characters: the companion and the bride. The archetype of comedy, pastoral and idyll.

3.

The sunset, autumn and death phase. Myths of fall, of the dying god, of violent death and sacrifice and of the isolation of the hero. Subordinate characters: the traitor and the siren. The archetype of tragedy and elegy.

4.

The darkness, winter and dissolution phase. Myths of the triumph of these powers; myths of floods and the return of chaos, of the defeat of the hero, and Götterdämmerung myths. Subordinate characters: the ogre and the witch. The archetype of satire (see, for instance, the conclusion of *The Dunciad*).

The quest of the hero also tends to assimilate the oracular and random verbal structures, as we can see when we watch the chaos of local legends that results from prophetic epiphanies consolidating into a narrative mythology of departmental gods. In most of the higher religions this in turn has become the same central quest-myth that emerges from ritual, as the Messiah myth became the narrative structure of the oracles of Judaism. A local flood may beget a folk tale by accident, but a comparison of flood stories will show how quickly such tales become examples of the myth of dissolution. Finally, the tendency of both ritual and epiphany to become encyclopedic is realized in the definitive body of myth which constitutes the sacred scriptures of religions. These sacred scriptures are consequently the first documents that the literary critic has to study to gain a comprehensive view of his subject. After he has understood their structure, then he can descend from archetypes to genres, and see how the drama emerges from the ritual side of myth and lyric from the epiphanic or fragmented side, while the epic carries on the central encyclopedic structure. Some words of caution and encouragement are necessary before literary criticism has clearly staked out its boundaries in these fields. It is part of the critic's business to show how all literary genres are derived from the quest-myth, but the derivation is a logical one within the science of criticism: the quest-myth will constitute the first chapter of whatever future handbooks of criticism may be written that will be based on enough organized critical knowledge to call themselves "introductions" or "outlines" and still be able to live up to their titles. It is only when we try to expound the derivation chronologically that we find ourselves writing pseudo-prehistorical fictions and theories of mythological contract. Again, because psychology and anthropology are more highly developed sciences, the critic who deals with this kind of material is bound to appear, for some time, a dilettante of those subjects. These two phases of criticism are largely undeveloped in comparison with literary history and rhetoric, the reason being the later development of the sciences they are related to. But the fascination which *The Golden Bough* and Jung's book on libido symbols have for literary critics is not based on dilettantism, but on the fact that these books are primarily studies in literary criticism, and very important ones.

In any case the critic who is studying the principles of literary form has a quite different interest from the psychologist's concern with states of mind or the anthropologist's with social institutions. For instance: the mental response to narrative is mainly passive; to significance mainly active. From this fact Ruth Benedict's *Patterns of Culture* develops a distinction between "Apollonian" cultures based on obedience to ritual and "Dionysiac" ones based on a tense exposure of the prophetic mind to epiphany. The critic would tend rather to note how popular literature which appeals to the inertia of the untrained mind puts a heavy emphasis on narrative values, whereas a sophisticated attempt to disrupt the connection between the poet and his environment produces the Rimbaud type of *illumination,* Joyce's solitary epiphanies, and Baudelaire's conception of nature as a source of oracles. Also how literature, as it develops from the primitive to the self-conscious, shows a gradual shift of the poet's attention from narrative to significant values, this shift of attention being the basis of Schiller's distinction between naive and sentimental poetry.

The relation of criticism to religion, when they deal

with the same documents, is more complicated. In criticism, as in history, the divine is always treated as a human artifact. God for the critic, whether he finds him in *Paradise Lost* or the Bible, is a character in a human story; and for the critic all epiphanies are explained, not in terms of the riddle of a possessing god or devil, but as mental phenomena closely associated in their origin with dreams. This once established, it is then necessary to say that nothing in criticism or art compels the critic to take the attitude of ordinary waking consciousness towards the dream or the god. Art deals not with the real but with the conceivable; and criticism, though it will eventually have to have some theory of conceivability, can never be justified in trying to develop, much less assume, any theory of actuality. It is necessary to understand this before our next and final point can be made.

We have identified the central myth of literature, in its narrative aspect, with the quest-myth. Now if we wish to see this central myth as a pattern of meaning also, we have to start with the workings of the subconscious where the epiphany originates, in other words in the dream. The human cycle of waking and dreaming corresponds closely to the natural cycle of light and darkness, and it is perhaps in this correspondence that all imaginative life begins. The correspondence is largely an antithesis: it is in daylight that man is really in the power of darkness, a prey to frustration and weakness; it is in the darkness of nature that the "libido" or conquering heroic self awakes. Hence art, which Plato called a dream for awakened minds, seems to have as its final cause the resolution of the antithesis, the mingling of the sun and the hero, the realizing of a world in which the inner desire and the outward circumstance coincide. This is the same goal, of course, that the attempt to combine human and natural power in ritual has. The social function of the arts, therefore, seems to be closely connected with visualizing the goal of work in human life. So in terms of significance, the central myth of art must be the vision of the end of social effort, the innocent world of fulfilled desires, the free human society. Once this is understood, the integral place of criticism among the other social sciences, in interpreting and systematizing the vision of the artist, will be easier to see. It is at this point that we can see how religious conceptions of the final cause of human effort are as relevant as any others to criticism.

The importance of the god or hero in the myth lies in the fact that such characters, who are conceived in human likeness and yet have more power over nature, gradually build up the vision of an omnipotent personal community beyond an indifferent nature. It is this community which the hero regularly enters in his apotheosis. The world of this apotheosis thus begins to pull away from the rotary cycle of the quest in which all triumph is temporary. Hence if we look at the quest-myth as a pattern of imagery, we see the hero's quest first of all in terms of its fulfillment. This gives us our central pattern of archetypal images, the vision of innocence which sees the world in terms of total human intelligibility. It corresponds to, and is usually found in the form of, the vision of the unfallen world or heaven in religion. We may call it the comic vision of life, in contrast to the tragic vision, which sees the quest only in the form of its ordained cycle.

We conclude with a second table of contents, in which we shall attempt to set forth the central pattern of the comic and tragic visions. One essential principle of archetypal criticism is that the individual and the universal forms of an image are identical, the reasons being too complicated for us just now. We proceed according to the general plan of the game of Twenty Questions, or, if we prefer, of the Great Chain of Being:

1.

In the comic vision the *human* world is a community, or a hero who represents the wish-fulfillment of the reader. The archetype of images of symposium, communion, order, friendship and love. In the tragic vision the human world is a tyranny or anarchy, or an individual or isolated man, the leader with his back to his followers, the bullying giant of romance, the deserted or betrayed hero. Marriage or some equivalent consummation belongs to the comic vision; the harlot, witch and other varieties of Jung's "terrible mother" belong to the tragic one. All divine, heroic, angelic or other superhuman communities follow the human pattern.

2.

In the comic vision the *animal* world is a community of domesticated animals, usually a flock of sheep, or a lamb, or one of the gentler birds, usually a dove. The archetype of pastoral images. In the tragic vision the animal world is seen in terms of beasts and birds of prey, wolves, vultures, serpents, dragons and the like.

3.

In the comic vision the *vegetable* world is a garden, grove or park, or a tree of life, or a rose or lotus. The archetype of Arcadian images, such as that of Marvell's green world or of Shakespeare's forest comedies. In the tragic vision it is a sinister forest like the one in *Comus* or at the opening of the *Inferno,* or a heath or wilderness, or a tree of death.

4.

In the comic vision the *mineral* world is a city, or one building or temple, or one stone, normally a glowing precious stone—in fact the whole comic series, especially the tree, can be conceived as luminous or fiery. The archetype of geometrical images: the "starlit dome" belongs here. In the tragic vision the mineral world is seen in terms of deserts, rocks and ruins, or of sinister geometrical images like the cross.

5.

In the comic vision the *unformed* world is a river, traditionally fourfold, which influenced the Renaissance image of the temperate body with its four humors. In the tragic vision this world usually becomes the sea, as the narrative myth of dissolution is so often a flood myth. The combination of the sea and beast images gives us the leviathan and similar water-monsters.

Obvious as this table looks, a great variety of poetic images and forms will be found to fit it. Yeats's "Sailing to Byzantium," to take a famous example of the comic vision at random, has the city, the tree, the bird, the community of sages, the geometrical gyre and the detachment from the cyclic world. It is, of course, only the general comic or tragic context that determines the interpretation of any symbol: this is obvious with relatively neutral archetypes like the island, which may be Prospero's island or Circe's.

Our tables are, of course, not only elementary but grossly over-simplified, just as our inductive approach to the archetype was a mere hunch. The important point is not the deficiencies of either procedure, taken by itself, but the fact that, somewhere and somehow, the two are clearly going to meet in the middle. And if they do meet, the ground plan of a systematic and comprehensive development of criticism has been established.

[*Other critics will continue the series,* MY CREDO, *in forthcoming numbers. In the Autumn 1949 number the critics were Leslie Fiedler, Herbert Read, Richard Chase, and William Empson.—*
Editors.]

NORTHROP FRYE

Myth, Fiction, and Displacement

"Myth" is a conception permeating many areas of contemporary thought: anthropology, psychology, comparative religion, sociology, and several others. My contribution is an attempt to explain what the term means in literary criticism today. Such an explanation must begin with the question: Why did the term ever get into literary criticism? There can be only one legitimate answer to such a question: because myth is and has always been an integral element of literature, the interest of poets in myth and mythology having been remarkable and constant since Homer's time.

There are two broad divisions of literary works, which may be called the fictional and the thematic. The former comprises works of literature with internal characters, and includes novels, plays, narrative poetry, folk tales, and everything that tells a story. In thematic literature the author and the reader are the only characters involved: this division includes most lyrics, essays, didactic poetry and oratory. Each division has its own type of myth, but we shall be concerned in this paper only with the fictional part of literature, and with myth in its more common and easily recognized form as a certain kind of narrative.

When a critic deals with a work of literature, the most natural thing for him to do is to freeze it, to ignore its movement in time and look at it as a completed pattern of words, with all its parts existing simultaneously. This approach is common to nearly all types of critical techniques: here new and old-fashioned critics are at one. But in the direct experience of literature, which is something distinct from criticism, we are aware of what we may call the persuasion of

587

continuity, the power that keeps us turning the pages of a novel and that holds us in our seats at the theatre. The continuity may be logical, or pseudo-logical, or psychological, or rhetorical: it may reside in the surge and thunder of epic verse or in some donkey's carrot like the identity of the murderer in a detective story or the first sexual act of the heroine in a romance. Or we may feel afterwards that the sense of continuity was pure illusion, as though we had been laid under a spell.

The continuity of a work of literature exists on different rhythmical levels. In the foreground, every word, every image, even every sound made audibly or inaudibly by the words, is making its tiny contribution to the total movement. But it would take a portentous concentration to attend to such details in direct experience: they belong to the kind of critical study that is dealing with a simultaneous unity. What we are conscious of in direct experience is rather a series of larger groupings, events and scenes that make up what we call the story. In ordinary English the word "plot" means this latter sequence of gross events. For a term that would include the total movement of sounds and images, the word "narrative" seems more natural than "plot," though the choice is a matter of usage and not of inherent correctness. Both words translate Aristotle's *mythos*, but Aristotle meant mainly by *mythos* what we are calling plot: narrative, in the above sense, is closer to his *lexis*. The plot, then, is like the trees and houses that we focus our eyes on through a train window: the narrative is more like the weeds and stones that rush by in the foreground.

We now run into a curious difficulty. Plot, Aristotle says, is the life and soul of tragedy (and by implication of fiction generally): the essence of fiction, then, is plot or imitation of action, and characters exist primarily as functions of the plot. In our direct experience of fiction we feel how central is the importance of the steady progression of events that holds and guides our attention. Yet afterwards, when we try to remember or think about what we have seen, this sense of continuity is one of the most difficult things to recapture. What stands out in our minds is a vivid characterization, a great speech or striking image, a detached scene, bits and pieces of unusually convincing realization. A summary of a plot, say of a Scott novel, has much the same numbing effect on a hearer as a summary

588

of last night's dream. That is not how we remember the book; or at least not why we remember it. And even with a work of fiction that we know thoroughly, such as *Hamlet*, while we keep in mind a sequence of scenes, and know that the ghost comes at the beginning and the duel with Laertes at the end, still there is something oddly discontinuous about our possession of it. With the histories this disappearance of continuity is even more striking. *The Oxford Companion to English Literature* is an invaluable reference work largely because it is so good at summarizing all the fictional plots that one has forgotten, but here is its summary of *King John:*

> The play, with some departures from historical accuracy, deals with various events in King John's reign, and principally with the tragedy of young Arthur. It ends with the death of John at Swinstead Abbey. It is significant that no mention of Magna Carta appears in it. The tragic quality of the play, the poignant grief of Constance, Arthur's mother, and the political complications depicted, are relieved by the wit, humour, and gallantry of the Bastard of Faulconbridge.

This is, more or less, how we remember the play. We remember Faulconbridge and his great speech at the end; we remember the death scene of Prince Arthur; we remember Constance; we remember nothing about Magna Carta; we remember in the background the vacillating, obstinate, defiant king. But what *happened* in the play? What were the incidents that made it an imitation of an action? Does it matter? If it doesn't matter, what becomes of the principle that the characters exist for the sake of the action, the truth of which we felt so vividly while watching the play? If it does matter, are we going to invent some silly pedantic theory of unity that would rule out *King John* as legitimate drama?

Whatever the final answer, we may tentatively accept the principle that, in the direct experience of fiction, continuity is the center of our attention; our later memory, or what I call the possession of it, tends to become discontinuous. Our attention shifts from the sequence of incidents to another focus: a sense of what the work of fiction was all *about*, or what criticism usually calls its theme. And we notice that as we go on to study and reread the work of fiction, we tend, not to reconstruct the plot, but to become more conscious of the theme, and to see all incidents as manifestations of it. Thus the incidents themselves tend to remain, in our critical study of the

589

work, discontinuous, detached from one another and regrouped in a new way. Even if we know it by heart this is still true, and if we are writing or lecturing on it, we usually start with something other than its linear action.

Now in the conception "theme," as in the conception "narrative," there are a number of distinguishable elements. One of them is "subject," which criticism can usually express by some kind of summarized statement. If we are asked what Arthur Miller's *The Crucible* is about, we say that it is about—that is, its subject is—the Salem witch trials. Similarly, the subject of *Hamlet* is Hamlet's attempt at revenge on an uncle who has murdered his father and married his mother. But the Olivier movie of *Hamlet* began with the statement (quoted from an unreliable memory): "This is the story of a man who could not make up his mind." Here is a quite different conception of theme: it expresses the theme in terms of what we may call its allegorical value. To the extent that it is an adequate statement of the theme of *Hamlet*, it makes the play into an allegory and the chief character into a personification of Indecision. In his illuminating study of *The Ancient Mariner*, Robert Penn Warren says that the poem is written out of, and about, the general belief that the truth is implicit "in the poetic act as such, that the moral concern and the aesthetic concern are aspects of the same activity, the creative activity, and that this activity is expressive of the whole mind" (italicized in the original). Here again is allegorization, of a kind that takes the theme to be what Aristotle appears to have meant primarily by *dianoia*, the "thought" or sententious reflexion that the poem suggests to a meditative reader.

It seems to me that a third conception of "theme" is possible, less abstract than the subject and more direct than an allegorical translation. It is also, however, a conception for which the primitive vocabulary of contemporary criticism is ill adapted. Theme in this third sense is the *mythos* or plot examined as a simultaneous unity, when the entire shape of it is clear in our minds.* The theme, so considered, differs appreciably from the moving plot: it is the same in substance, but we are now concerned with the details in relation to a unity, not in relation to suspense and linear progression. The

* In *Anatomy of Criticism*, I use *dianoia* in this sense: an extension of Aristotle's meaning, no doubt, but in my opinion a justifiable one.

590

unifying factors assume a new and increased importance, and the smaller details of imagery, which may escape conscious notice in direct experience, take on their proper significance. It is because of this difference that we find our memory of the progression of events dissolving as the events regroup themselves around another center of attention. Each event or incident, we now see, is a manifestation of some underlying unity, a unity that it both conceals and reveals, as clothes do the body in *Sartor Resartus*.

Further, the plot or progress of events as a whole is also a manifestation of the theme, for the same story (i.e., theme in our sense) could be told in many different ways. It is, of course, impossible to say how extensive the changes of detail would have to be before we had a different theme, but they can be surprisingly extensive. Chaucer's *Pardoner's Tale* is a folk tale that started in India and must have reached Chaucer from some West-European source. It also stayed in India, where Kipling picked it up and put it into the *Second Jungle Book*. Everything is different—setting, details, method of treatment —yet I think any reader, on whatever level of sophistication, would say that it was recognizably the same "story"—story as theme, that is, for the linear progression is what is different. More often we have only smaller units in common, of a kind that students of folklore call motifs. Thus in Hawthorne's *The Marble Faun* we have the motif of the two heroines, one dark and one light, that we have in *Ivanhoe* and elsewhere; in *Lycidas* we have the motif of the "sanguine flower inscrib'd with woe," the red or purple flower that turns up everywhere in pastoral elegy, and so on. These smaller units I have elsewhere called archetypes, a word which has been connected since Plato's time with the sense of a pattern or model used in creation.

In most works of fiction we are at once aware that the *mythos* or sequence of events which holds our attention is being shaped into a unity. We are continually, if often unconsciously, attempting to construct a larger pattern of simultaneous significance out of what we have so far read or seen. We feel confident that the beginning implies an end, and that the story is not like the soul in natural theology, starting off at an arbitrary moment in time and going on forever. Hence we often keep on reading even a tiresome novel "to see how it turns out." That is, we expect a certain point near the end at which linear suspense is resolved and the unifying

591

shape of the whole design becomes conceptually visible. This point was called *anagnorisis* by Aristotle, a term for which "recognition" is a better rendering than "discovery." A tragic or comic plot is not a straight line: it is a parabola following the shapes of the mouths on the conventional masks. Comedy has a U-shaped plot, with the action sinking into deep and often potentially tragic complications, and then suddenly turning upward into a happy ending. Tragedy has an inverted U, with the action rising in crisis to a peripety and then plunging downward to catastrophe through a series of recognitions, usually of the inevitable consequences of previous acts. But in both cases what is recognized is seldom anything new; it is something which has been there all along, and which, by its reappearance or manifestation, brings the end into line with the beginning.

Recognition, and the unity of theme which it manifests, is often symbolized by some kind of emblematic object. A simple example is in the sixteenth-century play, *Gammer Gurton's Needle*, the action of which is largely a great to-do over the loss of the needle, and which ends when a clown named Hodge gets it stuck in his posterior, bringing about what *Finnegans Wake* would call a culious epiphany. Fans, rings, chains and other standard props of comedy are emblematic talismans of the same kind. Nearly always, however, such an emblem has to do with the identification of a chief character. Birthmarks and their symbolic relatives have run through fiction from Odysseus' scar to the scarlet letter, and from the brand of Cain to the rose tattoo. In Greek romance and its descendants we have infants of noble birth exposed on a hillside with birth-tokens beside them; they are found by a shepherd or farmer and brought up in a lower station of life, and the birth-tokens are produced when the story has gone on long enough. In more complex fiction the emblem may be an oblique comment on a character, as with Henry James's golden bowl; or, if it is only a motif, it may serve as what T. S. Eliot calls an objective correlative.

In any case, the point of recognition seems to be also a point of identification, where a hidden truth about something or somebody emerges into view. Besides the emblem, the hero may discover who his parents or children are, or he may go through some kind of ordeal (*basanos*) that manifests his true character, or the villain may be unmasked as a hypocrite, or, as in a detective story, identified

592

as a murderer. In the Chinese play, *The Chalk Circle*, we have almost every possible form of recognition in the crucial scene. A concubine bears her master a son and is then accused of having murdered him by the wife, who has murdered him herself, and who also claims the son as her own. The concubine is tried before a foolish judge and condemned to death, then tried again before a wise one, who performs an experiment in a chalk circle, resembling that of the judgment of Solomon in the Bible, and which proves that the concubine is the mother. Here we have: (a) the specific emblematic device which gives the play its name; (b) an ordeal or test which reveals character; (c) the reunion of the mother with her rightful child; and (d) the recognition of the true moral natures of concubine and wife. There are several other elements of structural importance, but these will do to go on with.

So far, however, we have been speaking of strictly controlled forms, like comedy, where the end of the linear action also manifests the unity of the theme. What shall we find if we turn to other works where the author has just let his imagination go? I put the question in the form of this very common phrase because of the way that it illustrates a curious critical muddle. Usually, when we think of "imagination" psychologically, we think of it in its Renaissance sense as a faculty that works mainly by association and outside the province of judgment. But the associative faculty is not the creative one, though the two are frequently confused by neurotics. When we think of imagination as the power that produces art, we often think of it as the designing or structural principle in creation, Coleridge's "esemplastic" power. But imagination in this sense, left to itself, can only design. Random fantasy is exceedingly rare in the arts, and most of what we do have is a clever simulation of it. From primitive cultures to the *tachiste* and action paintings of today, it has been a regular rule that the uninhibited imagination, in the structural sense, produces highly conventionalized art.

This rule implies, of course, that the main source of inhibitions is the need to produce a credible or plausible story, to come to terms with things as they are and not as the story-teller would like them to be for his convenience. Removing the necessity for telling a credible story enables the teller to concentrate on its structure, and when this happens, characters turn into imaginative projections,

593

heroes becoming purely heroic and villains purely villainous. That is, they become assimilated to their functions in the plot. We see this conventionalizing of structure very clearly in the folk tale. Folk tales tell us nothing credible about the life or manners of any society; so far from giving us dialogue, imagery or complex behavior, they do not even care whether their characters are men or ghosts or animals. Folk tales are simply abstract story-patterns, uncomplicated and easy to remember, no more hampered by barriers of language and culture than migrating birds are by customs officers, and made up of interchangeable motifs that can be counted and indexed.

Nevertheless, folk tales form a continuum with other literary fictions. We know, vaguely, that the story of Cinderella has been retold hundreds of thousands of times in middle-class fiction, and that nearly every thriller we see is a variant of Bluebeard. But it is seldom explained why even the greatest writers are interested in such tales: why Shakespeare put a folk-tale motif into nearly every comedy he wrote; why some of the most intellectualized fiction of our day, such as the later works of Thomas Mann, are based on them. Writers are interested in folk tales for the same reason that painters are interested in still-life arrangements: because they illustrate essential principles of storytelling. The writer who uses them then has the technical problem of making them sufficiently plausible or credible to a sophisticated audience. When he succeeds, he produces, not realism, but a distortion of realism in the interests of structure. Such distortion is the literary equivalent of the tendency in painting to assimilate subject-matter to geometrical form, which we see both in primitive painting and in the sophisticated primitivism of, say, Léger or Modigliani.

What we see clearly in the folk tale we see less clearly in popular fiction. If we want incident for its own sake, we turn from the standard novelists to adventure stories, like those of Rider Haggard or John Buchan, where the action is close to if not actually across the boundary of the credible. Such stories are not looser or more flexible than the classical novels, but far tighter. Gone is all sense of the leisurely acquiring of incidental experience, of exploring all facets of a character, of learning something about a specific society. A hazardous enterprise is announced at the beginning and everything is rigorously subordinated to that. In such works, while characters

594

exist for the sake of the action, the two aspects of the action which we have defined as plot and theme are very close together. The story could hardly have been told in any other narrative shape, and our attention has so little expanding to do when it reaches the recognition that we often feel that there would be no point in reading it a second time. The subordination of character to linear action is also a feature of the detective story, for the fact that one of the characters is capable of murder is the concealed clue on which every detective story turns. Even more striking is the subordinating of moral attitude to the conventions of the story. Thus in Robert Louis Stevenson's tale, *The Body-Snatcher*, which is about the smuggling of corpses from cemeteries into medical classrooms, we read of bodies being "exposed to uttermost indignities before a class of gaping boys," and much more to the same effect. It is irrelevant to inquire whether this is really Stevenson's attitude to the use of cadavers in medical study or whether he expects it to be ours. The more sinister the crime can be felt to be, the more thrilling the thriller, and the moral attitude is being deliberately talked up to thicken the atmosphere.

The opposite extreme from such conventionalized fiction is represented by Trollope's *Last Chronicle of Barset*. Here the main story line is a kind of parody of a detective novel—such parodies of suspense are frequent in Trollope. Some money has been stolen, and suspicion falls on the Reverend Josiah Crawley, curate of Hogglestock. The point of the parody is that Crawley's character is clearly and fully set forth, and if you imagine him capable of stealing money you are simply not attending to the story. The action, therefore, appears to exist for the sake of the characters, reversing Aristotle's axiom. But this is not really true. Characters still exist only as functions of the action, but in Trollope the "action" resides in the huge social panorama that the linear events build up. Recognition is continuous: it is in the texture of characterization, the dialogue and the comment itself, and needs no twist in the plot to dramatize a contrast between appearance and reality. And what is true of Trollope is roughly true of most mimetic fiction between Defoe and Arnold Bennett. When we read Smollett or Jane Austen or Dickens, we read them for the sake of the texture of characterization, and tend to think of the plot, when we think of it at all, as a conventional,

595

mechanical, or even (as occasionally in Dickens) absurd contrivance included only to satisfy the demands of the literary market.

The requirement of plausibility, then, has the apparently paradoxical effect of limiting the imagination by making its design more flexible. Thus in a Dutch realistic interior the painter's ability to render the sheen of satin or the varnish of a lute both limits his power of design (for a realistic painter cannot, like Braque or Juan Gris, distort his object in the interest of pictorial composition) and yet makes that design less easy to take in at a glance. In fact we often "read" Dutch pictures instead of looking at them, absorbed by their technical virtuosity but unaffected by much conscious sense of their total structure.

By this time the ambiguity in our word "imagination" is catching up with us. So far we have been using it in the sense of a structural power which, left to itself, produces rigorously predictable fictions. In this sense Bernard Shaw spoke of the romances of Marie Corelli as illustrating the triumph of imagination over mind. What is implied by "mind" here is less a structural than a reproductive power, which expresses itself in the texture of characterization and imagery. There seems no reason why this should not be called imagination too: in any case, in reading fiction there are two kinds of recognition. One is the continuous recognition of credibility, fidelity to experience, and of what is not so much lifelikeness as life-liveliness. The other is the recognition of the identity of the total design, into which we are initiated by the technical recognition in the plot.

The influence of mimetic fiction has thrown the main emphasis in criticism on the former kind of recognition. Coleridge, as is well known, intended the climax of the *Biographia Literaria* to be a demonstration of the "esemplastic" or structural nature of the imagination, only to discover when the great chapter arrived that he was unable to write it. There were doubtless many reasons for this, but one was that he does not really think of imagination as a constructive power at all. He means by imagination what we have called the reproductive power, the ability to bring to life the texture of characterization and imagery. It is to this power that he applies his favorite metaphor of an organism, where the unity is some mysterious and elusive "vitality." His practical criticism of work he admires is concerned with texture: he never discusses the total

596

design, or what we call the theme, of a Shakespeare play. It is really fancy which is his "esemplastic" power, and which he tends to think of as mechanical. His conception of fancy as a mode of memory, emancipated from time and space and playing with fixities and definites, admirably characterizes the folk tale, with its remoteness from society and its stock of interchangeable motifs. Thus Coleridge is in the tradition of critical naturalism, which bases its values on the immediacy of contact between art and nature that we continuously feel in the texture of mimetic fiction.

There is nothing wrong with critical naturalism, as far as it goes, but it does not do full justice to our feelings about the total design of a work of fiction. We shall not improve on Coleridge, however, by merely reversing his perspective, as T. E. Hulme did, and giving our favorable value-judgments to fancy, wit, and highly conventionalized forms. This can start a new critical trend, but not develop the study of criticism. In the direct experience of a new work of fiction we have a sense of its unity which we derive from its persuasive continuity. As the work become more familiar, this sense of continuity fades out, and we tend to think of it as a discontinuous series of episodes, held together by something which eludes critical analysis. But that this unity is available for critical study as well seems clear when it emerges as a unity of "theme," as we call it, which we can study all at once, and to which we are normally initiated by some crucial recognition in the plot. Hence we need a supplementary form of criticism which can examine the total design of fiction as something which is neither mechanical nor of secondary importance.

By a myth, as I said at the beginning, I mean primarily a certain type of story. It is a story in which some of the chief characters are gods or other beings larger in power than humanity. Very seldom is it located in history: its action takes place in a world above or prior to ordinary time, *in illo tempore*, in Mircea Eliade's phrase. Hence, like the folk tale, it is an abstract story-pattern. The characters can do what they like, which means what the story-teller likes: there is no need to be plausible or logical in motivation. The things that happen in myth are things that happen only in stories; they are in a self-contained literary world. Hence myth would naturally

597

129

have the same kind of appeal for the fiction writer that folk tales have. It presents him with a ready-made framework, hoary with antiquity, and allows him to devote all his energies to elaborating its design. Thus the use of myth in Joyce or Cocteau, like the use of folk tale in Mann, is parallel to the use of abstraction and other means of emphasizing design in contemporary painting; and a modern writer's interest in primitive fertility rites is parallel to a modern sculptor's interest in primitive woodcarving.

The differences between myth and folk tale, however, also have their importance. Myths, as compared with folk tales, are usually in a special category of seriousness: they are believed to have "really happened," or to have some exceptional significance in explaining certain features of life, such as ritual. Again, whereas folk tales simply interchange motifs and develop variants, myths show an odd tendency to stick together and build up bigger structures. We have creation myths, fall and flood myths, metamorphosis and dying-god myths, divine-marriage and hero-ancestry myths, etiological myths, apocalyptic myths, and writers of sacred scriptures or collectors of myth like Ovid tend to arrange these in a series. And while myths themselves are seldom historical, they seem to provide a kind of containing form of tradition, one result of which is the obliterating of boundaries separating legend, historical reminiscence, and actual history that we find in Homer and the Old Testament.

As a type of story, myth is a form of verbal art, and belongs to the world of art. Like art, and unlike science, it deals, not with the world that man contemplates, but with the world that man creates. The total form of art, so to speak, is a world whose content is nature but whose form is human; hence when it "imitates" nature it assimilates nature to human forms. The world of art is human in perspective, a world in which the sun continues to rise and set long after science has explained that its rising and setting are illusions. And myth, too, makes a systematic attempt to see nature in human shape: it does not simply roam at large in nature like the folk tale.

The obvious conception which brings together the human form and the natural content in myth is the god. It is not the connexion of the stories of Phaethon and Endymion with the sun and moon that makes them myths, for we could have folk tales of the same kind: it is rather their attachment to the body of stories told about Apollo

598

and Artemis which gives them a canonical place in the growing system of tales that we call a mythology. And every developed mythology tends to complete itself, to outline an entire universe in which the "gods" represent the whole of nature in humanized form, and at the same time show in perspective man's origin, his destiny, the limits of his power, and the extension of his hopes and desires. A mythology may develop by accretion, as in Greece, or by rigorous codifying and the excluding of unwanted material, as in Israel; but the drive toward a verbal circumference of human experience is clear in both cultures.

The two great conceptual principles which myth uses in assimilating nature to human form are analogy and identity. Analogy establishes the parallels between human life and natural phenomena, and identity conceives of a "sun-god" or a "tree-god." Myth seizes on the fundamental element of design offered by nature—the cycle, as we have it daily in the sun and yearly in the seasons—and assimilates it to the human cycle of life, death, and (analogy again) rebirth. At the same time the discrepancy between the world man lives in and the world he would like to live in develops a dialectic in myth which, as in the New Testament and Plato's *Phaedo*, separates reality into two contrasting states, a heaven and a hell.

Again, myths are often used as allegories of science or religion or morality: they may arise in the first place to account for a ritual or a law, or they may be *exempla* or parables which illustrate a particular situation or argument, like the myths in Plato or Achilles' myth of the two jars of Zeus at the end of the Iliad. Once established in their own right, they may then be interpreted dogmatically or allegorically, as all the standard myths have been for centuries, in innumerable ways. But because myths are stories, what they "mean" is inside them, in the implications of their incidents. No rendering of any myth into conceptual language can serve as a full equivalent of its meaning. A myth may be told and retold: it may be modified or elaborated, or different patterns may be discovered in it; and its life is always the poetic life of a story, not the homiletic life of some illustrated truism. When a system of myths loses all connexion with belief, it becomes purely literary, as Classical myth did in Christian Europe. Such a development would be impossible unless myths were inherently literary in structure. As it makes no difference to

599

that structure whether an interpretation of the myth is believed in or not, there is no difficulty in speaking of a Christian mythology.

Myth thus provides the main outlines and the circumference of a verbal universe which is later occupied by literature as well. Literature is more flexible than myth, and fills up this universe more completely: a poet or novelist may work in areas of human life apparently remote from the shadowy gods and gigantic story-outlines of mythology. But in all cultures mythology merges insensibly into, and with, literature. The Odyssey is to us a work of literature, but its early place in the literary tradition, the importance of gods in its action, and its influence on the later religious thought of Greece, are all features common to literature proper and to mythology, and indicate that the difference between them is more chronological than structural. Educators are now aware that any effective teaching of literature has to recapitulate its history and begin, in early childhood, with myths, folk tales and legends.*

We should expect, therefore, that there would be a great many literary works derived directly from specific myths, like the poems by Drayton and Keats about Endymion which are derived from the myth of Endymion. But the study of the relations between mythology and literature is not confined to such one-to-one relationships. In the first place, mythology as a total structure, defining as it does a society's religious beliefs, historical traditions, cosmological speculations—in short, the whole range of its verbal expressiveness—is the matrix of literature, and major poetry keeps returning to it. In every age poets who are thinkers (remembering that poets think in metaphors and images, not in propositions) and are deeply concerned with the origin or destiny or desires of mankind—with anything that belongs to the larger outlines of what literature can express—can hardly find a literary theme that does not coincide with a myth. Hence the imposing body of explicitly mythopoeic poetry in the epic and encyclopaedic forms which so many of the greatest poets use. A poet who accepts a mythology as valid for belief, as Dante and Milton

* See "An Articulated English Program: A Hypothesis to Test," *PMLA*, September 1959, pp. 13-19. My only reservation to the argument of this article is that it seems strange not to require from Ph.D. students (p. 16) some knowledge of the degrees by which they did ascend—that is, some scholarly understanding of the connexion between mythology and literature.

600

accepted Christianity, will naturally use it; poets outside such a tradition turn to other mythologies as suggestive or symbolic of what might be believed, as in the adaptations of Classical or occult mythological systems made by Goethe, Victor Hugo, Shelley, or Yeats.

Similarly, the structural principles of a mythology, built up from analogy and identity, become in due course the structural principles of literature. The absorption of the natural cycle into mythology provides myth with two of these structures; the rising movement that we find in myths of spring or the dawn, of birth, marriage and resurrection, and the falling movement in myths of death, metamorphosis, or sacrifice. These movements reappear as the structural principles of comedy and tragedy in literature. Again, the dialectic in myth that projects a paradise or heaven above our world and a hell or place of shades below it reappears in literature as the idealized world of pastoral and romance and the absurd, suffering, or frustrated world of irony and satire.

The relation between myth and literature, therefore, is established by studying the genres and conventions of literature. Thus the convention of the pastoral elegy in *Lycidas* links it to Virgil and Theocritus, and thence with the myth of Adonis. Thus the convention of the foundling plot, which is the basis of *Tom Jones* and *Oliver Twist*, goes back to Menandrine comedy formulas, thence to Euripides, and so back to such myths as the finding of Moses and Perseus. In myth criticism, when we examine the theme or total design of a fiction, we must isolate that aspect of the fiction which is conventional, and held in common with all other works of the same category. When we begin, say, *Pride and Prejudice*, we can see at once that a story which sustains that particular mood or tone is most unlikely to end in tragedy or melodrama or mordant irony or romance. It clearly belongs to the category represented by the word "comedy," and we are not surprised to find in it the conventional features of comedy, including a foolish lover, with some economic advantages, encouraged by one of the parents, a hypocrite unmasked, misunderstandings between the chief characters eventually cleared up and happy marriages for those who deserve them. This conventional comic form is in *Pride and Prejudice* somewhat as the sonata form is in a Mozart symphony. Its presence there does not account for any of the merits of the novel, but it does account for its conventional,

601

133

as distinct from its individual, structure. A serious interest in structure, then, ought naturally to lead us from *Pride and Prejudice* to a study of the comic form which it exemplifies, the conventions of which have presented much the same features from Plautus to our own day. These conventions in turn take us back into myth. When we compare the conventional plot of a play of Plautus with the Christian myth of a son appeasing the wrath of a father and redeeming his bride, we can see that the latter is quite accurately described, from a literary point of view, as a divine comedy.

Whenever we find explicit mythologizing in literature, or a writer trying to indicate what myths he is particularly interested in, we should treat this as confirmatory or supporting evidence for our study of the genres and conventions he is using. Meredith's *The Egoist* is a story about a girl who narrowly escapes marrying a selfish man, which makes many references, both explicitly and indirectly in its imagery, to the two best-known myths of female sacrifice, the stories of Andromeda and Iphigeneia. Such allusions would be pointless or unintelligible except as indications by Meredith of an awareness of the conventional shape of the story he is telling. Again, it is as true of poetry as it is of myth that its main conceptual elements are analogy and identity, which reappear in the two commonest figures of speech, the simile and the metaphor. Literature, like mythology, is largely an art of misleading analogies and mistaken identities. Hence we often find poets, especially young poets, turning to myth because of the scope it affords them for uninhibited poetic imagery. If Shakespeare's *Venus and Adonis* had been simply a story about a willing girl and an unwilling boy, all the resources of analogy and identity would have been left unexplored: the fanciful imagery appropriate to the mythical subject would have been merely tasteless exaggeration. Especially is this true with what may be called sympathetic imagery, the association of human and natural life:

> No flower was nigh, no grass, herb, leaf, or weed,
> But stole his blood and seem'd with him to bleed.

The opposite extreme from such deliberate exploiting of myth is to be found in the general tendency of realism or naturalism to give imaginative life and coherence to something closely resembling our own ordinary experience. Such realism often begins by simplifying

602

its language, and dropping the explicit connexions with myth which are a sign of an awareness of literary tradition. Wordsworth, for example, felt that in his day Phoebus and Philomela were getting to be mere trade slang for the sun and the nightingale, and that poetry would do better to discard this kind of inorganic allusion. But, as Wordsworth himself clearly recognized, the result of turning one's back on explicit myth can only be the reconstructing of the same mythical patterns in more ordinary words:

> Paradise, and groves
> Elysian, Fortunate Fields—like those of old
> Sought in the Atlantic Main—why should they be
> A history only of departed things,
> Or a mere fiction of what never was?
> For the discerning intellect of Man,
> When wedded to this goodly universe
> In love and holy passion, shall find these
> A simple produce of the common day.

To this indirect mythologizing I have elsewhere given the name of displacement. By displacement I mean the techniques a writer uses to make his story credible, logically motivated or morally acceptable—lifelike, in short. I call it displacement for many reasons, but one is that fidelity to the credible is a feature of literature that can affect only content. Life presents a continuum, and a selection from it can only be what is called a *tranche de vie*: plausibility is easy to sustain, but except for death life has little to suggest in the way of plausible conclusions. And even a plausible conclusion does not necessarily round out a shape. The realistic writer soon finds that the requirements of literary form and plausible content always fight against each other. Just as the poetic metaphor is always a logical absurdity, so every inherited convention of plot in literature is more or less mad. The king's rash promise, the cuckold's jealousy, the "lived happily ever after" tag to a concluding marriage, the manipulated happy endings of comedy in general, the equally manipulated ironic endings of modern realism—none of these was suggested by any observation of human life or behavior: all exist solely as story-telling devices. Literary shape cannot come from life; it comes only from literary tradition, and so ultimately from myth. In sober realism, like the novels of Trollope, the plot, as we have noted, is

603

135

often a parody plot. It is instructive to notice, too, how strong the popular demand is for such forms as detective stories, science fiction, comic strips, comic formulas like the P. G. Wodehouse stories, all of which are as rigorously conventional and stylized as the folk tale itself, works of pure "esemplastic" imagination, with the recognition turning up as predictably as the caesura in minor Augustan poetry.

One difficulty in proceeding from this point comes from the lack of any literary term which corresponds to the word "mythology." We find it hard to conceive of literature as an order of words, as a unified imaginative system that can be studied as a whole by criticism. If we had such a conception, we could readily see that literature as a whole provides a framework or context for every work of literature, just as a fully developed mythology provides a framework or context for each of its myths. Further, because mythology and literature occupy the same verbal space, so to speak, the framework or context of every work of literature can be found in mythology as well, when its literary tradition is understood. It is relatively easy to see the place of a myth in a mythology, and one of the main uses of myth criticism is to enable us to understand the corresponding place that a work of literature has in the context of literature as a whole.

Putting works of literature in such a context gives them an immense reverberating dimension of significance. (If anyone is worrying about value judgements, I should add that establishing such a context tends to make the genuine work of literature sublime and the pinchbeck one ridiculous.) This reverberating significance, in which every literary work catches the echoes of all other works of its type in literature, and so ripples out into the rest of literature and thence into life, is often, and wrongly, called allegory. We have allegory when one literary work is joined to another, or to a myth, by a certain interpretation of meaning rather than by structure. Thus *The Pilgrim's Progress* is related allegorically to the Christian myth of redemption, and Hawthorne's story, *The Bosom Serpent*, is related allegorically to various moral serpents going back to the Book of Genesis. Arthur Miller's *The Crucible*, already mentioned, deals with the Salem witch trials in a way that suggested McCarthyism to most of its original audience. This relation in itself is allegorical. But if *The Crucible* is good enough to hold the stage after McCarthyism has become as dead an issue as the Salem trials, it would be clear that

604

the theme of *The Crucible* is one which can always be used in literature, and that any social hysteria can form its subject matter. Social
hysteria, however, is the content and not the form of the theme itself,
which belongs in the category of the purgatorial or triumphant
tragedy. As so often happens in literature, the only explicit clue to
its mythical shape is provided by the title.

To sum up. In the direct experience of a new work of literature,
we are aware of its continuity or moving power in time. As we become both more familiar with and more detached from it, the work
tends to break up into a discontinuous series of felicities, bits of vivid
imagery, convincing characterization, witty dialogue, and the like.
The study of this belongs to what we have called critical naturalism
or continuous recognition, the sense of the sharply focused reproduction of life in the fiction. But there was a feeling of unity in the
original experience which such criticism does not recapture. We
need to move from a criticism of "effects" to what we may call a
criticism of causes, specifically the formal cause which holds the
work together. The fact that such unity is available for critical study
as well as for direct experience is normally symbolized by a crucial
recognition, a point marking a real and not merely apparent unity
in the design. Fictions like those of Trollope which appeal particularly to critical naturalism often play down or even parody such a
device, and such works show the highest degree of displacement and
the least conscious or explicit relationship to myth.

If, however, we go on to study the theme or total shape of the
fiction, we find that it also belongs to a convention or category, like
those of comedy and tragedy. With the literary category we reach a
dead end, until we realize that literature is a reconstructed mythology, with its structural principles derived from those of myth. Then
we can see that literature is in a complex setting what a mythology
is in a simpler one: a total body of verbal creation. In literature,
whatever has a shape has a mythical shape, and leads us toward
the center of the order of words. For just as critical naturalism studies
the counterpoint of literature and life, words and things, so myth
criticism pulls us away from "life" toward a self-contained and autonomous literary universe. But myth, as we said at the beginning,
means many things besides literary structure, and the world of words
is not so self-contained and autonomous after all.

605

137

Mythology into Psychology:
Deux ex Machina into God Within

LILIAN R. FURST

"Hier ist eine von den Gränzen des alten und neuen Trauerspiels," Schiller wrote to Goethe in a letter[1] of 22 January 1802. This intriguing comment is made in the context of a correspondence about Goethe's *Iphigenie auf Tauris* which was then being rehearsed for performance at the Weimar court theater. Three days earlier Goethe had sent Schiller a copy "des gräcisierenden Schauspiels,"[2] as he called it with a certain ironic detachment from the play he had originally written in prose in 1779 and re-worked into verse in 1786. "Ich bin neugierig, was Sie ihm abgewinnen werden," Goethe adds, as if to solicit Schiller's advice about this drama, which continued to trouble him despite the success it has already achieved. Though Schiller's response was by and large reassuring, he did express serious strictures regarding the figure of Orestes:

> Orest selbst ist das Bedenklichste im Ganzen; ohne Furien
> ist kein Orest, und jetzt da die Ursache seines Zustands nicht
> in die Sinne fällt, da sie bloss im Gemüth ist, so ist sein Zustand
> eine zu lange und zu einförmige Qual, ohne Gegenstand; hier ist
> eine von den Gränzen des alten und neuen Trauerspiels. Möchte
> Ihnen etwas einfallen, diesem Mangel zu begegnen, was mir freilich
> bei der jetzigen Oekonomie des Stücks kaum möglich scheint; denn
> was ohne Götter und Geister daraus zu machen war, das ist schon
> geschehen. Auf jeden Fall aber empfehl' ich Ihnen die Orestischen
> Scenen zu verkürzen.

Schiller's comment is important not so much for its diagnosis of a flaw in Goethe's play as for its sounding of larger issues implicit in the adaptation of Classical subjects to the modern stage. Without "Gods and spirits," Schiller concedes, Goethe had done as much as could be done. But does Orestes's state of perturbation make sense once he is stripped of the pursuing Furies, and the crisis is located "merely in his mind," Schiller objects. His criticism points to a problem central to modern versions of Classical myths. In the process of modernization, which entails naturalization into a cultural, ethical, social, and theological milieu very different from that of Antiquity, the beliefs which had buttressed the myth are superseded by others more in consonance with a contemporary conception of the reciprocal relationships between human beings and between man and God. When Classical conformity to a ritualistic mythology is replaced by the modern aspiration to psychological realism, a new set of dramatic criteria, expectations — and problems — is raised. Foremost among them is the requirement of psychological plausibility. That is the thrust of Schiller's disquiet about Goethe's portrayal of Orestes: when the Furies, the visible reason for his derangement in the Classical theater, are removed not merely as stage trappings but as a principle of causation, and the source of his condition resides "bloss im Gemüth," how convincing is his lengthy torment? It is in this predicament that Schiller recognized "eine von den Gränzen des alten und neuen Trauerspiels."

The figure of Orestes is not the only instance of this problem in *Iphigenie auf Tauris.* Throughout the play Goethe has consistently transferred the motivation from the mythological into the psychological. The nature and the implications of this change are particularly evident in the denouement, where Goethe's departure from the mythological and Euripidean models is most striking. He reinterprets the mythological matrix in the cohesive terms of the inner psychological conflicts within the protagonists and the interaction between them. In so doing, he effects a radical alteration of the Classical material, converting it into an eloquent testimony to the Weimar Humanism of the 1780s. But though the changes that Goethe makes infuse a sense of urgency and of relevance into a remote and perhaps outlandish subject from Antiquity, they also provoke questions of psychological credibility not projected by Classical drama.

In Euripides's *Iphigeneia in Tauris,* as in the mythological paradigm which it follows closely, the resolution of the plot is brought about by the startling intervention of a *dea ex machina.* The release of Orestes and Pylades from captivity and imminent death and their return to Greece together with Iphigeneia can be accomplished only by a supernatural mechanism after natural human endeavors have failed. Iphigeneia, the priestess of Diana in Tauris, had recognized in the two Greeks she is ordered to sacrifice her brother and his friend Pylades. In an attempt to save them and to escape with them, she practises a studied deception, conniving with Orestes and Pylades to outwit Thoas, the barbarian king of Tauris, who had decreed the human sacrifice. The strangers steal from the temple the sacred image of Diana, which was to redeem Orestes from the curse of the Furies, and under the shelter of Iphigeneia's falsehoods they embark to flee the island. Their stratagem is foiled, however, by an element beyond their control, which suggests even before the final denouement that human beings cannot govern their own destiny. For the wind suddenly veers, stranding the fugitives' ship offshore. Thoas catches them, and in his fury is about to "throw them down/the steep cliff, or impale their bodies on sharp spikes."[3]

This is the moment when the goddess Athena appears aloft above the temple to bid Thoas to "cease to rage" (l. 1448), to desist from pursuit, and to let the Greeks return to their homeland in peace. Promptly and without a murmur of protest the barbarian accedes to the goddess's bidding in submission to her superior authority:

> Goddess Athena, when the gods speak to a man
> and he will not believe them, then he is a fool.
> I am not angry with Orestes and his sister
> though he has taken the image. What honor is there
> in setting ourselves against the gods, who have the power?
> Let them go to your country, let them take the image
> and there establish it with all good auspices.
> So also I shall send these women back to Greece
> and happiness. Such is your will and command.
> I shall disband the force I raised against the Greeks,
> and my ships, goddess, in accordance with your will.
>   (lines 1449-1459)

So Iphigeneia is saved, and the impending tragedy is averted, but only through recourse to a *dea ex machina*.

It was not this contrived ending alone that was unacceptable to Goethe. He spurned the entire conspiracy of deception devised by Pylades to doublecross Thoas, and thereby altered the Classical plot in its very essentials. The change in the denouement from Euripides's *Iphigeneia in Tauris* to Goethe's *Iphigenie auf Tauris* devolves logically from the central metamorphosis of the mythological material, and can only be understood in this context. The flagrant deceit practised by Iphigeneia against her host and protector Thoas in the Classical and the Euripidean format is shunned by Goethe's Iphigenie as an inadmissible act of betrayal. To her it represents a betrayal first of the trust Thoas has bestowed on her as the guardian of the temple. Her sense of responsibility and obligation is no doubt heightened by his consideration for her, indeed his attachment to her, which is revealed in the first act[4] of *Iphigenie auf Tauris* when Thoas seeks her hand in marriage. Her rejection of his proposal is the immediate cause of the reinstatement of the death sentence on strangers found on the island. Nevertheless, despite this recrudescence of savage mores on Thoas's part, there is a human, personal link between him and Iphigenie, not just the authoritarian bond between ruler and subject. In resisting Pylades's scheme of deception, Goethe's Iphigenie is heeding to a voice

> die mich warnt,
> Den König, der mein zweiter Vater ward,
> Nicht tückisch zu betrügen, zu berauben. (lines 1640-43)

Even more compelling is her adamant refusal to betray the principles of truthfulness and integrity that are sacrosanct to her. That "truthtelling and lying" are the thematic as well as the moral crux of the drama has been cogently documented by Peter Salm.[5] Iphigenie seeks the touchstone of her morality and the practical guide to her conduct in "mein eigen Herz" (l. 1648), which must remain "ganz unbefleckt" (l. 1652) and "befriedigt" (l. 1648), as she repeatedly tells Pylades in her confrontation with him (Act iv, scene iv). While his standpoint is that of a sober expediency, hers is a commitment to a lofty idealism. The major conflict in Goethe's version is thus an internal one within Iphigenie's mind between her spontaneous loyalty to her brother, her ethical allegiance to Thoas, and her intuitive fidelity to her inviolable beliefs, which predicate absolute standards of veracity, even towards her opponents, and even at her own risk.

The conflict is resolved by Goethe's invention of Iphigenie's confession to Thoas. This is not just a deviation from the Classical myth but an inversion of both its moral and its dramatic design. Far from participating in the trickery perpetrated on Thoas, Goethe's Iphigenie decides to take him into her confidence by disclosing Pylades's plan of escape and appealing to his humane instincts to grant life and liberty to the prisoners. Her action is a flamboyant expression of her faith in the imperatives of the God within.[6] Her judgment is validated by reliance on the inner truth of the heart, which in turn stems from the individual's accord with the divinity. When Thoas chides her, "Es spricht kein Gott; es spricht dein eignes Herz," her immediate rejoinder is: "Sie reden nur durch unser Herz zu uns" (lines 493-4). She derives her strength from the postulate of an essentially benevolent deity, who wills man's salvation by instilling into the pure of heart a clear consciousness of the right course. This is patently a late eighteenth century conception of the relationship of man and God, and also a manifestation "von sedimentiertem Christentum,"[7] very far removed from the capricious and at times malicious gods of Antiquity. What is more, this new inti-

mate rapport between man and God authorizes a degree of autonomous self-determination on the part of the individual wholly alien to
Classical culture. After Iphigenie has made her crucial decision in
favor of openness towards Thoas but before her actual confession,
she challenges the gods to live up to the image she cherishes of them:
"Rettet mich/Und rettet euer Bild in meiner Seele!" (lines 1716-6).

The outcome justifies her faith. Thoas responds to her eloquent
plea with the magnanimous forgiveness on which she had staked her
hopes. The resolution that is accomplished in Euripides by supernatural intervention is attained in Goethe through almost superhuman
generosity. The final reconciliation is brought about not by an un-
predictable outer agency, but by the conscious ethical choices of the
protagonists. The extraneous paraphernalia of the gods has been replaced by an internal moral force so that the release of the Greeks
from Tauris is in effect the externalization of an inner state of grace.
The displacement of the mythological dependence on an outer cosmos of gods by the eighteenth century trust in the privileged prescripts of the heart results in a fundamental modulation of the motivation of the denouement. The consequent discrepancy between
the Classical model and its modern incarnation was already sketched
by Hegel:

> Bei Euripides raubt Orest mit Iphigenien das Bild der Diana.
> Dies ist nichts als ein Diebstahl. Thoas kommt herzu und gibt
> Befehl, sie zu verfolgen und das Bildnis der Göttin ihnen
> abzunehmen, bis dann am Ende in ganz prosaischer Weise Athene
> auftritt und dem innezuhalten befiehlt. . . . Thoas horcht sogleich
> . . . Wir sehn in diesem Verhältnis nichts als einen trockenen
> aüsserlichen Befehl von Athenes, ein ebenso inhaltloses blosses
> Gehorchen von Thoas Seite. Bei Goethe dagegen wird Iphigenie
> zur Göttin und vertraut der Wahrheit in ihr selbst, in des Menschen
> Brust.[8]

The transformation of the mythological *deus ex machina* into
an eighteenth century God within has contradictory implications.
On the one hand, the psychological causation of the denouement
is certainly one of the factors that makes Goethe's *Iphigenie* "so
erstaunlich modern und ungriechisch,"[9] as Schiller described it.
Its considerable appeal to audiences in Weimar around the turn of
the century can be attributed to their recognition of a distinctly
contemporary problem beneath the Classical patina. On the other
hand, the heavy emphasis on the inner element in the action is a
potential source of difficulties, as Goethe himself realized. "Das
Stück," he told Eckermann on 1 April 1827, "hat seine Schwierig-
keiten. Es ist reich an innerem Leben, aber arm an äusserem." Yet

he went on categorically to affirm: "Dass aber das innere Leben hervorgekehrt wird, darin liegt's."[10]

In practice, the difficulties inherent in *Iphigenie* are not those to which Goethe seems to allude. The dearth of outer action and the preponderance of "inner life" has not proven prejudicial to its successful performance on stage, at least not before discerning audiences. The dissatisfactions voiced most frequently center rather on the problematical nature of the play's credibility, specially in its resolution of the potentially tragic conflict. Goethe expressed his own doubts in his outspoken verdict that *Iphigenie* struck him (in 1802) as "ganz verteufelt human."[11] Schiller, too, experienced a certain disaffection: "Ich habe mich sehr gewundert, dass die *Iphigenie* auf mich den günstigen Eindruck nicht mehr gemacht hat, wie sonst."[12] The fulcrum of the objections to the play is invariably its ending. The most trenchant censure is contained in a late essay by Adorno:

> Das Unzulängliche der Beschwichtigung, die Versöhnung
> nur erschleicht, manifestiert sich ästhetisch. Die verzweifelte
> Anstrengung des Dichters ist überwertig, ihre Drähte werden
> sichtbar und verletzen die Regel der Natürlichkeit, die das
> Stück sich stellt. Man merkt die Absicht und man wird vers-
> timmt. Das Meisterwerk knirscht in den Scharnieren: damit
> verklagt es den Begriff des Meisterwerks.[13]

Writing in the wake of Adorno, Hans Robert Jauss asserts: "Der nicht ausgetragene Konflikt des Zivilisationsdramas wird durch die Harmonie der Schlusszenen nur mühsam verschleiert."[14] More specific and dispassionate attempts have also been made recently to pinpoint the sources of the widely acknowledged unease that *Iphigenie* arouses. Martin Mueller, in his perspicacious book, *The Children of Oedipus,* suggests that the predicament stems from the nature of its implicit assertion, i.e. "the possibility of reconciliation without loss."[15] The characteristically eighteenth century idealization of Greece leads to the evocation of a realm of " 'sweetness and light' " (p. 64) that achieves a "precarious victory over a world of bondage and terror" (p. x). This theodicy of love and hope asks to be accepted as an act of faith. Iphigenie herself, in the exorcising of the demons, appears as a secular redeemer. To see her in this light, "protects the play from misinterpretation as the embodiment of a passive humanitarianism. Iphigenia's achievement appears on the contrary as an act of great daring born from suffering" (p. 91). However, such a reading must prompt further questions, which again revolve around the issue of credibility; as Mueller concedes:

"the comparison with the redemptive sufferings of Christ forces us to ask in what sense Iphigenia's act could be called sacrificial. What is the price she pays to make 'redemption' possible? And if she does not pay a price, is such redemption credible?" (p. 91). While Mueller's inquiry hinges on the figure of Iphigenie, Erich Heller's focuses on Orestes. Heller deems the play "lyrically, but not dramatically true"[16] on the grounds that there is no real evil in the world Goethe portrays, and that Orestes's guilt is incommensurate with a purely human redemption so that the effectiveness of that redemption is hardly convincing. Though Heller's arguments smack at times of an almost bathetic commonsensicality,[17] basically his criticisms reiterate those of Schiller when he points out that: "All the evil inherent in the mythological pattern taken over from the Greeks is considerably reduced in stature so as to lose an essential degree of reality" (p. 41). In other words, "without Gods and spirits," as Schiller put it, with the brutality of the mythological curse mitigated into a psychological state of guilt, how much credibility does Orestes still have? If, on the other hand, his agitation has an authentic cause beyond a psychosis, how persuasive is the gospel of loving humanity as a releasing force? And if Thoas is not the vindictive barbarian but the eighteenth century noble savage that the ending proves him to be, how menacing is the situation? How grave a risk[18] is Iphigenie taking with her apparently daring confession to Thoas in view of his sentimental chivalry towards her and his assurance: "Ich bin ein Mensch" (l. 502)? Thoas's initial promise to let Iphigenie go, if such be the wish of the goddess Diana, is singled out in a recent study of *Iphigenie auf Tauris* as an anticipatory indication of the happy outcome[19] quite independent of Iphigenie's impact on Thoas. Such a hypothesis, apart from its tenuous foundation in the text, ignores the central action, i.e. the change in Iphigenie's relationship to Thoas consequent upon the discovery of Orestes and Pylades. Nonetheless, the very possibility of shortcircuiting the plot by the a priori supposition of a happy ending is surely a reminder of the fine balance between the threat of tragedy hanging over Goethe's *Iphigenie* and the affirmation of an optimistic vision that overcomes the potential for evil. If the play is ultimately to carry conviction, it must establish equally the reality of that evil and the power of good to conquer it.

The questions raised about the authenticity of the play's motivation, like the doubts cast on the validity of its characterization from Schiller onwards, spring from the demand that *Iphigenie* satisfy those expectations that it has itself projected. This becomes clear through comparison with the Greek model. There is no place and no

need in Euripides's *Iphigeneia in Tauris* for any discussion of Thoas's
abrupt tergiversation in response to Athene's intervention. It has its
undisputed justification within the framework of a mythological
system of beliefs that follow the rationale of their innate irration-
ality. But as soon as the mythological creed is excised, other criteria
are brought to bear on the action. By transforming the *deus ex machina* into the God within, Goethe opened the door to the kind of objections commonly directed against his play. When Classical mythology is transposed into modern psychology, when the mythological
curse is internalized as a neurotic conflict,[20] the conventions of ritual yield to those of realism. Orestes's dementia can well be interpreted as a psychopathological state, "das Zeichen eines habituell
gewordenen Misstrauens, geistig vererbt, und in Angst, Argwohn,
Blindheit sich steigernd zur Panik von Gewalttaten."[21] His vision is
one of determinism and despair, fixated on the trauma of the past.
The problem that Goethe explores is one that does not concern
Euripides: by what means can Orestes be freed from the persecution
dogging him for the death of his mother. To Euripides, that question is superfluous because the answer is contained in the public
mythological model: only through divine grace in the form of the
goddess's direct intervention. To Goethe it is a moral, psychological,
and personal issue, whose solution lies in the natural human domain.
Orestes, like Coleridge's Ancient Mariner, is redeemed by sublime
gestures of altruistic love. Whether this bespeaks "ein romantisches
Element,"[22] as Adorno would have it, is of no great importance.
What matters is that the situation is envisaged not in the mechanistic
terms of Classical mythology but as a unique dilemma of modern
individual psychology. As a result of this basically different perspective, Goethe's *Iphigenie* invites standards of judgment which
would be wholly inappropriate in regard to Euripides's *Iphigeneia*.
Because the thrust of Goethe's version is towards psychological
veracity, it elicits the yardstick of plausibility. So while the supernatural is acceptable without demur in the mythological structure,
the superhuman is suspect in the context of a psychological realism.

Goethe's *Iphigenie* is not an isolated example of the farreaching
changes consequent upon the transformation of the *deus ex machina*
into the God within. Racine's *Iphigénie* testifies to the same phenomenon. The parallelism of direction between the two dramas is
the more striking in view of the signal divergences between them.
Not only do they treat different phases of Iphigenie's life, Racine
dealing with her fate in Aulis, while Goethe uses the episode in
Tauris. More telling than the disparity of the actual thematic basis
is the heterogeneity of the moral and theological climate into which

the Classical material is adapted. Racine's *Iphigénie* dates from 1674 when Jansenism carried considerable force in France; Goethe's *Iphigenie* derives from the 1780s, the heyday of Weimar Humanism. That the two plays espouse antithetical theodicies is, therefore, hardly surprising. In place of the benign gods of the later eighteenth century who can be conjured to fulfill the promise of *agape* invested in them by a trusting mankind, the Racinian god is a malignant "mangeur d'hommes,"[23] imperious and cruel, willfully extorting horrible sacrifices, far closer indeed to the often oppressive gods of Antiquity than his idealized Enlightenment successor. Yet despite this central difference, the process of modernization revealed by Racine's *Iphigénie* is remarkably similar to that in Goethe's drama.

Like the German version, the French deviates most significantly from the Classical paradigm in its denouement, though this entails in Racine's case a less extensive restructuring of the Classical material. Racine remains more faithful than Goethe to the mythological and Euripidean outline in his plot. Iphigeneia is to be sacrificed by her father, Agamemnon, as an act of propitiation to the gods. Her death is the price to be paid for favorable winds and victory in the Trojan war; it is not a test of faith, as in the Biblical story of Abraham and Isaac, nor an atonement for guilt, but simply a sort of bribe, a symbol of unconditional subjugation to the gods' whims. Agamemnon, after some struggle, and Iphigeneia herself, with a resigned compliance, submit to the divine decree, although her mother, Clytemnestra, and her lover, Achilles, are rebelliously indignant exponents of an alternative social and moral ethos that challenges the dominant assumptions by championing the autonomous rights of the individual.

In the event, Iphigeneia is saved. In Classical mythology, as in the Euripidean drama, the goddess Diana snatches her from under the knife by substituting a deer:

> And the miracle happened. Everyone
> distinctly heard the sound of the knife
> striking, but no one could see
> the girl. She had vanished.
> The priest cried out, and the whole army
> echoed him, seeing
> what some god had sent, a thing
> nobody could have prophesied. There it was,
> we could see it, but we could scarcely
> believe it: a deer
> lay there gasping, a large
> beautiful animal, and its blood ran
> streaming over the altar of the goddess.[24]

The *dea ex machina* was patently as unpalatable to Racine as to Goethe. In his preface he confronts the predicament posed by the ending:

> Quelle apparence que j'eusse souillé la scène par le meurtre
> horrible d'une personne aussi vertueuse et aussi aimable
> qu'il fallait représenter Iphigénie? Et quelle apparence
> encore de dénouer ma tragédie par le secours d'une déesse
> et d'une machine, et par un métamorphose, qui pouvait
> bien trouver quelque créance du temps d'Euripide, mais
> qui serait trop absurde et trop incroyable parmi nous? [25]

Racine's discourse arouses suspicion both through the double re-iteration of the slippery concept of "apparence" as the keystone of an argument that is made to seem more rational than it is, and through the twin rhetorical questions with their emotionally laden appeal to a presumptive common consensus. The voiced fear of of-fending the audience's sensibilities by the horrible murder of an in-nocent, virtuous young princess disregards the fact that in the Clas-sical version Iphigeneia is not in fact put to death, but whisked away to Tauris. Though she languishes there in exile, she is eventually re-stored to her homeland and reunited with the remnants of her fam-ily, so that the final outcome is not as negative as Racine suggests. What evidently troubles him above all is the violation of the Neo-classical creed of *vraisemblance* that a supernatural solution would involve. Since tragedy was expected to deal seriously with lofty moral and even metaphysical themes, it could not include *le mer-veilleux,* i.e. the wholly incredible, only at the utmost *le vraisemb-lable extraordinaire.*[26] Racine's rejection of the *dea ex machina* as "trop absurde et trop incroyable parmi nous" is a manifestation of his respect for the dramatic tenets of his age.

His strategy for compromise between the theatrical imperatives of his day and the prescripts of Classical mythology is ingenious. He introduces into the plot the figure of Eriphile, whom he had discovered in Pausanias, and "sans lequel je n'aurais jamais osé entreprendre cette tragédie."[27] The clandestine daughter of Helen and Theseus, Eriphile is "une autre Iphigénie,"[28] a mirror image other to the titular persona, identical in name and in age, but oppo-site in position and character, an orphan, an exile, a captive in love with her captor, Achilles, tormented by jealousy and envy of the security of family, home, and love which she so woefully lacks and which the daughter of Agamemnon so eminently possesses. It is this other Iphigénie who had been designated as the victim, the scape-goat, the substitute sacrifice whose death serves to propitiate the gods. But in the manner of Eriphile's death, Racine had made another momentous modification. For it is a suicide: on the sacrificial altar she plunges the knife into her own heart (l. 1776) before the officiating priest can lay hands on her. So her death, as Odette de Mourgues has pointed out, "bien qu'elle soit en principe décidée par les dieux, n'en est pas moins l'aboutissant logique de la destruction opérée en elle-même par l'amour et la haine."[29] Like Goethe, Racine transforms the *deus ex machina* into a god/demon within. The force of human passion within, as terrifying as the incalculable gods without, becomes in Racine's rendering the activating mainspring of the tragedy. The sacrifice is here personal and internal in motivation, triggered by rage, guilt, and misery, not the consummation of an inscrutable external edict. The link between cause and effect is psychological rather than theological; its inevitability is that of a psychopathological state of mind, not the enactment of an ordained ritual. The portrayal of Eriphile is, therefore, "a psychological study of the destructiveness of passion as it lures the self into betrayal and humiliation."[30]

Through the addition of Eriphile, Racine has devised a subterfuge which succeeds in circumventing the two major problems inherent for him in the mythological material. The harsh punishment of a visibly guilty persona satisfies the desire for a moralistically apposite closure. It is even arguable that the unhoped for reprieve of the virtuous Iphigénie could be seen as an instance of that divine grace so salient to Jansenism. Even more important, the avoidance of the obviously miraculous is in conformity with the principle of *vraisemblance.* Yet for all its palpable advantages from the point of view of his contemporaries, Racine's adaptation has serious drawbacks too. In softening the impact of incidents too prominent a part of the well-known model to be entirely ignored, Racine had debilitated, perhaps even distorted, the Classical myth. The presence of Eriphile in fact creates at least as many problems as it seems to solve. The energy of the play's internal logic is blunted when the sacrifice is no longer the fulfillment of the gods' gratuitous wishes, but the result of a human failing. Eriphile's suicide, while wholly convincing from the behavioristic and moral angle, is in various ways dramatically precarious. First, it is not integrated into the play's central theme, the confrontation between man and the gods. Eriphile, in her solipsism, seems bereft of that immediate awareness of the gods that breeds the questioning stance of the other protagonists. Secondly, she has no intrinsic function in the plot other than as the scapegoat; though already mentioned in the first act (lines 153-6, 237-42, 345-52), she does not actually appear until

the second act. Thirdly, her death, as an act of private despair, is
stripped of the ethical significance of a consciously chosen self-
sacrifice. Finally, it is her intrusion that creates that sexual triangle
that may well make the play more modern, but which diverts attention from the main conflict between man and the gods. The earthly
rivalry comes to overshadow the greater, overarching contest of will
between the divine prerogative and human self-assertion. The threat
of the gods' arbitrary malevolence is defused by the late revelation
of their covert justice in their choice of Eriphile as sacrifice:

> Le Dieu qui maintenant vous parle par ma voix
> M'explique son oracle, et m'instruit de son choix.
> Un autre sang d'Hélène, une autre Iphigénie
> Sur ce bord immolée y doit laisser sa vie. (lines 1747-50)

Having set in motion the violent mechanism of human passions by
their initial oracle, the gods then deflect its course by the surprising
interpretation of their edict. This may be taken as evidence of the
"intrikate Zweideutigkeit göttlicher Willkür, die Racines Tragödie
auf den Gipfel treibt."[31] But this ambivalence, which follows from
the addition of Eriphile, leads to an uncertainty of purpose that results from the attempt to graft a psychologically motivated suicide
onto the mythological model. The essentially collective theological
axis of the myth as of the Euripidean drama is weakened, while the
shift of emphasis to individual, and in particular, to erotic psychology, though plausible enough in itself, raises questions of dramatic
congruity as weighty as the issue of *vraisemblance* that Racine was
endeavoring to settle by this stratagem. At a deeper level, the problem of credibility is never satisfactorily solved in *Iphigénie* because
the new psychological motivation from the god within does not fit
well into the tracks left by the *deus ex machina.* The outcome is a
play that has been described as belonging to the "category of instructive failures,"[32] and that could be said to cast psychology as
its *ex machina* device.

The conformation of the "boundary between ancient and modern tragedy," to which Schiller referred in a somewhat cryptic and
elliptical manner, can now be delineated with greater precision. That
boundary is crossed with the specifically modern concern with the
subjectivity of the individual. It is the inner struggles of Iphigenie
and of Eriphile that are the focus of interest in Goethe's and Racine's versions, and it is from their personal decisions that the denouement devolves. This preoccupation with the intimate recesses
of the individual heart and mind fosters a very high degree of in-
ternalization. Outer dramatic action between the protagonists is a

precipitate and a reflection of the paramount inner conflict within the protagonists. Such a centering on the individual obviously predicates a primarily psychological approach, a reinterpretation of myth in terms of inter- and, above all, intrapersonal stresses and strains. Again it is Schiller, with the intuitive understanding of a practising dramatist, who first grasped the tenor of Goethe's *Iphigenie*. In that same letter to Goethe of 22 January 1802, he designated "Seele" as "den eigentlichen Vorzug" of the drama, elaborating on this insight with the observation:

> Es gehört nun freilich zu dem eigenen Charakter
> dieses Stücks, dass dasjenige, was man eigentlich
> Handlung nennt, hinter den Coulissen vorgeht, und
> das Sittliche, was im Herzen vorgeht, die Gesinnung,
> darin zur Handlung gemacht ist und gleichsam vor
> die Augen gebracht wird.[33]

Schiller's word "soul" may not feature in the vocabulary of literary criticism today, but it catches with extraordinary acuity that transposition into the personal realm of the individual that occurs in both Goethe's and Racine's reenactment of the Classical myth.

The process of modernization of myth is bound to engender a tension between the model from Antiquity and its modern reincarnation. As a process it is of necessity simultaneously subversive and creative. It is subversive in its marked tendency to a critical dissolution of myth as the mythical dimension becomes merely a shadowy second level onto which the characters extend through their past, and which gives them a kind of dual identity. That mythical dimension is also eroded through the infiltration into its timeless, archetypal contours of a contemporary psychology (and theodicy). The relationship to the mythic paradigm may become so tenous as to forfeit the benefits of its allusive intertextuality. On the other hand, that very shortfall can itself be creative. "Das Unzulängliche ist produktiv," Goethe declared, applying his dictum to his own play: "Ich schrieb meine 'Iphigenia' aus einem Studium der griechischen Sachen, das aber unzulänglich war. Wenn es erschöpfend gewesen wäre, so wäre das Stück ungeschrieben geblieben."[34] The exhaustive study of the source may be exhausting to the poet's own creativity. The old exists to serve the new, and it can best do so not by spawning a spectral revival but by prompting an original, independent work. When myth is turned into a metaphor for psychodrama, the troubled marriage of mythology and psychology can beget brilliant modern offspring.[35]

LILIAN R. FURST · *University of Texas at Dallas*

14   COMPARATIVE LITERATURE STUDIES

NOTES

1. *Briefe,* ed. Fritz Jonas (Stuttgart, Leipzig, Berlin, Wien: Deutsche Verlagsanstalt, 1895), vi, 337.
2. Letter to Schiller, 19 January 1802, *Goethes Werke* (Weimar: Böhlau, 1894), Abt. 4, *Briefe,* xvi, No. 4471, p. 11.
3. Euripides, *Iphigeneia in Tauris,* trans. Richard Lattimore (New York: Oxford Univ. Press, 1973), p. 63, lines 1402-3. All subsequent line numbers refer to this edition.
4. *Goethes Werke* (Weimar: Böhlau, 1889), Abt. 1, x, 13, lines 246-50. All subsequent line numbers refer to this edition.
5. Peter Salm, "Truthtelling and Lying in Goethe's *Iphigenie,*" *German Life & Letters,* 34 (July 1981), 351-58.
6. Recent critics have argued that Iphigenie's actions are prompted as much by self-assertiveness and a desire for personal autonomy. "Freiheit ist, woraus Iphigenie handelt und was sie will," Theodor Adorno claims in his essay "Zum Klassizismus von Goethes *Iphigenie,*" in *Noten zur Literatur,* iv (Frankfurt: Suhrkamp, 1974, p. 26). If she were to stay with the aging Thoas, who wishes an heir, her autonomy would be prejudiced, and with it her Kantian right towards herself and, indeed, even her humanity. Adorno's suggestion has been taken up by Wolfdietrich Rasch, *Goethes "Iphigenie auf Tauris" als Drama der Autonomie* (München: Beck, 1979, pp. 25-6) and by Hans Robert Jauss, "Racines und Goethes *Iphigenie*" in Rainer Warning (ed.), *Rezeptionsästhetik. Theorie und Praxis* (München: Beck, 1975, pp. 377-78.
7. Adorno, *Noten zur Literatur,* iv, 9.
8. Georg Wilhelm Friedrich Hegel, *Ästhetik,* ed. Friedrich Bassenge (Berlin: Aufbau Verlag, 1955), p. 245.
9. Letter to Gottfried Körner, 21 January 1802, *Briefe,* vi, 335.
10. Johann Peter Eckermann, *Gespräche mit Goethe,* ed. Conrad Höfer (Leipzig: Hesse & Becker, 1913), p. 568.
11. Letter to Schiller, 19 January 1802, *Briefe,* xvi, 11.
12. Letter to Gottfried Körner, 21 January 1802, *Briefe,* vi, 336.
13. Adorno, *Noten zur Literatur,* iv, 26-7.
14. Jauss in Warning (ed.), *Rezeptionsästhetik,* p. 377.
15. Martin Mueller, *Children of Oedipus and other essays on the imitation of Greek Tragedy 1550-1800* (Toronto, Buffalo and London: Univ. of Toronto Press, 1980), p. 92.
16. Erich Heller, "Goethe and Tragedy," *The Disinherited Mind,* 3rd. ed. (New York: Barnes & Noble, 1971), p. 41.
17. Heller, *The Disinherited Mind,* p. 42: "For surely there is no 'cure' for the murder of a mother."
18. cf. Rasch, *Goethes "Iphigenie auf Tauris",* pp. 99 and 107; and Jauss, in Warning (ed.), *Rezeptionsästhetik,* pp. 357-58.
19. Rasch, *Goethes "Iphigenie auf Tauris",* p. 107: "Der gute Ausgang des Dramas ist also schon durch dieses Gelöbnis des Königs vorbereitet und wird nicht erst durch Iphigenies Einwirkung auf Thoas erreicht."
20. Adorno, *Noten zur Literatur,* iv, p. 29.
21. Arthur Henkel, "Die 'verteufelt humane' *Iphigenie,*" *Euphorion,* 59 (1965), 11.
22. Adorno, *Noten zur Literatur,* iv, 30.
23. Roland Barthes, *Sur Racine* (Paris: Editions du Seuil, 1963), p. 49.
24. Euripides, *Iphigeneia at Aulis,* trans. W. S. Merwin and George E. Dimock, Jr. (New York: Oxford Univ. Press, 1978), p. 94, lines 2121-33.
25. Jean Racine, Preface to *Iphigénie* (Paris: Larousse, 1965), p. 28. All subsequent line numbers refer to this edition.
26. cf. R. C. Knight, "Myth in Racine: A Myth?" *L'Esprit Créateur,* 16, No. 2 (Summer 1976), 99.
27. Racine, Preface to *Iphigénie,* p. 28.
28. Racine, *Iphigénie,* p. 126, line 1749.
29. Odette de Mourgues, *Autonomie de Racine* (Paris: Corti, 1967), p. 153.
30. Mueller, *Children of Oedipus,* p. 41.

31.Jauss in Warning (ed.), *Rezeptionsästhetik,* p. 363.

32.Mueller, *Children of Oedipus,* p. viii.

33.*Briefe,* vi, 339.

34. Friedrich Wilhelm Riemer, *Mittheilungen über Goethe* (Berlin: Duncker & Humboldt, 1841), ii, p. 716; 20 July 1811.

35. This article develops a paper presented at the VIIIth Triennial meeting of the American Comparative Literature Association, Santa Barbara, 25 March 1983.

The Plague in Literature and Myth

THE PLAGUE IS FOUND EVERYWHERE IN LITERATURE. IT BELONGS TO the epic with Homer, to tragedy with *Oedipus Rex*, to history with Thucydides, to the philosophical poem with Lucretius. The plague can serve as background to the short stories of Boccaccio's *Decameron*; there are fables about the plague, notably La Fontaine's "Les Animaux malades de la peste"; there are novels, such as Manzoni's *I Promessi Sposi* and Camus' *La Peste*. The theme spans the whole range of literary and even nonliterary genres, from pure fantasy to the most positive and scientific accounts. It is older than literature—much older, really, since it is present in myth and ritual in the entire world.

The subject appears too vast for a brief exploration. Undoubtedly, but a descriptive enumeration of literary and mythical plagues would be of little interest: there is a strange uniformity to the various treatments of the plague, not only literary and mythical but also scientific and nonscientific, of both past and present. Between the matter-of-fact, even statistical account of Defoe in his *Journal of the Plague Year* and the near hysteria of Artaud in *Le Théâtre et la peste*, the differences, at close range, turn out to be minor.

It would be exaggerated to say that plague descriptions are all alike, but the similarities may well be more intriguing than the individual variations. The curious thing about these similarities is that they ultimately involve the very notion of the similar. The plague is universally presented as a process of undifferentiation, a destruction of specificities.

This destruction is often preceded by a reversal. The plague will turn the honest man into a thief, the virtuous man into a lecher, the prostitute into a saint. Friends murder and enemies embrace. Wealthy men are made poor by the ruin of their business. Riches are showered upon paupers who inherit in a few days the fortunes of many distant relatives. Social hierarchies are first transgressed, then abolished. Political and religious authorities collapse. The plague makes all accumulated knowledge and all categories of judgment invalid. It was traditionally believed that the plague attacks the strong and young in preference to the weak and old, the healthy rather than the chronically ill. Modern authorities do not believe that great epidemics really singled out any particular individuals or categories. The popular belief must have arisen from the fact

Texas Studies in Literature and Language
XV.5 (Special Classics Issue 1974)

that it is more surprising and shocking to see the death of the young and healthy than of the old and the sick. The scientific view, it must be noted, fits the eternal ethos of the plague just as well and better than the popular tradition. The distinctiveness of the plague is that it ultimately destroys all forms of distinctiveness. The plague overcomes all obstacles, disregards all frontiers. All life, finally, is turned into death, which is the supreme undifferentiation. Most written accounts insist monotonously on this leveling of differences. So does the medieval *danse macabre*, which, of course, is inspired by the plague.

This process of undifferentiation makes sense, obviously, and poses no special problem in the sociological sphere. The belief that a great plague epidemic can bring about a social collapse is not difficult to accept or irrational in any way; it can be based on positive observation. At the beginning of the modern age, when plague epidemics had not yet disappeared and the spirit of scientific investigation was already awakened, texts can be found that clearly distinguish the medical plague from its social consequences and yet continue to see a similarity. The French surgeon Ambroise Paré, for instance, writes:

At the outbreak of the plague, even the highest authorities are likely to flee, so that the administration of justice is rendered impossible and no one can obtain his rights. General anarchy and confusion then set in and that is the worst evil by which the common wealth can be assailed; *for that is the moment when the dissolute bring another and worse plague into the town.* (emphasis mine)

This sequence of events is perfectly positive and rational. The reverse sequence is no less so. A social upheaval can bring about conditions favorable to an outbreak of the plague. Historians still argue whether the Black Death was a cause or a consequence of the social upheavals in the fourteenth century.

Between the plague and social disorder there is a reciprocal affinity, but it does not completely explain the confusion of the two that prevails not only in innumerable myths but in a good number of literary plagues, from ancient times to contemporary culture. The Greek mythical plague not only kills men but provokes a total interruption of all cultural and natural activities; it causes the sterility of women and cattle and prevents the fields from yielding a crop. In many parts of the world, the words we translate as "plague" can be viewed as a generic label for a variety of ills that affect the community as a whole and threaten or seem to threaten the very existence of social life. It may be inferred from various signs that interhuman tensions and disturbances often play the principal role.

In the passage just quoted, Paré separates what primitive thought unites—the medical and social components of the mythical plague. His language, however, is interesting. The social components are described as *another and worse plague*. Anarchy is a plague; in a sense, it is even more of a plague than the disease itself. The former unity is broken, and yet it is remembered and preserved in the stylistic effect of using the same word for two distinct and yet curiously inseparable phenomena. The medical plague has become a metaphor for the social plague; it belongs to what we call literature.

Judging from the role of the plague in Western literature up to the present, this metaphor is endowed with an almost incredible vitality, in a world where the plague and epidemics in general have disappeared almost altogether.[1] Such vitality would be unthinkable, of course, if the social "plague" were not always with us, as fear or as reality, in some form or other. This fact is not enough, however, to account for the more obscure and yet persistent aspects of the metaphoric configuration as well as for what appears to be the real need it fulfills with a great many writers. Indeed, an analysis of significant texts reveals definite analogies between the plague, or rather all great epidemics, and the social phenomena, real or imagined, that are assimilated to them. One such text belongs to Dostoevsky's *Crime and Punishment*. Raskolnikov has a dream during a grave illness that occurs just before his final change of heart and at the end of the novel. He dreams of a worldwide plague that affects people's relationships with each other. No specifically medical symptoms are mentioned. It is human interaction that breaks down, and the entire society gradually collapses.

He dreamt that the whole world was condemned to a terrible new strange plague that had come to Europe from the depths of Asia. . . . Some new sorts of microbes were attacking the bodies of men, but these microbes were endowed with intelligence and will. Men attacked by them became at once mad and furious. But never had men considered themselves so intellectual and so completely in possession of the truth as these sufferers, never had they considered their decisions, their scientific conclusions, their moral convictions so infallible. Whole villages, whole towns and peoples went mad from the infection. All were excited and did not understand one another. Each thought that he alone had the truth and was wretched looking at the others, beat himself on the breast, wept, and wrung his hands. They did not know how to judge and could not agree what to consider evil and what good; they did not know whom to blame, whom to justify. Men killed each other in a sort of senseless spite. They gathered together in armies against one another, but even

---

[1] Concerning the symbolic significance of disease in modern literature, see the suggestive article of Gian-Paolo Biasin, "From Anatomy to Criticism," *MLN*, 86 (December, 1971), 873–890.

on the march the armies would begin attacking each other, the ranks would be broken and the soldiers would fall on each other, stabbing and cutting, biting and devouring each other. The alarm bell was ringing all day long in the towns; men rushed together, but why they were summoned and who was summoning them no one knew. The most ordinary trades were abandoned, because every one proposed his own ideas, his own improvements, and they could not agree. The land too was abandoned. Men met in groups, agreed on something, swore to keep together, but at once began on something quite different from what they had proposed. They accused one another, fought and killed each other. There were conflagrations and famine. All men and things were involved in destruction. The plague spread and moved further and further.

The plague is a transparent metaphor for a certain reciprocal violence that spreads, literally, like the plague. The appropriateness of the metaphor comes, obviously, from this contagious character. The idea of contagiousness implies the presence of something harmful, which loses none of its virulence as it is rapidly transmitted from individual to individual. Such, of course, are bacteria in an epidemic; so is violence when it is *imitated*, either positively, whenever bad example makes the usual restraints inoperative, or negatively, when the efforts to stifle violence with violence achieve no more, ultimately, than an increase in the level of violence. Counterviolence turns out to be the same as violence. In cases of massive contamination, the victims are helpless, not necessarily because they remain passive but because whatever they do proves ineffective or makes the situation worse.

In order to appreciate Raskolnikov's dream, we must read it in the context of Dostoevsky's entire work, of that self-defeating mixture of pride and humiliation characteristic of Raskolnikov and other Dostoevskian heroes. The victims of the plague seem to be possessed with the same desire as Raskolnikov. Each falls prey to the same megalomania and sees himself as the one and only superman: "Each thought that he alone had the truth and looked with contempt at the others."

This desire implies a contradiction; it aims at complete autonomy, at a near divine self-sufficiency, and yet it is *imitative*. The divinity this desire is trying to capture never fails, sooner or later, to appear as the divinity of someone else, as the exclusive privilege of a model after whom the hero must pattern not only his behavior but his very desires, insofar as these are directed toward objects. Raskolnikov worships Napoleon. The possessed imitate Stavrogin. The spirit of worship must combine with the spirit of hatred. To reveal the secret of this ambivalence, we need not turn to someone like Freud. There is no secret at all. To imitate the desires of someone else is to turn this someone else into a rival as well as a model. From the convergence of two or more desires on the same object, conflict must necessarily arise.

The mimetic nature of desire can account for the many contradictions in the Dostoevskian hero; this one principle can make his personality truly intelligible. Imitative desire necessarily generates its own living obstacles and comes to view this failure as a sign of the model's omnipotence, as convincing proof, in other words, that this model is the right one, that the door he keeps so tightly shut must be the door to heaven. Mimetic desire cannot keep its illusions alive without falling in love with its own disastrous consequences and focusing more and more on the violence of its rivals. The mimetic attraction of violence is a major topic of Dostoevskian art. Thus, violence becomes reciprocal. In the dream of the plague, the expressions "each other, one another" recur constantly. The great Dostoevskian novels describe mimetic breakdowns of human relations that tend to spread further and further. The dream of the plague is nothing but the quintessential expression of the Dostoevskian crisis; and, as such, it must extend that crisis to the entire world, in truly apocalyptic fashion.

From Dostoevsky, I would like to turn to another writer, Shakespeare, who appears very distant but is really very close in respect to the problem at hand. I want to compare the dream of the plague, a specific passage in *Crime and Punishment*, to a specific passage in a work of Shakespeare, the famous speech of Ulysses in *Troilus and Cressida*, a text that rests, in my view, on the same conception of a cultural crisis as the dream of the plague in Dostoevsky.

First, it must be observed that *Troilus and Cressida* revolves entirely around a view of mimetic desire analogous if not identical to the one just detected in Dostoevsky. The topic of the play is the decomposition of the Greek army stalled under the walls of Troy. Disorder begins at the top. Achilles imitates Agamemnon, both in the sense that he seriously aspires to his position, he wants to become the supreme ruler of the Greeks, and in the sense that he derisively mimics and parodies the commander-in-chief. Mimetic rivalry spreads from rank to rank and brings about a complete confusion:

> So every rank
> Exampled by the first pace that is sick
> Of his superior, grows to an envious fever
> Of pale and bloodless emulation.

These lines remind us of Raskolnikov's dream: "They gathered together in armies against one another, but even on the march the armies would begin attacking each other, the ranks would be broken and the soldiers would fall on each other."

Mimetic desire also dominates the two protagonists. No less than the political and the military, the erotic aspect of the play is an affair of worldly ambition, competitive and imitative in character. We would have to call Cressida "inauthentic" if we did not suspect that the ideal of autonomous desire by which she will be judged is itself a fruit of rampant imitation. The lovers are always open to the corruptive suggestion of spurious models or to the even worse advice of Pandarus. They are really nonheroes, always caught in a game of deception and vanity which is to real passion what the behavior of the army is to genuine military valor.

No individual or psychological approach can do justice to the scope of the phenomenon. That is why the high point of the play is that speech in which Ulysses describes a crisis so pervasive and acute that it goes beyond even the most radical notion of social crisis.

The central concept, Degree, from the Latin *gradus*, means a step, a measured distance, the necessary difference thanks to which two cultural objects, people, or institutions can be said to have a *being* of their own, an individual or categorical identity.

> Oh, when degree is shaked,
> Which is the ladder to all high designs,
> The enterprise is sick! How could communities,
> Degrees in schools and brotherhoods in cities,
> Peaceful commerce from dividable shores
> . . . .
> But by degree, stand in authentic place?
> Take but degree away, untune that string,
> And hark, what discord follows! Each thing meets
> In mere oppugnancy. The bounded waters
> Should lift their bosoms higher than the shores,
> And make a sop of all this solid globe.
> Strength should be the lord of imbecility,
> And the rude son should strike his father dead.
> Force should be right, or rather, right and wrong,
> Between whose endless jar justice resides,
> Should lose their names, and so should justice too.

The image of the untuned string clearly reveals that the cultural order is to be understood on the model of a melody, not as an aggregate, therefore, a mere collection of heterogeneous objects, but as a "totality" or, if we prefer, a "structure," a system of differences commanded by a single differentiating principle. Degree in the singular seems to define a purely social transcendence, almost in the sense of Durkheim, with the difference, however, that cultural systems in Shakespeare are always liable to collapse; and it is with such collapse, obviously, not with the systems themselves, that the tragic writer is preoccupied.

If mimetic desire has an object, it is Degree itself; Degree is vulnerable to criminal attempts from inside the structure. The thought appears irrational, but it is not. It does not mean that Degree is something like an object that could be appropriated. It means exactly the opposite. If Degree vanishes, becomes "vizarded" when it becomes an object of rivalry, it is precisely because it is really nothing but the absence of such rivalries in a cultural order that remains functional. The crisis, therefore, is a time of most frantic ambition that becomes more and more self-defeating. As these ambitions are mimetically multiplied, reciprocal violence grows and the differences dissolve; the "degrees" leading to the object and the object itself disintegrate. It is an ambition, therefore, that "by a pace goes backward / With a purpose it hath to climb."

As in Dostoevsky's text, all constancy of purpose disappears, all useful activities are interrupted. The desire in each man to distinguish himself triggers instant imitation, multiplies sterile rivalries, produces conditions that make society unworkable through a growing uniformity. The process is one of undifferentiation that passes for extreme differentiation— false "individualism." Finally, even the most fundamental distinctions become impossible. Shakespeare writes that "Right and wrong . . . lose their names," and this is duplicated almost to the letter in Dostoevsky: "They did not know how to judge and could not agree what to consider evil and what good; they did not know whom to blame, whom to justify."

In both texts the dominant idea, more explicit in Shakespeare, is that regular human activities, however reciprocal their final results, can take place only on a basis of nonreciprocity. Constructive relationships of any type are differentiated. Ulysses certainly betrays a strong hierarchical and authoritarian bias. One should not conclude too hastily that the interest of his speech is thereby diminished. The concepts with which he operates, the very notion of the cultural order as a differential system susceptible of collapse, imply the essential *arbitrariness* of cultural differences.

When the difference goes, the relationship becomes violent and sterile as it becomes more symmetrical, as everything becomes more perfectly identical on both sides: "*Each thing meets in mere oppugnancy.*" It is a relationship of *doubles* that emerges from the crisis. We would misunderstand this relationship if we interpreted it as a *coincidentia oppositorum*, in the tradition of philosophical idealism, or as a mere subjective reflection or hallucination, in the vein of psychological "narcissism," an approach adopted by Rank, for instance, in his essay on Don Juan and the *double*.

With Shakespeare, as earlier with the playwrights of classical antiquity, the relationship of *doubles* is perfectly real and concrete; it is the fundamental relationship of the tragic and comic antagonists. It is present among the four *doubles* of *A Comedy of Errors*, where it is almost identical to the relationship defined in *Troilus and Cressida* and dramatized in all of Shakespeare's plays. The fact that the *doubles* constantly run into each other in a desperate effort to part ways can be viewed either in a tragic or in a comic light. This is as true of Dostoevsky as it is of Shakespeare. The relationship of conflictual symmetry and reciprocal fascination portrayed in the novels is fundamentally identical to what is attempted very early in the short story entitled *The Double*.

Thus, the speech of Ulysses closely parallels Raskolnikov's dream of the plague. In both these texts the authors find a way to conceptualize and generalize the same type of relationship that, in the rest of the work and in his other works, is developed in dramatic or novelistic form. The convergence of these two writers is particularly striking in view of their obvious differences of language, period, style, genre, etc. In order to be complete, the parallel should also include, on Shakespeare's side, the metaphor of the plague; and, of course, does. In the passage quoted above, the idea of disease occurs repeatedly. Even though it does not play as prominent a role as in Raskolnikov's dream, the plague proper is not absent; it figures among the various and more or less natural disasters that accompany the crisis, as in a kind of mythical orchestration:

> What raging of the sea, shaking of the earth,
> What plagues and what portents, what mutiny
> Divert and crack, rend and deracinate
> The unity and married calm of states
> Quite from their fixture!

Looking back upon the preceding remarks, we must note that we are no longer dealing with a single theme, with the isolated plague, but with a thematic cluster that includes, besides the plague or, more generally, the theme of epidemic contamination, the dissolving of differences and the mimetic *doubles*. All these elements are present both in the text of Shakespeare and in the text of Dostoevsky. I shall give more examples later, and they will show that this same thematic cluster almost never fails to gather around the plague in a great many texts that may appear to have very little in common. Some of the elements may be more emphasized than others; they may appear only in an embryonic form, but it is very rare when even one of them is completely missing.

First, however, we must complete our thematic cluster. Another element, which has not yet been mentioned, may be the most important of all, the *sacrificial* element. This sacrificial element may be limited to the assertion that all the death and suffering from the plague is not in vain, that the ordeal is necessary to purify and rejuvenate the society. Here is, for example, the conclusion of Raskolnikov's dream: "Only a few men could be saved in the whole world. They were a pure chosen people, destined to found a new race and a new life, to renew and purify the earth." Something very similar is present in Artaud's *Le Théâtre et la peste*: "The theater like the plague is a crisis which is resolved by death or cure. And the plague is a superior disease because it is a total crisis after which nothing remains except death or an extreme purification." Death itself appears as the purifying agent, the death of all plague victims or a few, sometimes of a single chosen victim who seems to assume the plague in its entirety and whose death or expulsion cures the society, in the rituals of much of the world. Sacrifices and the so-called scapegoat rituals are prescribed when a community is stricken by "the plague" or other scourges. Our thematic cluster is even more common in myth and ritual than in literature. In *Exodus*, for instance, we find the "ten plagues" of Egypt together with the incident of Moses stricken with leprosy and cured by Yahweh himself. The "ten plagues" are a worsening social breakdown, which also appears in the form of a destructive rivalry between Moses and the magicians of Egypt. Finally we have a strong sacrificial theme in the death of the firstborn and the establishment of the passover ritual.

The sacrificial element is sometimes an invisible dimension, something like an atmosphere that pervades every theme but cannot be pinpointed as a theme; its status must be ascertained. An analysis not of the entire Oedipus myth, but of the mythical elements that appear in Sophocles' tragedy, *Oedipus the King*, may help shed some light upon that problem.

In the opening scenes of the tragedy, the city of Thebes is in the throes of a plague epidemic; and the solution of the crisis becomes a test of power and prestige for the protagonists, Oedipus, Creon, and Tiresias. Each of these would-be doctors tries to place the blame on another, and they all turn into each other's *doubles*. Here, too, the tragic process is one with a worsening "crisis of Degree," one with the plague itself, in other words. The tragic conflict and the plague are in the same metaphoric relationship as in Dostoevsky or Shakespeare, except, of course, that this metaphoric character is less explicit, as if the task of uncovering the element of violence hidden behind the mythical plague were initiated by Sophocles but less advanced than in the work of the two other writers.

In the light of our analyses, the tragic conflict of *Oedipus the King* amounts to nothing more and nothing less than a search for a scapegoat, triggered by the oracle, which says, "a murderer is in your midst; get rid of him and you will be rid of the plague." How could a single individual, even the worst offender, be responsible for whatever social catastrophe may be at stake in the "plague"? Within the confines of the myth, however, not only is the significance of the strange medicine unquestioned, but its efficacy is actually verified. We must assume that the prescription works, that the discovery of the "culprit" cures the plague. The reciprocal witch hunt brings the crisis to a climax; then, the focusing of the guilt on Oedipus and his expulsion constitute a genuine resolution. The whole process is comparable to a "cathartic" purge.

A fascinating possibility arises. Even though the reasons adduced are quite mythical, the reality of the cure may be a fact. Behind the entire myth there could be a real crisis, concluded by the collective expulsion or death of a victim. In this case the oracle would be truthful in part. What is true is not that there is, as a "real culprit," a man who bears alone the entire responsibility for the plague. Such a man cannot exist, of course. The oracle is really talking about a victim who is "right," in the sense that against and around that victim everyone can unite. Oedipus may well be the right scapegoat in the sense that the accusation against him really "sticks" and restores the unity of the community. This restoration is tantamount to a "cure" if, as Sophocles himself appears to suggest, the plague is the same crisis as in Shakespeare or Dostoevsky, a crisis of mimetic violence. The polarization of all fascination and hatred on a single victim leaves none for the other *doubles* and must automatically bring about their reconciliation.

How can the required unanimity be achieved if no one among the potential victims is likely to be either much more or much less guilty than anyone else? How can the mythical "guilt" become solidly fixed on a more or less random victim? The mimetic *doubles* are concretely alike; there is no difference between them. This means that at any time even the smallest incident, the most insignificant clue, can trigger a mimetic transfer against any *double* whatsoever. The positive effect of such a transfer, the end of the crisis, must necessarily be interpreted as a confirmation of the "oracle," as absolute proof that the "real culprit" has been identified. A faultless relationship of cause and effect appears to have been established.

The process just described implies that the random victim must be perceived as a "real culprit," missing before and now identified and punished. This random victim, in other words, will never be perceived as random; the "cure" would not be operative if its beneficiaries realized the randomness of the victim's selection.

All this goes without saying, and yet it needs very much to be said because the unperceived consequences of these facts may be decisive for the myth as a whole. We just said that the entire responsibility for the crisis is collectively transferred upon the scapegoat. This transfer will not appear as such, of course. Instead of the truth, we will have the "crimes" of Oedipus, the "parricide and the incest" that are supposed to "contaminate" the entire city. These two crimes obviously signify the dissolving of even the most elemental cultural differences, those between father, mother, and child. The parricide and the incest represent the quintessence of the whole crisis, its most logical crystallization in the context of a scapegoating project, that is, of an attempt to make that crisis look like the responsibility of a single individual. Even today, these and similar accusations come to the fore when a pogrom is in the making, when a lynching mob goes on a rampage. The ideas of parricide, incest, and also infanticide always crop up when cultural cohesion is threatened, when a society is in danger of disintegration. The nature of the crimes attributed to Oedipus should be enough to make us suspect that we are dealing with some kind of lynching process. And this suspicion has been present for many years; it has prompted many investigations. Unfortunately, scholars keep looking for a possible link that could be historically documented between the Oedipus myth and some particular scapegoat-type ritual. The results have been disappointing. The question of relating myth to ritual or ritual to myth is a circle that can be broken here by asking a more decisive question about the possible origin of both in a spontaneous lynching process that must necessarily remain invisible because of its very efficacy.

If the collective transfer is really effective, the victim will never appear as an explicit scapegoat, as an innocent destroyed by the blind passion of the crowd. This victim will pass for a real criminal, for the one guilty exception in a community now emptied of its violence. Oedipus is a scapegoat in the fullest sense *because he is never designated as such*. For the genuine recollection of the crisis, which allows for no differentiation whatever between all the *doubles*, the two differentiated themes of the myth are substituted. The original elements are all there, but rearranged and transfigured in such a way as to destroy the reciprocity of the crisis and polarize all its violence on the wretched scapegoat, leaving everybody else a passive victim of that vague and undefined scourge called "the plague." A lynching viewed from the perspective of the lynchers will never become explicit as such. In order to apprehend the truth, we must carry out a radical critique that will see the mythical themes as systematic distortion of the former crisis.

The spontaneous scapegoat process now appears as the generative process of myth, the true *raison d'être* of its themes and notably of the plague, which must be viewed, I believe, as a mask for the crisis leading to the scapegoat process, not only in the Oedipus myth but in countless other myths of the entire world.

Oedipus, it will be said, is a religious hero as well as a villain. This is true, and it is no objection—far from it—to the genesis just outlined. The difference between the founding process of myth and the scapegoat processes we may know of and understand is that the first, being the more powerful, literally goes full circle from unanimous hatred to unanimous worship. The juxtaposition of the one and the other is intelligible. If the polarization of the crisis upon a single victim really effects a cure, this victim's guilt is confirmed, but his role as a savior is no less evident. That is why Oedipus and behind him the more remote but parallel figure of the god Apollo appear both as bringers of the plague and as benefactors. This is true of all primitive gods and other sacred figures associated with the mythical "plague." They are both the accursed divinities that curse with the plague and the blessed ones that heal. This duality, it must be noted, is present in all primitive forms of the "sacred."

I have already suggested that the present hypothesis bears also on ritual, that a sacrificial action or immolation is generally found, frequently interpreted as the reenactment of a divine murder supposed to be the decisive event in the foundation of the culture. In the preparatory stages of a ritual immolation, symmetrically arranged antagonists hold warlike dances or real and simulated battles. Familial and social hierarchies are reversed or suppressed. These and many other features may be interpreted as traces of some "crisis of degree" climaxed by its habitual resolution, the collective transfer on a single victim. We may suppose that ritual tries to reenact this entire process in order to recapture the unifying effect mentioned earlier. There are sound reasons to believe that this purpose is generally achieved. Being still unable to perceive the threat that internal violence constitutes for primitive society, we cannot recognize in ritual a relatively effective protection against that threat.

If the preceding and obviously too brief remarks are not unfounded,[2] the conjunction between the plague and sacrificial ritual, first in primitive religion and later in literature, becomes fully intelligible. Primitive societies constantly resort to ritual against anything they call the plague. That may comprise very diverse threats ranging from the crisis of mimetic violence and less acute forms of internal tensions and aggressions to purely exterior threats that have nothing to do with reciprocal vio-

---

[2] For a more complete exposition of the collective transfer and single victim process as mythical genesis, see my *La Violence et le sacré* (Paris, 1972).

lence, including, of course, real pathological epidemics, even the plague in the modern scientific sense.

Ritual tries to reproduce a process that has proved effective against one kind of "plague," the most terrible kind, the epidemic of reciprocal violence that never becomes explicit as such. It is my opinion that the scapegoat process, through religious myths, notably the myths of the plague, plays a major role in disguising and minimizing the danger its own potential for internal violence constitutes for a primitive community. This minimization must be viewed in turn as an integral part of the protection that myth and ritual provide against this same violence.

Certain lines of Sophocles and Euripides make it hard to believe that these writers did not have an intuition of collective mechanisms behind the myths they adapted, an intuition that is still incomplete, perhaps, but far superior to ours. These mechanisms are still well attested historically. In the Middle Ages, for instance, social catastrophes, notably the great plague epidemics, usually triggered persecutions against the Jews. Even though they have become less productive in terms of mythical lore, these mechanisms, quite obviously, are far from extinct.

We are now in a position to understand why the mythical plague is never present alone. It is part of a thematic cluster that includes various forms of undifferentiation and transgression, the mimetic *doubles*, and a sacrificial theme that may take the form of a scapegoat process. Earlier, I said that the plague, as a literary theme, is still alive today, in a world less and less threatened by real bacterial epidemics. This fact looks less surprising now, as we come to realize that the properly medical aspects of the plague never were essential; in themselves, they always played a minor role, serving mostly as a disguise for an even more terrible threat that no science has ever been able to conquer. The threat is still very much with us, and it would be a mistake to consider the presence of the plague in our literature as a matter of formal routine, as an example of a tradition that persists even though its object has vanished.

Not only the plague but the entire thematic cluster is alive, and its relevance to our current psychosociological predicament becomes evident as soon as specific examples are produced. The continued vitality of all our themes must correspond to a continued need to disguise as well as to suggest—the one and the other in varying degrees—a certain pervasive violence in our relationships.

I will give three examples, each so different from the other two and from the texts already mentioned, at least in terms of traditional literary values, that direct literary influence cannot account for the presence of the pattern. The first is Artaud's already mentioned *Le Théâtre et la peste*.

Much of this text is devoted to a strange account of the medical and social effects not of a specific outbreak but of the plague in general. In a long pseudoclinical disquisition, Artaud rejects all attempts at making the transmission of the disease a scientifically determined phenomenon; he interprets the physiological process as a dissolution of organs, which may be a kind of melting away, a liquefaction of the body or on the contrary a desiccation and a pulverization. This loss of organic differentiation is medically mythical but esthetically powerful because it patterns the pathological symptoms on the breakdown of culture, producing an overwhelming impression of disintegration. This apocalyptic vision is quite close to Dostoevsky's dream of the plague, but this time, in keeping with the destructive ethos of contemporary art, it is a cause for fierce jubilation.

At first glance it seems that, in spite of its intensity, the process of undifferentiation does not culminate in the *doubles*. The *doubles* are there, though—less explicit, to be sure, than in Dostoevsky and Shakespeare but unmistakable nevertheless—notably in those passages that hint at a purely spiritual contamination, analogous to the mimetic *hubris* of our first two examples.

Other victims, without bubos, delirium, pain, or rash, examine themselves proudly in the mirror, in splendid health as they think and then fall dead with their shaving mugs in their hand, full of scorn for other victims.

The proud self-examination is *hubristic* pride, reaching out for supreme mastery, even over the plague, immediately defeated, massively contradicted by the instant arrival of the disease. Still apparently intact, the victim dies, "full of scorn for the other victims." An unquenchable thirst to distinguish himself turns the apparently healthy man into a *double* of all other victims, his partners in violence and death. The mirror, everywhere, is an attribute of the *doubles*.

The sacrificial theme is there too: first, as earlier indicated, in the rejuvenation that the plague and its modern counterpart, the theater, are supposed to bring to a decadent world, but also in more subtle touches that may be limited, at least in one case, to one single word. At one point the author imagines some kind of surgical dissection performed on the victims not with just any knife but with a knife that, for no immediately apparent reason, is described as being made of *obsidian*. Anthropological literature knows of knives made of this material and used on human flesh, the Aztec sacrificial knives. In the context of our analyses, it is not excessive to suppose, perhaps, that the *couteau d'obsidienne*, in conjunction with the victims of the plague, was prompted by a reminiscence of human sacrifice.

The second example is the film work of Ingmar Bergman in which the plague, the dissolving of differences, the mimetic *doubles*, and the sacrificial scapegoat are recurrent themes. If one particular film should be mentioned in connection with the *doubles*, it is certainly *Persona*. Two characters only are constantly present, a nurse and her patient, a totally silent actress. The entire work is dedicated to the mimetic relationship of these two, never a communion, really, but the same violent dissolving of differences as elsewhere. Another film, *Shame*, makes the conjunction of the mimetic *doubles* and of a plaguelike contamination quite manifest. A senseless civil war is being fought between two perfectly undistinguishable parties. This absurd struggle of rival *doubles* gradually spreads into a general infection, a literal ocean of putrefaction. Here, as in many contemporary works, the old mythical plague literally merges with such positive threats as radioactive fall-out and industrial pollution, both of which "function," of course, exactly like the plague and constitute disturbingly appropriate "metaphors" of individual and social relations in a state of extreme degradation.

One may single out *The Seventh Seal* as one film of Bergman in which the interplay of all the elements in our thematic cluster is quite spectacular. The mimetic *doubles* are there, and Death is one of them. So is a real medieval plague with its cortège of Flagellants. In the midst of all this comes the brief suggestion of a mob scene, a collective transfer against a very random and at the same time quite significant *scapegoat*, an actor, a mime, the very personification of *mimesis*.

The third example is both literary and cinematic. It is the famous short story by Thomas Mann, *Death in Venice*, which was recently made into a film by Lucchino Visconti. My own comments are based on the short story, which remains, I believe, the more striking of the two in the present context.[3]

An older and famous writer, Aschenbach, goes to Venice for a rest. As he arrives, he notices another elderly man who clings desperately to a group of younger people. His modish attire and the rouge on his cheeks turn this pathetic figure into a monstrous mask of pseudo-youthfulness. Later, the protagonist will permit a hairdresser to paint his face and dye his hair, which makes of him the exact replica, the perfect *double*, of the grotesque vision encountered at the beginning.

In the meantime, at the hotel and on the beach, the artist has come under the spell of a Polish adolescent. The differences of age, language, and culture, as well as its homosexual character, make this silent attach-

---

[3] A paper on "The Plague in *Death in Venice*," by Ruth Ellen Perlman, a student at SUNY/Buffalo (Spring, 1972), first made me aware of the short story's relevance to the present investigation.

ment more than a mere transgression; it is really a destruction and a dissolution of the old man's entire life.

The sense of decay is heightened by the plague and the rumors of plague that are abroad in the city. The sacrificial theme is present, of course, first in the hero's dream of a primitive bacchanal during which animals are slaughtered and, no less decisively, in his sudden death the next morning, which seems a retribution for his surrender to the forces of cultural disintegration. The writer has become the very embodiment of the plague. He literally sides with the epidemic when he chooses not to inform the Polish family of its presence in Venice, thus increasing their exposure to danger. He delights in the plague, and the plague will literally die with him since, as he dies, everybody is leaving Venice and the drama is resolved.

In our three contemporary examples the plague and associated themes are all present; our entire cluster is strikingly intact. It even has more thematic consistency than in Sophocles, Shakespeare, or Dostoevsky. The plague is a less transparent metaphor in Thomas Mann and Artaud than in *Crime and Punishment, Troilus and Cressida*, and even *Oedipus the King*. This very opacity confers to the plague a great evocative and esthetic power. The *doubles*, too, appear in a light of romantic mystery, in contrast with the unadorned severity of the tragic rapport.

Such opacity, it must be noted, belongs to myth—distinguished, of course, from its tragic adaptations—as well as to modern literature. If we limited ourselves to these chronological or cultural extremes, which is what recent investigators tend to do, the conjunction between the plague, the *doubles*, and the sacrificial scapegoat would remain unintelligible. Many specialists, of course (for instance, the psychoanalysts), have all sorts of answers ready for us. Unfortunately, these ever-ready answers shed no real light on the texts. As for the literary critics, they usually reject not only these superficial answers—which is good—but also the question itself—which cannot be good. In a misguided effort to protect the integrity of literature against all possible enemies, they refuse the open and equal dialogue between literature and anthropology they themselves should promote. We should not cut off literature from the vital concerns of our age. We should not divorce esthetic enjoyment from the power of intelligence, even from scientific investigation. We cannot simply "enjoy" the plague and be quiet—like old Aschenbach, I suppose, awaiting in pure esthetic bliss whatever fate may lie in store for us.

I find Shakespeare more bracing than Aschenbach. One reason is that he does not despair of the truth. If we had not turned to him earlier, we could not have made sense out of our thematic cluster. The brightest light available is still there. Shakespeare does not use the plague as verbal violence against an indifferent world. He is not interested in words as shields or weapons in the dubious battle of individual *ressentiment*. What concerns him most is the myth and the truth of his own language.

In our contemporary examples, the thematic elements of our cluster are juxtaposed a little like colors on the flat surface of a modern painting. It takes Shakespeare to realize that these themes are not really on a par, that they are not really even themes, and that it is a misnomer to call them so. The plague is less than theme, structure, or symbol, since it symbolizes desymbolization itself. The *doubles*, on the contrary, are more than a theme; they are the unperceived reciprocity of violence among men. They are essential to the understanding of sacrifice as a mitigation, a displacement, a substitution, and a metaphor of this same violence. The closer the writer gets to the fundamentals of that process, the more the plague and other metaphors become transparent. Sacrificial values disintegrate, disclosing their origin in the unifying and reconciling effect of a spontaneous scapegoat. If the scapegoat process described above is the resolution of the crisis and the source of mythical meaning, it must also be the end of tragedy and the restoration of Degree. Shakespeare does not simply repeat; he reveals the entire process.

In *Romeo and Juliet*, for instance, it takes Shakespeare no more than six words to suggest our entire pattern of metaphoric and real interaction. The famous cry of the dying Mercutio, *A plague on both your houses*, is not an idle wish. It is already fulfilled in the endlessly destructive rivalry of these same two houses, Montagues and Capulets, who turn each other into perfect *doubles*, thereby bringing the plague upon themselves. At the end of the play, the Prince equates the death of the two lovers with the plague of their families: *See what a scourge is laid upon your hate*. The two statements are really the same. Both are uttered *in extremis*, as a revelation of the truth: the first by a dying victim; the second as the last judgment of the sovereign authority, always a sacrificial figure in Shakespeare, and a potential scapegoat.

The death of the lovers is the entire plague, in the sense that it represents the climax of the scourge, the plague finally made visible and, as a consequence, exorcised by its very excess; the plague is both the disease and the cure. A sacrificial death brings about the end of the crisis and the reconciliation of the *doubles*. Talking to Capulet, Montague aptly calls the victims *Poor sacrifices of our enmity*.

Thus, a scapegoat mechanism is clearly defined as the solution to the tragic crisis, the catharsis inside the play that parallels the catharsis produced by that play, the catharsis twice announced and proposed to the spectators at the very opening, in an enigmatic little prologue that contains literally no other idea: Romeo and Juliet, we are told,

171

Do with their death bury their parents' strife.
The fearful passage of their death-marked love,
And the continuance of their parents' rage,
Which, but their children's end, naught could remove,
Is now the two hours' traffic of our stage.

The word *catharsis* originally refers to the purifying effect of a particular sacrifice. Shakespeare needs no etymology to see through Aristotelian estheticism and to reveal in the most concrete and the most *dramatic* fashion that all drama is a mimetic reenactment of a scapegoat process. In his tragedies, Shakespeare reproduces the cathartic mechanism of all tragedy; but he underlines it so forcefully that he lays it bare, so to speak, forcing us to ask questions that run counter to the cathartic effect, questions that would tear the entire dramatic structure asunder if they were seriously asked.

In his comedies, Shakespeare openly derides the sacrificial pattern. In the Pyramus and Thisbe episode of *A Midsummer Night's Dream*, the play that comes immediately after *Romeo and Juliet*, he parodies the cathartic system of this first play. He comes closer to a full revelation of the sacrificial values hidden behind the plague and other mythical or tragic metaphors than our contemporaries, including those like Artaud, whose frontal attacks against sacrificial values ultimately regress into the crudest forms of sacrifice. Contrary to what we believe, we may not be in a position to criticize Shakespeare. He may be the one who criticizes us. Rather than trying to judge him from above, from a necessarily superior "modern" viewpoint, we should try to recover some major intuitions of his that obviously escape us. We must have lost them somehow and somewhere, unless, of course, they have yet to be grasped.

Stanford University
  Stanford, California

Myth Criticism:

Limitations
and
Possibilities

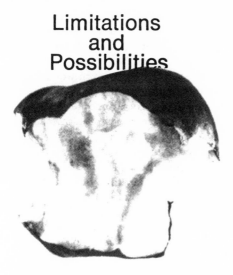

By E. W. HERD

In an address to a joint meeting of the Midwest Modern Language Association and the Central Renaissance Conference in April 1962, Northrop Frye referred to his work on the prophetic books of Blake and went on to say: "I had to learn something about myth to write about them, and so I discovered, after the book was published, that I was a member of a school of 'myth criticism' of which I had not previously heard."[1] Even today it is hardly possible to speak of a school of myth criticism, although the more extravagant devotees of this approach to literature, and their more fiery opponents, both tend to give the impression that myth criticism is a well-defined movement. Certainly it has become fashionable to accept an established lineage for myth criticism.

This form of criticism has suffered from the enthusiasm of some of its practitioners. It has developed a "cultism," to use Philip Rahv's

---

[1]Northrop Frye, "The Road of Excess," in *Myth and Symbol*, ed. Bernice Slote (Lincoln, Neb., 1963), p. 3.

phrase;[2] it has at times strayed too far from the discipline of literary criticism; and it has produced work of dubious value, where the emphasis has been on the origin or on the identity of the myth, and not on its function as a structural element in a work of literature. The opponents of myth criticism however seem in their turn to have been infected by this exuberance, and have attacked all interest in myth without sufficient discrimination. It cannot be denied that modern authors have been fascinated by the possibilities of myth in literature, and it is therefore necessary for the literary critic to examine the ways in which those possibilities are exploited and developed. This involves a fairly restricted and modest appraisal of the value of myth criticism; it demands concentration on the work of literature in which myths or mythical elements are discerned; and it requires the critic to consider the function of myth as part of the total structure of a given work.

There are five basic literary situations in which myth criticism can be used in this way. First, there is the work which avowedly sets out to retell an acknowledged myth. There are numerous examples of this type in the works of Thomas Mann: the *Joseph* tetralogy quite obviously, and also *Der Erwählte* (*The Holy Sinner*) and possibly the short story "Das Gesetz" ("The Tables of the Law"). In these cases it is necessary for the critic to refer to the original myth material in order to examine and evaluate the way in which Mann forms the given material into a literary structure. This will involve consideration of the author's attitude towards the original myth, of the way in which this attitude is communicated through the new form, of style and of structure. Secondly, there are works in which the author uses myth as a means of literary allusion, intended to attract the attention of the reader and to add significance to a theme or situation by means of illustration or parallel. In the novel *Riders in the Chariot* by the Australian Patrick White, there is a scene in which some drunken young Australians tie an elderly German Jew to a tree, and the details of the description—the incidental wounds on the Jew's hands, the action of a girl throwing an orange at him—are obviously, perhaps a little too obviously, designed to invoke the parallel of the Crucifixion. Kafka also uses mythical allusion in this way, particularly in *Der Hungerkünstler* (*The Hunger Artist*), and even Günter Grass in *Die Blechtrommel* (*The Tin Drum*) seems to be using myth for literary reference. More interesting to the critic than either of these uses of myth is its conscious use as a structural element. This use may be avowed or tacit. In a study of Zola's *Germinal*, Philip Walker has shown that in

---

[2]Rahv speaks of the "Cultism of myth, which is primarily an ideological manifestation." For a view of the varying attitudes towards myth as a basis of criticism the reader is referred to *Myth and Literature*, ed. John B. Vickery (Lincoln, Neb., 1966) in which Philip Rahv's article "The Myth and the Powerhouse" (quoted above) appears with those of a number of critics, some defending, some attacking myth criticism, some giving illuminating illustrations of its uses, others unconsciously demonstrating its abuses.

this case "it is not so much a matter of using myths for literary embellishment . . . as it is of consciously or unconsciously transforming myth into an expression of a new *Zeitgeist*."[3] Whether myth is so used consciously or unconsciously should not worry those whose sympathies lie with the New Critics, as the critic's concern here is not with the author's intentions but with the integral structure of the work. "It is not a matter of scattering here and there a few random images, but of weaving into the basically realistic fabric of the novel a multitude of analogies and metaphors arranged in a manner which is not at all haphazard, whether consciously intended by Zola or not" (Walker, p. 372). Particularly in the European novel of the twentieth century, writers have used myth in this way, the archetype being of course Joyce's *Ulysses*. It is also possible that a mythical pattern can emerge within the structure of a novel without conscious development by the author. The critic's task is then to show that this pattern forms a coherent and meaningful whole within the overall structure of the work. The mythical patterns which will emerge most frequently in this situation will be connected with the theme of the quest of the hero, and analogous themes such as the "rites de passage" and the descent into the underworld. There are difficulties to be encountered in this situation. Without external evidence it is just as impossible to prove that a mythical pattern is unintentionally present in a work as it is to prove that it is intended by the author. This however is a secondary consideration. If the critic discovers and demonstrates that such a pattern exists, he will be making meaningful comment on the structure of a work by means of textual analysis. An example of this situation might be found in Kafka's *Das Schloss* (*The Castle*). In this novel, the symbols of cavern and mountain which Maud Bodkin traces in *Paradise Lost* and the *Divine Comedy* are apparent at a first reading. The castle is set on the hill above the village, and K.'s first glimpse of it underlines its eminence and superiority above the petty world of the village. K. left the inn in which he had spent his first night in the village and went out into the brilliant winter morning.

> Nun sah er oben das Schloss deutlich umrissen in der klaren Luft und noch verdeutlicht durch den alle Formen nachbildenden, in dünner Schicht überall liegenden Schnee. Übrigens schien oben auf dem Berg viel weniger Schnee zu sein als hier im Dorf, wo sich K. nicht weniger mühsam vorwärts brachte als gestern auf der Landstrasse. Hier reichte der Schnee bis zu den Fenstern der Hütten und lastete gleich wieder auf dem niedrigen Dach, aber oben auf dem Berg ragte alles frei und leicht empor, wenigstens schien es so von hier aus.[4]

---

[3]Philip Walker, "Prophetic Myths in Zola," in *Myth and Literature*, p. 370.
[4]Franz Kafka, *Das Schloss* (Frankfurt, 1958), p. 13. "Now he could see the Castle above him, clearly defined in the glittering air, its outline made still more definite by the moulding of snow covering it in a thin layer. There seemed to be

Is this not that "flaming mount whose top / Brightness had made invisible," the mountain drenched in light, as a natural symbol of deity—a concept, as Maud Bodkin points out, which is certainly due in great part to the influence of Hebrew literature? The complementary image is that of the cavern.[5] In *The Castle* the village is described as consisting of low-roofed huts, and the action takes place almost entirely in the dark, low rooms: "Eine grosse Stube im Dämmerlicht. Der von draussen Kommende sah zuerst gar nichts" (p. 16) ("A large kitchen, dimly lit. Anyone coming in from outside could make out nothing at first" [Muirs, p. 15]). Then in the third chapter the cavern image is taken to an extreme—a characteristic element of Kafka's technique. K. is hiding from the innkeeper under a desk in the bar; Frieda comes to him, turns out the light, and the grotesque love scene takes place in this sordid hiding-place amongst the little pools of spilt beer and other refuse. And K. felt as though

> er verirre sich oder er sei so weit in der Fremde, wie vor ihm noch kein Mensch, eine Fremde, in der selbst die Luft keinen Bestandteil der Heimatluft habe, in der man vor Fremdheit ersticken müsse und in deren unsinnigen Verlockungen man doch nichts tun könne als weiter gehen, weiter sich verirren. (p. 45)[6]

The archetypal patterns are there, and can be traced repeatedly in Kafka's work, but the critic's task is to proceed from definition of the patterns to an examination of their function in the structure of the novel. Another difficulty presented by this type of situation is that discussion of archetypal patterns too easily leads via Maud Bodkin to C. G. Jung and to consideration of the "collective unconscious." As in the case of anthropology, psychology has its own terms of reference which cannot always be harmoniously married to the criteria of literary criticism. The danger can however be kept to a minimum by concentration on the literary text. The fifth situation is the most controversial. This is the situation of an author who claims himself, or who is claimed by critics, to be creating new myth. In Kafka's case the claim has been

---

much less snow up there on the hill than down in the village, where K. found progress as laborious as on the main road the previous day. Here the heavy snow-drifts reached right up to the cottage windows and began again on the low roofs, but up on the hill everything soared light and free into the air, or at least so it appeared from down below" (Franz Kafka, *The Castle*, trans. Edwin and Willa Muir, with an Introduction by Thomas Mann, New York, 1949, p. 11).

[5]For a discussion of the origins of mountain and cavern images, and their influence on European thought, see G. R. Levy, *The Gate of Horn* (London, 1963).

[6]"he was losing himself or wandering into a strange country, further than ever man had wandered before, a country so strange that not even the air had anything in common with his native air, where one might die of strangeness, and yet whose enchantment was such that one could only go on and lose oneself further" (Muirs, p. 55).

made by Wilhelm Emrich, but not altogether convincingly.[7] When a critic writes of the fictional narrator in Hawthorne's *The Blithedale Romance* that "Coverdale has not merely reformulated old myth; he creates a new myth relating man to nature and to the deity and dramatizing the mystery of life and death,"[8] he arouses expectations which are extremely difficult to satisfy. He must surely need to define his use of the term, before he can convince his readers that the pattern he is tracing is "new myth." He needs to do this particularly because the majority would consider "myth" to be something already generally accepted, and in this view "new myth" is a contradiction in terms. Nevertheless, writers such as Hermann Broch have postulated the need to create a literature that embodies a new mythic view of experience. The creative writer is free to do so, but the critic lacks the criteria by which to evaluate the term. The critic is faced in this situation by almost all the dangers pointed out by the opponents of myth criticism, and would seem to be making a postulation which cannot be supported by acceptable evidence. If the "new myth" has nothing in common with the patterns of established myths, the critic must have recourse to other disciplines to prove his point. If he is tracing a new structural pattern, there seems no cogent argument in terms of literary criticism for describing it as "myth," and nothing is really gained by doing so.

It may be somewhat timid to restrict the uses of myth criticism in this way. Every new trend in literary criticism has been hailed by its less cautious neophytes as a panacea, and it is this exaggeration which has made myth criticism suspect. Myth criticism can however profitably operate within the discipline of literary criticism as one approach among others, and it is most illuminating when it serves to elucidate the structure of a work. As a means of structural analysis it is in some cases indispensable, in others it opens vital new perspectives. Where myth has been consciously, and perhaps avowedly used by an author, the literary critic must make use of myth criticism; where myth is apparently an unconscious element in the structure of a work, the critic can reveal new insights into form and composition by identifying and analysing the structural pattern arising from the myth elements.

Amongst the novels of Hermann Broch there is an example of each type. In *Der Versucher* (*The Bewitchment*) he consciously attempted to use myth in a modern setting. In *Der Tod des Vergil* (*The Death of Vergil*) at least some of the mythical elements apparently emerged without deliberate effort on the author's part.[9] *Der Versucher* was the title given by the editor who published a version of the novel after

---

[7]See Wilhelm Emrich, "Symbolinterpretation und Mythenforschung" and "Die Bilderwelt Franz Kafkas," both in *Protest und Verheissung* (Frankfurt and Bonn, 1960).

[8]Peter B. Murray, "Myth in *The Blithedale Romance*," in *Myth and Literature*, p. 213.

[9]See Hermann Broch, *Briefe, Gesammelte Werke* (Zürich, 1957), VIII, 419; hereafter cited as *GW*.

Broch's death; it had been referred to by Broch as the "Bergroman" and in one letter as "Demeter." The first draft was probably completed in 1936. In the following year Broch began a revision of the manuscript, but progress was slow, and the second version was never completed. It is true that external circumstances were partly responsible for this—financial worries, family difficulties, the threatening political situation in Europe, all militated against finding the necessary peace and concentration. It would however be a mistake to conclude that external circumstances alone prevented Broch from completing the revised version. The method he had chosen to incorporate mythical elements into the novel was too close to the technique of Joyce and Thomas Mann, which he had already rejected. It was bound to lead to failure. Broch was fully aware of the inadequacy of his method, as can be seen from a letter to Friedrich Torberg, written on April 10, 1943 (*GW*, VIII, 185-186). The events of the novel are narrated by a doctor, who has given up a career in medical science and who has settled as village doctor in the Tyrol essentially on account of his doubts concerning the validity of the purely rational, scientific approach to knowledge. In this figure Broch has created an observer who attempts to preserve a balance between the spheres of the rational and of the irrational, which Broch claimed to be a characteristic of myth.[10] The irrational is presented in two contrasting characters. The arrival of the false prophet, Marius Ratti, plunges the village community into a chaotic dissolution of all values. Marius is a demagogue, a mystic and a fanatic whose dream is to restore the Golden Age by appeasing the productive powers of earth and by forcing the mountain to yield up its hidden gold. The earth can only be assuaged by the banning of the machine and by the sacrament of chastity. Marius' fanaticism and demonic power over this isolated village community reach their peak in the celebration of a ritual folk-festival on the mountain, which his madness turns to bloody reality in the sacrificial death of a young girl. The critic can demonstrate various mythical motifs here—the pure priest and the sacrifice of the virgin, which is to guarantee safe descent into the underworld of the old mine in the mountain. But the critic's next and more important task is to examine the function of these elements of myth. He must consider whether there is not here confusion in the use of myth. On the one hand the mythical pattern points to the present, since the tempter's role clearly offers a representation of events in Nazi Germany, and the attempt is made by means of the myth-pattern to transform historical reality into the abstract and universal. On the other hand the myth-motifs point back to a prehistorical past. The creation of a valid cosmogony, Broch's goal in the creation of "new myth," is frustrated by that same procedure which Broch

---

[10]See Hermann Broch, "Die mythische Erbschaft der Dichtung," in *GW*, VI, 239-248.

had condemned in the work of Joyce and Thomas Mann, the return to traditional myth-material. This is even more evident in the characterisation of the second figure intended to represent the irrational. Since the account of events is controlled from the point of view of the doctor-narrator, the reader is required to reject the words and actions of Marius as demonic seduction and impious nonsense, and to accept more positively the antagonist of Marius, the wise old Mother Gisson (whose name is easily recognised as an anagram of Gnosis). Mother Gisson is presented as a Great Mother figure, steeped in the secrets of the earth, drawing her knowledge and her wisdom from intuitive understanding of the cycle of death and fertility, in clear opposition to Marius who is ignorant of the true meaning of death and whose gospel of chastity derives from his sexual impotence. Marius' claim to knowledge is empty and false because he is cut off from love and the fullness of life. In these terms the distinction may carry conviction, but when the dying Mother Gisson attempts to formulate the secret of her knowledge, she uses language which is by no means clearly distinguished in style or even in vocabulary from the pseudo-mystical rantings of Marius (*GW*, IV, 545-550). The similarity between the would-be healthy wisdom of Mother Gisson and the intended corruptness of Marius' irrationalism repeatedly obtrudes in the use of language, and degrades the mythical Great Mother to an unconvincing novel-character, to a romantic concept. The critic cannot content himself with merely indicating that Mother Gisson is a Demeter figure,[11] but he must show by structural and stylistic analysis that it is not possible to bring Demeter back to life in the novel so easily, dressing her up in Tyrolean costume and sending her out into the woods to gather herbs. The use of myth remains on the level of intellectual intention and is at variance with the function of the characters in the novel. Broch seems guilty of playing an intellectual game with mythical allusion, as could also be said of Thomas Mann in *Der Tod in Venedig* (*Death in Venice*).[12]

It is impossible to approach a novel of this type without recourse to myth criticism, but the example quoted of the second type, Broch's *The Death of Vergil*, offers a much greater and more rewarding challenge. Here the myth critic has no such obvious sign-posts to guide him as in *The Bewitchment*. Close examination of the structure of this intricately architectured novel is necessary to elucidate the myth patterns which illuminate the total structure and the different layers of meaning. It is possible to discern several myth patterns which recur in *The Death of Vergil*, but two are dominant and can be identified as the theme of descent into the underworld and the theme of the night-sea-journey. They can be traced throughout the four books of the novel, and their

---

[11]See Felix Stössinger, "Nachwort des Erzählers," in Hermann Broch, *GW*, IV, 575.

[12]See E. W. Herd, "Myth and Modern German Literature," in *Myth and the Modern Imagination,* ed. M. Dalziel (Dunedin, N.Z., 1967), pp. 60-63.

function in the structural pattern can be determined. Let us consider briefly the motif of the night-sea-journey. The novel begins with the arrival one evening in Brundisium of the ships bringing Augustus and Virgil back from Greece, opening with a description of the sea, which has undertones of premonition. It is particularly important to notice that the motifs in the first section of the novel which are most directly relevant to this interpretation are to be found in a much earlier version, the short prose sketch, *Die Heimkehr des Vergil* (*The Return of Vergil*) (*GW*, X, 203-214). They were not therefore subsequently introduced into the novel to meet the demands of a structural plan, but seem to have suggested themselves to the author when he was concerned primarily with the problem of death. Even in the earlier version there are motifs which are of considerable importance for the purposes of myth criticism, and they are further developed in the novel. The waves of the sea are "stahlblau und leicht," the sky "perlmuttern," the loneliness of the sea is "sonnig und doch so todesahnend," the harbour is crowded with ships and boats "mit solchen, die gleichfalls dem Hafen zustrebten oder die von dorther kamen," from the shore can be heard "die Töne des Lebens," and it is evening. What is described here in the opening lines of the novel is not quite a sea-journey and it is not yet night. It is the situation of "noch nicht und doch schon," a phrase which is one of the leitmotifs in the novel, since the sea-journey, although over for the imperial squadron, is present not only as a presupposition but is indicated in the picture of the ships setting out from the harbour, which Virgil observes and strives to fix in his memory. Night has not yet fallen, but the colours of evening are all muted and dull—steely blue and mother-of-pearl. The idea of night is given in the motif of the loneliness of the sea in contrast to the boisterous companionship of the crowds in the streets of the port, and is intensified by the adjective "todesahnend." The account of the last eighteen hours of Virgil's life, which comprises the span of the novel, begins therefore with what seems on the surface to be an ingenuous piece of nature-description, but which "not quite and yet already" contains the image of the night-sea-journey, which then reappears at the beginning of the fourth part to depict the final journey into death. This last part, entitled "Äther: die Heimkehr" ("Air: The Homecoming") takes up the gentle murmuring at the end of the previous part which lulled Virgil to sleep. It echoes in the fading consciousness of the poet and turns into the murmuring of water, which is to bear him on his last journey. He bids farewell to the activity and life of this world—a reversal but also an intensification of the motif at the beginning of the novel—although he is still accompanied by many vessels under a mother-of-pearl, leaden sky. The ferryman, who determines the course at the beginning, can, like all other characters and phenomena, only accompany him so far, and the night-sea-journey ends in loneliness. As we know from Jung, Kerényi and others, the night-sea-journey is an archetype, but not one which has been fixed by an established literary tradition. Broch would seem in this case to have freed himself from the restrictions of the literary traditions of myth and to have succeeded in incorporating archetypal patterns harmoniously into the structure of the novel.

It has not been possible in the space of this essay to do more than hint at illustrations of the methods of myth criticism which seem from the review in the first part to offer the greatest possibilities for the study of literature. The general conclusions from this review have already been expressed by Charles Moorman: "In literary scholarship, it has never been sufficient to delineate a source; the scholar must show how that source is used in the work at hand, how it itself becomes a tool of creation. To be able to show how the poet uses myth and, in doing so, to concentrate not on the identity of the myth, but on its function, not on its closeness to the known pattern, but on the changes which the poet effects in that pattern, not on origin, but on use would seem to me to constitute the proper aim of the myth critic."[13] Seen in this light myth criticism is neither revolutionary nor esoteric, but is an extension of proven techniques.

University of Otago
Dunedin, New Zealand

---

[13]Charles Moorman, "Myth and Medieval Literature: *Sir Gawain and the Green Knight*," in *Myth and Literature*, p. 175.

THE REINTERPRETATION OF THE MYTHS

By GILBERT HIGHET

NO ONE knows when the Greek legends were created, or by whom. But they have lived for more than three thousand years, they have entered nearly all the literatures of modern Europe and the Americas, and some of them are part of our daily thought and conversation. They are far less destructible than men, or nations. Even the religion of which they were once a part has perished, and its temples are ruined; but the myths live on, with the deathless youth which breathes from the statues of Apollo and his sister Artemis.

At the present time, the most interesting development of classical influence in modern thought is the reinterpretation and revitalization of the Greek myths. This is going on in two different fields, and apparently in two different directions. One is almost wholly literary, and mainly dramatic. The other has produced a great deal of literature indirectly, and will produce more, but is primarily psychological and philosophical.

II

For century after century men have been re-telling the Greek legends, elaborating some and neglecting others. They have sought different beauties and values in them, and, when they gave them conscious interpretations, have educed from them many different kinds of truth. However, there are three main principles on which the myths can be interpreted. One is to say that they describe *single historical facts*. The second is to take them as symbols of *permanent philosophical truths*. The third is to hold that they are reflections of *natural processes, eternally recurring*.

Many of the myths are about human beings, and gods in human shape; so they need hardly be changed to be interpreted as accounts of historical events. This kind of interpretation began in Greece itself, with the brilliant Euhemeros. He explained all the legends—divine, human, and semi-human—as being ennobled versions of the exploits of real warriors and chiefs long ago, who had been changed into gods by their admiring tribes. And indeed, an essential part of Greco-Roman religious and political thought was the idea that men, by showing superhuman excellence, could become gods. The most famous instance was that of Hercules, who made his way up to heaven through his twelve labors and his heroic death. Alexander the Great was treated as a god during his lifetime. After his example, it was not too difficult to deify dead emperors, if they had done great services to mankind, and to worship Caesar as the Saviour and the Prince of Peace.

Again, some Christian writers believe that the legends about pagan divinities were really stories about the devils who went to and fro upon the earth before the birth of Christ. This is the interpretation given by Milton. In "Paradise Regained," Satan reproaches Belial for suggesting that the best way to tempt Jesus would be to "set women in his eye and in his walk"; and he implies that the "sons of God," who the Bible says "went in unto the daughters of men," were really Belial and his companions masquerading as the Greek deities:

> Have we not seen, or by relation heard,
> In courts and regal chambers how thou lurk'st,
> In wood or grove, by mossy fountain-side,
> In valley or green meadow, to waylay
> Some beauty rare, Calisto, Clymene,
> Daphne, or Semele, Antiopa,
> Or Amymone, Syrinx, many more,
> Too long—then lay'st thy scapes on names adored,
> Apollo, Neptune, Jupiter, or Pan,
> Satyr, or Faun, or Silvan?

Then some scholars hold that the warrior heroes, Achilles, Agamemnon, Ajax, and their peers, were personifications of warring tribes, and that their victories and deaths represented the conquests of one clan or another during the great migrations. Historians of religion think that many of the myths in which a god is associated with an inferior personage reflect religious revolutions, in which the worship of one deity was replaced by that of another. For example, if a divinity usually known in human shape is described as occasionally transforming himself into an animal, or killing an animal, or being accompanied by an animal, that would mean that the worship of the animal was abolished, replaced by the cult of the anthropomorphic god, and only dimly remembered. Finally, many legends are believed to record great inventions or advances in civilization: the "culture-hero" Dionysus or Bacchus represents the discovery of wine, Triptolemus and Hiawatha the discovery of agriculture, the Argonauts the exploration of the unknown seas east of the Mediterranean, the Golden Fleece the wealth of the new Black Sea trade, and Prometheus the discovery of fire, metal, and the handicrafts on which civilization is built.

Myths have also been thought to be symbols of important processes, either in the external world or in the soul. Max Müller, the German naturalized Englishman who was one of the founders of comparative philology, held that nearly all the myths symbolized the grandest phenomenon in the physical universe: the passage of the sun through the heavens every day and through the twelve signs of the zodiac every year. Thus, he interpreted almost every hero, from Hercules and his twelve labors and his flaming death to Arthur and his round table and his twelve knights, as a sun-myth. Even before him, C. F. Dupuis had declared that Jesus was really the sun, and his twelve disciples the signs of the zodiac. This theory is not now generally accepted. One of the books which helped to explode it was a very amusing essay by J. B. Pérès called "How Napoleon never existed"; it proves that Napoleon Bonaparte (whose name means "certainly Apollo, from the *bona parte,* the good region of the East") was really the sun, while his twelve marshals were the Ram, the Bull, the Heavenly Twins. . . .

A large group of myths has been associated with the processes of reproduction, sexual and agricultural, and with the connection made between these two processes in the primitive mind. The leader in this field of interpretation is Sir J. G. Frazer, with "The Golden Bough." He pointed out how the mysteries of birth and death, sowing and harvest, winter and spring were reflected in the legends of Demeter and Persephone, Venus and Adonis, Isis and Osiris. There is something of this in our own Christmas story. For there is no evidence in the Bible that Jesus was born in December; but it seems right that the infant saviour should be born about the winter solstice, to bring new life to a world apparently cold and dead. Our rejoicing round the Christmas tree is a relic of a pagan winter ritual, which used the evergreen as a symbol of the longed-for resurrection that would come in the spring.

Psychologists now regard myths as expressions of permanent but unacknowledged psychical attitudes and forces. This interpretation was launched by Sigmund Freud. He pointed to the many parallels between famous and widespread legends and the symbols which occur in dreams to represent (under an acceptable disguise) powerful instinctive drives. And he gave a Greek legendary name to one of the most powerful, the son's love of his mother and jealousy of his father. He called it, after the tragedy of the house of Thebes, the Oedipus complex. The parallel attitude, in which the daughter loves her father and is jealous of her mother, he called the Electra complex, because it recalls the tragedy of the princess who hated her proud, cruel mother, Clytemnestra. The self-adoration and self-absorption which may make a man or woman dead to the whole external world were first and most graphically found in the mythical youth who died for love of his reflection in a pool: so, after Narcissus, the neurosis is called narcissism.

Freud's suggestions are now being elaborated by C. G. Jung, both in his books and in the periodical Eranos, which he sponsors. The essence of this interpretation of the myths is that they are symbols of the desires and passions which all mankind feels but does not acknowledge. Girls wish to be surpassingly beautiful and to marry the richest, noblest, handsomest man in the world, who will find them in spite of the neglect and hostility of their family and their surroundings. They relieve the tension of this desire by saying that it has already come true, by retelling or rereading the story, and by identifying themselves with its heroine Cinderella. Boys wish to be the only object of their mothers' love and to expel all their competitors, of whom father is the chief. They do so by telling the story of a gallant young man who, as part of his adventurous career, kills an unknown old man who turns out to be his father, and marries a beautiful queen who turns out to be his mother. Oedipus, Cinderella, Helen of Troy, Don Juan, Robin Hood, Aladdin or Gyges, David the slayer of Goliath or Jack-the-giant-killer, Sindbad or Ulysses, Hercules or Samson or Paul Bunyan—all these characters are not so much historical individuals as projections of the wishes, passions, and hopes of all mankind. The great legends, and even the great symbols—such as the mystic flower and the mystic numbers three, seven, and twelve —keep recurring throughout human history and human literature, not only in Europe but all over the world. They are constantly being remodeled. They emerge again and again as superstitions, or foundations of great creeds, or universal patterns of art and ritual. Jung calls them "archetypes of the collective unconscious": patterns in which the soul of every man develops, because of the humanity he shares with every other man. Every married couple dreams of having a child which will be not imperfect, not even ordinary, but superb, the solver of all problems, good, strong, wise, heroic. This dream becomes the myth of the miraculous baby. And, in the deepest sense, the dream is true. Every baby is a miracle.

According to Jung, it is because of this universality that

the great myths can be attributed to no one author, and can
be rewritten again and again without losing their power.
The work done on them by many generations of taletellers
and listeners is truly "collective." They represent the inmost
thoughts and feelings of the human race, and therefore they
are—within human standards—truly immortal.

Yet we must not think that all legends are saccharine
wish-fulfilments. Certainly the Greek myths are not. There
is need of a book which will analyze them, tracing the manifold relations which link them to the myths of other nations
and to the more conscious art of the Greeks, and explaining
how they differ from other groups of legends. One essential
difference is that many of them are tragic: the stories of
Narcissus, Arachne, Syrinx, Phaeton, Oedipus himself. They
knew, the wise Greeks, that the realization of the extreme
wishes of mankind usually leads to disaster. Cinderella lives
happily ever after. But Oedipus blinds himself and goes into
exile. Hercules, with his own superhuman body changed to
an instrument of torture, burns himself to death.

III

Meanwhile, in literature, work of remarkable vitality has
been produced by a number of modern authors who have
been retelling Greek myths as plays or stories—occasionally
giving them a modern setting, but more frequently retaining
the ancient milieu and characters. Oddly enough, few of
them actually treat the myths as symbols of the unconscious
or seem to be familiar with psychological research. On the
contrary, they prefer to use the legends as the Greek poets
did, making them carry contemporary moral and political
significance.

Although this movement has outposts in several other
countries, its base is in modern France, and its activities there
are by far the most fertile and interesting. Its leader is
André Gide, who began as long ago as 1899 with "Philoctetes" and "Prometheus Drops His Chains," followed by a

play, "King Candaules," on the strange legend of Gyges. He then turned to other methods of presenting the problems that obsess him, but his work continued to presuppose a classical outlook in his readers. In 1931 he returned to Greece with a terse and shocking drama on Oedipus; and his latest is a prose tale in the form of autobiography, "Theseus," embodying some material from his unfinished "Considerations on Greek mythology."

Not all the dramatists in the neo-Hellenic school can be called disciples of Gide; yet they have all adopted many of his attitudes to myth, transforming and sometimes distorting the legends in the same way as he does; and they share something of his basic spiritual outlook. The chief plays of this group include Jean Cocteau's "Antigone," "Orpheus," and "The Infernal Machine"; Jean Giraudoux' "Amphitryon 38," "The Trojan War Will Not Take Place," and "Electra"; Jean Anouilh's "Orpheus," "Antigone," and "Medea"; and Jean-Paul Sartre's "The Flies."

Before we consider these plays in detail, we might ask why so many modern playwrights have gone to Greek mythology for their plots. There are several different answers.

First, they are in search of themes which can be treated with strong simplicity—themes which have enough authority to stand up without masses of realistic or "impressionist" detail to make them convincing. (The same tendency is exemplified in contemporary music by Stravinsky's "Oedipus Rex," and even better in art by the paintings of Chirico and the sculptures of Maillol.)

Then these themes are not only simple in outline, but profoundly suggestive in content—and it is here that the neo-Hellenic dramatists join hands with the psychologists, for they know that every great myth carries a deep significance for the men of every age, including our own. Thus, under the German occupation of France, by rehandling the legends of Antigone and Orestes, Anouilh and Sartre were able to deal with the problem of resistance to an unjust but apparently irresistible authority, not only more safely but much more broadly than if they had invented a contemporary plot. Similarly, because one element of tragedy is the audience's foreknowledge of the coming disaster, there was a deeply tragic quality in Giraudoux' play showing all the efforts and sacrifices made by statesmen on both sides to avoid the Trojan war, which was being forced on them by the passionate folly of mobs and demagogues. Since his play was produced in 1935, it was not only a Greek but a contemporary tragedy.

Also, since the French intellectuals are always defending themselves against the Olympians, Gide and Cocteau and the others find a certain relief in humanizing, debunking, and even vulgarizing some of the formidable old traditions. By bringing the myths nearer to humanity, they make them more real. On the other hand, they also find the myths to be inexhaustible sources of poetry. One of the gravest defects of modern drama is that it lacks imaginative power. It is quick, clever, sometimes thoughtful, always realistic. But the great dramas of the world do not stay on the ground. They leave it and become poetry. Because of the modern world's emphasis on material power and possessions, it is extremely difficult to write a contemporary play which will rise, at its noblest moments, into poetry; but contemporary problems, treated as versions of Greek myths, can be worked out to solutions which are poetic, whether the poetry is that of fantasy or that of tragic heroism.

In form, these plays are restrained without being rigidly classical. Except for Cocteau's "The Infernal Machine," they observe the unities of time and place closely but unobtrusively, and all maintain the indispensable unity of action. They are all in completely modern prose, which in Cocteau and Giraudoux often mounts into poetic eloquence, and in both these two and the others often descends into vulgarity and slang. The chorus of Greek tragedy appears only vestigially: a few women talking flat prose in Gide's "Oedipus," a single commentator (like the Chorus of "Henry V") in

Anouilh's "Antigone" and Cocteau's "Antigone" (where Cocteau himself took the rôle at the first performance). But there is an interesting experiment in bridging the gap between audience and actors, in André Obey's "The Rape of Lucrece." A masked pair of Narrators, male and female, sit at the sides of the stage throughout the action. Sometimes they report offstage incidents, sometimes they comment on the events shown on the stage, sometimes they speak for crowds, and now and then they quote the poem of Shakespeare on which the play is based: "poor bird," they say, and "poor frighted deer," *pauvre biche effrayée,* which is changed in the last words of the drama to *pauvre biche égorgée,* "poor slaughtered deer."

The plots are almost always the same in outline as the myths on which they are based. They could scarcely be different. It would be ridiculous to write a play proving that Julius Caesar was not assassinated, or that Troy was never captured and burnt. What can be done, though, is to take the story of Caesar's murder or the fall of Troy, and give it new implications, explain the facts in an odd and interesting way, cast strange lights on the characters involved, and, by remodeling values, motives, and results, to emphasize the infinite uncertainty and complexity of human life. Every writer who attempts to create anything alive on a basis of myth must add, or subtract, or alter.

One distinguished French novelist has destroyed, or inverted, a very famous legend—not because he dislikes Greek and Roman poetry but because he prefers nature to statuesque heroism. This is the Provençal writer Jean Giono, who tells us in his autobiography that the discovery of Vergil was a revelation as blinding for him as a religious conversion. He has written several works designed to recapture in prose the pastoral and animistic richness he feels in classical literature. In his "Birth of the Odyssey" he tells the story of the return of Odysseus, situates it in a fertile countryside more like southern France than barren Ithaca, and reduces the

hero himself to a nervous and aging liar, who invented the
stories about the Cyclops, and Scylla and Charybdis, and so
forth, merely in order to account for the years he spent en
route living with bewitching women like Circe, and to compensate for his shabbiness and timidity as he approaches his
home. His yarns are picked up by a blind old guitarist, who
makes them into new ballads and sings them round the countryside.

The details of this story are carefully calculated to be anti-
heroic. For instance, Odysseus is terribly afraid of Antinous,
the strong young athlete with whom his wife Penelope has
been living in adultery; but, getting into an argument, he hits
Antinous by accident, puts him to flight, chases him, and sees
him caught in a landslide that throws him mutilated into the
sea. Hence the tale that Odysseus killed all the suitors of
Penelope. Instead of the faithful old dog Argus, a pet mag-
pie recognizes the returning Odysseus; but, to avoid being detected by Antinous, he crushes it to death. In one version of
the legend, he was at last killed unwittingly by his own son—
not Telemachus, but Circe's child Telegonus. Giono's book
ends with the rebellious Telemachus preparing to murder
his father in cold blood. Although the story is ingenious and
the descriptions vivid, the inversion of the heroic saga of
Odysseus is pretty artificial. Such an unsubtle and pacific
character would never even have regained his home, far less
fought successfully through ten years of war at Troy.

Apart from this instance, the modern French taletellers
and playwrights keep the outlines of the legends; but they
rehandle them in such a way as to bring out unexpected
truths. For instance, there is not much authority for believing
that Hector and Odysseus made a concerted effort to avert
the Trojan war by negotiation, but were forced into it by
unknown hotheads; yet it is certainly plausible that the two
cautious heroes should have planned for peace rather than for
war. And although Giraudoux, in inventing a blustering
militarist and an excited propagandist to precipitate the con-

flict, has created characters more appropriate to modern Germany and France than to Bronze Age Greece, the anachronism does not vitiate the main truth he is conveying.

Anouilh's "Orpheus" is unlike most of the others, because it is entirely modern in setting and yet almost unintelligible without knowledge of the myth. The story is that Eurydice, wife of the master musician Orpheus, died suddenly; that he, by the power of his music, gained entrance to the world of the dead and was allowed to bring Eurydice back—on condition that he would not look at her before they reached the living world; that he forgot his promise, lost her forever, and wandered about in despair until he was torn to pieces by the savage maenads of Thrace. In Anouilh's play, Orpheus is a café violinist who meets a touring actress in a railway station, and falls in love with her, but loses her when he insists on questioning her about her previous lovers. She is given back to him by a mysterious Monsieur Henri (who would be quite meaningless if he were not understood as part of the Greek myth) on condition that he shall not look her in the face until morning. But he asks her again for the whole truth, and stares her in the face, and loses her again in death. His failure is a symbol of the fact, worked out in such detail by Proust, that a lover cannot keep from trying to find out everything about his sweetheart's life, even if it will kill their love.

In Gide's cynical little story, "Prometheus Drops His Chains," Prometheus has left the crag on which he was crucified; but he still keeps his eagle as a pet, and feeds it on his own vitals. Why? Because he likes to see it looking handsome; and because he, like each of us, enjoys having a private eagle, not hanging round his neck like a dead albatross, but loving him and living on his heart's blood. And Gide's "Oedipus" —in which one of Oedipus' sons writes a book closely corresponding to works written by two of Gide's disciples, and where the Sphinx is only the monstrous enigma of life, intimidating every youth, but ready to disappear as soon as the youth answers its riddle with the word "man" (that is, by

asserting that human nature creates its own standards) —
surely this play, in which everyone is corrupt but proud, is a
reflex of Gide himself and of the corrupt but proud children
of his spirit. Of all these neo-Hellenic works, Giraudoux'
"Amphitryon 38" is the richest in its power of revealing unexpected truths about great subjects: the love of husband
and wife, the power of any woman over any man (even a god
in man's disguise), and the relation of man and the gods.

All these playrights are good psychologists; and they have
all discovered new and yet credible motives for the actions
recorded in mythical tradition. In his autobiography of
Theseus, Gide says that when Ariadne gave him a thread to
guide him back out of the monster-haunted labyrinth, she
was really trying to attach him to herself; that this was why
he later abandoned her on a desert island; and that, when he
"forgot" to hoist the white sails which would tell his father
he was safe (thus indirectly causing his father's suicide and
his own accession to the throne), he did not really forget, any
more than he forgot Ariadne on Naxos. In the same book
Oedipus says that he put out his eyes, not to punish himself,
but to punish them for not seeing what they ought to have
seen. Creon is usually the typical harsh tyrant; but in Anouilh's "Antigone" he explains very coolly and patiently that,
so far from being cruel, he is merely an administrator of law
and order and efficient government, an ideal nobler than any
individual's private code of morals. Yes, and after the tragedy, after Antigone has hanged herself, after Creon's own
son has denounced him and killed himself, after his own wife
has cut her throat, he only sighs heavily and goes off to do his
duty by presiding at a Cabinet meeting: a death as complete,
though not as tragic, as those of the others. The most striking
reinterpretation of motives, if not the deepest, is in Cocteau's
"The Infernal Machine," where the Sphinx, although a deity
vastly more powerful than the arrogant young Oedipus, tells
him her secret because he has charmed the human part of her,
but, as Nemesis, looks on with pity at the fulfilment of his

burning ambition, the ambition favored by the gods: that he shall supplant his father, and win the kingdom, and marry his mother, and, after the fuse has burnt down to the explosive, be shattered in the ruins of his own strength. "They kill us for their sport."

André Gide, a recent Nobel Prize-winner, stands apart from all the others as an inventor of repulsive new episodes and vicious motives. For more than two thousand years men have rehearsed the awful history of the Labdacids; but Gide was the first to suggest that the sons born of Oedipus' unknowing incest were deliberately, and not without success, trying to seduce their sisters. The story of Candaules and Gyges, as told by Herodotus (and retold by Gautier), is spicy enough: the king is so proud of his wife's beauty that he hides his vizier Gyges in the bedroom to watch her undressing. But Gide makes the king, in a phenomenal access of generosity, leave the room and tell Gyges to substitute for him that night. Theseus, in the legend, carried off both Ariadne and her sister Phaedra. But Gide says that he told Ariadne he had taken a fancy to her young brother, that she connived at her brother's corruption, and that Phaedra was then smuggled aboard in the disguise of the disappointed boy. Bad taste on Gide's level, like Nero's poetry or Gaudi's architecture, is as difficult to achieve as good taste, and is at least as rare. Theseus is not the most attractive of mythical champions, but Gide gives him that peculiarly cynical type of sexual immorality which most of Gide's heroes carry as proudly as an oriflamme. "I never like leaving a desire unsatisfied," he says as he turns from one sister to another; " it is unhealthy." And even Ariadne's scarf, which lovers of poetry have always known as a pathetic token of her betrayal and her loneliness, the scarf with which she waft her love to come again to Naxos —Gide has succeeded, consciously or unconsciously, in defiling even that slight thing. In his story it blows off Ariadne's head, and is picked up by Theseus, who at once, and publicly, wraps it around him as a loincloth.

All these authors are eager to keep their plays from being remote, archaic, unreal. Therefore, although they do not deliberately put anachronisms on the stage, they make the language as modern as they can, and frequently lapse into vulgarities of detail and expression. In Giraudoux' "Electra" an angry wife talks of having to light her husband's cigars and filter his coffee. Helen of Troy, like a modern Frenchwoman, says Paris may desert her for a while "to play bowls or fish for eels." In Sophocles' "Antigone" there is a sentry who reports Antigone's crime in comparatively blunt and simple language; but in Anouilh's "Antigone" there are several sentries, and they accentuate the lonely virginal idealism of the heroine by very coarse conversations about getting drunk and going to a brothel. In Cocteau's "Orpheus" the poet is torn to pieces because he submits in a poetry competition the oracular phrase "Madame Eurydice Reviendra Des Enfers," the initial letters of which form the commonest French obscenity. Gide (except in his early "Philoctetes") tries deliberately to be banal, because he thinks heroics are false while banality is real. One example will be enough. After Oedipus discovers his sin and rushes out to blind himself, Gide makes the chorus remain on stage. Instead of keeping silence or chanting a song of pity and terror, it breaks out into infuriatingly trivial comments:

> "It's all just a family affair: nothing to do with us . . .
> He's made his bed, and now he's got to lie in it."

But in spite of such eccentricities, the best of these plays are very fine, and even the worst of them contain striking and memorable thoughts. Tragedy must rise above the realities of every day, upon the wings of imagination and emotion. The great tragedians have known this necessity, and have used many means of fulfilling it: vivid descriptions like the beacon-speech in Aeschylus' "Agamemnon"; striking stage-pictures like the storm in "King Lear" and the sleeping Furies in "The Eumenides"; symbols like the crimson carpet in "Agamem-

non," the jester's skull in "Hamlet," the hand-washing in
"Macbeth"; metrical richness, both dramatic and lyrical;
physical suffering like that of Prometheus, Philoctetes,
Orestes, Othello, Gloucester, Phèdre; and, above all, supernatural appearances—omens, divinities, spirits of health, or
goblins damned. Yielding to the decline in taste and the con-
traction of imagination, most modern playwrights do not
even attempt such bold effects: or, if ever, do so awkwardly
and unconvincingly. However, the French neo-Hellenic
dramatists, stimulated by the example of their predecessors
and strengthened by the myths which they are using (or
which are using them), employ several of these effects to en-
noble their work.

A powerful new symbol for the sense of guilt which is
basically weakness and cowardice was created by Sartre in
"The Flies," when he showed the blood-guilty city of Argos
infested with a plague of fat black blowflies, and the Furies
themselves threatening Orestes in the shape of monstrous
bloodsucking flies. Flies annoy, and weaken, and in swarms
even terrify, but they rarely kill. With energy and decision,
by killing some and driving others away and ignoring the rest,
one can survive. "The Flies" was produced when France was
occupied by the Germans. Again, in Cocteau's "The Infernal
Machine," Jocasta, the pitiful, nervous, but still beautiful
queen, enters leading Tiresias, the blind seer who foresees
her tragedy. Her scarf trails behind her, and Tiresias treads
on it. She cries:

"I am surrounded by things that hate me! This scarf has been
choking me all day. It hooks onto branches, it rolls itself
around axles, and now you tread on it. . . . It's terrifying! It
will kill me."

That is indeed the scarf with which she hangs herself; and in
the last scene she appears (visible only to the blinded eyes of
Oedipus) with it bound around her neck.

In the same play, the wedding of Oedipus and his mother is
treated with masterly tact and imagination. The couple, left

alone in the bridal chamber, are exhausted by the coronation
ceremonies, the long processions, the heavy robes: they move
and live half-asleep in an uneasy dream. Oedipus falls asleep
just as he has thrown himself down to rest, across the mar-
riage-bed, his tired head lolling over the foot of it. And his
head rests on the empty cradle (once his own) which Jocasta
kept in memory of the child she lost; and then, as he sleeps,
she rocks the cradle.

The authority of legend makes it easier for a playwright
to introduce the supernatural in a mythical play than in a
contemporary drama. The French dramatists are not as a
rule content with imitating the traditional appearances of
supernatural beings in Greek drama. They prefer to give
their creations new forms. The flies of Sartre are one such
creation. The Furies also appear in Giraudoux' "Electra": as
little girls who gradually grow into maidens and then into
tall powerful women, while the revenge of Orestes approaches its maturity. In the same play, a vulture is seen in
the last act, at first floating very high above the head of the
doomed Aegisthus, and then gradually, gradually planing
lower. Cocteau's "Orpheus" is really a surrealist extrava-
ganza, clever but silly. However, it contains one impressive
deity: Death. Neither a crowned phantom nor a winged
angel, she appears as a beautiful impassive young woman,
who puts on a surgeon's white coat and mask, and, while her
patient Eurydice is dying, directs the manipulation of machines as intricate and terrifying as those of modern hospitals.
No horseman, no skeleton reaper could be so effective for
today. But the most impressive of all these figures is the
Sphinx in Cocteau's "The Infernal Machine." At first only
a girl whom young Oedipus meets on the road, she changes
into a winged monster, half-woman, half-lioness; and the
proud hero falls before her, bewitched and aghast.

Much might be said of the eloquence of Giraudoux, who
wrote exquisite prose, and whose characters talk in flashingly
vivid images, following the French dramatic tradition of

raisonnement, brilliant disquisitions on abstract themes. If anything, his characters do discuss too much. But Giraudoux and Cocteau are the only two of these writers whose style reaches real splendor at great moments. One example will suffice. When Oedipus falls before the Sphinx, he is paralyzed. He shouts "I *will* resist!" And she replies:

It is useless to close your eyes, to turn your head away. My power does not lie in my gaze nor in my song. When I act, I am defter than a blind man's fingers, swifter than a gladiator's net, subtler than the lightning, stiffer than a charioteer, heavier than a cow, more dutiful than a schoolboy wrinkling his brows over a sum, more rigged and sailed and anchored and balanced than a ship, more incorruptible than a judge, greedier than the insects, bloodier than the birds, more nocturnal than an egg, more ingenious than an Oriental torturer, more deceitful than the heart, more supple than the hand of a thief, more fateful than the stars, more diligent than the snake as it moistens its prey with saliva; I can secrete and produce and abandon and wind and ravel and unravel so that when I will these knots of mine they are tied, and when I think them they are tightened or loosened; so delicate that you cannot grasp them, so pliant that you feel them like a creeping poison, so hard that if I let them slip they would maim you, so taut that a bow could draw a note of divine anguish from the bond between us; clamped like the sea, like the pillar, like the rose, thewed like the octopus, complicated like the mechanics of a dream, invisible above all else, invisible and majestic like the blood in the veins of a statue, a thread binding you in the multiple swirls and twists of a stream of honey falling into a cup of honey.

We began this essay by asking why these playwrights chose Greek legends for their subjects. The central answer is that the myths are permanent. They deal with the greatest of all problems, the problems which do not change, because men and women do not change. They deal with love; with war; with sin; with tyranny; with courage; with fate: and all in some way or other deal with the relation of man to those divine powers which are sometimes felt to be irrational, sometimes to be cruel, and sometimes, alas, to be just.

WILLIAM A. JOHNSEN

Myth, Ritual, and Literature after Girard

The nineteenth-century dream of the comparative method, so spectacularly successful in natural science, economics, and linguistics, has remained for literary intellectuals tauntingly unfulfilled, backing up into provocative but unstable analogies between comparative structural analyses of myth, ritual, and literature. The chronological derivation of myth from ritual, or ritual from myth, and literature from both, in the early part of this century, especially by the Cambridge Ritualists (Fraser, Harrison, Murray, Cornford¹), and in Freud's anthropological speculations, was prudently reduced to logical derivation by the 1950s. Lévi-Strauss had chosen synchronic linguistics, which put aside the question of language's origin, as the model for structural anthropology. Neumann borrowed "sequence-dating" from Flinders Petrie to rule anachronism out of depth psychology's parallel development of individual and cultural consciousness. Universally recurring archetypes became, for Northrop Frye, the metahistorical building blocks for literature as a whole. What remained as the transcultural authority for these universally recurring archetypes, sequences, and structures was, in Edward Said's oppositional term for structuralism, the "totalitarianism of mind."¹ Homologies followed from the common structuring principles of the human imagination of every time and place. Structure, as the key to all explanation, could not itself be further explained.

René Girard has consciously positioned himself to follow through on the consequences of comparison. Beginning in the do-

116

main of myth, ritual, and literature, this means nothing less than to make good on the dream of a hypothesis that ultimately accounts for the generation of all cultural forms. One future for the systematic study of literature made possible by Girard becomes the comprehending of the relation of the modern to myth, ritual, and literature as a whole. This essay will argue "after Girard" in two related ways: "according to" his hypothesis, as well as estimating what "follows" from its explanatory power. I leave the contentious sense of "getting after" Girard to those who are captured by the contemporary myth that being critical in the human sciences means discarding without further consideration any hypothesis that claims by comparison to be superior to others.

Mensonge romantique et vérité romanesque (1961), translated as *Deceit, Desire, and the Novel* (1965),[3] Girard's first book, is founded on the kind of historical threshold that is everywhere in his work. Man once acknowledged his own incompleteness in deferring to the superior beings of the gods, kings, or nobility. Imitation was to properly follow their example, with no thought of equality. When the Enlightenment rationalized divinity for man's sake, there was no further excusing any deficiency of human autonomy. Yet fictional texts show this promise unfulfilled, to each alone; to mask this private shame, all pretend to possess the sufficiency that each lacks. Each must copy the apparent originality of others, without giving himself away as a rank imitator. Such imitation among "equals" can only lead to rivalry, with the disciple reaching for whatever object the model has indicated as desirable, as the apparent source of his autonomy. In early stages, the model can deny any coquetry, and the disciple can deny any rivalry; but in later stages of "deviated transcendency" the disciple will find divinity not in objects themselves, but only in those who reject him. Modern desire is metaphysical, a fight over increasingly elusive and intangible goals. Sadism and narcissism become the decisively modern masks of autonomy, the expression of being desired while wanting (lacking) nothing, rejecting all.

Such a profound revolution in the way desire is understood could not but evolve as well a theory of consciousness and the unconscious, instincts and their repression. Furthermore, it leads to a radical revision, within the human sciences, of theories of prohibition, then ritual, then myth, and finally culture itself, the

117

201

process of hominization. If desire depends on a model for instruction, then the repression and prohibition of desires cannot be the restraining of instinctual drives, or the tabooing of instinctually indicated desirables. If desire is imitative, then prohibition and tabooing must be a restraint of imitation itself—in particular, the mimesis of appropriation, but more generally, of all intersubjectivity. Religious ritual can no longer be (for believers and skeptics alike) the "symbolic" or imaginary exorcizing of spiritual or instinctual agencies, a primitive form of metaphoric inoculation against real micro- and macrobic invasion. Instead, it becomes an effective if misunderstood restructuring of imitation as a potentially catastrophic behavior.

Girard's method is appropriately comparative, appropriately initiated in nineteenth-century material, but distinctive in the seriousness that he allows literary as intellectual (ultimately, scientific) labor. Girard first develops this mimetic hypothesis on the authority of his comparison of nineteenth-century European fiction, which proposes two rival traditions for the novel: the *romantic*, which reflects, without comprehending, the mediation of desire, and the *romanesque* (novelistic), which reveals it. The romanesque work of Stendhal, Proust, and Dostoyevsky learns, first in others, finally in itself, the pretensions of romantic (autonomous) desire.

How does *La Violence et le sacré* (1972), *Violence and the Sacred* (1977),[4] make good on the scientific potential of the novelistic tradition? First, by suggesting violence as an intra- and transcultural constant that enables comparison of all cultural forms. Nothing more closely resembles a violent man than another, from within or without the culture, and nothing better consolidates this resemblance than their mutual conflict. But if we learn, following Girard, to associate violence with the erasing of differences, what do we do with our modern enlightened presupposition that differences, not similarities, breed conflict? Girard turns this presupposition of peaceful equality back on itself: What powerful modern institution could cultivate a presupposition so different from the primitive horror of the Same? The discrepancy between primitive and modern ideas about difference leads to a significant distinction between primitive and modern culture, based on their ratios of preventive to curative procedures for expelling violence from the

118

community. After some extremely suggestive paragraphs on the superior efficacy of the judicial system for incarnating divine vengeance, before which all are equal, he turns to the primitive world of preventive procedures. The return to modern ritual and myth occurs, up to this point in Girard's writing, mostly in the margins of something else, especially his readings of Freud.[5] Our itinerary here will be to summarize Girard's hypothesis for cultural mimesis, as the key to primitive myth and ritual. Next we will observe his unique sense of the role of literature for *desymbolizing* myth and ritual (especially novelistic fiction, Greek and Elizabethan drama, and the tradition he names *l'écriture judéo-chrétienne*). As we proceed, we will relate Girard's theory to those of others, especially Claude Lévi-Strauss, Walter Burkert, Jean-Pierre Vernant, and Northrop Frye. Finally, we will consider the potential future of Girard's theory ("after Girard") for the myths and rituals of modern culture, especially in coordination with Edward Said on literary representations of the myths and rituals of imperialism.[6]

If violence travels so well, what keeps it from spreading like a contagion, enveloping and breaking down a whole community? Sometimes nothing works (any longer), as in the case of the Kaingang tribe in Brazil; their transplantation, which has deprived them of their hereditary enemy (everyone else), has left them to an internal bloodfeuding certain to wipe them out in a generation. Put another way, a community, hominization itself, is sustainable only in the presence of some working solution to the contagion of spontaneous violence. All societies that have survived, or that have survived long enough to have entered history, must have had some answer of varying effectiveness. If violence is a constant, what permissible variables effectively contain it? Prohibition and ritual. If one reverses the proliferation of modern theories of psychic complexes, agencies, and archetypes (which resemble all too closely the primitive myths of the gods as sufficient cause) in favor of the mimetic hypothesis, prohibition and ritual can be seen as the restraint of imitation itself. In particular, the restrained mimesis is that of appropriation: father, then son, reaching for the same object made irresistible by the indication of each other's rivalry. Primitive prohibition also taboos all other indications of doubling as signs of incipient violence: mirrors, representations, twins. If Girard is a more economical psychologist than Freud, he is a more down-

119

to-earth anthropologist than Lévi-Strauss. Primitive rituals do not put twins to death as organizational misfits, scandalous signs of two applying for the structural position reserved for one. Adults' reasons for putting children to death are abominably mistaken, but hardly philosophical. For Girard, primitives are not to be understood as proto-structuralist intellectuals; behind the issue of structuralism there is always the more crucial issue of a social order threatened by, yet generated from, violence misunderstood as a divinity.[7]

If taboos prohibit imitation, ritual legislates its effects. Ritual functions by imitating the progress of spontaneous violence. Because it is eminently imitable, violence spreads easily, uninterrupted until it has exhausted itself with the peace that follows the satisfaction of violence by imitating its finale of all against (the last) one. In spontaneous violence, each is the other's enemy; as it ends, one is the enemy of all. Ritual legislates this process: the ritual victim substitutes for each one's enemy. Because violence erases differences, one can stand as the enemy of all, their monstrous double. The double valence of the *pharmakos*, defiled as monstrous yet holy in his office, is *sacer*, sacred. Girard's mimetic hypothesis comprehends those discussions of symbolic action that terminate themselves in the circular answers of ambivalence, human duplexity, and undecidability as the last word.

Freud saw the father, as Hubert and Mauss saw ritual, as at once a potent source and unexplainable explanation of contradictory commands: "I am your progenitor; I am your enemy." Girard analyzes the Freudian father within the context of Freud's theoretical attempt to reconcile a mimetic with an instinctual model of desire (*Violence and the Sacred*, Ch. 7). In the chapter of *Massenpsychologie und Ich-Analyse* (1921) on identification, Freud identifies the father as the child's primary model, whose place he would take everywhere (*an allen seinen Stellen treten*).[8] In the child's mental life, identification with the father (mimetic) and a cathexis toward the mother (instinctual) develop side by side, until he sees the father in the way of the mother. His way blocked to the object by the father, who had helped to identify it as desirable, his identification now (*jetzt*) takes on a hostile coloring: the son would take that place (*zu ersetzen*) as well (*auch*). Girard brilliantly queries the offhandedness of *auch*: Does this mean that the child warily observed, up until now, the incest taboo meant to prohibit conflict? How can we account for this special category of the mother in the child's mental life, among the "everywheres" of the father, otherwise sufficiently comprehensible through the father's mediation of the son's desire?

Girard follows Freud's discussion of the Oedipus complex to *Das Ich und das Es* (1923), where a primary desire for the mother, originating in the son, now preempts the *nebeneinander* development of the father's mediation.[9] Thus Freud has chosen an instinctual theory of desire over a mimetic theory. Furthermore, because the father no longer prepares the way he will later block, he (and/or patriarchal culture in general) is absolved of any responsibility for scandalously drawing the unsuspecting child into rivalry. He is absolved as well of responsibility for his own "ambivalence"; the instincts now serve the god-function, determining the fate of every modern Oedipus. Although it deserves fuller treatment elsewhere, a coordination of feminist theory with Girard might begin here, by considering Freud's profoundly influential decision to blame the instincts (that is, the body, nature itself) for the regrettable ambivalence of the father for the child, and how that is the same as blaming women.[10] Such a beginning in a critique of Freudian myth could follow out Girard's provocative (but essayistic) suggestion for primitive culture, that the negative symbolization in myth and ritual of menstrual blood responds to "some half-repressed desire to place the blame for all forms of violence on women" (*Violence and the Sacred*, p. 36).

To sketch out this future, let us follow Girard's reading over Freud's shoulder, to pay yet closer attention to Freud's development of his theory. In the *Massenpsychologie*, father-identification is at first healthy, competitive, an intimate, active sparring that prepares the son to assume in due time his manly prerogatives (*Dies Verhalten hat nichts mit einer passiven oder femininum Einstellung zum Vater (und zum Manne Überhaupt) zu tun, es ist viehlmehr exquisit männlich*). Once the father is seen as blocking the path to the mother, however—or once the mother refuses the "advances" of the son in the name of some absent adult male, who may or may not exist—father-identification becomes identical with the wish (*wird identisch mit dem Wunsch*) to *take* (*zu ersetzen*), not to assume or inherit eventually, the father's place. We see that

121

the language of father-identification now clearly voices violent rivalry, the son wishing to contest the Father-in-the-way, head on, for the *same* place.

In the chapter of *Das Ich und das Es* on the "Über-Ich," Freud refers to his earlier discussion in *Massenpsychologie*. Although he repeats the phrase about father-identification taking on a hostile coloring, he no longer finds it identical to a previous father-identification now recklessly (that is, threateningly) exercised in a forbidden place. Rather, the intensification of sexual desire for the mother precedes the recognition of the father as an obstacle (*ein Hindernis*; p. 37) Father-identification changes into a violent rivalry that had not before existed, "a wish to get rid of his father in order to take his place with his mother" (*wendet sich zum Wunsch, den Vater zu beseitigen, um ihn bei der Mutter zu ersetzen*). The universal logic behind the universal prohibition of incest identifies women of every human society as the source of violence to be legislated, isolated. Like violence, they are sacred (*Violence and the Sacred*, pp. 219-20). When we trace the customary history of the development of sacrificial substitution, given its most popular form by Robert Graves,[11] back toward its origins (totemic animal substitutes for *pharmakos*, who substitutes for *tyrannos*, who was once sacrificed for the queen), we must think past the premature termination of this sequence of substitutions in the cultic figure of the *magna mater*. Her sacred ambivalence, definitively mapped in Neumann's work,[12] derives, like the king's, from a prior role as a sacrificial victim.

At this point we must bring ourselves back from the interminable deconstruction of other theories which, as Said suggests,[13] easily confuses the power to critique cultural mythology with the ability to contest its influence with an alternative. Girard is reading Freudian theory to recover the mimetic hypothesis, which would place violent rivalry within the domain of cultural, not natural propagation, within the domain of pedagogy, not instinct, and for social reciprocity, not for repression.

How, then, does Girard's mimetic reading of father-identification differ? First, the child who follows the familial and cultural indications of the father as a proper model is the last to learn that imitation is rivalry—that father-identification is appropriative, patricidal. Forbidden "this" place, he can only assume that the father's ambivalence, his mercurial change of attitude, is a rejection justified by the son's failure; and he can only conclude that such failure has been measured before an especially desirable object. Violence will thereafter indicate the desirable, an obstacle (*ein Hindernis*) the surest sign of an opportunity to retrieve the full being denied him. Subsequent identifications will take on the coloring of the ambivalent father-identification.

The consequences of such a reading open up a future for the practice of psychoanalysis apart from myth and ritual, and the possibility of situating this practice in a diachronic plan.[14] By recognizing the compelling yet arbitrary nature of the distinction between those places where imitation is required or prohibited, treatment can avoid the parallel fetishism of adjustment and perversion. It can comprehend at once the function of prohibition, and the perspicacity of those unfortunate analysands who cannot blind themselves to its arbitrary nature (*Violence and the Sacred*, p. 172).

The ambivalence of the father as the primary model and obstacle who influences all subsequent identifications can only occur, Girard insists, in a patriarchal culture where the father's role is weakened but not yet effaced (*Violence and the Sacred*, p. 188). Freud tried to generate the incest taboo historically by arguing, in *Totem and Taboo*, that in Darwin's horde the king is father of all and is killed by his "sons" in sexual jealousy over "his" women. In remorse for this killing, or in "delayed obedience," the men prohibit themselves incest and commit themselves to exogamy. Following the mimeticization of Freud's psychology, Girard depaternalizes Freud's anthropological theory as well. Prohibition prevents rivalry: for the single murder of a single father, Girard substitutes rite as the mimesis of spontaneous violence, saving Freud's essential insight of collective violence as the origin of totem and taboo. Thus the mimetic hypothesis explains the ambivalence of the sacred as well as the father (or mother). Ritual prepares a sacrificeable victim by making him violate every taboo, by making him everyone's rival. Before such a rival all are united. He is the savior as well as the scourge because he is signed with the sacred, with the beneficial resources of sacrifice itself. Such awe can easily transform the enemy after his sacrifice, into the progenitor who

123

allows his own sacrifice, who makes laws, who establishes prohibitions against his (former) misbehavior and even requires sacrifice to keep the peace he alone provides.

Walter Burkert's *Homo Necans*, which appeared in the same year as *Violence and the Sacred*, is a prodigious garnering of the literature of myth and ritual, under a hypothesis in many ways akin to Girard's reading Freud.[15] Like Girard, Burkert is interested in relating classical studies to anthropology and psychology. He suggests the origin of the gods in the prohibition of some prior act of collective violence, but he derives prohibition from the *psychologisme* of Paleolithic hunters who regret the killing of the animal they have hunted, because they belatedly identify with their victim. In reaction, they set this animal off limits; eventually this difference becomes sacred. The weak link is the dynamic that Burkert shares with Freud in *Totem and Taboo*; guilt, or remorse for murder, energizes a universal system of prohibitions. How could one moment of remorse (putting aside for now the problem of where that moment of remorse comes from) maintain its influence throughout human culture? The mimetic hypothesis has a superior scientific value that can be exampled in the hunt, but it can function equally well for an agricultural society. A being who draws back from claiming an object, for the sake of another or in fear of another's desire, has acknowledged and limited the dangerous power of the mimesis of appropriation. Hunters circling their prey reinforce mimetically each other's reluctance to lay the first hand (which could provoke a second), to get too close to being on the other side with the victim. Prohibition and ritual legislate this prudence into protocols that insure peace by making certain no one else gets mixed up with the victim's sacred difference.[16]

By showing the persistent influence of archaic ritual violence on the cultural forms of democratic Athens, Louis Gernet provided the historical scholarship required to evaluate the speculative profusion of the Cambridge Ritualists, who saw ritual sacrifice behind every king, every tragedy. Jean Pierre Vernant, Pierre Vidal-Naquet, and Marcel Detienne have followed out Gernet by structuralizing the observation of misrule becoming rule in ritual (as in literature) as a regulation of man's ambiguous nature: Oedipus as Everyman, *homo duplex, tyrannos-pharmakos*.[17]

To the persistent observation that Oedipus plays all the roles,

124

father-brother, son-lover, savior-scourge, Vernant brings the structuralist hypothesis of binary opposition composing all symbolic forms. To play everyone is nevertheless to play by the iron rules of structuration: the king must ultimately suffer reversal to the opposite pole of anathema. But what is the answer to binary opposition itself as a hypothesis? Mind? How can this *tyrannos* serve as both tyrant and king; how can this *pharmakos* be the cure and the scourge of the city?[18] Girard's rethinking of structuralism, in its early stages, parallels deconstructive thinking. Such orders can never be neutral, philosophical. Oppositions are privileged, interested, worldly; they make a difference for someone's sake.

Who benefits from each role that Oedipus plays? The proper opposition to watch is not that of scourge versus savior, but the opposition of each to the city, the one posed against all, which Girard insists is the primary sign of sacrificial reconciliation, the origin of all symbolic representation, of symbolicity itself.[19] To see the play of the *pharmakos* as undecidable is, in one sense, true. (Here Girard follows Derrida.) The identification of the victim is truly arbitrary—s/he is no more guilty of contagious violence than is anyone else. Yet to terminate analysis in ambiguity is to play along with the purification that tragedy comes to, to ignore the final decision (*de-cidere*) that always occurs at the moment purgation requires: the perepeteia of the hero.

In Girard's reading, Sophocles intolerably delays this expected moment of decisiveness as Oedipus tries to dodge his "fate." Girard's attention to such delays and reservations marks off his reading from those of Freud, Burkert, Vernant, the archetypalists, and Frye. What interests mythographers like Lévi-Strauss (or Robert Graves, for that matter) in *Oedipus Tyrannos* is a unidirectional, irresistible homology to another myth, leading as soon as possible to the myth of myth.[20] The myth, whether Classical or Freudian, never expresses any doubt about Oedipus's guilt. Audiences, whether in Athens or New York, consolidate themselves in impatient opposition to Oedipus's obstinate resistance to admitting what they already know.

But Girard suggests that certain literary works, especially in times of social crisis (modern fiction, Greek and Elizabethan tragedy, *l'écriture judéo-chrétienne*), desymbolize the myths that corroborate violent rituals of social cohesion. Sophocles goes part way, according to Girard, in calling the certitude of Oedipus's guilt into question. To follow out Sophocles, we must delay our accusation of *hamartia* against an Oedipus who is the only intellect, temper, or unconscious out of control. Girard would have us see that Creon, Tiresias, and even Jocasta give way to anger in their turn. Each becomes a mimetic rival to the other as each accuses the other of the same crimes, for the sake of the city's institutions. Sophocles rejoins the reciprocity between antagonists that myth decides. The play itself contains, as many have argued, uncertain evidence for Oedipus's guilt. The account of one or many murderers of Laios is never verified, nor is the context of that account, whether it was given before or after the Herdsman found Oedipus as king.[11] Even if the play more or less acquiesces to the myth's account of Oedipus's guilt, audiences, following Aristotle, agree rather on the all-too-human sin of pride, and the causal link of either sin to plague is never verified by the play's conclusion. Vernant concludes as well that Sophocles locates an unstructurable ambiguity between Oedipus as Everyman and the social positions that would name him. But Girard takes Vernant's discussion beyond ambiguity, arguing that Vernant's own observation of Oedipus as scapegoat (*bouc émissaire*) as well as *pharmakos* critically identifies the structuring principle of the myth that Sophocles discovers: "The traces of religious anathema unearthed in tragedy should be regarded not as anachronistic survivals from a primitive past but as being in the nature of an archaeological find" (*Violence and the Sacred*, p. 84).

Violence and the Sacred openly acknowledges the priority of Gernet, Vernant, Benveniste, and Derrida. In each case Girard attempts a comprehension of their work. The mimetic hypothesis accounts for the ambiguity of the sacred in ritual (Gernet, Vernant) and in language (Benveniste, Derrida), but also for its partial demythologization in Sophocles.

If Girard is a brilliant reader of others, he is also particularly gifted in finding answers for the most stubborn misreadings of his own work. *Violence and the Sacred* first encountered an antireferential prejudice that prohibited any belief that myth (or, more generally, religion) could refer to anything outside itself, and a pseudo-scientific skepticism that knew all truth claims are now obsolete. Almost immediately Girard began to answer with the medieval "texts of persecution," documents composed of the same stereotypes as the myths he analyzes in *Violence and the Sacred*.[22] Furthermore, he insists that his reading of mythology and primitive religion, which scandalizes contemporary notions of textuality, is the method of reading that everyone uses for these medieval texts, which describe how Jews poisoned wells, caused stillbirths, and cast evil eyes until all problems were cured by their elimination. Girard defies any reader to argue with this modern consensus which shows the contemporary literary intellectual's version of textual practice as an anachronism. Who would deny (1) that there are real persecutions behind such texts, even when independent corroboration is impossible; (2) that the intention of the authors of persecution, to find the single cause, is knowable; (3) that we can, with certainty, replace the persecutors' interpretation, which we know, with our own (the victims are not guilty, and their persecutors know not what they do), with an interpretation that is theoretically and morally superior?

As in the case of Lévi-Strauss, Burkert, Mary Douglas, or, more generally, the fields of psychology, anthropology, and biblical scholarship, to ask who is the more competent specialist is to foreclose all futures for the disciplines except departmental snobbery.[23] The only course, even in those cases where Girard seems to have read lightly (or not at all), is to follow the theory that comprehends all this work, even if it comes from one who has earned no credits in the field or the clinic, but who puts "the literature" to best use.

The most influential modern theorist for the relation of myth and ritual to literature has been Northrop Frye. In one of the most famous sentences of *Anatomy of Criticism* (1957),[24] Frye argued that literary structure derives logically, if not chronologically, from myth and ritual. This strategic retreat from the contested question of generative origins consolidated Cornford on comedy, Aristotle on tragedy, Jung and Neumann on romance, and the best local authority on the pertinence of myth, ritual, and the primitive for modern writing.

Frye has been outmoded by the journalists of critical theory because of the questions he strategically, but only momentarily, set aside: in particular, the question of why literary structure resembles the structure of myth and ritual. Such questions have occupied both Frye and Girard for more than twenty years. Such

127

mythical lustrations as Lentricchia's *After the New Criticism* (1980),²⁵ which washes its hands of Frye after 1970, are necessarily ignorant of Frye's later work.

Frye's anatomy presents the constituting literary structure as the story of a dying and resurrecting god, whose motive is to resolve the loss of identity between the human and natural world. Frye correlates the recurring narrative myths of comedy, romance, tragedy, and irony into a monomyth, the story of one being who rises, sets, and returns like the sun: the spirit of comedy for the regeneration of society is reborn in a young man of mysterious birth, the knight of romance, who becomes the king of tragedy, who becomes the *pharmakos* of irony whose *sparagmos* feeds a new comedy.

Why does literature follow myth and ritual, according to Frye? Because it wants to. That is, the motive for literature is to articulate the desirable already comprehended most clearly in myth and ritual, which are the structural building-blocks of the imagination. Myth narrates the adventures of beings empowered to do whatever they want. The "Theory of Modes" sees a descent in literary history from the classical to the modern period, in the hero's power of action, and a descent in narrative myths from the most powerful heroic actions to the least, ending in modern literature's preference for ironic myth and mode.

But why is literature as a whole headed in the opposite direction from the desirable? Frye describes this progress as displacement: accommodating the dream of literature to the pressure of the reality principle at any. given historical moment. This gap between myth and mode, the relation between myth and history, and the corresponding underdetermination of the relation of secular to sacred scripture is still a pressing issue in Frye's work.²⁶ Yet a term like "displacement" suggests that Frye begins by seeing literature measured against the norm of myth and ritual. Frye's earliest attempt to reconcile the historical descent of modes with the cyclical return of myth was to suggest that the modern interest in the ironic victim, in primitive cult and ritual, signifies the *sparagmos* of myth, a successful sacrifice, which sacramentally fortifies the emerging spirit of a new comic society.

What would a mimetic reading of Frye look like? Like Girard, Frye defines desire interdividually, in the sense that he defers plot-

128

ting the intentions and desires of single authors whose only wish is to make a work, until such work accumulates in the archetypal phase, where collectively recurrent desires and their prohibition articulate a dream of identification, all the world absorbed by one desiring human form. That is, human desires become legible as the drives that cultural prohibitions imperfectly restrain. Frye's theory of identification in *Anatomy of Criticism*, the "motive for metaphor" in *The Educated Imagination* (1964),[27] follows Freud: to identify is to absorb. In the *Massenpsychologie*, the ambivalence of father-identification, from which all future forms of identification take their coloring, behaves like a derivative of the oral phase, "*in welcher man sich das begehrte und geschätzte Objekt durch Essen einverleibte und es dabei als solches vernichtete. Der Kannibale bleibt bekanntlich auf diesem Standpunkt stehen; er hat seine Feinde zum Fressen lieb, und er frisst nur die, die er lieb hat*" (67) ("in which the object that we long for and prize is assimilated by eating and is in that way annihilated as such. The cannibal, as we know, has remained at this standpoint; he has a devouring affection for his enemies and only devours people of whom he is fond" [37]). Such a desire for identification/absorption is, in the language of *Deceit, Desire, and the Novel*, "ontological sickness," an attempt to appropriate for one's own depleted resources the greater being of the other.[28]

As we have seen, the mimetic hypothesis absolves the disciple of any instinctive, violent urge to appropriate, referring such accusations back to their mediators. If desire is mediated, if prohibitions control the consequences of mimesis, then archetypes can be understood as "articulating" the desires that cultural prohibitions project onto the disciples. The progressive displacement of desire in Frye's "Theory of Modes," read mimetically, becomes, adapting Raymond Williams's phrase, "the long devolution," literature's progressive desymbolization of *mythic* desires, projected by prohibition and ritual as instinctive, as originating in nature, in the child. This devolution culminates in the modern period. The modern interest in myth and ritual is not a historical residue, not a return, but an archaeological dis-covery of the roots of all human societies in violent sacrifice.

Frye identifies literary structure with the *pharmakos* (which Derrida quotes approvingly[29]) and, like Vernant, uses "scapegoat"

129

as a synonym. Girard uses *pharmakos* and scapegoat, respectively, to distinguish between the reflection and revelation of victimization. When we see that Jews and witches are scapegoats, we see the dynamic invisible to the persecutor-author, the dynamic that structures the text. A text that talks openly about victimization has a scapegoat theme, whose structure, then, is post-sacrificial.

For Girard "scapegoat" is a term in the West's development of the precious critical vocabulary of social relations, generated by the comparative studies of cultures, religions, and languages. But comparison must not prematurely terminate itself by regarding all cultures as equally ethnocentric, racist, sexist. Such collective, comparative labor, on such an unprecedented scale, suggests an anthropological or even logological motive of our culture. We have improved our comprehension of all cultural languages by minimizing our own; when positive rules of kinship (which cross-cousin one should marry) desymbolize, we are left with only the minimal prohibitions necessary to forestall violent rivalry.

Girard pursues the consequences of comparative religion in the nineteenth century beyond the premature termination in collecting homologies between the Bible and other stories of dying and resurrecting gods. He goes on to ask, "What makes such comparisons possible?" His answer is: "Judeo-Christian writing," which emphasizes the innocence of the persecuted: Joseph in Egypt is not guilty of desiring to replace his "father" everywhere. The capacity to see those who are sacrificed as marked with the sign of the perfectly innocent victim makes possible the fundamental distinction between reflection and revelation of scapegoating.

Frye's positing of myth as the structural paradigm for literature, and his commitment to expel all value judgment as comparative class determination, proposes the equivocal position of regarding any hero's *sparagmos* as good as any other, only arbitrarily authorized by a dominant interest. Dionysus would do just as well. A mimetic rereading of Frye's heroic categories would be less resigned to Zeus's criminal sexual practice as the articulation of the desirable. Zeus's desire is transgressive, mythologically attracted to obstacles, prohibitions, taboos. All such "heroic" crimes are signs of the sacrificial origin of the divinity in a plague of rivalry resolved by his expulsion.

If one theorizes the historical preference for Judeo-Christian

130

writing over other local myths in Western literature as something more than class privilege, "the long devolution" (the mimetic reading of the "Theory of Modes") is the contest of violence and nonviolence, the two logoi of Satan and the Paraclete, the accuser and the advocate, respectively, of the persecuted (*The Scapegoat*, Chs. 14, 15). Following Frye according to Girard recovers the prematurely "outmoded" future of "literature as a whole," in relation to myth and ritual, as the revelation of violence from an emerging post-sacrificial comprehension.

For Frye, the scapegoat structure in modern literature is the victory of the obstacle or reality principle over the solar hero of romance, who bears the dream of literature. A mimetic reading of mode suggests that modern literature finalizes Western literature's *thematization* of the scapegoat mechanism. The sacred power of queens as well as kings was inherently unstable, was earned through victimization; they are victimized again when anything goes wrong because they are the sole cause of violence and/or peace. The secularization of violent myth and ritual sustains, over time, the dissolution of violent difference between the turbulent audience and its heroes. An ironic hero who proves his power is less than ours is, in effect, our victim. The vertiginous rise and fall of leadership in modern societies replays this devolution in a matter of years. The parallel desymbolization of social and literary forms forces us to consider that the crowd dynamic, not some reality principle or unique character flaw, is responsible for social crisis.

Let us conclude our following of Girard's theory by seconding the credit he gives to literature's "quasi-theoretical potential,"[30] by considering two writers who consciously project work before and after the post-sacrificial revelation of violence. Shakespeare, in *King Lear*, deals with those who, because they do violence in the name of peace before scriptural revelation, cannot know what they do. Orwell, in *Nineteen Eighty-Four*, examines those of an anthropological post-critical age who know exactly what they are doing. (These are but two texts for Girard's future that have been temporarily deferred by his fifteen-year centering on the Bible. If Girard never writes separately on *Nineteen Eighty-Four*, his comments on the modern totalitarian state in *Job* remain extremely useful; and the amount and quality of his work on Shakespeare make it certain that he will turn eventually to *King Lear*.)

131

Frye refers repeatedly to a Shakespeare who returns to myth and ritual as the bedrock of drama. For Girard, Shakespeare is equally important in a mimetic tradition: as an imitator not of universal forms, literary genres, or nature, but of the social play of imitation itself. Shakespeare's reading of conflictive mimesis is not a structuring of the play by archetypes, but a revelation of how stereotypes of persecution control the machinations of the characters.

Even in England's prehistory, desire is already modernized, metaphysical: to mimetically contend for the father's blessing is to fight over nothing, for nothing comes of nothing. After a somewhat perfunctory description of real estate ("plenteous rivers, and wide-skirted meads"; I, i, 65), *King Lear* nowhere pays any further attention to whatever wealth, privileges, and pleasures follow from taking the father's place everywhere.

The play begins in apparently arbitrary donations and rescensions of paternal blessing which only the mimetic hypothesis can clarify. Gloucester equalizes Edmund to Edgar, but mocks his getting, and talks offhandedly about sending him off again. Yet when Gloucester looks to Lear, he doesn't know what he is doing. Too late will he know that, when he had eyes, he could not see.

To be more precise, Gloucester and Kent don't know why Lear has made a contest to decide what everyone already knows. If Gloucester and Kent know that Lear prefers Albany to Cornwall, Cordelia before her "stepsisters," it can only mean that Lear has performed such "decisions" before. Why is it necessary to go through all this again?

Lear requires this repetition because previous instances have been somehow unsatisfactory. Why hasn't Lear ever gotten what he wants, and why does this failure happen again and again? Girard explains the obsessive failures of metaphysical desire as having nothing to do with desiring defeat. A disciple drawn to insuperable obstacles is still interested in victory, but the only meaningful victory will be over the kind of obstacle that has defeated him previously.

Lear first asks Goneril which daughter loves him best. Goneril was once Lear's only daughter, in a time when such questions were inconceivable; but subsequent paternal blessings have been divided, first in half, then in thirds. Cordelia alone has never suffered this critical diminution of being. Goneril says (as she always has, with progressively diminishing returns) that she loves him best—she presents no obstacle to his desire. His dissatisfaction, signaled by his public reservation of a more ample third for another daughter, can only scandalize her anew. Regan is a more violent contestant that Goneril. She forcibly removes all rivals to Lear's desire: she is enemy to her sister, as well as to all other "joys." Yet Regan's claim of superior difference is likewise annulled.

Why is Cordelia loved best by all? The temptation (to which Kent, and audiences at large, usually succumb) is to take Cordelia's side against all these *other* snobs and hypocrites. But how could such a daughter ever have become the favorite of such a father? The most lucid response is the simplest: this ritual only repeats, in an exacerbated form, what has always happened. The father is unsatisfied by those daughters who love him without reserve, and he is drawn rather to that daughter who does as he does, reserving a portion of her love to some rival.

It is to such rivals for Cordelia that Lear now turns, first by vanquishing Kent's paternal intercession for Cordelia, then by intervening between the competition of France and Burgundy. Burgundy, who would be the establishment suitor of Frye's comic archetype, obeys Lear's prohibition. Burgundy, like Cornwall and Albany, is vanquished as a rival for the daughter's love. But when Lear urges France, the comic suitor, away from loving where he hates, France, like Cordelia, opposes Lear's desire:

> Fairest Cordelia, that art most rich being poor,
> Most choice forsaken, and most loved despised,
> Thee and thy virtues here I seize upon.
> Be it lawful I take up what's cast away.
> Gods, gods! 'Tis strange that from their cold'st neglect
> My love should kindle to inflamed respect (I, i, 250-55)

"Most" modifies both "choice" and "forsaken," "loved" and "despised." That any action could make the one most worthless, most precious, is incomprehensible to France. Therefore he attributes such magic to the gods, not to Lear. The Father's imperious obstacle inflames France's re-gard, re-spect. Paternal violence indicates the desirable. The prohibition against rivalry makes desire transgressive. Violence is the Father of all.

133

Gloucester blames the "machinations" of Edgar's rivalry on the gods as well, but it is Edmund, and not a messenger from the oracle at Delphi, who tells him his son would replace him everywhere. The quasi-theoretical power of *King Lear* is remarkable. Here are Frye's archetypes of tragic and comic action within the dynamic of a single stereotype of persecution—tragic from the point of view of the victim, comic to the society that profits by his expulsion. The symmetry of such a dynamic does not reflect the untranscendable structure of Mind. Symmetry is the consequence of the mimetic rivalry of age and youth for elusive goals. Edmund consciously mimics the stereotype of Gloucester's anticipation of the other's violence, youth's comic agenda of replacing the aged everywhere.

It should be clear by now that to decide who gets the blame, to expel all the bastards, demonstrates the futility of all violent mythologies. All are guilty, yet none does offend. All (even Edmund) are applying preventive measures to forestall the violence they suspect in others; all are one with Lear's intent that "future strife be prevented now." Goneril ungratefully plots against her father immediately after receiving his "blessing," because she is certain Lear's riotous knights provoke her, grow dangerous in prompting a sign of ingratitude that would require Lear's redress. Goneril and Regan already suspect that their mercurial father (like other retiring father figures in Shakespeare's plays) could arbitrarily take back what he has given. When Oswald faithfully breeds an occasion of insult to Lear (to justify the preventive measures Goneril knows she must take), one of Lear's knights sees this insult as only the latest in a series.

> KNIGHT: My lord, I know not what the matter is; but to my judgement your Highness is not entertained with that ceremonious affection as you were wont. There's a great abatement of kindness appears as well in the general dependents as in the Duke himself also and your daughter.
>
> . . . .
>
> LEAR: Thou but rememb'rest me of mine own conception. I have perceived a most faint neglect of late, which I have rather blamed as mine own jealous curiosity than as a very pretense and purpose of unkindness. (I, iv, 55-67)

134

Jealous curiosity fathers rivalry everywhere. Albany insulting Lear is an especially incredible accusation. We are shown nothing in the play to suggest that he would ever insult the king, or even rival Cornwall (another rumor). If Cornwall is well known to be "fiery," sufficiently susceptible to retributive violence, we must remember our first glimpse of these fraternal rivals, when Albany and Cornwall act in unison to restrain Lear's violence against Kent: "Dear sir, forbear!" (I, i, 162). Violent reciprocity, once initiated, is a runaway mechanism whose cause is mythical, a plague for which everyone blames everyone else.

King Lear blames women; *King Lear* exonerates all the accused. The difference between the father and the play, the proper name and the title, is the difference, *a real difference*, between reflecting and revealing the scapegoat mechanism. The voices of the fathers begin in coarse play on the place of Edmund's unlawful getting; Lear immediately associates Cordelia's independence to the barbarous, anthrophagous Scythians. The alacrity with which Lear curses each of his daughters in turn a beast, monster, rhymes with the servant who sums this fear of contagion: "If she live long,/ And in the end meet the old course of death,/Women will all turn monsters" (III, vii, 100-102). Women are monstrous doubles, pretenders to autonomy. They are contaminated by the sacred, which is to be plagued by all that threatens social order.

> O, how this mother swells up toward my heart!
> Hysterica passio, down, thou climbing sorrow;
> Thy element's below. Where is this daughter? (II, iv, 54-56)

"Hysterica passio" connects "mother" to "daughter"; their element—like madness, misrule, lechery—is properly below, what violent rivalry leads Regan to name, perhaps by synecdoche, but perhaps not, "the forfended place" (V, i, 11). Prohibition fathers transgressive desires, fetishized desirables. The sacred is behind the play's mercurial veneration and fear of women, and violence is behind the sacred. Lear's madness is his raving fear of being contaminated by the infernal regions of the feminine: "There's hell, there's darkness, there is the sulpherous pit; burning, scalding, stench, consumption" (IV, vi, 127-28).[31]

That future strife may be prevented now, sister contends with sister, brother and brother-in-law with brother, father with son,

135

godson, daughter, bastards all. But the decisive blow can never be struck, and such "plays" of violence can only end for those who renounce their own stereotypes of persecution in humility before the abominable spectacle of breakaway violence.

> The weight of this sad time we must obey,
> Speak what we feel, not what we ought to say.
> The oldest hath born most: we that are young
> Shall never see so much, nor live so long. (V, iii, 324-27)

Whether we follow the folio reading or the quarto, the speaker is a son, godson (Edgar), or son-in-law (Albany) who "ought to" stick up for his own side, youth, the spirit of comedy. Instead, in all humility, this choral voice defers to age. This same humble deference characterizes Lear and Cordelia's reconciliation to each other. Captured by their rivals, they renounce divine autonomy, prestige, all that violence promises for all the father's places. It is sufficient to be father of this daughter, daughter of this father.

But that is not all. When Shakespeare frustrates a narrative expectation uncertainly placed in Holinshed between pagan myth and English dynastic history to rob Lear of Cordelia in the end, he reveals the "things hidden since the foundation of the world." The play enacts the last possible occasion when all could still unilaterally renounce these scandalous repetitions of mimetic entanglements for peace. Because they live before Judeo-Christian revelation, they cannot know the day and the hour. It is futile to prosecute any sides, to contest comic myth and tragic myth against each other. *King Lear* forgives all those who know not what they do.

But what of us, the beneficiaries of the precious critical terminology of a fundamental anthropology, interdividual psychology, and the Judeo-Christian scriptures? What forgiveness for those who have eyes yet cannot see?

Let us re-gard, re-spect a text that we, as literary intellectuals, have twice modernized (after its publication in 1949, and after its resuscitation in 1984), each time putting it behind us with the same complacency with which Lentricchia outmodes New Criticism and Northrop Frye: Orwell's *Nineteen Eighty-Four*. Furthermore, let us test the future of Girard's theory this time against Edward Said, a self-confessed opponent of "religious criticism" (although secular

136

criticism, Said's alternative, is opposed solely to the title of Girard's work).[32]

The critic's job, according to Said, is not to serve wall-to-wall discourses that absorb any individual, resisting voice. Criticism must limit theory (rather than spreading it) by localizing, circumscribing its itinerary from one site to another. A sanative interest in delimiting theory, however, faces its own challenge of premature limitation. Said unpersuasively restricts the travel of his reading of Orientalism to other archival formations, and he resigns himself philosophically, despite the example of his own passionate resistance, to culture as an exclusionary mechanism.[33]

Both Said and Girard agree on the cultural strength that the West derives from its anthropological interests, but Said has a more ominous vision of what these "interests" are. Balfour, he reminds us, defended England's imperium in Egypt, a culture with an admittedly greater cultural pedigree, because it was Europe alone that could make such a comparison (*Orientalism*, p. 32). Yet what makes the work of Girard and Said compatible is their belief in the critical power of individual texts to reveal, as well as reflect, cultural mythology. For Girard, this critical position (Said's term is "strategic location") is achieved by the power of theory to be more scientific, more reductive than the dominant discourse; for Said, criticism *places* the worldliness of a dominant theory, influential texts, showing by inference where theory does not or cannot extend.

Now we may turn to two related considerations: the worldliness of theory and text in Orwell's novel *Nineteen Eighty-Four* and the worldliness of the novel as theory, as text, from 1949. This second consideration can be subdivided into three related categories: (1) the historical moment of the novel's composition—in general, the work of cultural historians, British studies specialists, Bernard Crick, as well as the personal reminiscences of family and friends; (2) the predictive value of the novel, over thirty-five years, for the year 1984 which made "Orwellian" a parody of the signifying power of symbolic language; (3) most interestingly, the imagined world of its own composition. *Nineteen Eighty-Four* is attributed to an anonymous, post-1984 scholiast who looks back complacently on 1984 as we do now, with no sense of limits on its knowledge of Winston's limits.

137

What is the place of a scapegoat hypothesis in a worldly text like *Nineteen Eighty-Four*? Winston, as the last man in a venerable European tradition, maintains the historical animus against Jews, women, and Orientals, but Oceania has suppressed the modern critical vocabulary of anti-Semitism, sexism, and racism. Propaganda efficiently applies some hidden theoretical model for violent unanimity, transferring enmity the way the "capitalists" transferred luggage and laundry onto someone else's back. The two-minute hate, which provokes Winston's diary, conforms to Girard's analysis of the scapegoat mechanism: (1) the characteristic preparation which qualifies a sacrificial victim; (2) the moment of oscillation, the crisis of difference, when violence apparently ranges at will, to choose its victims; (3) the technique of transference; (4) the order of polarization, where everyone is united in opposition to a single victim responsible for all their troubles; (5) and finally, the sacred peace attributed to the divinity that follows the successful resolution of the sacrificial crisis.

The narrator places us so that we can see what Winston ought to see, a classic demonstration of scapegoating. (1) Sacrificial victims chosen outside the group to be unified must be rehabilitated, incorporated so that they can stand for the whole community; victims from inside must be estranged, to separate them from potential allies who might enter the conflict on their behalf. The double valence of familiar and stranger essential to the proper victim is well satisfied by Goldstein's qualifications: betrayer, parodist of Newspeak, Jew. (2) The moment of oscillation is when the ritual re-enacts the crisis of degree, the moment when the whole community could fall into a violent, interminable conflict, into a loss of difference, because everyone has become everyone else's enemy. Not only does the contest of violent hatred oscillate back and forth between Big Brother and Goldstein (like the contest of violent mastery between Oedipus and Creon, or Bacchus and Pentheus), but Goldstein is also surcharged with the image of non-differentiation: he bleats like a sheep (a classic sacrificial animal), he stands for the faceless Asiatic hordes. (3) Violent antagonism is channeled, transferred to Goldstein; everyone hates the same man, the Enemy of the People. Thus (4) the community is united in polar opposition to their single common enemy, who is responsible for all crimes, all treacheries. Finally (5), there is the theophanic moment, when the god for whom the sacrifice is performed appears, to give his blessing. The sandy-haired woman sitting by Winston who offers her savior, Big Brother, a prayer is essential for blocking recognition of the real mechanism. The transcendent god is the misrepresentation of human violence successfully transferred, channeled to a single victim, which produces peace for everyone else.

Winston makes an important observation that could lead to a full critical understanding of the scapegoat mechanism: the arbitrariness of the victim. Winston sees that the collective animus against Goldstein is charged like an electric current, polarized, abstract, capable of being directed at Big Brother or Julia as well as at Goldstein. Characteristically, this observation doesn't make it into his diary, his text, but it is clearly there as already understood by us.

Why? It will take the rest of this essay to give an answer, but perhaps you are already anticipating that I will finally succumb to a theoretical snobbism attributed to all non-Girardian critics who minimize the quasi-theoretical potential of literary texts. You may suspect that I will show up Winston and/or Orwell before (me and) Girard, the way Culler reads Flaubert as a hesitating anticipation of what we already know.

The first answer is that we are all already accused of being theoretical snobs by Orwell himself. The text is structured so that reader and narrator are assumed to know full well what Winston at best suspects. This would remain true to Orwell's text even if, or when, we do exceed Orwell's understanding of totalitarianism. As I hope to show, it is not the possession of superior theoretical knowledge alone that characterizes the strategic location of the reader of *Nineteen Eighty-Four* in whatever after-year. Rather, it is the scandal of such knowledge coexisting hypocritically (in the most literal sense) with violent mechanisms of social cohesion no longer misunderstood as divine.

If our interest is in the worldliness of text and theory, then surely the place to begin is with the Oceanic ambitions for the Eleventh Edition of the Newspeak Dictionary: " 'The Eleventh Edition is the definitive edition,' he said. 'We're getting the language into its final shape—the shape it's going to have when nobody speaks anything else. When we're finished with it, people like you

139

will have to learn it all over again. You think, I dare say, that our chief job is inventing new words. But not a bit of it. We're destroying words—scores of them, hundreds of them, every day. We're cutting the language to the bone. The Eleventh Edition won't contain a single word that will become obsolete before the year 2050.'"[34] The theoretical potential of *Nineteen Eighty-Four* is strikingly different from the postmodernism of new criticisms and new novels, in covert ideological harmony with the modernization of underdeveloped labor and nations. Modernization is only apparently the production of new forms; "ungood" is a linguistic device for setting aside the history in language that might resist a purification to perfect instrumentality.

> "It's a beautiful thing, the destruction of words. Of course the great wastage is in the verbs and adjectives, but there are hundreds of nouns that can be got rid of as well. It isn't only the synonyms; there are also the antonyms. After all, what justification is there for a word which is simply the opposite of some other word? A word contains its opposite in itself. Take 'good,' for instance. If you have a word like 'good,' what sense is there in having a whole string of vague useless words like 'excellent' and 'splendid' and all the rest of them? 'Plusgood' covers the meaning, or 'doubleplusgood' if you want something stronger still. Of course we use those forms already, but in the final version of Newspeak there'll be nothing else. In the end the whole notion of goodness and badness will be covered by only six words—in reality, only one word. Don't you see the beauty of that, Winston? It was B.B.'s idea originally, of course," he added as an afterthought. [45-46]

What does our attention to the worldliness of Orwell's text, and the worldliness of our privileged, strategic location of superior theory in relation to the year 1984, require us to see in the world projected by the Eleventh Edition? A structuralist model of language, of course, a system of pure differences with no positive terms; but also a deconstruction of these oppositions as interested, anything but pure. Finally, the polarization of good/ungood as a violent structuration, the linguistic parallel to the scapegoat mechanism. From a Girardian perspective, the oppositions that structuralists are so fond of collecting (and that post-structuralists are so fond of deconstructing) occur because there are ultimately only two sides to any violent resolution. We see not how language works

140

by "itself" (we are not fooled by Syme's theory) but how it is to *be* worked, for ideological purposes, in the future. Structural oppositions that dissolve the referential power of symbolic thought are themselves deconstructed, to disable the language and the literature of the past that it renders obsolete.

This is the key to the work that Smith, as a literary intellectual, is asked to do with the public record, the social text. It is not simply (as Winston seems to think) the legitimation of the Party's day-to-day interests, but involves the transformation of daily life into a system of pure oppositions with no positive terms—a network of pure intertextuality that renders the material reality of any opposition to the State obsolete, ungood, vaporized. We know, even better than Winston, how unworldly his manuscript evidence of Party misrepresentation is, against the Party's textual power, or even against O'Brien's offhand claim of authorship of *The Theory and Practice of Oligarchical Collectivism*.

How, then, is Winston's diary contained in the worldliness of *Nineteen Eighty-Four*? What happens to the potential value of what Winston has seen, for the necessary inventory of Oceania's traces on him? *Nineteen Eighty-Four* in fact begins with Winston coming home for lunch after the Two-Minute Hate, to begin his diary: "For whom, it suddenly occurred to him to wonder, was he writing this diary? For the future, for the unborn. His mind hovered for a moment round the doubtful date on the page, and then fetched up with a bump against the Newspeak word *doublethink*. For the first time the magnitude of what he had undertaken came home to him. How could you communicate with the future? It was of its nature impossible. Either the future would resemble the present, in which case it would not listen to him, or it would be different from it, and his predicament would be meaningless" (7). We see how well, in Winston's *rezeptiontheorie*, the structures of opposition embedded in social and linguistic forms erase the future, *by nature*, in advance.

Such structures dog Winston's view of Julia as well, as he desires and hates her by turns. When she sends him something to read, he already knows she belongs to one of two oppositions, the Party or the Brotherhood. She becomes the sign of Winston's remedial education in Room 101, where he learns to transfer the violence that threatens him: "Do it to Julia!"

141

How can we estimate what has happened to the potential for "critical elaboration" in Winston's recognition of the arbitrary sign of the victim, his knowledge that violence could have chosen another? Two aspects of Girard's theory will help us read the cultural order of Oceania. (1) Girard disagrees with Frazer and the Cambridge Ritualists, by insisting that primitives are not hypocrites. The social link missing from the victim, which allows collective violence against it to remain unanswered, is not a conscious criterion for choice. The scapegoat is not seen as sacred because he is victimizable, but victimizable because he is seen as sacred. (2) Girard's mimetic model makes unnecessary Freudianism's proliferation of psychic agencies, especially an unconscious produced and repressed by a fleeting recognition of incestuous desires. *Doublethink*, directed toward the recognition of violence's arbitrary signification of The Enemy of the People, unites all Oceania in a post-Frazerian *hypocritical* practice of sacrifice. Furthermore, each shares a post-Freudian unconscious produced not by a fleeting recognition of incestuous desires, but by doublethinking the arbitrary transfer of violence and then doublethinking itself, the trace of the trace. Doublethink becomes the primary psychic agency, solid enough for Winston's mind to bump into, in the passage above.

We watch Winston fail to understand the founding of the symbolic in unanimous violence, which allows only two sides to any question, in the clothes philosophy of Oceania. Forced to wear uniforms, Winston and Julia politicize taking them off. Winston dreams of Julia's gesture of throwing her clothes aside, which seems to "annihilate a whole culture, a whole system of thought, as though Big Brother and the Party and the Thought Police could all be swept into nothingness by a single splendid movement of the arm" (29). Similarly, Winston dutifully asks his prole-informant if the capitalists wore tophats. The yes-or-no answer Winston's question allows cannot compare with what the prole offers him when he mentions that tophats could be hired for the occasion. We can see how radically this shifts the ground of understanding power, from the acquisition of property whose signified value is accepted, constant, natural, to the regulated envy and obsolescence of arbitrated symbols of (violently, mimetically contested) being.[35]

It is hard not to sense Orwell's justifiable pride in the acuteness of his own down-and-out fieldwork during the 1930s.

Although Winston's diary becomes more worldly, more interested in both circumstantial detail and theory, it never overcomes the influence of O'Brien, seen in the first chapter:

> Momentarily he caught O'Brien's eye. O'Brien had stood up. He had taken off his spectacles and was in the act of resettling them on his nose with his characteristic gesture. But there was a fraction of a second when their eyes met, and for as long as it took to happen Winston knew—yes, he *knew!*—that O'Brien was thinking the same thing as himself. An unmistakable message had passed. It was as though their two minds had opened and the thoughts were flowing from one into the other through their eyes. "I am with you," O'Brien seemed to say to him. "I know precisely what you are feeling. I know all about your contempt, your hatred, your disgust. But don't worry. I am on your side!" And then the flash of intelligence was gone, and O'Brien's face was as inscrutable as everyone else's. [13]

Winston never followed out the consequences of his critical consciousness of the scapegoat mechanism in the Two-Minute Hate, even to the point of entering it in the diary, because O'Brien understands, always already, precisely what he feels, thinking exactly what Winston thinks. The diary remains only interpersonal communication written, finally, for O'Brien, not analysis of the social text for some future. Like Winston's reductive formula for dismissing the future of his diary, the opposition of history and writing misplaces the real option of usable political analysis. Winston's "knowledge" of O'Brien is as dangerously totalized as the screen version of Goldstein.

But if O'Brien is Winston's future reader, so is the narrator of *Nineteen Eighty-Four*—and, following the narrator, so are we. If Winston is victimized by O'Brien's gaze of comprehension, how are we to place the understanding that we have been assumed by Orwell to share with the narrator, as we look back to 1984? Where did this narrator's knowledge of Winston's thought come from, and what is the context, the world of our own critical understanding?

We seem unable or unwilling to protect theory from modernization. The rise and fall of critical fame is *fama*; the model

143

behind the turbulence of the institution of criticism is the *turba*, which also requires a Girardian reading. It would be hypocritical— *hypocriticism*, in fact—to blind ourselves to the cyclothymia of the critical languages of anti-Semitism/orientalism, racism, and sexism, before the perdurable violence they comprehend. The cultural strength of critical theory for the future is now decided by the mechanism of news: not just advertising, whose model is mimetic desire, but the turbulence and the modernizing of public attention itself.

NOTES

1. See James George Frazer, *The Golden Bough* (London: Macmillan, 1911–15), 12 vols. Most pertinent to this discussion is *The Scapegoat* (1913). For Jane Harrison, see *Prolegomena to the Study of Greek Religion* (London: Cambridge University Press, 1927). The second edition contains essays by Gilbert Murray and F. M. Cornford.

2. Edward Said, "The Totalitarianism of Mind," *Kenyon Review* 29 (March 1967): 256–68.

3. René Girard, *Mensonge romantique et vérité romanesque* (Paris: Bernard Grasset, 1961); *Deceit, Desire, and the Novel* (Baltimore: Johns Hopkins University Press, 1965).

4. René Girard, *La Violence et le sacré* (Paris: Bernard Grasset, 1972); *Violence and the Sacred* (Baltimore: Johns Hopkins University Press, 1977).

5. See René Girard, "Interdividual Psychology," *Things Hidden since the Foundation of the World* (Stanford: Stanford University Press, 1987), pp. 283–431, but also *Job: The Victim of His People* (Stanford: Stanford University Press, 1988), 111–23.

6. This essay takes the position that one must follow the most comprehensive theory of the relation between myth, ritual, and literature. For an alternative approach that maps all mythographers without choosing between them, see William G. Doty, *Mythography* (University: University of Alabama Press, 1986). The choice being argued in this essay isn't who (not) to read, but how to read them all. One ought to read *everything* by Freud, Gernet, Lévi-Strauss, Frye, Vernant, and Burkert *again*, from a mimetic hypothesis.

7. For Girard on Lévi-Strauss, see especially *Violence and the Sacred*, Ch. 9. Pages 328–32 of *La Violence et le sacré* were cut from what is now the first paragraph on p. 240 of *Violence and the Sacred*. See

also Chs. 8 and 9 in *To Double Business Bound* (Baltimore: Johns Hopkins University Press, 1978).

8. Sigmund Freud, *Massenpsychologie und Ich-Analyse* (Leipzig: Internationaler Psychoanalytischer Verlag, 1921); *The Standard Edition of the Complete Psychological Works of Sigmund Freud*, trans. James Strachey (London: Hogarth Press, 1961), 19:66.

9. Sigmund Freud, *Das Ich und das Es* (Leipzig: Internationaler Psychoanalytischer Verlag, 1923); *The Standard Edition of the Complete Psychological Works of Sigmund Freud*, trans. James Strachey (London: Hogarth Press, 1955), Vol. 18.

10. Sarah Kofman, "The Narcissistic Woman: Freud and Girard," *Diacritics* 10 (September 1980): 36–45; Toril Moi, "The Missing Mother: The Oedipal Rivalries of René Girard," *Diacritics* 12 (Summer 1982): 21–31; Mary Jacobus, "Is There a Woman in This Text?," *New Literary History* 14 (Autumn 1982): 117–41. The reading of Girard in these essays is sacrificial: Girard is blamed for excluding women. Like Freud, he resents their self-sufficiency. Further, Kofman argues that Girard fears the female genitalia, which he will only refer to in Freud's German. Can the patriarchy be undone by a few women clad in trenchcoats, lurking in the bushes by Lake Lagunita? A real dialogue between Girardian and feminist theory might take up the following issues: (1) Girard's theory comprehends the patriarchal dynamics that exlude (sacralize) women; (2) the mimetic theory denies patriarchal and matriarchal "essentialism," the autonomy of narcissism as well as coquetry; (3) Girard's commitment to the quasi-theoretical potential of literary texts might challenge the emerging orthodoxy of diagnosing as masochistic Virginia Woolf's unilateral renunciation of masculine competition, anger, violence. *A Room of One's Own* (1929) insists that masculine violence is mimetic, metaphysical, contagious. Men dominate the world by crediting themselves with twice the being of women. Resentment alternates with veneration (cyclothymia), which can provoke women's writing into doubling male competitive "hysteria," blocking the possibility of seeing things nonviolently, in themselves. See Adrienne Rich, "When We Dead Awaken: Writing as Revision," in *On Lies, Secrets, and Silence: Selected Prose, 1966–78* (New York: Norton, 1979); Elaine Showalter, *A Literature of Their Own: British Women Novelists from Brontë to Lessing* (Princeton: Princeton University Press, 1977); Jane Marcus, "Art and Anger," *Feminist Studies* 4 (1978): 66–99. Despite playing an important part in the renaissance of Woolf studies, these essays add themselves to the depressing tradition of diagnosticians who know better than Woolf herself the

145

cause and cure of her illness. Perhaps we could finally try out Woolf's own hypothesis: that being angry was like being mad.

11. Robert Graves, *Greek Myths* (Harmondsworth: Penguin Books, 1972).

12. See especially Erich Neumann, *The Origins and History of Consciousness* (Princeton: Princeton University Press, 1970) and *The Great Mother* (Princeton: Princeton University Press, 1972). Neumann explains the sacred ambivalence of the feminine as "dynamic reversal," the point when a "good" feminine archetype mercurially turns against consciousness.

13. Edward Said, *The World, the Text, and the Critic* (Cambridge: Harvard University Press, 1983), esp. Ch. 8.

14. Jean Michel Ourghourlian, *Un Mime nommé desir* (Paris: Bernard Grasset, 1982).

15. Walter Burkert, *Homo Necans* (Berkeley: University of California Press, 1983); also see *Structure and History in Greek Mythology and Ritual* (Berkeley: University of California Press, 1979); *Greek Religion* (Cambridge: Harvard University Press, 1985).

16. See the papers from a 1983 conference in which both Girard and Burkert participated, in *Violent Origins*, ed. Robert G. Hamerton-Kelly (Stanford: Stanford University Press, 1987). For the first mimetic reading of Burkert's hunting hypothesis, see Andrew McKenna, "Introduction," *René Girard and Biblical Studies, Semeia 33* (Decatur, Ga.: Scholars Press, 1985), pp. 5–6.

17. Louis Gernet, *The Anthropology of Ancient Greece*, trans. John Hamilton, S.J., and Blaine Nagy (Baltimore: Johns Hopkins University Press, 1981); Jean Pierre Vernant et Pierre Vidal-Naquet, *Myth et tragédie en Grèce ancienne* (Paris: François Maspero, 1972); *Myth et tragédie en Grèce ancienne, T.II* (Paris: Éditions La Découverte, 1986); Detienne et Vernant, *Les Ruses de l'intelligence* (Paris: Flammarion, 1974).

18. See Vernant, "Ambiguité et renversement," In *Myth et tragédie*, pp. 101–31.

19. Girard, *Violence and the Sacred*, pp. 234–36; *Things Hidden since the Foundation of the World*, pp. 99–104.

20. Claude Lévi-Strauss, *Structural Anthropology*, trans. Claire Jacobson and Brooks Grundfest Schoepf (New York: Basic Books, 1963), pp. 206–31.

21. Sandor Goodhart, "Leskas Ephaske: Oedipus and Laius' Many Murderers," *Diacritics* 8:1 (Spring 1978): 55–71.

22. "Discussion avec René Girard," *Esprit* 429 (Novembre 1973): 528–63; "Interview," *Diacritics* 8:1 (Spring 1978): 31–54: Girard, *Things*

146

Hidden since the Foundations of the World, pp. 126–38; René Girard, *Le Bouc émissaire* (Paris: Grasset, 1982); trans. Yvonne Freccero as *The Scapegoat* (Baltimore: Johns Hopkins University Press, 1986).

23. See *L'Enfer des choses: René Girard et la logique de l'economie*, ed. Paul Dumouchel et Jean Pierre Dupuy (Paris: Grasset, 1982); *René Girard et le probleme du Mal*, ed. Michel Deguy et Jean-Pierre Dupuy (Paris: Grasset, 1982); *Disorder and Order: Proceedings of the Stanford International Symposium* (Sept. 14–16, 1981), ed. Paisley Livingston, in *Stanford Literature Studies* 1 (1984); *Violence et vérité: autour de René Girard*, ed. Paul Dumouchel (Paris: Grasset, 1985); *Violence and Truth, On the Work of René Girard*, ed. Paul Dumouchel (Stanford: Stanford University Press, 1988); for a full bibliography of primary and secondary sources, see *Stanford French Review* 10:1–3 (1986).

24. Northrop Frye, *Anatomy of Criticism* (Princeton: Princeton University Press, 1957).

25. Frank Lentricchia, *After the New Criticism* (Chicago: University of Chicago Press, 1980), pp. 3–26. For a more complex assessment of Frye, see *Centre and Labyrinth: Essays in Honour of Northrop Frye*, ed. Eleanor Cook, Chaviva Hošek, Jay Macpherson, Particia Parker, and Julian Patrick (Toronto: University of Toronto Press, 1983), especially the essay by Paul Ricoeur.

26. Northrop Frye, *The Secular Scripture* (Cambridge: Harvard University Press, 1976): *The Great Code* (New York: Harcourt Brace Jovanovich, 1982).

27. Northrop Frye, *The Educated Imagination* (Bloomington: Indiana University Press, 1964).

28. See my essay, "The Sparagmos of Myth Is the Naked Lunch of Mode: Modern Literature as the Age of Frye and Borges," *boundary 2* 8 (Fall 1980): 297–311.

29. Jacques Derrida, *Dissemination*, trans. Barbara Johnson (Chicago: University of Chicago Press, 1981), p. 132.

30. Girard, "Introduction" to *To Double Business Bound*, pp. vii–xvi. See also "Lévi-Strauss, Frye, Derrida and Shakespearean Criticism," *Diacritics* 3 (Fall 1973): 34–38; "Myth and Ritual in Shakespeare: *A Midsummer Night's Dream*," in *Textual Strategies: Perspectives in Post-Structural Criticism*, ed. Josué V. Harari (Ithaca: Cornell University Press, 1979), pp. 189–212; "To Entrap the Wisest": A Reading of *The Merchant of Venice*," in *Literature and Society*, ed. Edward Said (Baltimore: Johns Hopkins University Press, 1980), pp. 100–119; "Comedies of Errors: Plautus-Shakespeare-Molière," in *American Criticism in the Post-Structuralist Age*, ed. Ira Konigsberg

147

(Ann Arbor: University of Michigan Press, 1981), pp. 68–96; "Hamlet's Dull Revenge," *Stanford Literature Review* 1 (Fall 1984): 159–200.

31. I have found the following essays useful: Esther Fischer-Homberger, "Hysterie und Misogynie—ein Aspekt der Hysteriegeschichte," *Gesnerus* 26: 1–2 (1969): 117–27; Madelon Gohlke, " 'I wooed thee with my sword': Shakespeare's Tragic Paradigms," in *Representing Shakespeare: New Psychoanalytic Essays,* ed. Murray M. Schwartz and Coppélia Kahn (Baltimore: Johns Hopkins University Press, 1980), pp. 170–87; Coppélia Kahn, "Excavating 'Those Dim Minoan Regions': Maternal Subtexts in Patriarchal Literature," *Diacritics* 12 (1982): 32–41. See also Lawrence R. Schehr, "King Lear: Monstrous Mimesis," *SubStance* 11:3 (1982): 51-63; Michael Hinchliffe, "The Error of King Lear," *Actes du Centre Aixois de Recherches Anglaises* (Aix: Université de Provence, 1980).

32. Said, *The World, the Text, and the Critic,* pp. 290–92.

33. Edward Said, *Orientalism* (New York: Pantheon, 1978), pp. 23, 45; and *Blaming the Victim,* ed. Edward Said and Christopher Hutchins (London: Verso Books, 1988), p. 178.

34. George Orwell, *Nineteen Eighty-Four* (New York: New American Library, 1982), pp. 45–46.

35. See especially Dumouchel and Dupuy, *L'Enfer des choses.*

148

FRANCESCO LORIGGIO

Myth, Mythology and the Novel: Towards a Reappraisal

Reopened today, the dossier on myth and its relation to literature, the novel in particular, puts us face to face with issues that are intimidating. It is not just that the first of the terms, myth, has been variously handled by philosophers, anthropologists, psychoanalysts and theologians or that in the last few decades we have been us littérateurs, more and more sensitive to the rumblings occurring in and coming from other domains. Even the restrictions our rider imposes (within literature, the novel) cannot allay our discomfort. The perfect interdisciplinary object, a text, myth is at the same time a device that serves to encode and to decode: it convenes all the components of communication, in a manner ambiguously circular.

There is, in short, a preliminary problem, and it has to do less with the definition of myth than with its role in the production and the reception of texts, and less with either than with their interdependence. In dealing with myth, poets, novelists, dramatists have always relied on the social sciences, especially anthropology and psychoanalysis (Frazer, Freud and Jung, or, later, Lévi-Strauss, Eliade, Turner, have been archival and theoretical guides). Whence the impression that myth is one of those topics that brings the extrinsic into literature, that, being determined 'outside,' the borrowed notions, once 'inside,' affect literary works through the traces they retain of the original formulations. By contrast, the presence of myth within criticism shifts the emphasis on the dialectics, the dynamics of creation and interpretation. The matter now becomes an internal one. Where the definition of myth has been derived from is an important question but it grafts on the more primary concern about the effect of myth on the writer, the reader and the text. So that the final step of an assessment of the relation between myth and literature would have to be the fitting of the peculiarities of each individual conception to its position in the processes by which literature is made or understood.

Of course this duality does not contradict the views about myth that the sources of the writers and the critics have promoted. Indeed, it could be argued that all definitions must have built into them at least some

0319-051x/84/1104-0501 $01.25/©Canadian Comparative Literature Association

acknowledgment of reception. Fully summarized, in its most conventional version myth has been: (1) a story (2) about gods or exemplary figures, narrating events of a time before or beyond history and periodically re-enacted (ritually or, in psychoanalysis, as a symptom). That in reality social scientists have privileged some qualities at the expense of others is probably due to the extensions the parts of the definition permit. As (1), myth is a system of signs, therefore also essentially 'false'; as (2), its main property is its efficacy: it is, to those who reiterate it, also an essentially 'true' story. In this century each of these aspects — the 'material content' or the 'intensity' whith which it is experienced, to recall Cassirer's famous opposition[1] — has linked to specific approaches. For early functionalists such as Malinowski or historians of religion such as Mircea Eliade scientific analysis of the narrative of myth yields little information, and less that is pertinent, if it is not preceded by an examination of what the narrative does.[2] For structuralists such as Lévi-Strauss the mythical text is not only accessible to science but is the only depository of valid data.[3] Yet no school or single author has managed to completely expunge the pragmatic element from its account of myth. When Lévi-Strauss tells us that the Oedipus story reconciles logical alternatives which in real life must continue to collide, is he not talking, however surreptitiously, of the social relevance of myth?[4]

The last decade has, if anything, further stressed these priorities. One can perhaps see this more directly in Germany, where a rereading of the very rich local tradition on myth (going back to Schelling, Herder, the Romantics) has involved philosophers, sociologists and literary theorists and has focused quite overtly on the legitimating power of myth, on its impact on communication.[5] But, again, it is also evident in other countries and with authors who have chosen other routes and have other interests. Recently, the semanticist Thomas Pavel has revisited Eliade's

---

1 E. Cassirer, *The Philosophy of Symbolic Forms. II: Mythical Thought* (New Haven: Yale University Press 1953) 5

2 Of B. Malinowski see his *Magic, Science and Religion* (New York: Doubleday n.d.) 96 and 108. For M. Eliade see his *Myth and Reality* (New York: Harper & Row 1963) 1-20.

3 C. Lévi-Strauss, 'La Structure des mythes,' in *Anthropologie structurale* (Paris: Plon 1958) 227-55

4 M. Frank, *Der kommende Gott: Vorlesungen über die neue Mythologie* (Frankfurt a/M: Suhrkamp 1983) 77. Also important is K.-H. Bohrer, *Mythos und Moderne: Begriff und Bild einer Rekonstruktion* (Frankfurt a/M: Suhrkamp 1983).

5 Lévi-Strauss, 239

hypothesis about the existential, ritualistic effectiveness of myth to suggest that in societies which adopt two-tiered ontologies and admit the possibility that a sacred, 'true' reality may coexist side by side with a profane, 'false' one, the mythical text can be classified with non-fictional genres.[6] G.S. Kirk, in his book on myth,[7] Marcel Detienne, J.-P. Vernant and the rest of the contributors to the number the journal *Le Temps de la Réflexion* has devoted to the same topic, have, instead, downplayed the connection with ritualism or with religion. For them the term 'myth' does cover stories about gods but it can be adequately applied to stories of folkloric nature, to genealogies, proverbs, old wives' tales, general hearsay. Rather than a text it designates a field. So much so that it could easily be replaced by the adjective 'mythic.'[8] On one issue only is there common ground between these various authors. Whatever it is one considers to be mythical, it must be operative. Sacred or profane, 'true' or 'false,' myth must be differentiated from other texts in that it can be used to interpret them (while the reverse may or may not be true: it clearly is not with 'sacred' texts).

But the backdrop can still be enlarged. The cultural horizon in which the revival of myth we are witnessing today situates itself allows us to discern analogies in otherwise distant and disparate items. Gadamer's rehabilitation of prejudice, of pre-judgment, as a hermeneutic concept, as a way of fore-knowing[9]; the debate, ongoing within psychology, about the role of belief-systems in cognition[10]; notions such as that of script ('a predetermined, stereotyped sequence of actions that define a well-known situation'[11]) now current in artificial intelligence or that of secondary modeling system ('communication structures built as superstructures upon a natural linguistic plane [myth and religion, for

6 T. Pavel, 'The Borders of Fiction,' *Poetics Today* 4, No. 1 (1983) 83-8

7 G.S. Kirk, *Myth: Its Meaning and Its Function in Ancient and Other Cultures* (Cambridge: Cambridge University Press 1973) 30ff

8 See M. Detienne, 'Une Mythologie sans illusion,' *Le Temps de la Réflexion* 1 (1980) 50-3, for a good summary of an argument that is espoused by all contributors to that issue of the journal.

9 H.-G. Gadamer, *Wahrheit und Methode* (Tübingen: J.C.B. Mohr 1975) 261ff.

10 Recent surveys of the issues are in R.P. Abelson, 'Differences Between Belief and Knowledge Systems,' *Cognitive Science* 3 (1979) 355-66 and D.A. Norman, 'Twelve Issues for Cognitive Science,' *Cognitive Science* 4 (1980) 1-32.

11 R.C. Schank and R.P. Abelson, 'Scripts, Plans, and Knowledge,' in P.N. Johnson-Laird, P.C. Wason, eds., *Thinking: Readings in Cognitive Science* (Cambridge: Cambridge University Press 1977) 422

example]'[12]) developed by Soviet semioticians: all these phenomena center on the processes whereby knowledge is attained or produced and all of them refract and are refracted back on that self-interrogation, that reappraisal of the founding principles all analytical disciplines have been engaged in during the last two or three decades of their history. Social or not, the sciences have their own question of myth to contend with, and it impinges on their premises, as the many investigations on the convergences, as well as the divergences, between models, archetypes, metaphors and myth amply demonstrate. We read in the work of an eminent epistemologist: 'An examination then reveals that science and myth overlap in many ways, that the differences we think we perceive are often local ... may turn into similarities elsewhere and that fundamental discrepancies are results of different aims rather than of different methods trying to reach one and the same "rational" end ... .'[13]

In other words, if how meaning is constituted and/or assigned is the topos of the century, through myth literature partakes of that topos and the intellectual climate it embodies emblematically. Compromised though their theoretical framework may be, social scientists are not called upon to minister to domains as permeated with and exposed to myth as literary texts will be. Nor is the bond between the object and its study, between language and metalanguage as strong, as necessary elsewhere. True enough, literature and criticism are not synonymous entities. Nevertheless, quite aside from the rest (literature can represent its interaction with criticism), in some not unreasonable sense the gist of literature lies in the hypostasis it has attached to it. It demands a reply, a commentary, and that reply and that commentary may be structured according to the same precepts of the text and which the text may be vehicling. We do not know, we do not have memory of myths if not by way of their carriers, of the texts which repeat them. Implicit in such specularity is not only the idea that literature's and criticism's modernity may also be ascertained by means other than the ones we have been accustomed to (and which have highlighted the linguality, the linguistics of the texts) but a reaffirmation of literature's cognitive vocation.

Set against parameters of this sort, both the achievements and the deficiencies of the reflection on myth as it has taken place in the past can perhaps be better appreciated. The most authoritative works on the subject, those of the early Frye, seem, when reread, strikingly ambivalent.

12 J. Lotman, *The Structure of the Artistic Text* (Ann Arbor: Michigan University Press 1977) 9

13 P. Feyrabend, *Against Method* (London: NLB 1975) 296

On the one hand, Frye's conceptual apparatus is very much in tune with the perception of the issues we have today. In such recapitulatory essays as 'The Archetypes of Literature,' looking for the patterns mythological repertories furnish us, scanning the texts to see if or how they suit those patterns is justified on the basis of antecedence. Myth simply predates, comes first, historically ('Total literary history moves from the primitive to the sophisticated ... the search for archetypes is a kind of literary anthropology, concerned with the way that literature is informed by preliterary categories such as ritual, myth and folktale'[14]) and logically ('The myth is the central informing power that gives archetypal significance to the ritual and archetypal narrative to the oracle. Hence the myth *is* the archetype ... . These sacred scriptures are consequently the first documents that the literary critic has to study to gain a comprehensive view of the subject. After he has understood their structure, then he can descend from archetypes to genres ...'[15]). From this angle of vision, the fact that the models are narrative is not the drawback it might have appeared to be one or two decades ago. It reminds us that the decline of the great macronarratives, be they the Bible or Marx's eschatology, has left untouched narrativity *per se*: in actual everyday practice stories are created and deciphered through the mediation of other stories, and not of the symbolic notation of the logician. The form of the model may thus depend on orientation more than anything else, the narrativist, like some scientists, being preoccupied with how we behave rather than with how we should be behaving. On the other hand, Frye's main aspiration seems to be to improve methods of classification, and in this, his disregard for notation notwithstanding, he is closer to structuralism and affiliates. As the latter could envisage a system of systems governing individual works, so in *Anatomy of Criticism* the quest encompasses all genres and all culture-specific myths.[16] The procedures leading to the taxonomies also recall those of the structuralists. Originating patterns are postulated; they are then analyzed and projected on to the texts. Here, however, form does matter. Frye's models consist of actions and agents whose attributes, singly or in combination with others, give rise to the criteria applied in the cataloguing: the degree of superiority or inferiority to other men and the environment will put the hero in mythical, realistic, satiric or romance-like structures; as an *alazon*, a *pharmakos* or an *eiron* he will

---

14 N. Frye, 'The Archetypes of Literature,' in *Fables of Identity* (New York: Harcourt, Brace & World 1963) 12

15 Ibid. 15-17

16 N. Frye, *Anatomy of Criticism* (Princeton: Princeton University Press 1957) 215

be ensured a certain status in each of these plots, which in turn may be comic if they end happily, tragic if they end unhappily etc. Models, that is, are always endowed with some rudimentary content. Missing is any in-depth treatment of myth's narrativity, as a story and as a special story, before it is filled in with historical values. Frye is not unaware that myth may antecede in the social sciences and literary theory as well. In the 'Tentative Conclusion' to *Anatomy of Criticism* he does ask himself whether 'the verbal structures of psychology, anthropology, theology, history, law, and everything else built out of words' may not 'have been informed or constructed by the same kind of myths and metaphors that we find, in their original hypothetical form, in literature.'[17] (His answer is a cautious yes. 'Perhaps we shall eventually decide,' he says, alluding to Freud's description of the Oedipus complex, 'that we got it the wrong way round: that what happened was that the myth of Oedipus informed and gave structure to some psychological investigations ... .'[18]) And he does realize how inevitable, for someone who devotes all his work to myth and its function, certain intellectual encounters may be. In *The Great Code*, his latest book and a book he himself declares much indebted to Gadamer, Ricoeur and Ong,[19] Frye brings all modern criticism under the aegis of hermeneutics. But the two strains never meet: we are never told, in that book or elsewhere, in any extended fashion, how we are to take the ubiquity of myth, how its recurrence in literature and criticism interferes with, enriches or generally conditions our interpretations.

If we move from critical theory to the texts and, starting from the only gap Frye has left open to us, worry not so much about genres and filled-in taxonomies as about plain narrativity and its status in and for novelistic structure, what we notice first are the similarities. The novel externalizes, as it were, the cognitive dimension of production and reception. Nothing better typifies that area of fiction the concept of myth circumscribes for us than the prestige it confers on precedence, on the beginning.

This is undoubtedly more evident with the first and most influential of the poetics of myth developed by literature in our century, which is associated with modernism. The mythical man a James Joyce, a Herman Broch, a Thomas Mann envisions is always looking back for a pattern. It

17 Ibid. 352

18 Ibid. 353

19 N. Frye, *The Great Code* (New York: Harcout, Brace & Jovanovich 1982) xix

is an 'archaizing attitude,'[20] a 'life in quotation'[21] which generates a distance to then abolish it by retrieval. The writer is in sympathy with these ideals and these procedures. For him too, myth belongs to other times and other places, to an elsewhere to be elicited. Except that the recovery does not quite occur. Irrespective of the project or the structure (a work may rewrite a myth to reflect contemporary themes and topic or locate the story in a modern setting and refer to myth), the novel can never coincide with the past it is resuscitating. The very essence of the material evoked, which usually comes from specific sources, forbids it. Thus also a second aspect. Not only are the sources often authors and single texts, but the authors and the single texts — Hesiod, Homer, Ovid, *The Iliad, The Odyssey, The Metamorphoses*, and so on — are those which have nurtured the whole tradition of Western High Culture. Scriptural, with a Joyce, a Broch, a Mann myth is effective in proportion to its inactuality: models are immaculately preserved yet available to an ever diminishing public.

But our century has seen at least another attempt to relate myth to literature. The stance countering modernism surfaced, very opportunely, in the Sixties, with the demise of that movement, and has been most cogently voiced by Leslie Fiedler. It advocates a closer alliance between literature and the urban, industrial world, the 'media mass-produced and mass-distributed by machines,'[22] hence a fiction which would deify, rather than antiquity, 'Hitler and Stalin, John Kennedy and Lee Oswald ... or Jean Harlow and Marilyn Monroe and Humphrey Bogart, Charley Parker and Louis Armstrong and Lennie Bruce, Geronimo and Billy the Kid, the Lone Ranger and Fu Manchu and the Bride of Frankenstein,'[23] along with Superman and other comic book heroes.

Fiedler's proposal has not met with much critical success. In part, the lack of favour is due to the competition (the most eloquent spokesmen for modernist myth were the practitioners themselves, authors of indisputable reputation. Fiedler is a critic and does not seem to have inspired any major writers). For the greater part, it is due to that perduring mental habit which continues to keep the study of classical or primitive myths separate from the study of modern myths even when the social

---

20 T. Mann, 'Freud and the Future,' in *Essays of Three Decades*, trans. H.T. Lowe-Porter (New York: Knopf 1947) 424

21 Ibid. 425

22 L. Fiedler, 'Cross the Border — Close the Gap,' in *Collected Essays* (New York: Stein and Day 1971) 481

23 Ibid. 482

sciences have ceased doing so. Like a Detienne or a Vernant, Fiedler widens the scope of his definition. Without renouncing the modernist device of allusion, he changes its finality, adds to it. The poetics of popular art he abides by promotes a tradition that has its abode in Northern lore and American culture (the exhortation to 'cross out those overpaid accounts'[24] to Parnassus and the Mediterrenean basin dates back to Whitman). The history of the genre is greatly affected. Whereas the modernist view incorporates the novel in a discourse initiating literarily but not novelistically in mythical discourse, proceeding to an epic phase, then to the bourgeois fiction of the problematic hero and completing its cycle with the twentieth-century return to myth, Fiedler does not require us to go that far into the past. For him modes of diffusion are criteria sufficiently decisive. In his writings the birth and rise of the novel are transposed to Gutenberghian society, a milieu modern and incomparable and which, by reordering hierarchies, by establishing the primacy of prose over verse, sets the stage for the prosperous future the genre was to enjoy in later centuries. For the same reasons, the sources of the novel need not be literary, inscribed in texts. The cultural past is now rooted in a period, Romanticism or thereabouts, whose effects are still with us, or is constantly created and recreated by the electronic media. It can therefore also exist euhemeristically. Ecumenical, demotic, the patterns are daily reasserted anew. Or, to reformulate it starting from the other side, distance having been reduced, abolished, the present is always archaic, always original. In Fiedler's version, semantic, ontological barriers dissolve. John Kennedy and Frankenstein can both be mythical. Not insignificantly, among the subgenres of Fiedler's larger category is the New Journalism, which reports on non-fictional topics in a fictional style, treats, in Norman Mailer's phrase, 'History as the Novel, the Novel as History.'[25]

In spite of the differences in circulation, appeal, authority, these two positions cannot but be thought of together. Not simply because they confirm literature's concern with how knowledge and understanding are produced, generated. Fiedler confronts us with a novel which, instead of searching for foundations, is aiming to be itself foundational, which proclaims itself ready to serve as source, as reference for other texts. This brings a further perspective to the debate on myth. In recent years literary studies has had more than its share of dichotomies whose

24 Quoted in Fiedler, 481.

25 This is the subtitle of N. Mailer's *The Armies of the Night* (New York: Signet Books 1968).

inventorial space cuts across thematic borders. The dyad coined by Roland Barthes and pitting the *texte de jouissance* against the *texte du plaisir* or the *scriptible* against the *lisible* or the subsequent polarity his terms fostered (*illisible/lisible*) come quickly to mind.[26] Within archetypal criticism, Frye and J. White have distinguished narratives employing myth explicitly from narratives in which myth is implicit, the mythological from the mythical.[27] But these dualities, theoretically neutral, hide, sanction, strong empirical and historical allegiances. Between Frye or Barthes and the T.S. Eliot of the celebrated review of *Ulysses*, for whom the 'mythical method'[28] inaugurates a new era in fiction, the jump is minimal: it is the James Joyce, the Thomas Mann or equivalent, the writer of the *scriptible*, the *illisible*, of the mythological, who embodies what is worthwhile in the twentieth-century novel. To say, as Fiedler does, that the mythical is also a plausible option, that literature can have a more active cultural function, relativizes modernist preferences, but more than that it exposes the asymmetry, the discrepancy of modernist premises and modernist antinomies: the real impugned, the *lisible*, the mythical, comprises more texts, synchronically or diachronically. Split into two oppositional halves, myth has this advantage over other approaches to the novel: that it mobilizes every facet, that, before channeling them towards a single dénouement, it shows how the cognitive, the structural and the evaluative, the question of the beginning and the question of the literariness interlock one into the other.

The particulars of these connections and the sense emanating from them, their relevance for the novel as we might conceive it today, can be grasped only through the texts. Let us then look in greater detail at the way the novel summons the past or articulates its own presentness.

Works such as *Ulysses* are actually large, protracted analogies. A number of devices can procure the liaison with the archaic materials, the model patterns. Titles, chapter headings are the most usual, but names of characters or notes at the end of the book will also do. Some novelists have tried outright juxtaposition: the protagonist of John Bowen's *A World Elsewhere* interpolates parts of the Philotectes myth,

26 For R. Barthes's oppositions see his *S/Z* (Paris: Seuil 1970) and *Le Plaisir du texte* (Paris: Seuil 1973). The 'lisible'/'illisible' opposition has been best described by P. Hamon in 'Note sur les notions de norme et de lisibilité en stylistique,' *Littérature* 14 (1974) 114-22.

27 See N. Frye, 'Myth, Fiction and Displacement,' in *Fables of Identity*, 36ff. and J.J. White, *Mythology and the Modern Novel* (Princeton: Princeton University Press 1971) 8.

28 T.S. Eliot, 'Ulysses, Order and Myth,' *Dial* 85, No. 5 (1923) 483

which he is rewriting, in his autobiographical story; Ann Quin's *Passages* is arranged typographically so that mythical correspondences may appear, in separate columns, next to the straight narrative, as in the following excerpt:

| Depicted on vase:
Wheels suspended
in Palace of
Hades/Persephone.
Two kinds solid
and spoked. | Decision between madness and security is imminent.

Approach of death-madness the only way out?[29] |

Parallel making does have its rules and regulations. The same analogy may be distributed among several characters or one character may benefit of several analogues. Mixed references are not infrequent (in Joyce's *Ulysses* semitic sources often complement classical ones; in Wolfe's *Of Time and the River* a chapter is entitled 'Faustus and Helen'). But the crucial precepts are intentionality and perceptibility. To be operative, the parallel of the mythological novel must be systematic and visibly anchored to the logic of the text. If they are not continuous, the devices will have no influence over plot and narration. Conversely, motivation will be for nought if it is obscure, if it is not given the right textual, surface expression. When in the early pages of *Doktor Faustus* we read about the 'horrible bargain'[30] compacted by the protagonist, we know what is being recalled: we are expecting it. In the 'Cyclops' episode of *Ulysses* the less than intrepid Bloom will honour the past constantly evoked on his behalf by puffing his cigar in the nationalist's face. But, again, the analogy must be properly activated. A certain equilibrium is necessary. Too many allusions and the work slides dangerously close to the rewriting of the myth, not enough allusions or allusions not immediately discernible and the work will be deprived of the benefits obtaining with the analogy.

Where the analogy is adequately formed, the explicitness of the intertextuality has its repercussions on the intratextuality. Each quotation is a kind of literary anamnesis: with the sources, it announces

29 Quoted in J.J. White, *Mythology and the Modern Novel*, 186.

30 T. Mann, *Doctor Faustus*, trans. H.T. Lowe-Porter (London: Secker and Warburg 1949) 4

genealogies, traditions (many other authors throughout the centuries may have resorted to that one specific allusion). The influx of external data foregrounds, magnifies internal processes. Semantically, the allusion will signal to us that we are facing a text of hybrid referentiality. Besides the world populated by the modern-dress characters and subject to verisimilitude, we must be prepared to accept a world endowed with the attributes generally connoted by the adjective 'mythical' and which is literary by statute. We are asked to suspend disbelief, to respect the demands of realism and to perceive the text as fictional and realistic illusion as a convention among others. Structurally, the myths in the texts will function like an extra fabula[31]: conjured up in fragments but always carrying, synecdochically, the whole with them, they provide the text with ready-made simulacra of the characters and of the events narrated or still to be narrated. Both paradigmatic and syntagmatic relations are involved. Mythological references tend first of all to enhance the text's 'depth,' since to fulfil their role they must be able to tie in and bear witness to internal tensions, the division of the narration in levels. The fabula system transplanted from the outside reinforces coherence but also acts as the norm from which the modern variant can deviate, therefore ratifying, by counterpoint, the individuality of a work. Now centripetal, now centrifugal, analogies will install a dialectic at the heart of a novel's organization. Modern trajectories may scale down the superhuman deeds of the mythical characters, may be counterinformational plots. Ulysses of the crafty mind, the master rhetorician, becomes Bloom the prudent or, in Alberto Moravia's *Il disprezzo*, Molteni, the reluctant writer of 'B' film scripts. Penelope is the oversexed Molly or Emilia Molteni, the wife faithful more out of custom than for real love. Or, it may, the analogy, infer the rite beneath the prosaic, degraded modern gesture, infuse order in 'the panorama of futility which is contemporary history' (it is Eliot's justification of the mythical method[32]). Syntagmatically, the extra fabula is also fully equipped. Contracts, trials, deficiencies and reintegrations, all the stages of the hero's progress are there. The plot of the modern variant can refuse some of the specific contents of the parallel story. It cannot reject the diegetic program, the macrocontent the text has summoned. We know what choices await the character for whose fabula the Oedipus myth has been exhumed and his

---

31 The term is, of course, derived from Russian Formalism. See B. Tomachevsky [Tomaševskij], 'Thématique,' in T. Todorov ed., *Théorie de la littérature: Textes des formalistes russes* (Paris: Seuil 1965) 263-307.

32 T.S. Eliot, 483

personal flair and excentricity are, narrationally, of no great matter. The concept of prefiguration, whereby parts of the plot are foreshadowed by the analogy, is central to the criticism of the mythological novel. The privileges and/or limits of the writer (it has been a rule of thumb in force at least since Poe's 'Philosophy of Composition' that to tell stories one must know the ending in advance) are passed on to the reader. In *Ulysses*, in *Doktor Faustus*, in *A World Elsewhere* events do not occur; they co-occur. The narration is deliberately inserted in a system of traces, of declared similarities. It predicts itself. As receivers we are always dealing with two stories, one of which is over when we begin the other. We are constantly rereading, or, if to be a critic is, in its lowest common denominator, to have already read, reading critically.

Semantically, structurally, the mythological novel is not difficult to place. Most rubrics devised for the classifying of metafictional narratives would offer some compatible criteria. John Barth's notion of literary 'exhaustion,' of a literature which, having run out of plots, falls back on those already recorded, is a case in point.[33] Another is Gérard Genette's category of the *hypertextuel*, a section of the larger domain of the *transtextuel* (wherein goes all literature to the second degree) housing the texts that imitate other texts.[34] But the suggestive associations come to us from tradition. A *Ulysses*, a *Doktor Faustus* can be profitably compared to the enriched narratives of the past. They are works that adapt within and to a modern prose genre procedures akin to those of allegorical and figural forms (both of which require recourse to other texts and depend on materials, on patterns serving to encode and to decode: for patristic and medieval hermeneutics events in the Old Testament anticipate events in the New Testament).[35]

Given the properties of the mythological novel, the mythical text could be defined, very simply, as a text allowing no prefiguration and no metafictional extensions. This, however, would not do complete justice to the complexity of the original opposition. Even if they lack the range of the systematic allusion, the novelist does have other methods by which to organize the coherence of his works. Until the twentieth century, references to classical antiquity, used then to embellish or to fortify

---

33 J. Barth, 'The Literature of Exhaustion,' in M. Bradbury ed., *The Novel Today* (Glasgow: Fontana/Collins 1977) 70-83

34 For the terms 'transtextuel' and 'hypertextuel' see chapter 1 of G. Genette's *Palimpseste* (Paris: Seuil 1982).

35 The pioneering text on these forms is E. Auerbach's 'Figura,' now in *Scenes from the Drama of European Literature* (New York: Meridian Books 1959) 11-76.

a sentence or a paragraph and bearing upon the narration in its totality only cumulatively through recurrence, were themselves one of them. As frequent as mythological metaphors in the eighteenth- or nineteenth-century novel and also of local expediency are proverbs and generalizations. They relate to their context by announcing the class the characters or the events described fit into, by setting for them public, ideal parallels. In Balzac's *Les Paysans* we often find passages such as the following: 'Le paysan a pour sa demeure l'instinct qu'a l'animal pour son nid ou pour son terrier, et cet instinct éclatait dans toutes les dispositions de cette chaumière. D'abord, la fenêtre et la porte ... .'[36] What superlativeness, what universality does the initial statement bestow on the 'chaumière'! In this other passage, from the translation of Giovanni Verga's *I Malavoglia*, the proverb functions almost like a title: 'The house by the medlar tree was full of people. The proverb says: "Sad is the house where there is the wake for the husband!" All those who walked past, seeing the poor Malavoglia standing at the doorway with grimy faces and hands in their pockets, shook their heads and said: "Poor comare Maruzza! Now trouble has come to her house!" '[37] Still other devices are the pedagogical clauses, the appeals to the reader. These may call upon one's ability to process textual units (*Les Paysans*: 'Quelqu'un qui se serait rappelé le pavillon comme il est décrit plus haut, l'aurait cru rebâti ...'[38]) or one's knowledge of the author's other works (*Les Paysans*: 'On a pu voir ailleurs le personnage d'un régisseur songeant à ses intérêts et à ceux de son maître [voir *Un début dans la vie: Scènes de la vie privée*[39]]) or one's expertise as a member of a group (*Les Paysans*: 'Quiconque a voyagé dans le Midi, dans l'Ouest de la France, en Alsace, autrement que pour se coucher à l'auberge ... doit reconnaître la vérité de ces observations ...'[40]) and may be retrospective or prospective (*Les Paysans:* Mais le général comptait, comme on va le voir, sans son Gaubertin'[41]).

All of the above should interest us, but pedagogical clauses and appeals to the reader particularly. For they can be attributed to a specific voice, the author's or his surrogate. Insofar as it names the entities taking

36 H. de Balzac, *Les Paysans*, in *La Comédie humaine* (Paris: Seuil 1966) VI, 20

37 G. Verga, *The House by the Medlar Tree*, trans. R. Rosenthal (Berkeley and Los Angeles: University of California Press 1984) 40

38 Balzac, 62

39 Ibid. 44

40 Ibid. 60

41 Ibid. 48

part in the fictional contract, the novel of the eighteenth or the nine-teenth century engages in its own sort of metafiction. But precisely, it is a metafiction achieved intratextually, by fractioning the text, instead of in-tertextually, by duplication, as in the mythological novel. Though the knowledge guaranteeing structural cohesiveness is outside of the novel, it is invoked by operations which, by bringing the process of enunciation into the enunciated, leave their mark in the text.

To underscore the role of these breaks in the flow of the narration, it is enough to rejoin them to their twentieth-century future. The pages which in works such as *Les Faux-Monnayeurs* or *Point Counter Point* are en-trusted to implied author or his figurehead (a writer of fame or some in-dividual aspiring to become one) can be considered expansions of the authorial intrusion, have as their antecedents those pages which guide us through the maze of gestures and faces. The device Gide's and Huxley's works are best noted for epitomizes all the ambiguities of the pedagogical clause or the appeal to the reader. As a form of specularity, *mise en abyme*, increases textual fragmentation. As a miniaturized analogy of a portion of text which may look backward or forward to events already happened or still to happen, it can provide some degree of readability or further complicate the structure with the expectations it creates. As both, it lays bare the strategy of a whole lineage of fiction. Contrary to mythological allusions, which buttress narratives with other narratives, *mise en abyme* can in some occasions be the manifestation of a profound pessimism about narration and its fate. *Les Faux-Monnayeurs, Point Counter Point*, even Proust's *Recherche*, rest on the conviction that nar-ration is no longer feasible. The story escapes the control of the author, is not finished or not begun; essayism, confession, argumentation enter the text. The final outcome are novels such as Nabokov's *Pale Fire*, in which the commentary overtakes the narrative, or Giorgio Manganelli's *Nuovo commento*, a string of footnotes to a non-existent text, a work in which narration is always postulated but always absent.

A third term must then be introduced in the opposition between mythological and mythical fiction. Mythological novels have in common with the novels of the authorial intrusion the intent to reinforce, to clarify narration. They differ from them in the means: the allusion is im-personal, usually not enunciated. Voice also distinguishes mythological novels from novels employing proverbs or generalizations, which, though they are a 'savoir a priorique,'[42] 'des unités de sens de longue

---

42 C. Grivel, 'Esquisse d'une théorie des systèmes doxiques,' *Degrés* 24-25 (hiver 1980-81) d1

durée,'[43] something like collective short short stories, are of intratextual application only and can be attributed to speakers, to the author. In this, by implying that a narrative can directly, without mediating interventions, affect other narratives, a *Ulysses*, a *Doktor Faustus* is in reality closer to mythical novels: both overestimate narration.

Complicities, connections such as these prove that the concept of myth must be worked into a theory of the novel.[44] But, to repeat an observation we made at the beginning of our foray into the realm of structure, inclusion is not without its price. Myth revises, and drastically, accepted assumptions. Any text, of any type (we know how many intrusions, how many appeals to the reader, how many proverbs serial novels contain) can be mythical, if it generates the appropriate consensus. Yet the very possibility that the mythical may be more easily accosted sociologically, may be a theoretical virtuality, a notion formally not verifiable, makes it problematical: after all, the other categories *can* be described. The embarrassment does not diminish when we sidestep the question of diffusion on the grounds that it is the narrativity that is retained of a text received as mythical and that, some texts fulfilling that requirement better than others, some measure of formal differentiation can and must be contemplated. Our survey of the techniques of textual structuring seems to indicate that metafictionality has been a permanent condition of the novel. This willy nilly turns the mythical into a project. Simple narration precedes the novel historically and logically but within the genre simplicity is not the rule.

To account for some of the procedures of the mythical novelist, Benveniste's now long-standing discrimination between *discours* and *histoire* is still of the greatest convenience.[45] The terms, it might be remembered, designate forms of linguistic usage. The first, held together by deixis, by the spatio-temporal coordinates harking back to a first per-

---

43 Ibid. d19

44 The risk is that of incompleteness, and it is a serious one. A good instance is J. Kristeva's *Le Texte du roman* (The Hague: Mouton 1970). In this book the author recognizes (p. 15) the 'capital importance' of the twentieth-century return to myth for an overall view of the novel, but informs us that it falls outside the scope of her study. Yet one of her conclusions is that the novel is to be allocated, within Western discourse, to the ideology of the sign. Since a Joyce or a Mann resort to devices whose function echoes those of patristic typology and of figural methods and can be linked to the expedients used by eighteenth- and nineteenth-century novelists, one cannot but suspect her metahistory.

45 É. Benveniste, 'Les Relations de temps dans le verbe français,' in *Problèmes de linguistique générale* (Paris: Gallimard 1966) 237-50

son speaker, attests of the role of subjectivity in language. The second alludes to the features of the third-person component, to a situation in which, speaker participation excluded, events appear to tell, to narrate themselves. Taken at face value, the strategy of the mythical novelist consists primarily in avoiding *discours*. Save for that of a first person narrator, who is represented (he is a character), no voices explicitly carrying references to other texts or directions for reading are to infiltrate the text. What is prohibited, in sum, are the devices by which all that can detract from the events and narration is brought into the text. The subtraction of the voices has as its corollary the subtraction of the contents they enunciate. Not every mythical writer can fully obey the prescriptions of one of the earliest decalogues of detective fiction, which disallowed (because they 'hold up the action'), among other things, 'long descriptive passages,' 'literary dallying with side issues,' 'subtly worked out character analysis,'' "atmospheric preoccupations," '[46] but they are symptomatic.

Several consequences follow. Free of deictics, *histoire*, if we accept Benveniste's determination of it, is mute, silent language. Thus, the elimination of the authorial intrusion would leave the novel with only one voice: that of the characters. Reticence also reducing verticality, surface and deep structures becoming less easily separated, the text can appear to be without breaks, uniform, homogeneous. Semantically, both the absence of references to analogous texts and the absence of interventions returns the novel to one space-time continuum. There is no extra fabula, no past to contrast to the contemporariness of the characters, nor does the 'here and now' from which the author addresses the reader or comments on the events stand out against the 'then' of the story. No dialectic between the levels mars the unity of the text. It is why works such as Nicholas Meyer's *The Seven-Percent-Solution* (in which Freud helps Sherlock Holmes to overcome his cocaine habit) or Philip José Farmer's *To Your Scattered Bodies Go* (in which Sir Francis Burton encounters Mark Twain, the real life model for Lewis Carroll's Alice, apemen and moon dwellers), while reminiscent of mythological novels in their mixture, cannot belong to that category. The characters, often fixtures of the collective imagination when they are book-originated, are only name tags: they do not send back to any specific story they might come from. The text can conjoin the worlds they imply into a superordinate one, with its own uninterrupted time and space. This is why, too,

---

46 S.S. Van Dine, 'Twenty Rules for Writing Detective Stories,' in H. Haycroft ed., *The Art of the Mystery Story* (New York: Scribner's 1946) 191-2

the function of proverbs, generalizations, clichés changes as soon as they are imbedded in the narration, where, no longer attached to the system of supervising voices, they have no effect on the events.

It should scarcely need pointing out that to insist on only an ideological interpretation of the mythical, to only denounce the transparency it may be founded on would be only to opt for the most facile, most comfortable solution. The story in which narration pretends to tell itself is no less constructed than the story which openly displays its functioning. To decry the illusion because it is an illusion is to deny the mythical the prerogative accorded to other texts, to reproach it for what is elsewhere appreciated: form. The fact is that homogeneity, unity does not have to be identified with popular literature. It is, again, a goal of literature as such. For a Cesare Pavese, a very refined writer and one who delved into the question of myth most thoroughly, the novelist's task is to reconcile 'the rhythm of contemporary life,' rendered with 'the same causal immediacy of a Cellini, a De Foe, a chatterbox met at a café,' with a 'contemplative detachment,' the penchant for structures which are 'intellectual' and 'symbolic.'[47] Free indirect discourse, which is a purely literary phenomenon (it has no parallel in natural speech) and whose fortunes, incidentally, grew out of the provisional eclipse of authorial presence in the late nineteenth century, combines voice and narration, first person and third person. For his own part, the writer striving to reach the public beyond the very confined group readership differences of social rank and education create, does not always clash with the 'serious' author. One recalls the briskness of the dialogues in the works of Chandler and Hammett, how formally motivated they are, how they let narration take charge without any hitches, any retardations. The poetics of reduction puts severe constraints on mimesis. The mythical writer cannot 'faire concurrence à l'État Civil,'[48] a program, this, which would commit him to epic totality and oblige him to insert specialized information (about upper or lower class life, about places the average reader has not seen) he would then have to normalize through commentary and/or allusion. Not detail but actuality is his concern. In the James Bond type of thriller a name, a passing reference to the colour of someone's skin is enough to set in motion an entire encyclopedia of cultural data. A lot can be left unsaid. Quick to seize on to the local, transitory issues, mythical particulars update the universal without disturbing narration.

47 C. Pavese, 'Intervista alla radio,' in *Letteratura americana e altri saggi* (Toronto: Einaudi 1962) 294. My translation.

48 Balzac, 'Avant-Propos,' *La Comédie humaine*, I, 52

Literarily, what is at stake with myth, then, is, together with textual coherence, textual time. Narratology has examined at some length the different durational values of each of a work's strata. It has shown how fabula systems, patterned on the anthropological, cultural models of a society, have a longer life-span, historically, than plots and the techniques of exposition they entail, and how these last longer than discourse materials, which experience the fastest turn-over.[49] The notion of textual polychrony does much to specify our dichotomies. Proverbs, generalizations (when linked to a voice) or mythological allusions install both a continuity and a discontinuity into the text: the time of the events is a time gone by, but it is analogous to authorial time and can be explained by it. Being able to count on an extra fabula derived from a canonic, chronologically distant narrative, the mythological novel, especially, can enhance the slowness, the resilience of the past vis-à-vis the topsy-turvy present, while ensuring, by means of the symmetries, that some of that constancy remain with the contemporaneity being depicted. In literature mythology buys time. Allying the text to a before still in force (and the persistence of which is part of what is being narrated) propels it into the future: the structure will be as valid tomorrow or fifty years from now as it is today. On the opposite end, the mythical, which has no hiatus to exploit, whose levels are less distinct, is more firmly tied to the present. Much like myths, which if they refer to constellations have a seasonal periodicity and if they refer to the sun and the moon must be reinvented daily and bring to mind, as Lévi-Strauss has remarked,[50] the serial novel, the literature of the industrial age, the novel will, at one stage of its history, have at its disposal the alternative of quality, of the structure that stays and the alternative of quantity, of repetition.

It is here that the discussion on the congruences or incongruences between the uses of myth that the novel, literary theory and the social sciences have made should begin. One aspect of this, at least, must be mentioned.

Myth, we have said, is a test-case for criticism for the way it contradicts and amends some influential dichotomies. To the degree that the extra fabula encourages deviation, stylistic and otherwise, mythological novels are unreadable. However, to the degree that the same fabula endows them with clearly perceivable directives they are also eminently readable, and will be all the more so in the long run. With the works of a

---

49 See C. Segre, 'Narrative Structures and Literary History,' *Critical Inquiry* 3 (1976) 271-9.

50 C. Lévi-Strauss, *L'Origine des manières de table* (Paris: Plon 1968) 104-6

Joyce, a Broch, a Mann, second readings better actualize the suggestions of the devices governing their structure. Mythical novels, readable by virtue of the subject matter and/or their form (organized to elicit, to facilitate consensus), will suffer the other, contrasting fate: when deprived of the context from which they receive their persuasiveness, they are practically unreadable, become different than what they were. In mythological texts the discrepancy between the time of the events and the time of interpretation is congenital to the structure. In mythical texts it is not: a science fiction novel will be fiction and no longer science fiction once its immediacy is dispersed, once its predictions and fantasies are common reality.

But the relation between time, the text and interpretation is more far-reaching yet. With mythological novels critical analysis is almost tautological. The patterns criticism requires for its reading are well preserved but the allusions, the symmetries the text privileges constitute already an interpretation of the source. With the mythical novel interpretation cannot get to its object of study without modifying it. The text will seek to abolish the embodiments of the distance between the story and the structuring or receiving consciousness, but distance is what criticism must continuously claim for itself in order to survive. The problem is one every social science which has thought about its premises or about its data-gathering methods has had to come to grips with.[51] Not by coincidence, in literary theory it has been most vividly illustrated in a work about myth. In the last essay of Barthes's *Mythologies* myth is composed of two sign-systems, one of which can act as signifier to the other. In the combinations that ensue, the signified of the first system can be full, as end term of the first system, or empty, as starting term of the second system or just maintain a neutral position in the two-levelled larger system. To the three possible structurings correspond modes of emission and reception of myth. The producer of myths and the mythologue, whose job it is to demystify mythical structures, to show them for what they are, are to be dissociated from the consumer, who is the only one perceiving the mythical process in full working order, as an 'inextricable whole of meaning and form.'[52] To apprehend mythical semiosis, to decipher myth the critic must therefore be careful not to re-

51 For the problem of the observer as it pertains to anthropology and the social sciences in general C. Lévi-Strauss's 'Place de l'anthropologie et problèmes posés par son enseignement,' in *Anthropologie structurale*, 396ff. and 'L'Œuvre du *Bureau of American Ethnology* et ses leçons,' in *Anthropologie structurale deux* (Paris: Plon 1973) 7off. are still very useful texts.

52 R. Barthes, *Mythologies*, trans. A. Lavers (London: Jonathan Cape 1972) 124

spond to its dynamics. He must arm himself with an aloofness which will dislocate him from the society he lives in. For better or for worse, the knowledge he gains is that of one who is 'outside' by choice. Barthes himself was later more uncertain about the theoretical foundation of the mythologue's function. In *Éléments de sémiologie* a metalanguage is a language to subsequent metalanguages,[53] in *Leçon* voluntary, professional exteriority is, finally, 'insoutenable.'[54] We may ourselves wonder if the mythologue can be a mythologue without being a consumer, if he is not a consumer of some other, more restricted belief-system. But for now it is sufficient to notice that outsidedness can be temporal as well as spatial. The literary poetician must by definition be out of 'sync' with mythical texts. He must first de-actualize them, retrodate them. As myth presents it to us, the novel may be the paramount genre it is also because it records in full, in both of its manifestations, criticism's predicament.

Carleton University

53 R. Barthes, 'Éléments de sémiologie,' in *Le Degré zéro de l'écriture* suivi de *Éléments de sémiologie* (Paris: Gonthier n.d.) 167

54 R. Barthes, *Leçon* (Paris: Seuil 1978) 36-7

Philip Rahv

THE MYTH AND THE POWERHOUSE

One must know how to ask questions: the question is who was Ariadne and which song did the sirens sing?—FRIEDRICH GEORG JUENGER.

Much has been written of late about myth. What it is and what it will do for us has been widely debated, yet I cannot see that any clear statement of the intrinsic meaning of present-day mythomania has emerged from the discussion. The exponents of myth keep insisting on its seminal uses, appealing indiscriminately to Yeats and Joyce and Mann and other examplars of the modern creative line, while the opponents point to the regressive implications of the newfangled concern with myth, charging that at bottom what it comes to is a kind of nebulous religiosity, a vague literary compromise between skepticism and dogma, in essence a form of magico-religious play with antique counters in a game without real commitments or consequences.

To be sure, not all exponents of myth are of one type. Some make no excessive claims; others have turned into sheer enthusiasts who blow up myth into a universal panacea, proclaiming that the "reintegration of the myth" will not only save the arts but will lead to no less than the cure of modern ills and ultimate salvation. So extravagant have been their claims that even Jacques Maritain, who is hardly to be accused of a naturalistic view of myth, has been moved to rebuke them, primarily for confusing metaphysical and poetic myths, that is confusing the fictions composed by the poet *qua* poet (which may be called myths, if at all, only in a loose analogical sense) with the great myths deriving their power solely from the belief that men have in them.[1] For myth actually believed in is not understood as a symbolic form, competing with other such forms, but as truth pure and simple.

Now why should a distinction so elementary be generally overlooked by the cultists of myth? For the very good reason, obviously,

that it is this very cultism which enables them to evade the hard
choice between belief and unbelief. After all, now that the idea of
myth has been invested in literary discourse with all sorts of intriguing
suggestions of holiness and sacramental significance, one can talk
about it as if it were almost the same thing as religion, thus circumventing the all-too-definite and perhaps embarrassing demands of
orthodoxy even while enjoying an emotional rapport with it. At the
same time, myth having been somehow equated with the essence of
poetry, it becomes possible to enlist its prestige along with that of religion. The mythomaniac puts himself in the position of speaking
freely in the name both of poetry and religion without, however, making himself responsible to either. But it should be evident that in the
long run neither benefits from so forced a conjunction. It deprives
them equally of specific definition and commitment; and this, I take
it, is the implicit point of M. Maritain's critical remarks.

The discussion of myth has led some literary men to undertake
interpretations of it in terms of its origins and fundamental import
in the history of culture. Such interpretations are in the main more
wishful than accurate, running counter to the findings at once of
such noted philosophical students of myth as Ernst Cassirer and anthropologists and ethnologists like Malinowski, Jane Harrison, Lord
Raglan, A. M. Hocart, S. M. Hooke, et al. The fact is that the current literary inflation of myth is not in the least supported by the
authoritative texts in this field of study. Typical is the approach of
a distinguished literary critic, who on the subject of myth proceeds
entirely without discretion. Myth is for him "the cartograph of the
perennial human situation," and he contends that in myth alone can
we hope to encounter "a beckoning image of the successful alliance
of love and justice, the great problems of the race from its dark
beginnings." In other words: Back to myth if you want to be saved!
It leaves one wondering how that sort of thing can possibly be squared
with anything to be found, for instance, in the late Professor Cassirer's
numerous, painstaking, and truly imaginative inquiries into myth.
What we do realize in reading Cassirer, however, is that contemporary mythomania makes for the renewal in our time of the symbolic-
allegorical treatment of myth favored by the romantics, who saw in
myth a source of higher teachings and ultra-spiritual insights, converting it into a magic mirror that reflected their heart's desire. As Cas-

sirer observes, the romantic philosophers and poets in Germany were the first to embrace myth with rapture, identifying it with reality in the same way as they identified poetry with truth: from then on "they saw all things in a new shape. They could not return to the common world—the world of the *profanum vulgus*."[2] The cultism of myth is patently a revival of romantic longings and attitudes.

It seems as if in the modern world there is no having done with romanticism—no having done with it because of its enormous resourcefulness in accommodating the neo-primitivistic urge that pervades our culture, in providing it with objects of nostalgia upon which to fasten and haunting forms of the past that it can fill with its own content. And the literary sensibility, disquieted by the effects of the growing division of labor and the differentiation of consciousness, is of course especially responsive to the vision of the lost unities and simplicities of times past. Now myth, the appeal of which lies precisely in its archaism, promises above all to heal the wounds of time. For the one essential function of myth stressed by all writers is that in merging past and present it releases us from the flux of temporality, arresting change in the timeless, the permanent, the ever-recurrent conceived as "sacred repetition." Hence the mythic is the polar opposite of what we mean by the historical, which stands for process, inexorable change, incessant permutation and innovation. Myth is reassuring in its stability, whereas history is that powerhouse of change which destroys custom and tradition in producing the future—the future that at present, with the fading away of the optimism of progress, many have learned to associate with the danger and menace of the unknown. In our time the movement of history has been so rapid that the mind longs for nothing so much as something permanent to steady it. Hence what the craze for myth represents most of all is the fear of history. But of that later. First let us turn to the genetic approach to myth developed by the scholars in this field, comparing it with some of the literary notions which, by infusing myth with the qualities that properly belong to art, have brought about widespread confusion as to the differences between the mythic and the aesthetic mode of expression.

The most commonly accepted theory among scholars is the so-called ritual theory defining myth as a narrative linked with a rite.

The myth describes what the ritual enacts. A mode of symbolic expression objectifying early human feeling and experience, the myth is least of all the product of the reflective or historical consciousness, or of the search for scientific or philosophical truth. Though satisfying "the demands of incipient rationality . . . in an unfathomed world,"[3] it arises, basically, in response to ever-recurrent needs of a practical and emotional nature that are assumed to require for their gratification the magical potency of a sacral act. Its originators, as S. M. Hooke writes, "were not occupied with general questions concerning the world but with certain practical and pressing problems of daily life. There were the main problems of securing the means of subsistence, of keeping the sun and moon doing their duty, of ensuring the regular flooding of the Nile, of maintaining the bodily vigor of the king who was the embodiment of the prosperity of community. . . . In order to meet these needs the early inhabitants of Egypt and Mesopotamia developed a set of customary activities directed toward a definite end. Thus the coronation of a king . . . consisted of a regular pattern of actions, of things prescribed to be done, whose purpose was to fit the king completely to be the source of the well-being of the community. This is the sense in which we shall use the term 'ritual.' "[4] Cassirer uses the term in much the same sense, as for example, in his comment on the mythic tale of Dionysus Zagreus: "What is recalled here is neither a physical nor historical phenomenon. It is not a fact of nature nor a recollection of the deeds or sufferings of a heroic ancestor. Nevertheless the legend is not a mere fairy tale. It had a *fundamentum in re;* it refers to a certain 'reality.' . . . It is *ritual.* What is seen in the Dionysiac cult is explained in the myth."[5] As for the Greek myths with which we are most familiar, Hooke sees them as the fragments of a very antique pattern that in becoming separated from ritual gradually acquired an independent life through poetic formulation. Thus both the Minotaur and Perseus myths manifestly involve an underlying ritual pattern of human sacrifice developed in a stage when myth and ritual were still one. And to comprehend that unity one must keep in mind, as Lord Raglan puts it, that "in the beginning the thing said and the thing done were inseparably united, although in the course of time they were divorced and gave rise to widely differing literary, artistic and religious forms." It is clear that both *epos* and *logos* evolved out of *mythos.* But that this evolu-

256

tion is irreversible the literary expatiators of myth fail to grasp.

The primitive significance of myth is not to be disclosed by scrutinizing ancient poetry. "It is as vain to look to Homer for the primitive significance of myth," writes A. M. Hocart, "as it would be to seek it in Sir Thomas Malory." The epic, though a medium of mythological lore, is at the same time, as Susanne M. Langer observes, "the first flower, or one of the first, of a new symbolic mode—the mode of art. It is not merely a receptacle of old symbols, namely those of myth, but is itself a new symbolic form, great with possibilities, ready to take meaning and express ideas that have had no vehicle before."[6] Poetic structure transforms the mythic material, disciplining and subjecting it to logical and psychological motives that eventually alienate it from its origins. To take the fact that myth is the common matrix of many literary forms as an indication that myth is literature or that literature is myth is a simple instance of the genetic fallacy. Myth is a certain kind of objective fantasy to which literature has had frequent recourse for its materials and patterns; but in itself it is not literature. The literary work is mainly characterized by the order and qualitative arrangement of its words; myths, on the other hand, as Miss Langer notes, are not bound to "any particular words, nor even to language, but may be told or painted, acted or danced, without suffering degradation or distortion. . . . They have no meter, no characteristic phrases, and are just as often recorded in vase-paintings and bas-reliefs as in words. A ballad, however, is a composition. . . ."[7] We know that *Oedipus Rex* is based on a mythic ritual. But the question is, what chiefly affects us in the play? Is it the myth, as such indifferent to verbal form, serving as Sophocles' material, or his particular *composition* of it? The Oedipus myth has its own power, to be sure, but one must distinguish between this power and that of the dramatic embodiment the poet gave it. And by confusing these different powers the inflators of myth are able to credit it with properties that really belong to art.

Moreover, the mythic imagination is a believing imagination. Attaching no value to fictions, it envisages its objects as actually existing. Conversely, the imagination of art, a relatively late development in the history of human mentality, is marked above all by its liberation from the sheerly actual and material. Art achieves independence as it gradually detaches itself from myth. The poetic image, Cassirer notes, attains "its purely representative, specifically 'aesthetic' function only as the magic circle with which mythical consciousness surrounds it is broken, and it is recognized not as a mythico-magical form, but as a particular sort of *formulation*." Then what is meant by saying that not only the great epic and dramatic poets but even the best lyric poets seem to be possessed by a kind of mythic power? Cassirer's reply is that in those poets "the magic power of insight breaks forth again in its full intensity and objectifying power. But this objectivity has discarded all material constraints. The spirit lives in the world of language and in the mythical image without falling under the control of either." Word and image, which once affected the mind as awesome external forces, have now cast off effectual reality, becoming for the literary artist "a light, bright ether in which the spirit can move without let or hindrance. This liberation is achieved not because the mind throws aside the sensuous forms of word and image, but because it uses them both as organs of its own, and thereby recognizes them for what they really are: forms of its own self-revelation."[8]

This type of historical analysis of the relation between art and myth is unlikely to interest the cultists. For what is the mind's recognition of its own creations if not an advance toward freedom? But it is freedom which is refused by those who wish to re-mystify the world through myth or dogma. This new-fashioned freedom is still largely untried by the generality of men. Why not keep it so, thus saving them from its perils? In literature this has prompted the endeavor to establish what might well be called a poetics of restitution— restitution for the disenchantment of reality carried through by science, rationality, and the historical consciousness. It is only natural that in such a poetics, ruled by schematic notions of tradition, the liberation of art from the socio-religious compulsions of the past should be taken as a calamity—a veritable expulsion from Eden. And how is Eden to be regained? Inevitably some of the practitioners of this poetics discovered that myth answered their purpose much better than tradition. After all, the supra-temporality of myth provides the ideal refuge from history. To them, as to Stephen Dedalus in *Ulysses,* history is a nightmare from which they are trying to awake. But to awake from history into myth is like escaping from a nightmare into a state of permanent insomnia.

But if the road back to genuine mythic consciousness is closed, what is still open is the possibility of manipulating ideas of myth. And that is precisely the point of my objection. For myth is not what its ideologues claim it to be. Though the common matrix of both, it is neither art nor metaphysics. In fact, both art and metaphysics are among those superior forces which culture brought to bear in its effort to surmount the primitivism of myth. Dialectical freedom is unknown to myth, which permits no distinction between realities and symbols. The proposition that "the world of human culture . . . could not arise until the darkness of myth was fought and overcome"[9] is no doubt historically valid. Witness the struggle against it in Greek philosophy, as for instance in the animadversions on mythic tales in the *Phaedrus*. Socrates, walking with his companion by the banks of the Ilissus, calls those tales "irrelevant things," declining to put his mind to them by reason of their uselessness in his search for self-knowledge. Even if instructive in some things, the one thing they cannot impart is ethical enlightenment: the question of good and evil is beyond myth and becomes crucial only with the emergence of the individual, to whom alone is given the capacity at once to assent to the gift of self-knowledge and to undergo its ordeal.

Individuality is in truth foreign to myth, which objectifies collective rather than personal experience. Its splendor is that of the original totality, the pristine unity of thought and action, word and deed. The sundering of that unity is one of the tragic contradictions of historical development, which is never an harmonious forward movement but "a cruel repugnant labor against itself," as Hegel described it with unequaled insight. It is the paradox of progress that humanity has proven itself unable to assimilate reality except by means of "the alienation of human forces." In order to recover the potency of myth civilized man would first have to undo the whole of his history; and when some literary intellectuals dream of this recovery they are manifestly reacting against the effects of self-alienation at the same time that they exemplify these effects with appalling simplicity. What Marx once called "the idiocy of the division of labor" must have gone very far indeed if people can so drastically separate their theories of life from their concrete living of it! (The "idiocy" results from the fragmentation of vital human functions, since, as Marx said, "together with the division of labor is given the possibility, nay, the actuality, that spiritual activity and material activity, pleasure and work, production and consumption, will fall to the lot of different individuals.")

It is not unimaginable that in the future the paradox of progress will be resolved and acting and thinking reintegrated. We can be certain, however, that a conquest so consummate will take place not within our civilization but beyond it, on the further shore of historical necessity, when man, at long last reconciling nature and culture within himself, will no longer be compelled to purchase every gain in freedom with the loss of wholeness and integrity. Admittedly that too is probably a dream, but it is at least a possible dream and so long as civilization lasts perhaps an indefeasible one. The fulfilment it promises is the hope of history—and its redemption. And inconceivable as that fulfilment may seem to us at present, it will be brought about through the real processes of history or not at all—never through the magic potion of myth.

I said above that the craze for myth is the fear of history. It is feared because modern life is above all an historical life producing changes with vertiginous speed, changes difficult to understand and even more difficult to control. And to some people it appears as though the past, all of it together with its gods and sacred books, were being ground to pieces in the powerhouse of change, senselessly used up as so much raw material in the fabrication of an unthinkable future. One way certain intellectuals have found of coping with their fear is to deny historical time and induce in themselves through aesthetic and ideological means a sensation of mythic time—the eternal past of ritual. The advantage of mythic time is that it is without definite articulation, confounding past, present, and future in an undifferentiated unity, as against historical time which is unrepeatable and of an ineluctable progression. The historical event is that which occurs once only, unlike the timeless event of myth that, recurring again and again, is endlessly present.

The turn from history toward myth is to be observed in some of the important creative works of this period, as Joseph Frank has shown in his remarkable essay "Spatial Form in Modern Literature." He quotes Allen Tate as saying that Ezra Pound's *Cantos* in their "powerful juxtapositions of the ancient, the Renaissance, and the modern worlds reduce all three elements to an unhistorical miscellany, timeless and without origin." Frank analyzes *The Waste Land, Ulysses, Nightwood* and other literary works along the same lines, establishing that while on one level they seem to be dealing with "the clash of historical perspectives induced by the identification of contemporary figures and events with various historical prototypes," in practice they make history unhistorical in that it is sensed as "a continuum in which distinctions of past and present are obliterated . . . past and present are seen spatially, locked in a timeless unity which, even if accentuating surface differences, eliminates any feeling of historical sequence by the very act of juxtaposition. The objective historical imagination, on which modern man has prided himself, and which he has cultivated so carefully since the Renaissance, is transformed in those writers into the mythical imagination for which historical time does not exist."[10] Frank offers no social-historical explanation of this retreat from history; he is simply concerned with it as an aesthetic phenomenon expressing itself in "spatial form."

Perhaps for that very reason he too readily assumes that the mythic imagination is actually operative in the writers he examines. But the supplanting of the sense of historical by the sense of mythic time is scarcely accomplished with such ease; the mere absence of the one does not necessarily confirm the presence of the other. For my part, what I perceive in Pound and Eliot are not the workings of the mythic imagination but an aesthetic simulacrum of it, a learned illusion of timelessness. We should not mistake historical retrospection, however richly allusive and organized in however "simultaneous" a fashion, for mythic immediacy and the pure imaginative embodiment of a perpetual present. In point of fact, the polemical irony which the poems both of Pound and Eliot generate at the expense of modern society in itself attests to a marked commitment toward history. Are not these poets conducting a campaign against history precisely in the name of history, which they approach, however, with mythic prepossessions, that is to say without either dynamism or objectivity, responding to its archaistic refinements while condemning its movement? The truth is that they are as involved in historicism as most contemporary writers sensitive to the "modern situation," but in their case the form it takes is negative. Willy-nilly they express the age, that few would deny is historicist through and through.[11] As Eliot himself once wrote, if a poet is "sincere, he must express with individual differences the general state of mind—not as a duty, but because he cannot help participating in it." Eliot is plainly a more "sincere" poet than Pound, and he is also a religious man; and it is necessary to uphold the distinction between religion and myth. His religiousness, which has temperamental as well as deep social roots, hardly disallows the cultivation of historical awareness. This may well explain why he has always been able to curb his "mythicism," so that it is but one of the several tendencies in his work rather than its motive-power. As a literary critic he is seldom inclined to hunt for mythological patterns, whose task it seems to be to reduce the history of literature to sameness and static juxtaposition; more typically he searches for those alterations of sensibility that are historically illuminating and productive of significant change.

It is Pound who in his later phase is wholly in the throes of "mythicism." But, far from being a reincarnation of an ancient imaginative mode, it is really but another sample of modern ideology, applied to poetry with frenetic zeal in an effort to compensate for loss of coherence. In the *Cantos* time neither stands still as in myth nor moves as in history; it is merely suspended. As for Joyce's *Ulysses,* it seems to me that the mythological parallels it abounds in provide little more than the scaffolding for the structure of the novel; and only critics fascinated by exegesis would mistake it for the structure itself. Those parallels do not really enter substantively into the presentation of the characters. The manner in which Bloom is identified with Odysseus and Stephen with Telemachus is more like a mythic jest or conceit, as it were, than a true identification. To be sure, it reflects the somewhat scholastic humor of the author; but its principal function is that of helping him organize his material. In that sense it has more to do with the making of the novel than with the reading of it—for as readers we find both Stephen and Bloom convincing because they are firmly grounded in the historical actualities of Joyce's city, his country, and Europe as a whole. It is in *Finnegans Wake,* far more than in *Ulysses,* that the mythic bias is in ascendant, the historical element recedes, and the language itself is converted into a medium of myth.

Finnegans Wake is the most complete example of "spatial form" in modern literature. Joseph Frank's definition of that form is extremely plausible, yet I cannot agree that it is a mythic form in any but a very limited analogical sense. It is best understood, to my mind, as the aesthetic means devised for the projection of a non-historical or even anti-historical view of history. The most one can say of this form is that it reflects a mythic bias. But this bias is by no means independent of historicism, of which it·is a kind of reactionary distortion or petrifaction.

There is a good deal of evidence supporting this conception of "spatial form." Thus in his book, *The Protestant Era*, Paul Tillich lists the main premises of the non-historical interpretation of history, and we find that one such premise is that "space is predominant against time; time is considered to be circular or repeating itself infinitely." What is the inner meaning of this spatializing of time? From Tillich's philosophical standpoint it means that time is being detached from history and yielded back to nature. In other words, the contradiction between history ánd nature is resolved in favor of the latter. Tillich defines time, in terms reminiscent of Schelling and Bergson, as the dimension of the dynamic, creative, and qualitative, whereas space he defines as the static and quantitative. If this contrast is valid, then one can only conclude that the attempt to re-spatialize time implies a defeatist attitude toward history, an attitude that in the long run makes for cultural regression.

Further premises of the non-historical interpretation of history are that "salvation is the salvation of individuals from time and history, not the salvation of a community through time and history," and that history is to be understood as "a process of deterioration, leading to the inescapable self-destruction of a world era." It is not difficult to recognize here some of the components of "mythicism." As an ideology "mythicism" is of course not to be equated at all points with its artistic practice. One must distinguish between the cultism of myth, which is primarily an ideological manifestation, and the literary works in which myth is made use of in one way or another. In Joyce the ideology is hardly perceptible, but you will find it in Eliot and a somewhat secularized version of it in Pound. Some critics write about Thomas Mann as if he too were enlisted in the service of myth. This is a mistake, I think. *Joseph and His Brothers* is not so much a mythic novel as a novel on mythic themes. In this narrative it is the characters, not at all the author, who confound past and present in their experience of that "pure time" which transcends

both. Furthermore, in his recreation of myth Mann is heavily indebted
to the Freudian psychology; and psychology is inherently anti-mythic.
The Freudian method is a special adaptation of the historical method
in general. Freud's early efforts to fit his theory into a biological
framework were of no avail; and now it is clear, as W. H. Auden
has so well put it, that Freud, "towers up as the genius who perceived that psychological events are not natural events but historical
and that, therefore, psychology, as distinct from neurology, must be
based on the presuppositions . . . not of the biologist but of the
historian."

Not a few characteristics of "mythicism" are brought into Tillich's exposition under the heading of the "mystical" approach to
history, against which he argues in the name of historical realism.
This is a perspective that he evaluates as a creation of the West,
especially in so far as it stands under Protestant influence. "For historical realism the really real appears in the structures created by the
historical process," he writes. "History is open to interpretation only
through active participation. We can grasp the power of historical
being only if we are grasped by it in our historical experience."[12] His
analysis, combining certain Marxist concepts with the religious variant
of existential thought, repudiates all attempts to escape the present
for the sake of the unreal past of archaism or the equally unreal future
of utopianism. It is a view resistant to attitudes of religious pessimism
toward the historical world and even more so to the mythic dissolution of it in the eternal past of ritual.

The fear of history is at bottom the fear of the hazards of freedom. In so far as man can be said to be capable of self-determination,
history is the sole sphere in which he can conceivably attain it. But
though history, as Tillich affirms, is above all the sphere of freedom,
it is also the sphere in which "man *is determined* by fate against his
freedom. Very often the creations of his freedom are the tools used
by fate against him; as, for instance, today the technical powers
created by him turn against him with irresistible force. There are
periods in history in which the element of freedom predominates, and
there are periods in which fate and necessity prevail. The latter is
true of our day. . . ."[13] An analysis of this type, largely coinciding
with the Hegelian-Marxist idea of historical tension and crisis, sufficiently accounts for the retreat from history toward myth. In our

time the historical process is marked far more by loss and extremity than growth and mastery, and this fact is interpreted by the spokesmen of traditionalism as completely justifying their position. The mythic principle appeals to them because of its fixity and profoundly conservative implications. But the hope of stability it offers is illusory. To look to myth for deliverance from history is altogether futile.

In literature the withdrawal from historical experience and creativeness can only mean stagnation! For the creative artist to deny time in the name of the timeless and immemorial is to misconceive his task. He will never discover a shortcut to transcendence. True, in the imaginative act the artist does indeed challenge time, but in order to win he must also be able to meet *its* challenge; and his triumph over it is like that blessing which Jacob exacted from the angel only after grappling with him till the break of day.

In criticism the reaction against history is shown in the search for some sort of mythic model, so to speak, to which the literary work under scrutiny can be made to conform. The critics captivated by this procedure are inclined to take for granted that to identify a mythic pattern in a novel or poem is tantamount to disclosing its merit—an assumption patently false, for the very same pattern is easily discoverable in works entirely without merit. Implicit here is the notion that the sheer timelessness of the pattern is as such a guaranty of value. What is not grasped, however, is that the timeless is in itself nothing more than a pledge waiting for time to redeem it, or, to vary the figure, a barren form that only time can make fecund. And Blake said it when he wrote in his "Proverbs of Hell" that "eternity is in love with the productions of time."

1 Jacques Maritain: *Creative Intuition in Art and Poetry* (New York 1953), p. 180ff.

2 Ernst Cassirer: *The Myth of the State* (New Haven 1946), p. 5.

3 A. N. Whitehead: *An Anthology* selected by F. S. C. Northrop and Mason Cross (New York 1953), p. 475.

4 S. M. Hooke: in *Myth and Ritual* (London 1949), p. 6.

5 Ernst Cassirer: *Op. cit.* p. 42.

6 Susanne M. Langer: *Philosophy in a New Key* (New York 1948), p. 160ff.

7 Susanne M. Langer: *Feeling and Form* (New York 1953), p. 274ff.

8 Ernst Cassirer: *Myth and Language*, p. 97ff.

9 Ernst Cassirer: *The Myth of the State*, p. 298.

10 Joseph Frank in *Criticism:the Foundations of Modern Literary Judgment*, edited by Mark Schorer, Josephine Miles, and Gordon McKenzie (New York 1948), p. 392.

11 "Historicism," writes Karl Mannheim, "has developed into an intellectual force of extraordinary significance. . . . The historicist principle not only organizes, like an invisible thread, the work of the cultural sciences (*Geisteswissenschaften*) but also permeates everyday thinking. Today it is impossible to take part in politics, even to understand a person . . . without treating all those realities we have to deal with as having evolved and as developing dynamically. For in everyday life, too, we apply concepts with historicist overtones, for example, 'capitalism,' 'social movement,' 'cultural process,' etc. These forces are grasped and understood as potentialities, constantly in flux, moving from some point in time to another; already on the level of everyday reflection we seek to determine the position of our present within such a temporal framework, to tell by the cosmic clock of history what the time is"—*Essays on the Sociology of Knowledge* (New York 1952), p. 84.

12 Paul Tillich: *The Protestant Era* (Chicago 1948), p. 71ff.

13 *Ibid*, p. 186.

MYTHOLOGY

(For the Study of William Blake)

By MARK SCHORER

IT is time to argue that the central problem in William Blake, a puzzling poet, is not mysticism at all, as has been generally supposed, but mythology; a mythology which the poet, for reasons both of temperament and of history, was forced to invent; and for the materials of which he turned to a wide variety of documents, some of which are mystical. Like his admirer, Yeats, Blake might have written,

> I made my song a coat
> Covered with embroideries
> Out of old mythologies
> From heel to throat;

and when Blake seems to be a mystic, he is usually only mistaking the embroideries for the coat itself.

Myths are those universal artifacts by which we continually struggle to make our multitudinous experience intelligible to ourselves. A myth is a large, controlling image (and a mythology is an articulated body of such images, a pantheon) which gives philosophical meaning to the facts of ordinary life, that is to say, which has organizing value for experience. Without such images, experience is chaotic and fragmentary, merely phenomenal. All real convictions involve a mythology—either in its usual, broad sense, in which it is embodied in literature or in ritual or in both, and in which it has application to the whole of a society and tends to be religious, or in a private sense alone, in which it remains in the disembodied realm of fantasy, and in which it tends to be obsessive and fanatical.   This is not to say that sound myths, of general application, necessarily support religions; rather, that they perform the historical functions of religion: they unify experience in a way that is satisfactory to the whole culture and to the whole personality.   Philip Wheelwright, from the point of view of an uncommon philosophical theism, argues understandably that "the very essence of myth" is "that haunting awareness of transcendental forces peering through the cracks of the visible universe."   And while it is true, as Durkheim pointed out, that myth suggests the "sacred" rather than the "profane" (in aesthetic terms, the Secondary rather than the Primary Imagination), that is, the enormous area of experience into which technology cannot usefully enter rather than the relatively small area which it is capable of elucidating, that is not to make religious experience proper more than a portion of the larger area.   That myth cannot be so limited is made clear by our own civilization, which seems to be struggling toward a myth which will be explicitly (and, one desperately hopes, satisfactorily) ethical.   "In our time," Thomas Mann has said, "the destiny of man presents its meaning in political terms," and in this usage, politics may, I believe, be subsumed under ethics.   Wars may be described as the clash of mythologies; and a society such as ours in this century which is basically disorganized is the result of a number of antithetical and competing mythologies which fail to adjust themselves.

Belief is secondary.   We habitually tend to overlook the fact that, as human beings, we are rational creatures not first of all, but last of all, that civilization emerged only yesterday from a primitive past that is at least relatively timeless.   Belief organizes experience not because it is belief but because belief itself depends on a controlling imagery and is the intellectual formalization of that imagery.   Christianity, as a basic set of images, has commanded the unanimous faith of millions; as a system of belief capable of a wide variety of dogmas, it has commanded the intellectual assent of hostile sectarian groups. Likewise, shall we say—although on a much smaller scale—such a more recent mythology as socialism. All those systems of abstractions which we call ideologies activate our behavior, when they do, only because they are themselves activated by images, however submerged. An abstraction is a generalization, and you cannot have a generalization without the concrete things to be generalized. In this sense, myth has priority over belief. And in this sense, one may even concur with Hume's offensive remark that "there is no such passion in human minds, as the love of mankind, merely as such"; for this passion, like all others, must have an image, real or ideal, as its object. Malinowski, writing of primitive myths, says, "They never explain in any sense of the word; they always state a precedent which constitutes an ideal and a warrant for its continuance, and sometimes practical directions for the procedure." This is to say, I think, that myth does not "illustrate" belief, but gives it a base to operate upon. Myth is fundamental, the dramatic representation of our deepest instinctual life, of a primary awareness of man in the universe, capable of many configurations, upon which all particular opinions and attitudes depend.

In their most fragmentary forms, these images have come to be known in modern writing as fictions, and they apply in all fields of inquiry, in science, in politics, jurisprudence, and economics, no less than in religion and history and morals. And even when, as in modern civilization, they multiply and separate and tend to become abstract, and the images themselves recede and fade (". . . we live in an intricacy of new and local mythologies, political, economic, poetic, which are asserted with an ever-enlarging incoherence," writes Wallace Stevens)—even then they are still the essential substructure of all human activity. Most profoundly, of course, they apply in literature, and fiction is a happily chosen word precisely because of its literary suggestiveness: great literature is impossible without a previous imaginative consent to a ruling mythology which makes intelligible and unitive the whole of that experience from which particular fables spring and from which they, in turn, take their meaning. Without myth—let us say, without adequate myth, for, to cite Malinowski again, myth, continually modified and renewed by the modifications of history, is in some form "an indispensable ingredient of all culture"—without adequate myth, literature ceases to be perceptual and tends to degenerate into mere description; thus, for example, the prevailing and tiresome realism of modern fiction. When we feel that we are no longer in a position to say what life means, we must content ourselves with telling how it looks. Those of our novelists who have transcended realism have done so by a bootstrap miracle, by supplying the myth themselves: Mann, with his artificial use of literary myth; Joyce, who in addition attempted to distill specifically modern developments such as psychology into their mythical essences; Kafka, and the rather disturbing dramatization of neurosis. In a disintegrating society such as this, literature, before it can proceed with other business, must become the explicit agent of coherence. Serious artists, in the realm of the imagination, must be like Hart Crane's tramps in their cross-country freight cars: "They know a body under the wide rain." All readers are aware that the chief energies of modern poets have been expended not simply in writing poetry but in employing poetry to discover its indispensable substructure, a useable mythology, that is, one which will account for and organize our competing, fragmentary myths. T. S. Eliot is the most familiar example: here excursions into anthropology and orientalism preceded the final compromise, apparently satisfactory to the poet, with Christian orthodoxy. The example of Yeats is no less spectacular and more systematic: years devoted to the exploration of magic and spiritualism and all the disreputable purlieus of mysticism were combined with a late interest in politics, and the curious melange seems to have served its purpose. Hart Crane—and Americans generally have found the material for their myths nearer at hand than modern Europeans,

having until now to take less into account—ingeniously but un-
successfully utilized a combination of American Indian legend
and modern American industrialism in the construction of his
single sustained work. Older poets and poets less given to self-
questioning, like Robert Frost, were apparently quite comfortable
in employing the available myth of the independent American
democrat for which a younger man no longer finds historical
sanction; thus Delmore Schwartz, with great brilliance, tries to
read mythical significances—of internationalism, I believe—in
his own biography. One could multiply the instances. The hunt
for the essential image, or series of them, goes on everywhere today; but the problem is hardly new.

The Elizabethans, who seemed to enjoy an intellectual flexi-
bility denied to men since the middle of the 17th Century, employed an enormous variety of myth. It is a striking fact that
—although the conflict between Pan and Christ was often sharp
—they embodied their cultural needs as successfully in classical
mythology as in the nearer Christian myth, and that, for example,
their aggressive nationalism found its expression with possibly
greater ease in the former. But on the merely decorative, the
pictorial, the rococo side, they ransacked and temporarily exhausted the myths of Greece and Rome, and throughout the 17th
Century poetry began to move away from classical mythology altogether. It is no accident that this movement began rather abrupt-
ly with Donne, who was among the first of the poets to reflect the
developments of science explicitly, following a critical mood first
expressed by Bacon, who is the fountainhead of these developments. (The historical irony here is that, when the same impulse
was applied to language itself, as by Hobbes, the poetic style of
Donne became an impossibility.) The measure of Dryden and
Pope may be taken up to a point in these terms: Dryden has ma-
jesty because the pagan and the Christian myths are still moder-
ately available to him; Pope—a shallower spirit who contented
himself with the new and inadequate myth—has a sustained ele-

gance only and moments of superb refinement, for when he employs the older myths at all, they are now available to comedy alone. The history of epic is instructive, for the many critics of the old epic formula—which involved supernatural machinery, in practice usually derived from pagan myth—did not foresee that when the formula was demolished, epic itself would vanish; the discredited machinery became the vehicle of *mock* epic. Nor have we yet achieved a shifting from the old heroic reference, the supernatural, to a new, presumably the social; for in this realm too many myths are still competing and there is no certainty.

If epic poetry is impossible without an adequate and explicit mythology, so too is the greatest lyric poetry. One may in this connection compare such moderns as Hardy and the later Yeats with their contemporary, Bridges. The recurrent triviality of this poet (". . . I love beauty, and was born to rhyme") results from the fact that he does not really regard poetry seriously, but as a mere ornament to life. Such a view reduces the composition of poetry to the arrangement of ornaments. Very pretty things may result, but they would hardly satisfy the demands which the greatest lyric poets place upon themselves. (The difference is eloquently embodied in this contrast: while Yeats was struggling to break down the barriers of mind by associating himself with societies for psychical research, Bridges was attempting to impose barriers on language by founding and operating a society to purify the language). Didactic and informative poetry, on the other hand, can do well enough with nearly any mythical material—as witness the eclecticism of *The Testament of Beauty*—or even with the myth that has not been articulated. This will explain the prevailing temper of 18th Century poetry, most of which we must designate not as poetry at all, for, in spite of its increasing solemnity, it fails in an important kind of seriousness. Solemnity has of course nothing to do with seriousness: many of Blake's lyrics are light verse, but they are more "serious" than Wordsworth at his pompous or Shelley at his frenetic norm; the poems of Prior, minor as they may be, are yet more "serious" than those of Addison; or Yeats's Crazy Jane songs than Bridges' sonnets on "The Growth of Love." Everyone will agree that 18th Century poetry, as the decades passed, became solemn enough, but few will contend that it became more serious than, let us say, Prior had been, or Pope at his most vindictive and comic. Employing, sometimes in only the most remote way, the myth of contemporary science, 18th Century poetry more and more took to itself as well the *functions* of science, which are exposition and description; these are not the functions of major poetry, but they justify the tag, "the age of prose." Thus, in the 18th Century, poetry at its very best was elegant, as Pope's; impressively severe, as Johnson's; stunningly vituperative, as Churchill's; at its second level, it was sometimes worthily prosaic, as Thomson's and Dyer's; more often, merely prosaic, as Blair's, Young's, Akenside's, and so on. It was all these things and other things besides, but it was hardly grand. The great limitation of 18th Century poetry is that it is thin: it means no more than it intends to mean.

Did Coleridge, translating Schiller, perceive the problem?

> The intelligible forms of ancient poets,
> The fair humanities of old religion,
> The Power, the Beauty, and the Majesty,
> That had their haunts in dale, or piny mountain,
> Or forest by slow stream, or pebbly spring,
> Or chasms and wat'ry depths: all these have vanished.
> They live no longer in the faith of reason!
> But still the heart doth need a language, still
> Doth the old instinct bring back the old names. . . .

William Blake, who cried with malice,

> Lo the Bat with Leathern wing,
> Winking & blinking,
> Winking & blinking,
> Winking & blinking,
> Like Doctor Johnson,

did perceive the problem. Writing at the end of a century whose poetic product seemed with very few exceptions unutterably dreary to him, he wanted above everything perhaps to return grandeur to poetry; and to this effect alone, he knew, myth was indispensable.

Unlike some poets of his time, Blake attempted almost no use of the figures and conventions of classical mythology. They were not, and, in that age, he felt, could not have been used in any organic fashion; for these myths were, in Coleridge's term, "exploded," and, as Douglas Bush points out, only Collins seemed to have any inclination to use them more significantly than as decoration. Decoration did not interest Blake, and the classical mythology enters his work at only four or five points, most of these in his juvenile efforts. He was wholly aware of its degraded place in the decor of the 17th and 18th Centuries:

> Bloated Gods, Mercury, Juno, Venus, & the rattle traps of Mythology & the lumber of an awkward French Palace are thrown together around Clumsy & Ricketty Princes & Princesses higgledy piggledy.

It was a mythology without meaning for Blake under the circumstances, first petrified and now corroded, of possible use to the poet interested in "delicate conceits," of no use whatever to one busy "with the terrors of thought." It might be supposed that the naturalistic basis of Greek myth would have indisposed Blake to it in any situation; but this is not true. He was fully acquainted with its naturalistic basis ("The ancient Poets animated all sensible objects with Gods or Geniuses," etc.) but his objection was to its systematization (". . . thus began Priesthood; Choosing forms of worship from poetic tales"). His most frequent image for systematization was petrifaction, and a good image this is for a condition which is intended to suggest the impossibility of further intuitional activity. A very fundamental reason for Blake's rejecting an older mythology and insisting on his own, then, was to disassociate his utterance from the literalness, the externality, to which older myths had been subjected; a literalness and externality so fast that the myths seemed no longer adaptable to fresh historical situations. The example of Keats and Shelley, who found the old mythology still quite limber, did not alter Blake's point of view; as he was more robust, so he was also more brash than they.

Coleridge argued that the agent which destroyed the classic myths was "the mechanical system of philosophy," and this is true enough; but it is not all of the truth. For the mechanical philosophy destroyed, just as clearly, the established Christian mythology. It is important to see that both Christianity and the mechanical system of philosophy entailed their *own* myths, Milton adequately representing one, Pope or Thomson the other. But vital remnants of the Christian myth remained, and these, working in terms of politics—for this was the necessary compromise if anything was to be saved from Christianity—cooperated with the antithetical myth of contemporary science until, by the time of the French Revolution, a new adjustment had been attained. Blake's problem was to find the metaphorical terms which would articulate and encompass both the Christian and the scientific myth, as well as those new terms which were the terms of the synthesis itself.

The Christian mythology, never so generally useful to English poetry as the pagan, was last successfully employed by John Milton. By deliberately turning his back on the new science, Milton managed to return a nearly orthodox view of a universe interpenetrated by God and his interests, and of man in immediate relation to God and answerable to him. Blake had the enormous good sense, along with many of his contemporaries in the 18th Century, to admire Milton (but in the major, rather than the minor poems), and while he was the only one among them who possessed genius, he had not perhaps the plastic kind of genius which could assimilate that rather terrific influence. He took the Christian mythology as Milton had employed it, with the emphasis on the creation and the resurrection—paradise lost and paradise regained—and, with the help of certain semi-mystical writings, and his own highly personal responses to the leading ideas of his age (responses capable of the most extraordinary transvaluations), manipulated it to his inclusive purposes. And in a sense he solved a problem which had existed throughout the whole literature of the century.

For the literature of the 18th Century is curious in that it reflects constantly two worlds and never brings them together. There is the world of affairs, of reason, of ethical notions, the world of mechanistic philosophy and of natural religion; all of which had its myth. And then there is that curious half-world of morbid fancy, of gothic titillation and unkempt bards, of garden ruins and Tahitian dinner guests and Chinoiserie and every manner of restless exoticism: all of which was an attempt to enrich the inadequate myth of the former. Often enough these two spheres appear in the same writer, as Thomas Gray, and even in the same work, but they never merge; one never helps to explain the other; they continue to involve their separate responses. No one in the century recognized the trouble although a good many writers observed the symptoms. A nearly unknown primitive poet, John Husbands, declared in 1731 that "the *Poetical* character has . . . been separated from the religious," which is as exact a statement of the *symptom* as one could wish for. But no one went further. Writers like Dennis, Addison, and Thomson, like Edward Young, Horace Walpole, Bishop Hurd, and the curious Wartons—all of whom asserted in one way or another the superiority of primitive genius and resisted the prevailing neo-classicism—all these still conceived of genius as operating rather on the second plane, the plane of fancy, than on the plane of imagination, which integrates sensibility and intellect. In one sense these writers were not wrong; for it is the primitive—Blake, Whitman, Lawrence—who brings these two realms of experience together most vigorously, if not usually most satisfactorily. The failure of the 18th Century worthies to make a distinction which was not explicitly made until the time of Coleridge—the distinction between a function which is external, decorative, static, and a function which is organic and organizing, "esemplastic" in Coleridge's big word—was not theirs but that of the century, or of the condition of contemporary metaphysics; failure it was, however, for it is exactly fancy which retains this separation between ordinary life and the life of the imagination. Yet their discussion and that gothic world of sensibility glued together by poets and novelists comprised the century's rather feeble if protracted attempt to fill the gap created by a departed mythology. The attempt was of course unsuccessful, for true and useful myth does not titillate, with fancy, but assimilates and modifies the facts of experience, with imagination. Juliet's moving fears of the tomb echo in all the charnel house poetry of the age—and in Blake, too—but how weakly, how theatrically, what lathe-and-plaster fears they are of an experience which, deprived in the imagination of its full consequences, is nearly meaningless, can only titillate.

The myth which the 18th Century could seriously employ was the austere, indeed, in its first manifestations, the barren myth of Newton—the myth of the mechanical universe (in other terms, of rationality), with its religious, ethical, and social ramifications. This is the picture which Milton was still able to reject: of a universe created by a God but from which that God, a mechanist, had withdrawn after his work was completed; a universe which operated on fixed and changeless principles which man could, to a point, understand by his reason; of a society comparably fixed and "rational," in which all things had their immutable place, their only obligation being to know it and to keep it. This view prevailed in the poetry which reflected the sober side of life, the world of affairs and of manners. That it occasionally resulted in such triumphs of social and ethical discursiveness as the *Epistle to Doctor Arbuthnot* and *The Vanity of Human Wishes* (although this, of course, is not an "original" poem, and Johnson hardly a deist), is to the credit of the poets in question, not of the myth. In the past the myth at its most fertile had provided a basis for comedy, for its ideal of society was as rigid as its picture of the universe, and allowed enormous ground for all manner of divagation; and if the comedy of the 18th Century was inferior to that produced in the second half of the preceding century, that is because the myth was already being corrupted by the agent most destructive to comedy—sentiment. The harder the universe became, the softer the heart. The stricter the conventions, the more outrageous the rebellious taste. When the glitter of the French drawing room became too bright for comfort, it was possible to substitute the gloom of a "gothic" hall, and even in gardens which had imitated Versailles, one could find space for a "grot" or a horrid ruin. The manners, like the poetry of the century, struggled continually to overcome the strictures of the myth. No less so religion: for the deeper the incursions which deism made into theology, or the more comfortable the parson became on a tavern settle—so, the more vigorous became the efforts of the revivalists, and the blacker the mood of the orthodox like Swift and Johnson. The century, like its greatest genius and many a lesser, died "like a tree, at the top first."

And the fault was in the myth. "Then tell me," Blake asked, "what is the material world, and is it dead?" What indeed had the picture of the universe presented by the mechanical philosophy to offer a poet who *was* serious, as no poet had been after the death of Milton, a poet who constantly felt the imperative and undeniable energy of life, who had—in the perhaps inadequate modern application of Yeats, for those convenient absolutes, good and evil, had already gone—the tragic sense and was therefore truly joyous? Joy is not the icy optimism of *The Essay on Man*, that highly enamelled structure which, in its closing lines, cracks widely enough to admit all the shocking anomalies of the age— the melancholy of Samuel Johnson, the despair of William Cowper, the madness of Christopher Smart. *"Vous criez 'Tout est bien' d'une voix lamentable!"* Nor are the alternatives to Pope— Johnson, Cowper, Smart—more useful to a poetry of joy than

Pope himself. Blake needed to construct a picture of the world—
a myth, if you please—which was in some sense the counterpart of
his experience of life; and the Newtonian order, in its mathematical denial of that dynamic expansiveness and fluidity which
energy connotes, was almost literally "death."   When we talk
of Blake and "the nothingness of matter" we must always remember that it was most often *that* "material world" which he
had in mind. He addressed this epigram "To God:"

> If you have form'd a Circle to go into,
> Go into it yourself & see how you would do.

Blake's experience—his   temperament—demanded   a   universe
which was above all "open," a universe which was not indifferent
to man but an extension of man, a universe in which all things
were in organic and active relationship with all others, and which
was constantly interpenetrated by these relationships. He could express his need in terms as hyperbolic as these:

> A robin redbreast in a cage
> Sets all heaven in a rage;

but it was nevertheless a peculiarly modern view: one thinks immediately of Bergson's vitalism, of Einstein's relativity, of Whitehead's "events," of Freud's fluid levels of consciousness, and of
I. A. Richards' "mental balances."   The tradition in which Pope
found his ideas assumed the "rational" Newtonian universe, and
deduced from that what seemed to be the inevitable conclusions
for man and society. But Blake, who jeered,

> To be, or not to be
> Of great capacity,
>   Like Sir Isaac Newton,

and always argued that "where man is not, nature is barren," began with his picture of man and from that deduced a comparable
society and a comparable cosmos. There is at least this to be
said for his innocence, or his arrogance: the static universe of the
18th Century did not fit the facts of scientific experience for very
long after it had failed the facts of poetic experience.

But all the time, out of these conflicting elements in the century, a new myth was in the making, was, one might almost say, being rescued from the ruins of religion. And this is as good an example as one can find of the interdependence of myth and history. For if, on the one hand, the myth of rationalism was construed to mean that society, like the universe, was static, and that men, like stars, were fixed by immutable law in the position to which they were born, that civilization in all time, past and future, was only an abstraction of the 18th Century itself; then also it could be argued that, within that frame of rationality, men could employ their reason not toward some academic understanding of the frame, but toward a new control of the frame and of themselves. Reason could be employed for revolutionary as well as for traditional purposes. Either way, it was useful to keep God—the old god —out of the universe; for divine interference is always confusing to that rational faculty on the superiority of which both arguments founded themselves. Thus that very deism which, in Pope, argued against man's progress, could also, as in Paine, be used to argue for it; and into this second tendency flowed the whole rich protest against authority of the noncomformist tradition. The new myth, therefore, finds its modern beginnings as far back as Bacon himself—("Bacon has broke that scare-crow Deity," Cowley wrote of authority)—and the beginnings of scientific investigation; in Bacon's precedent applied to religion, with the various insistence on the right to individual worship of 17th Century Protestantism; and in this protest summarized once and for all in that era by the metaphysical speculations of Locke and the argument of the *tabula rasa*. The myth is of man's native goodness, a vision of the liberated individual progressing into dignity when released from the most crushing forms of authority, whether economic, political, theological; the concept of regeneration not in the next world, but in this; the regeneration of the social man. This is the chiliastic hope of 17th Century Protestantism given specifically political form, the millennium conceived anew in terms not of graves burst open but of institutions broken down: perfectibility. If there is no merely logical incongruity present in this concept, a sharply logical incongruity exists between perfectibility and an utterly antithetical idea with which it cooperated, namely, primitivism. But it disturbed no one. For it is precisely this cooperation between these logical opposites, primitivism and progress, that marks the strictly religious antecedents of the new myth: for what are these concepts but political terms for the older conceptions of Eden and the Millennium, of paradise lost and paradise regained?

With the breakdown and bankruptcy of Christianity as such in the 18th Century, the dissenting myth, combined with science, passes over to politics completely, and ever since it has been politics which, in terms of the liberal ideal of progress and more recent, revolutionary revisions of that ideal, has performed the ethical functions of religion. The French Revolution, precisely because it was anti-ecclesiastical, was a revolution determined by values which politics had seized from a failing Christianity; the transmutation meant a certain immediate loss in the poetic value of the myth, and only if it was presented in reorganized terms of the old Christian imagery, as in Blake, or in a reorganized version of the older pagan imagery, as in Shelley, would it readily yield itself to poetic purposes. Nor should the ultimate failure of the myth in the life of the 19th Century prevent us from recognizing its character at the end of the 18th.

4

Literature and Myth

JOHN B. VICKERY

I

The history of literature everywhere attests to the closeness and complexity of the relation between literature and myth. The tragedians of classical Greece; the epic, lyric, and dramatic poets of the Renaissance; the representatives of English and German Romanticism in particular; and many of Europe's and America's finest modern novelists and poets all show us not only the impact of myth on literature but also the formal and functional resemblances between them. And what is true of Europe and America seems to hold good for Asia and Africa as well. In Asia, traditional literary modes such as the Nō drama are rooted in ancestral legends and rites, while in Africa artists such as Amos Tutuola deliberately reach back to the myths of their region in order to give form and continuity to their explorations of the novel as a genre. In short, the world's literature and its myths are so entwined that it is virtually impossible to give full consideration to the one without at least a significant measure of attention to the other.

But what is the nature of this relation? The question is simple. Unfortunately, the answer is not, for a variety of complex reasons. It is possible, nevertheless, to single out four aspects of the interrelation of myth and literature. These, needless to say, are by no means mutually exclusive. The most obvious is that which can be called the formal one. Here we are struck by the myriad ways in which myths resemble works of literature. Reading of, say, Prometheus' experiences and exploits in Hesiod or in Apollodorus resembles reading a macro-plot summary of the plays of Aeschylus and Percy Bysshe Shelley. One does not confuse the two, but one sees the similarities. The images of Prometheus nailed to Mount Caucasus and of Oedipus blinding himself, for instance, reverberate in myth as in literature just as the sacrificial and judgmental nature of both events is inherent in the renderings of mythographers as well as dramatists. In effect, then, myth and literature are interrelated because of their shared traits of narrative, character, image, and theme. This relation, however, is one of similarity and not of identity. In the main, the formal traits mentioned above occur in myth in a less developed, explicit, and sustained fashion than they do in literature. Actions are more arbitrary, motivation more simple and also enigmatic, and continuity and form more a matter of the perfunctory and ruptured than of design and resolution. This difference can be likened to that existing between certain biblical tales, such as that of Samson, and the developed genre of the short story.

When two things as vital as myth and literature are seen to bear markedly similar elements, it is inevitable to wonder whether one is responsible for the other's existence, and, if so, which occasions which, or whether there is no causal connection but merely isolated and accidental resemblances. This issue makes up the second aspect of the relation of myth to literature. Since the roots of myth and the earlier forms of oral literature are lost in prehistory, any answer is speculative. Nevertheless, both the number and degree of similarities between particular myths and specific works of literature make it highly improbable that they can all be ascribed to accident or coincidence. In effect, the question of origins becomes central here, for the answers, no matter how tenuous, will shape our critical attitudes. One view of the relation would stress the logical and temporal priority of myth over literature. According to this view, myth's formal properties are simple, elementary forms that naturally become more complex and diverse as society develops and changes and as authors become more aware of the possibilities and significances of myth. Such a view sees myth as culture's earliest mode of responding to its world. Literature together with religion, science, history, and philosophy are later developments from it. It is as if myth were a group of undifferentiated iron filings that in time were sorted out into various different patterns through the introduction of a number of magnets. To the extent that this view has a "causal" dimension, it might be described as a kind of pluralistic teleology.

Another view argues that the relation is a matter not so much of myth's priority to literature as of myth and literature's temporal or logical coincidence. Such a position derives much of its weight from a close study of the oral stage of human culture. Since much if not all of oral poetry originates in ritual functions and purposes, and since ritual is essentially a physical rendering or equivalent of myth, it follows that these earliest forms of poetry often deal with the same subjects as myth—the nature of the gods, the origin of the world, human beings, society, law, and the sundry interrelations of these. In short, the oral culture possesses in its myths, legends, and folktales what is tantamount to a literature save only for the lack of a written text. Needless to say, the differences between an oral and a written literature are considerable, but they do not obliterate the similarities or continuities of form. As a result, the relation between myth and literature that emerges in this view is less one of cause and effect or of generic evolution than one of differing social roles. That is to say, myth and literature differ in that one is sacred (at least so long as the culture at large believes in it) and the other secular or profane in the original sense. The role of the one is to encourage actual worship, that of the other to provide entertainment of an order that does not rule out moral reinforcement, social responsibility, and religious piety. The two come together in the concept of celebration, which weds work and play, activities later separated by literate cultures.

A third aspect of the connection between literature and myth concerns the historical and the specific. One cannot read much of either myth or literature without discovering that the former often serves as source, influence, and model for the latter. The most notable and sustained illustration of this role, of course, is the extent to which Western European literature resonates with classical, particularly Greek, mythology. Edmund Spenser, Christopher Marlowe, George Chapman, and Shakespeare, for example, show us how fraught with myth is the literature of the English Renaissance. Similarly, Pierre Corneille and Jean Baptiste Racine, like Vittorio Alfieri later, in works such as *Médée*, *Polyeucte*, *Andromaque*, and *Phèdre*, reveal the diffusion of those mythic figures from their native literature to that of France and the Continent. Later John Keats and Shelley use figures like Endymion and Prometheus even as Heinrich von Kleist and Ernst Theodor Amadeus Hoffmann do. What is the most striking about these and the multitude of other instances available is not only their number but the variety of forms that the relation is capable of taking. The same, of course, is true of nonclassical materials, such as the Bible, medieval figures like Faust and Tristan and Don Juan, and the Celtic tales of Cuchulain, Ossian, Finn, and Taliesin.

Literature uses mythological materials as direct source for events and characters in which transcription is the relation, but it also draws on myth for stimulus to original conceptions and formulations. A prime instance is the transformation wrought in the medieval and Renaissance legend of Faust by Johann Wolfgang von Goethe, who made of a knave a hero of human aspirations. And mediating these two renderings is that of Thomas Mann, who made of the same mythic protagonist a much more enigmatic and morally ambiguous figure. The function of influence need not necessarily be a positive or affirmative one. Alexander Pope, for instance, uses classical myths and allusions for incidental yet incisive contributions to his overarching satiric design. Before him Aristophanes did the same in such works as *The Thesmophoriazusae* and *Plutus*. Even more detached treatment of mythic materials appears in André Gide's *Prométhée mal enchaîné* and *Thésée* and in Jean Cocteau's *Orphée* and *La Machine infernale*. They range from moral satire of ancient but enduring modes of thought to witty yet haunting demonstrations of the modernity of myth and on to coolly ironic interrogations of the nature and functions of myth itself. Thus, the role of myth as model for literature may be as much iconoclastic as iconographic.

Another striking feature of this historical relation is the range of the diffusion of myth throughout its own culture and into that of other cultures. Mythic figures such as Ulysses, Prometheus, Hercules, Cain and Abel, and Orpheus have been traced in their literary apparitions throughout much of Europe, particularly in German, French, and English literature. And there is no single direction or migratory pattern to this diffusion. Writers are drawn to their own culture's myths, as Heinrich Heine, C. P. Cavafy, and Nelly Sachs demonstrate. But they are also fascinated with the structural, thematic, and narrative possibilities in myths quite alien to their immediate culture. The nineteenth-century American Herman Melville and the twentieth-century German Thomas Mann utilize the Egyptian deity and culture figure Osiris. The British novelist David Stacton goes to the Hindu god Shiva for a fictional locus, while the American John Berry seizes on Krishna. The German novelists Hans Jahnn and Guido Bachmann plunge back to the Babylonian epic hero Gilgamesh for their protagonist. And the Japanese novelist Kobo Abe invokes the Greek figure of Sisyphus, as did the French writer Albert Camus before him, in order to dramatize the existential ordeal and dilemma. Even more inclusive in his response to myth is the American poet Charles Olson, who finds poetic models in classical, Babylonian, Mexican, and Mayan mythology.

At the same time, it is important to recognize that the whole relation does not come down simply to a random plundering of myth by writers. In some cultures, the relation between myth and literature, whether oral or written, is direct and intimate, a fact apparent both in ancient Greek and contemporary African literature. But in other cultures, such as English and French, a body of literature (e.g., Greek or Roman) often serves as an intermediary between the dominant, classical myths and the native literatures. In still other cultures, we find some of the relations between myth and literature proving to be arbitrary and largely self- or group-determined. An obvious example is the recurring fascination with Eastern myths that American writers from Ralph Waldo Emerson, Henry David Thoreau, and Walt Whitman to Allen Ginsberg and Gary Snyder evince at the same time as they struggle furiously to embody the intrinsic myths of their native land. In sum, then, the historical relation obtains even in those writers, such as William Blake, J. R. R. Tolkien, Mervyn Peake, or E. R. Eddison, who seek to articulate their own personal or self-created mythologies.

The final relation between myth and literature is psychological insofar as it concerns itself with the dynamics of the two activities. Three issues stand out. The first is the attitude toward the production of myths and works of literature. Linguistically, both differ from activities such as science or commonsense empirical statements of descriptive or predictive fact. Neither Apollodorus' "Pluto fell in love with Persephone and with the help of Zeus carried her off secretly" nor T. S. Eliot's "Apeneck Sweeney spreads his knees / Letting his arms hang down to laugh" are read as records of historically actual events. Yet both are taken seriously, that is, held to possess meaning or significance or, in Bertrand Russell's words, to consist of "an idea or image combined with a yes-feeling." Belief or something similar to belief seems to be involved in both cases, yet not in the way of accuracy or truth of report-making utterances. Even members of a culture holding or revering a particular myth are not always prepared to assert its absolute truth even when convinced of its importance as a model of past or future events. And to persons outside of that culture its myths appear either unde-niably false, as John Milton viewed classical myth, or fictional, tales capable of reinforcing social or religious convictions, stimulating the imagination, or broadening human sympathies. And as such, they are of substantially the same order as works of literature. The existence of both drives us to recog-nize that these fictions are essential, that we need to define and classify their functions and to face (or evade) the possibility that fiction making is the central activity of the human mind.

A closely connected issue in the relation of myth and literature is the activity of storytelling, because often, for the serious student, the fact of lit-erature's existence outweighs the question of why literature does exist. Here myth's relation to the narrative dimension of literature is enlightening. Be-cause of the bizarre and puzzling nature of many mythical stories and because of our cultural detachment and distance from many of them, we are more likely to ask ourselves about the rationale for their existence. Why should an individual or a series of individuals tell about persons having fifty heads and a hundred hands, or about children cutting off parents' genitals, or about shape-changing, thieving, promiscuous deities? Why should a number of writers recount the exploits of a crippled child who acts violently toward a parent, rises to high office through his sagacity, discovers a terrible secret concerning himself and his parentage, leaves his homeland after destroying his vision, and dies in exile? And why for that matter should anyone ever tell any story at all?

The answer to all these questions would appear to be that the story form is the basic way we structure our awareness of the world. Because time figures in experience, all verbal efforts to render it seem to fall into or to de-rive from the story form. As levels of abstraction increase, the story form is less explicit, as one can see from the social and natural sciences. But for myth and literature the narrative activity remains paramount. Consequent-ly, they direct attention to the fact that the human world is a story-shaped one and that the human being lives surrounded by fictions. Faced with a world and with experiences that give rise to everything from wonder to tedium, the human mind turns to story in order both to explore and to es-cape, to celebrate and to query, those feelings. In short, both myth and liter-ature are the meeting point of minds warmed and bedeviled by their percep-tions of the world; they are the means by which active and passive responses to experience are fused, for in the writing-reading activity, the mood of idleness, as Keats saw, is one with the mood of energy.

While the nature of the relation between myth and literature is impor-tant in its own right, perhaps of even greater significance is the value it pos-sesses for the student of literature. Like the relation, that value is multiple and diverse. Essentially it engages several basic questions and provides a di-

versity of perspectives on them. The first of these questions concerns literature's source, where it came from logically and temporally. No ultimate answer is possible. But in approximate terms, one can say that literature comes
from the tradition of oral narrative and nonnarrative performance. In this
tradition myth and ritual occur both as subject and as form or event. Whether
myth ever existed historically anterior to the oral tradition is impossible to
say. But since thought is logically prior to speech or writing and since beliefs
precede their assertion, we can say this: myth—here regarded as the conviction or convictions, explained in various ways by the actions of beings superior in kind and degree to humans, that provide a rationale for existing patterns of belief and behavior—constitutes the religiosocial matrix from which
literature emerges as an endlessly self-complicating phenomenon.

A more immediate question confronting thoughtful readers is why
literature affects us as it does. Here again the relation with myth affords a
possible answer or line of investigation. Historically this question has had a
variety of responses—moral, religious, social, imaginative, historical, and
psychological. But it is difficult today not to feel that some form of the affective and the constructive powers of the individual psyche is the root of
explanation. That is, literature affects us through its capacity to construct
persons, scenes, and even worlds that arouse responses uncircumscribable
by rational knowledge or empirical description. The same is true of myth,
which, however socially vital, still leaves us with the tantalizing mystery and
puzzle as to its ultimate or real meaning. Myth's roots in religious ritual,
however, suggest that one of its central functions is to provide contact with
that transrational but empirical power called variously mana, orenda, or the
numinous. Even though the bulk of literature is secular, literature clearly
shares in the spiritual or emotional core of myth's power. Its role is to per-
petuate and focus the significance of that awe, wonder, and above all vitality
that is the human response to the experiential that lies both within and without the individual. To that extent, not only the forms of literature but also
its functions can be seen as displacements from those of myth.

In addition to the historical and psychological dimensions of these two
basic questions, there is a third, formalistic, value in the interrelation of
myth and literature. It is not enough to probe the origins and affective power
of literature; we also seek to appreciate or understand literature, to convey
to ourselves and others how we feel about it and what values we place on its
instances. Yet one of the most persistent features of this activity is our inclination to be parochial, provincial, or conventional in our judgments. The
artist's rage for disorder seems perennially to be countered by the reader's
passion for the familiar. Expectations and preconceptions about narrative,
subject matter, plausibility, tone, form, and related issues threaten appreciation and understanding. Though it may be neither a necessary nor a sufficient condition for the appreciation of literature, myth here too may exercise a positive value on the relation. Essentially, it can encourage readers to

move beyond limitations of place, time, and cultural perspective. Myth provides clues to the variability of literary forms and the defensibility of new ones. In so doing it renews or encourages catholicity of response. The adventures of the Argonauts, the grotesque appearance of Typhon, the familial violence of Cronus, the helter-skelter sexuality of Zeus, the rampages of Hercules, the amoral incitements of Dionysus, even the tedious genealogies and arbitrary conclusions such as "so much for that subject" all serve to alert us to the range of possibilities inherent in the act and art of storytelling. They also serve to point up the intricate relations, both congruent and incongruent, obtainable between form and content. And out of the interaction of these two avenues of suggestion, myth further bears in on the reader of literature the full and reverberant implications of both forms being a matter not only of what is said but of what is not said, a matter not only of declaration but also of interpretation.

II

Because of the antiquity and persistence of myth, its interrelations with literature are protean, and the perspectives from which they are viewed are multiform. Any historical overview has to recognize that the explicit interest of literary critics in myth is of recent vintage, scarcely more than a matter of late nineteenth- and twentieth-century concern. In other areas the interest is of an older order going back as far as the Stoics and Neoplatonists in philosophy. But for our purposes, the prevailing current extraliterary perspectives on myth are anthropological, psychological, sociological, and philosophical. Each has several distinctive emphases or points of view.

The anthropological perspective has at least three different groupings. The first and earliest of these is the Cambridge School, consisting of Sir James G. Frazer, Jane Harrison, and F. M. Cornford, which derived from the classical evolutionary views of E. B. Tylor and Andrew Lang. This group concentrates largely on Greek mythology, though in Frazer's *The Golden Bough* and elsewhere it casts a comparative net over a larger but looser body of materials. The central contention of its members lies in the ritual character of myth; they feel that ritual expresses in action an emotion or complex of emotions that in myth is expressed in words. In their eyes, since actions, such as ritual dances and gestures, may be developed more readily than is possible for the public or communal narratives of myth, ritual carries a measure of logical priority. They are also convinced that ritual is comparatively permanent in form whereas myth possesses a shifting and manifold character. For them, myth is not originally etiological but may become so when the emotions giving rise to the ritual lose their immediacy. At this point, the myths purport to explain the existence and origin of the rituals.

A quite different approach is found in those anthropologists who worked with, and developed within the general intellectual frame of reference of, Franz Boas with his concern with the factual, his skeptical and even negative view of generalization and speculation, and his emphasis on specific cultural context. For one thing, his insistence on fieldwork and the collecting of data led, in his studies of North American Indians such as the Bella Coola and Tshimian and in Ruth Benedict's of the Zuñi, to copious records of what those cultures themselves considered their myths to be. This led to the view that the genesis of myth was communal and cultural rather than individual and psychological. Their studies concluded that a single genealogical explanation of the origin and development of myth was not possible.

A third anthropological perspective on myth is that associated with structuralism and preeminently with Claude Lévi-Strauss, though others, such as Marcel Detienne, Harald Weinrich, and Georges Dumézil, are also involved. This view rejects both the evolutionary emphasis and the avoidance of generalization. Its shaping influences are three. One is Karl Marx's functional analysis of society as a global unit. Another comes from the structural linguists—notably Ferdinand de Saussure, Roman Jakobson, and Nikolay Trubetskoy—and their differentiation of synchronic and diachronic together with their stress on the primacy of the relational. And finally it reflects the Freudian or psychoanalytic emphasis on latent meanings and the techniques for discovering them. As a result, Lévi-Strauss regards myth as a particular kind of language possessing properties or features that are more complex than those of language. Myth is the antithesis of poetry in that its value and meaning persist throughout all translations.

Because of its linguistic nature, myth is composed of constituent units, but unlike the rest of language it possesses units unique to it. Such units are bundles of relations rather than isolated relations because mythological time is both synchronic and diachronic. That is to say, a given subject in a myth has different functions at different times within the narrative. As a result, the subject's meaning consists of all the relations obtaining between all the functions. Therefore, the meaning of a myth consists of all such relations of all the identifiable subjects it possesses. Analysis of these relations, the structuralist argues, reveals that any myth—construed as all the existing versions including interpretations of it—consists of polar and contradictory assertions or implications. These are progressively mediated by other conceptual formulations until the original contradiction is in a sense resolved. The language of myth expands the context of the original logical or metaphysical problem until it is translatable into issues of a social and moral order. Since these issues have socially structured solutions embedded in the culture, their equation with the logically insoluble problem enables the society and its members to continue to function.

Myth, then, is a conservative force dedicated to perpetuating social and mental existence by absorbing a culture's metaphysical and cosmological contradictions into its societal convictions and customs. Underlying this activity of myth is a logic, it is claimed, that differs from that of contemporary science only in its subject matter and not in its methodology or rigor. Such a logic, however, is not apparent from myth's manifest or surface narrative, which is full of discontinuity, arbitrariness, and repetitiveness. At the same time, myth exhibits, says Lévi-Strauss, an enormous measure of similarity in its manifestations from widely disparate geographical regions and cultures. It can do so only because these manifestations possess an underlying structural pattern that is both synchronic and diachronic. One of the chief indexes of this pattern is the pronounced tendency of myth to multiply similar narrative sequences, characters, and attributes. In sum, what the structural approach to myth stresses is that myths cohere in a kind of system. Their latent structure is as vital as their manifest content and they function on various levels — social, psychological, economic, cosmological, to mention only the most frequently adduced — but in the same basic way. They also underscore the polarities and antitheses of human experience, of which the most notable appears to be that between nature and culture. At the same time myths embody in their narratives balanced adjustments of emphasis and attitude that gradually approximate to a viable resolution of the initial dichotomy.

The second major intellectual perspective on myth is the psychological and in the main consists of the ideas of Sigmund Freud and Carl Jung and their followers and successors. For the early analysts myth was regarded as the dream of the race, which functioned in a cultural, social, public fashion much as the dreams of an individual did. Both myth and dream were symbolically constructed messages from the unconscious testifying to its problems, needs, and goals. Closer examination of actual myths in relation to actual dreams showed a significant structural difference in degree if not in kind. Condensation, displacement, and splitting dominate the dream mechanism. Myths reveal a narrative order, a selection of material or content, a temporal sequence, even a choice of symbol that betray a greater measure of conscious ordering. As a result, the psychoanalytic view came to ally myth less with dream per se and more with the daydream. In the latter the mechanisms of the unconscious still obtain but are modified by some impact of external reality.

All analysts from Freud, Otto Rank, Karl Abraham, and Sandor Ferenczi to Géza Róheim, Theodor Reik, and Erich Fromm agree that myth is preoccupied with the basic elements of human existence. Its topics, either manifestly or latently, are those of the child ego that in some measure may persist into adulthood. These include the hatred or the resentment of the father; the incestuous desire for the mother; infantile curiosity about sexuality as it manifests itself both in the parents and in the child's own developing behavior; the anxiety aroused by apprehensions and fantasies concerning physical and psychological acceptance and rejection; the terrors of being left alone in a strange and alien world that culminate in the fear of destruction represented most powerfully in the threat of castration; the network of personal rivalries both generational, as with siblings, and intergenerational, as with parents and children; and the longing for acceptance into a secure and independent state of existence identified with the adult world.

Natural events such as urination, defecation, copulation, masturbation, and menstruation, together with the feelings of aggression, anxiety, disgust, pride, and so on, that they arouse, are projected into fantasy form so as to reject or sublimate individual sexuality. To the extent that myths' projections entail reversals of real or actual interpersonal relations, as, it is claimed, happens in the Oedipal myth, myths are called paranoid, at least by early theorists such as Rank. Later analysts, especially those influenced by ego psychology, are more inclined to see myth and folklore generally as providing individuals and groups with fantasy escapes from socially imposed repressions such as taboos on incest or polygamy as well as from blockages of drives other than those of sex.

In contrast to the Freudian approach to myth, which sees it as deriving from other basic aspects of existence, Jung views myth as an inherent function of the human mind. Freud and Jung are related by their concern with the genesis and the forms of myth. Though their answers diverge significantly, each seeks to explain the production of myth by the human psyche and the meaning of its symbols, images, and narrative patterns. Jung's answers reflect his divergence from Freud in three key particulars. First, he shifts the genetic motive for myth from the libidinal impulse to a more encompassing concept of psychic maturation based on a recurring pattern of challenge and response. Second, Jung regards the unconscious as an irreducible symbolic structure, at least part of which is common to all individuals. That is, it is a reality that is untranslatable not because linguistic versions are not possible but precisely because they are possible and are limited to the status of versions. And finally, rather than postulating a psyche structurally given and largely determined in its response capacities during infancy, Jung proposes one that is the product of its own continuous development throughout time.

The Jungian psyche generates archetypal images that belong to the possibilities of imaginal representation inherited from the evolving totality of the human race's experience. Such images appear both in the individual's dreams—though not all dreams or all aspects of dreams are archetypal— and in the myths of the world. They do so in order to pose both the recurring threats of regression and the traditional modes of coping with those threats that human beings have experienced since they first began to struggle toward and into a consciousness of the world and of themselves. These polarities of regression and progression, self and world, inner and outer are represented in myth in the figures of mother and father. The ambivalence of reaction toward them, especially toward the former, testifies to the dangers as well as the benefits inhering in each pole. Facing, and coping with, these polarities—on the parts of the protagonist within the myth, the individual or group audience outside the myth, and the creator or narrator mediating between myth and respondents—yield those psychic transformations that not only symbolize but bring about the emergence of the truly individual person who is simultaneously creative and morally and culturally responsible.

The foremost sociological perspective on myth is the functionalist one advanced by Bronislaw Malinowski, who was influenced to some degree both by the Cambridge School and by the French school of sociology associated with Emile Durkheim. Durkheim saw myth as a significant aspect of the religious system operative in a society, being to language what ritual was to action. Perhaps because of his anthropological field experience in Melanesia, Malinowski minimizes the symbolizing role of myth. Instead he stresses the intimate connection between a tribe's sacred tales and its social organization, including such practical activities as agriculture and economics.

What myth does in his eyes is to provide the institutions and beliefs of a society with a charter, a justification capable of resolving conflicting claims whether of empirical fact or of rational argument. Because the realities of history, geography, politics, and economics are frequently inconsistent, a society needs and so creates a means of resolving the competing claims in a manner that seeks to ensure the persistence of the society itself. Myth does this by recounting events from a remote past about ancestors whose racial continuity with the tribe is balanced frequently by traits, powers, and relationships discontinuous with those of the tribe. In so doing, myths exert a justificatory force—sanctioning certain beliefs and actions and rejecting others—on the day-to-day life of their society. This role, argues Malinowski, rather than that of explaining or symbolically representing spiritual states or natural phenomena, constitutes the function of myth.

To determine precisely what any particular myth actually sanctions is far from simple. To see that sacred tales about flying witches or earliest ancestors emerging from holes in the earth are charters for certain clan or territorial rights is almost as incredible as the psychoanalytic identification of gold with feces or eyes with testicles in myths. Instead of taking the manifest content of myths at face value, one defines their meaning in cultural terms that take into account the society's view of the creatures and objects and actions referred to in the myths. To understand this view, one must grasp such things as the prevailing system of marriage and kinship, criteria of citizenship or tribal membership, and customary rights to territory such as hunting and fishing grounds.

Another aspect of Malinowski's functionalism, and one that follows from his field sources, is his discrimination among the prevailing narrative forms of a society. Not all stories are myths in the Trobriand Islands, only those regarded as true and of extreme age and sacred. Distinguished from myths are both legends and folktales. Legends are thought to be both true and factual, at least in part, but they possess no magical properties or efficacy and have no prescribed manner of telling. Folktales are fictional so far as belief is concerned, recounted dramatically, and identified with a particular teller or family. The crucial point of this differentiation is that Malinowski took these categories from the culture itself and from its members. In addition, he valued the total immediate, as well as mediate, context of myth. Thus, of equal importance are such factors as the occasion and location of myths' recital, the nature of the teller and the audience as well as the teller's devices and the audience's degree of participation, and the tribal attitude toward these narrative classifications.

The final perspective on myth is that of philosophy, where the principal names are those of the Neo-Kantian Ernst Cassirer and his American supporter Susanne Langer, though Philip Wheelwright has made significant contributions to the semantics, meaning, and symbolic function of myth in relation to literature. Even more recently there is the work of Roland Barthes, A. J. Greimas, and other semiologists, which radically alters the notion of myth. Barthes treats myth as both a system of signs and a system of beliefs. Society develops a system of beliefs in order to preserve its sense of its significance. The system of signs is based on the system of language and functions connotatively in such a way as to covertly produce meaning that appears to be natural or ultimate or "given" when in fact it is manufactured. Such an approach tends to concentrate on the range of sign-producing activities and on their contemporary forms rather than on the mythologies of prehistory and ancient times.

Historically, philosophy has had a good deal to say about myth, from the allegorical approach of the Sophists and Neoplatonists as well as Francis Bacon and the euhemeristic view of the Epicureans to the fusion of the two in Giambattista Vico's *La Scienza nuova*, the rationalistic treatment of Bernard le Bovier de Fontenelle, Voltaire, and the Encyclopedists, and the subsequent idealistic reaction of German Romanticism in the works of such thinkers as Johann Gottfried von Herder, Friedrich Schlegel, Friedrich Schelling, and Friedrich Nietzsche. But the directions philosophy has taken more recently with the analytic school, existentialism, pragmatism, and phenomenology have, in general, precluded its attending in any sustained fashion to myth.

Cassirer focuses on two topics or issues: the cultural role of myth as one of the symbolic forms by which human beings creatively apprehend existence, including their own, and the nature of mythical thinking or mythopoeic consciousness. Like Schelling, Cassirer regards myth as an independent expression of the human spirit that cannot be explained or reduced to any other cultural form such as language, art, or science. It does, however, have a significant relation to these and other symbolic forms, for all constitute progressive differences of consciousness. Human thought and, perhaps, language begin in an undifferentiated state in which image and entity, the ideal and the real coexist. With the gradual development of the human spirit and consciousness, the symbolic and significatory split off from the original matrix until they become separate and distinct modes aware of their individuality. Art, for instance, knows itself as art and also as not science or religion or myth. Each of these is essentially a human disposition to a particular mode of expression that gradually crystallizes into self-awareness and objective differentiation. Thus, as his study *The Myth of the State* reveals, Cassirer treats myth as a basic and ineradicable activity of human consciousness.

This activity of mythopoeic consciousness differs from that of philosophy or science in being neither rational nor intellectual. Its perceptions are not a matter of dispassionately registering objective entities. Instead, it is a question of concentratedly possessing in all its immediacy an aspect of external reality that includes the perceiver's vital emotions aroused by both the act and object of perception. Mythic perceptions, in short, are affect-saturated. As a result, one is capable of sensing real but nonexistent entities such as spirits, demons, divinities, or even ominous or benign shapes and locations. In whatever form mythic images present themselves to consciousness they do so with an aura of preternatural significance and power.

With such a mode of consciousness, not only the object but its causal connections are of a unique and dynamic order. The perceptual process disregards consistency, predictability, and even possibility in its contents and in its affects, while at the same time it stresses both the recurrent and the singular character of the awareness. In short, myth is, for Cassirer, a mode of consciousness that symbolically structures the world and a record of the mind's processes projected on to the external world. Its symbolizing activity, therefore, contributes to the human creation of a meaningful and so-called objective world. By so objectifying human emotions in image and symbol, myth serves the socially pragmatic function of generating a shared feeling and conviction of social and natural unity.

III

There are a number of other theories and approaches to myth, especially in the areas of comparative religion, the classics, comparative mythology, and folklore. The foregoing, however, represent not only the major recent influences but also a conspectus of the most common ways of viewing myth. With the possible exception of the Boasian approach, all are reflected in the approaches of literary critics. These approaches, in turn, represent not so much clearly defined methodologies as differing intellectual influences and personal predilections.

Earlier myth critics, such as Colin Still, G. R. Levy, William Troy, H. H. Watts, Francis Fergusson, Philip Wheelwright, and perhaps Alan Watts, stood fairly close to the Cambridge myth-and-ritual school, partly because it seemed to support their formalist preoccupations with the autonomy of the text. In some instances, an additional motivating factor was the longing, frequently subliminal, for a cultural surrogate—found in art—for the sanctions and solace of religion. Other critics were less concerned with the timeless pattern than with personal responses, especially of the author, sublimated into mythic narratives and images. Harry Slochower, Morton Seiden, Honor Matthews, and Claire Rosenfield exemplify this focus as well as the distinctive emphases of the Freudian and Jungian perspectives.

Though these approaches have not disappeared, they have been significantly modified by the appearance of other, more socially oriented focuses. Literary works, like tribal myths and rituals, have also been perceived as reflections—no matter how dim, oblique, and ambiguous—of their cultural setting and social dynamic, as in the works on American literature of Henry Nash Smith, Daniel Hoffman, R. W. B. Lewis, and Richard Slotkin. Concepts and images such as the "New Adam" and the "land as virgin" are seen as permeating a culture during certain historical epochs in much the same way as the myths of a tribal culture provide a sanction for its traditions and customs. Midway between these formal and social approaches are critics who share with Malinowski, A. Irving Hallowell, William R. Bascom, and other cultural anthropologists the emphasis on functionalism, but adapted to the nature and interpretive boundaries of the literary text. Critics such as Herbert Weisinger, Patricia Merivale, C. L. Barber, H. Bruce Franklin, and this author maintain a historical stance toward their subject, as seen by their concern with influence, derivation, and periodicity. At the same time, they concentrate on the myriad functions of myth as a factor in the text and in the interpretation. In short, they are probably concerned more with the particular ways in which myth merges with literary texts than with the fact or identification of its presence. Of the same general emphasis, though giving more attention to the formal aspects of the question, are recent studies by Lillian Feder and J. J. White.

One cannot emphasize too strongly that none of the foregoing groups of critics constitutes anything resembling a school. The unity among these critics, such as it is, comes from their shared interest in myth as a narrative, symbolic, and structural phenomenon that materially impinges on literature. Most myth critics, however, would probably subscribe to the following general principles. First, the creating of myths, the mythopoeic faculty, is inherent in the thinking process, and it answers a basic human need. Second, myth forms the matrix out of which literature emerges both historically and psychologically. Consequently, literary plots, characters, themes, and images are complications and displacements of similar elements in myths and folktales. How myth got into literature is variously explained by the Jungian racial memory, historical diffusion, or the essential similarity of the human mind everywhere. Third, myth not only can stimulate the creative artist, but it also provides concepts and patterns that the critic may use to interpret specific works of literature. Knowing the grammar of myth gives a greater precision and form to our reading of the language of literature. In recognizing that mythic features reside beneath as well as on the surface of a work, myth criticism differs substantially from earlier treatments of the mythological in literature. Fourth and last, the ability of literature to move us profoundly is due to its mythic quality, to its possession of mana, the numinous, or the mystery in the face of which we feel an awed delight or terror at the world. The real function of literature in human affairs is to continue myth's ancient and basic endeavor to create a meaningful place for human beings in a world oblivious of their presence.

The question of what the relation of literature and myth is leads logically to what the relation can contribute to our understanding of literature. Foremost is the capacity, shared with all good criticism, to sharpen our perception of theme, structure, imagery, and character in a specific work and their continuities and development throughout an author's canon. Through the relation we are able to reveal the transmogrifications of a single motif or figure such as Orpheus, Oedipus, or Ulysses in a period or several periods and to underline the ways a genre in a particular historical period, such as modern Continental drama, utilizes the materials of myth. We are also able to interpret a period or group of writers like those of the American renaissance as embodying a dominant myth or concatenation of myths. Finally, the relation can even lead, as we see preeminently from Northrop Frye, to an inclusive theory of literature. Recognition of the pattern of *sparagmos* ("the tearing apart of the sacrificial body") in *Tender Is the Night*, the rites of passage of the protagonist in *The Plumed Serpent*, or the role of divine king and scapegoat in James Joyce's HCE in *Finnegans Wake* uncovers significant aspects of these works that other forms of criticism slight. An awareness of myth enables the critic to isolate latent elements, which, like those of dreams, possess the force that vitalizes the manifest pattern. Shakespeare's tragic heroes, like Spenser's Garden of Adonis, Goethe's Walpurgis Night, Hermann Broch's meditations on Vergil, and Mann's bloody ritual temple dismemberment (in *Der Zauberberg*) resonate with primordial affect because individual genius was receptive to sources with mythic content.

Myths and rituals may also help gauge the unique features of literary works. For instance, identifying William Faulkner's Joe Christmas, Euripides' Pentheus, Henrik Ibsen's Dr. Stockmann, Fedor Dostoevsky's Prince Myshkin, or August Strindberg's Libotz as sacrifical scapegoats is but the first step. In terms of the myth model of the scapegoat, one is driven to ask of the texts a number of functionally specific questions, including why these characters were chosen, what differing kinds of communal sins they are to remove, what forms—physical, psychological, or social—the expulsion takes, and what view of the myth is implicit in the creative interaction of author and text. In the process the reader comes to a concrete and precise apprehension of how individual and cultural dynamics shape the character's fulfillment of his mythic role. Almost inevitably this approach leads to a comparative method that uses myth and archetype as the ground for thematic and dramatic comparison and differentiation. It follows the arc of the Promethean myth from Aeschylus to Shelley to Saul Bellow or that of the Oedipal myth from Sophocles to Alberto Moravia and Alain Robbe-Grillet or the permutations of the trickster from the classics through tribal tales to Goethe's *Reinecke Fuchs,* Melville's *The Confidence-Man,* and Mann's *Bekenntnisse des Hochstaplers Felix Krull,* not to mention Ted Hughes's *Crow.* In so doing it enriches our understanding of artist and age alike.

Such a concern for the emotional patterning in myth is peculiarly appropriate to the twentieth century's struggle to achieve a viable mode of psychic and cultural order. Writers as diverse as Nelly Sachs, George Seferis, C. P. Cavafy, and Federico García Lorca show us this connection unmistakably. Their immersion in the reality and unreality of the present in no way precludes their reaching out to the mythological figures and events of their cultures for the powers to endure. They may elect to see poetry and myth as converging on an intuitive knowledge that surpasses rational understanding, as Hermann Broch, Rainer Maria Rilke, William Blake, and perhaps Boris Pasternak do. Or they may, like Gide, Jean-Paul Sartre, Bertolt Brecht, Eugène Ionesco, and the contemporary American novelist John Barth, find in myth the relentlessly human wisdom resident in the bracing ironies of the narrative act, which for them exist both within and without the text. But whatever the stance toward, and the uses of, myth, literature draws on, perpetuates, and re-creates myth as vigorously today as in the past.

An equally important facet of this perspective is that it affords a unifying point of view that more nearly than any other derives from literature itself. Its key terms — myth and ritual — encompass that from which literature emerged; therefore, it is aligned with literature essentially, not accidentally, and in a way that social, political, philosophical, and religious concepts are not. Its terminology, perspective, and values are inherently and radically literary; to this extent, myth criticism is nonideological. Thus, whatever anthropologists may say about the meaning of the word "myth," critics legitimately extend or alter its sense to the needs of their own discipline. For instance, one speaks of the myth in Franz Kafka's work and refers to a projection of the author's psychoses. Used of *Ulysses,* say, myth means a formal extrapolation of, or structural parallel to, an ancient story. In some of D. H. Lawrence's short stories and short novels as well as in Ionesco's drama, myth may function as a satiric device offering both a contrast and a sense of continuity between the forms of life lived by ancient and contemporary humanity. Or myth may refer essentially to a new version of an old story, as in Robert Graves's *King Jesus,* Mann's *Joseph* series, Gide's *Thésée,* Faulkner's *Light in August,* and William Golding's *Lord of the Flies.* Here it describes what has been called the writer's "mythistoria," that is, "the circumambient atmosphere of his place and time."

In short, the multiplex relation of myth and literature demonstrates that the term may refer to the author, to his work, or to the society that attends to both. Accordingly, it acquires manifold dimensions: psychological, rhetorical, semantic, ideological, or sociological. What is essential is not reduction to a single definition but skill in discriminating the meaning relevant to the occasion. Through extended and sensitive development of these various dimensions — as Frye's *Anatomy of Criticism* shows us — myth criticism may help close the gap between formal analysis, whether semantic, rhetorical, or archetypal, and the functional, genetic concerns of the literary historian, biographer, and psychoanalyst.

While myth criticism endorses the autonomy and study of literature, it does not consign the critics to the vacuum-sealed containers of their own brains. Instead it links them to other disciplines, notably anthropology and psychology, and so broadens their approaches to, and their modes of experiencing, reality. It thus aspires to reverse the practical achievement of the New Criticism, which was to cut off the critic from direct access to the resources of science, sociology, and philosophy. By espousing the necessity of extraliterary knowledge for the critic while reserving the right to adapt that knowledge in accordance with the needs of literary study, myth criticism serves as a reminder of the dangers of concentrating too narrowly on limited areas and approaches. To avoid its own form of narrowness without resorting to a fuzzy ad hoc eclecticism is one of the premier and abiding challenges confronting this approach to literature.

IV

From the foregoing one might think a critical millennium is at hand. But as Gilbert Ryle once observed, intelligent theory always holds out the possibility of unintelligent practices. What concerns us here are the major general issues inherent in the subject. Though considerable simplification and some distortion may be inevitable, nevertheless we can perhaps distinguish four such issues, which carry, it is hoped, as much relevance as rhyme. They are the problems of definition, limitation, relation, and "inflation."

The first revolves around the question of whether in literature figures such as the dying god or scapegoat and actions such as rites of passage or quest journeys are actually myths and rituals of the sort recorded in a culture's sacred works (or its oral equivalents). That is to say, is the work itself a myth? This question, rightly perhaps, troubles anthropologists and comparative religionists more than literary scholars. The former groups are concerned with the possible confusions attendant on the multiplication of meanings for terms such as myth. For them, the term should be reserved for societal, communal narratives of a sacred or largely sacred order that sanction and reflect the existing cultural order and that either have at one time generated, or continue to generate, large-scale beliefs concerning either the actuality or meaningfulness of the narratives. But so long as one retains a firm grip on the mimetic character of literature and the modal concept of displacement, there should be little difficulty over such a use, for these notions will effectively preclude attributing to texts the sociocultural and spiritual functions of communal myths. Further, it is quite possible to envisage certain texts attaining for certain readers and writers the status of myth and ritual but operating on a personal level in which the factors of obsession and projection are prominent.

More important in general is the matter of definitional range. That is to say, may the term "myth" be applied to scholarly patterns such as Frazer's dying and reviving god; Mircea Eliade's eternal return; the several syncretistic formations of the hero by Joseph Campbell, Otto Rank, and Lord Raglan; Cassirer's notion of the state; and even more encompassing notions such as Frye's myths of detachment and concern or Jacques Ellul's of history and science? At what point, in short, does the definitional power of myth cease and that of other terms, such as concept, construct, and fiction begin? Might useful discriminations be made through the development and refinement of such terms as "para-myth," "meta-myth," and "proto-myth" for use in those areas outside the anthropological and sociological study of actual peoples' sacred narratives? An important related matter is the issue of allusion and its acceptable extensional range from explicit through oblique to implicit. Calling a character or scene mythic poses relatively little problem when names, titles, and undisplaced events or descriptions from classical, Celtic, Scandinavian, or some other mythology occur. But the situation is quite different when demands such as that of verisimilitude and other literary conventions intrude. In many ways the problem underlying this issue of allusion, and indeed the whole question of definition, is whether all or only some literature may be linked with myth or called mythic. And as with so many deceptively simple questions, there is much to be said on both sides.

Even more critical, at least in terms of what we say about the relations of myth to specific texts, is the problem of limitation. It raises, in its own way, the most vital and certainly the most enduring question of literary criticism, namely, whether patterns and interpretive significances are in a given instance discovered or created. The issue is one of, among other things, plausibility, the nature of the critical copula, and by extension the problems of value and identity. It is in the light of these issues that we have to examine specific assertions concerning the relation of literature to myth. Is, for instance, Faulkner's Dewey Dell an inverted Persephone, as has been claimed, or is the narrative form of *The Great Gatsby* that of the Grail quest?

At one time critics argued for the identity of myth and literature and the value of the myth in the context of the literature. Now critics are increasingly probing the relation in terms of the character and functions of not only analogy but also homology, in part because of the growing recognition that the awareness and use of myth in understanding literature need not be inimical to historical criticism, even though much myth criticism has been more heavily weighted toward formal and structural concerns. To the extent that this possibility is developed, it is likely that more myth studies devoted to single authors in their milieus or to limited historical periods will appear. If so, clearly specific cultural issues will gain greater prominence, not only in the act of textual interpretation but also in critical theory.

As soon as history and theory loom in the discussion, the general problem of relation between myth and literature moves to the fore. Apart from the question of whether a myth occurs in a particular work, there is the problem of how to construe the general relation. It is a function of meaning or significance rather than simply of sociohistorical existence. One way of construing the relation is the loosely psychological and religious or spiritual approach. It views myth as a series of latent, oblique, or untranslatable symbols recurring in literature because of their human centrality and power. Another view is that of Northrop Frye, who sees myth as constituting the structural principles or meaning of literature. Myth in its earliest manifestations is protoliterature insofar as its narrative sequences, recurring images, and dramatic actions are of the same order as those of oral and written literature, however much refined and shaped by history and culture. The language in which early myth is cast is the principal differentiating factor from other kinds of mental response to experience. With time, however, this language begins to function beyond what traditionally or originally was regarded as myth; it operates also in religion, philosophy, and expressions of social concern.

A third view gives a slightly different perspective on the relation of myth and literature by placing the emphasis for the meaning of myth on literature. Essentially the argument is that, from the literary standpoint, myth, viewed as an imaginative construct rather than a verbal formulation, has no meaning, though from other standpoints, such as the anthropological, it has. From this view, that of the literary critic, literature then functions as a commentary on myth, assigning to it values or significance that it does not in itself possess. To the extent that myth has a relatively determined written or oral form—a text, if you will—it is protoliterature and so a partial commentary on itself. Literature thus becomes the provider of specific meanings for particular myths so that the historical sequence of literary works involving a myth constitutes the open-ended totality of that myth's literary meaning.

The diversity of these views underscores the inventiveness of the human mind in seeing a single relation from differing perspectives. It also shows that the historical plurality of the relation is a result of the shifting cultural relevance and hence mode and content of myth. Myth has been successively located in the areas of religion, psychology, sociology, and now semiotics and popular culture. That fact surely must condition the particular features of the relation between literature and myth in a given culture or historical period. Classical literature is what it is, at least in part, because myth impinges on it from the region of religion. Neoclassical literature in Europe, by contrast, is dominated more by myths emanating from the realms of society and politics. Where the dynamic and viable forces of myth are located in modern national literatures is one of the tantalizing questions facing the contemporary student of the relation of myth and literature.

The problem of "inflation" has more revolutionary implications. It consists of two major issues, one of which stems from the logical aspects of the relation and the other from the relation's historical development. The first issue involves the matter of genre and the phenomenon of writing. Myth clearly has close and unmistakable relations to the major genres of poetry, drama, and the novel and these genres can be studied in terms of these relations. What is not clear is whether other genres of literature, say, autobiography and the personal essay, are also informed by myth. If they are not, why they are not becomes a matter of some moment if for nothing more than purposes of definition and classification. Is literature one unified verbal continuum or does it consist of at least two distinct subsets, one mythic and the other nonmythic? The subjective, afactually shaped features of autobiography and the essay are too well known to need arguing, so that it is difficult to see how, at least theoretically, these genres are not also related to myth. And if they are, what are we to say of adjacent genres such as biography and literary criticism itself? Still further beyond lies the question of the relation of myth to essentially nonliterary forms such as history, philosophy, the social sciences, and perhaps even the biological and physical sciences. For if, as we are told, there is only *écriture* in which the distinction between literary and nonliterary modes no longer obtains, how are we to adjudge the conflicting claims of traditionally and recognizably differentiable species of writing? Are facticity and truth values to be taken as convenient fictions, conceptual myths whose nature is completely heuristic? If so, what criteria and decision procedures will enable us to select among them those that are truly viable?

The historical dimension of the problem leads to a similar perplexity. The modern literary concern with myth was initially associated with the early representatives of modernism — William Butler Yeats, T. S. Eliot, Joyce, Rilke — then with the exponents of neoromanticism, surrealism, and religious conviction until by degrees it came, on the contemporary scene, to be represented by parodists, ironists, and black humorists from Jorge Luis Borges and Barth to Ionesco, Nabokov, Walker Percy, Günter Grass, John Updike, and John Hawkes. With them myth is not invoked as an ordering principle or as a vade mecum to spiritual power. Instead it is an essentially comic invitation to the infinite varieties of narrative proliferation and interpretive possibility. And this quality of parody and burlesque is not confined to literature's handling of myth. When we turn, for instance, to Lévi-Strauss's Bororo myths (notably M_1 and M_5) in *Mythologiques*, we find more than a touch of absurdist humor playing around the scenes and details, which is not to say that the Bororo do. And when one comes to comment critically on and to study seriously these instances of literature and myth, our traditional modes of treatment — sober in organization, cautious with evidence, dedicated to interpretive knowledge — themselves seem unable to capture the perceived and felt realities of the narratives, and by this failure they stand forth as almost parodies in themselves. Can it be — and there are already more than a few signs on the horizon — that criticism, like literature and myth, will increasingly become deliberately parodic as it endeavors to attest meaningfully to the age's dominant forms and perceptions of myth and literature?

Bibliography

This bibliography is intended to introduce the nonspecialist to some representative theories of myth and to studies of general or specific relations between myth and literature.

Albouy, Pierre. *Mythes et mythologies dans la littérature française*. Paris: Colin, 1969. An examination of the forms in which certain classical myths have been developed in French literature.

Aler, Jan, ed. *De Myth in de Literatuur*. The Hague: Mouton, 1964. Essays by Dutch scholars assessing the recurrence of ancient myths in modern literature.

Barber, C. L. *Shakespeare's Festive Comedy: A Study of Dramatic Form and Its Relation to Social Customs*. Princeton: Princeton Univ. Press, 1959. A seminal assessment of Shakespearean comedy in the light of the work of the Cambridge school.

Barksdale, E. C. *The Dacha and the Duchess: An Application of Lévi-Strauss's Theory of Myth in Human Creativity to Nineteenth-Century Russian Novelists*. New York: Philosophical Library, 1974.

Barthes, Roland. *Mythologies*. Paris: Seuil, 1957. English version, trans. and ed. Annette Lavers. New York: Hill and Wang, 1972. Semiological analyses of the myths of French daily life. Included is "Mythology Today," a useful introduction to his approach.

Bush, Douglas. *Mythology and the Renaissance Tradition in English Poetry*. Rev. ed. New York: Norton, 1963. A standard historical treatment of the subject.

Campbell, Joseph. *The Hero with a Thousand Faces*. 2nd ed. Princeton: Princeton Univ. Press, 1968. Develops a loosely Jungian "monomyth' of the hero's ritual quest in legend and literature.

Cassirer, Ernst. *The Philosophy of Symbolic Forms*. 3 vols. Trans. Ralph Manheim. New Haven: Yale Univ. Press, 1955. Volumes I and III treat, respectively, language and the phenomenology of knowledge; Volume II, subtitled *Mythical Thought*, is devoted to a Neo-Kantian treatment of the role and nature of myth.

Chase, Richard. *Quest for Myth*. Baton Rouge: Louisiana State Univ. Press, 1949. A survey of modern anthropological and psychological views of myth, with some indications of their applicability to literature.

Feder, Lillian. *Ancient Myth in Modern Poetry*. Princeton: Princeton Univ. Press, 1971. An examination of poets' thematic responses to myth, which the author · sees as structuring the unconscious experience.

Fergusson, Francis. *The Idea of Theater*. Princeton: Princeton Univ. Press, 1949. Explores plays from Sophocles to Shakespeare as ritual expressions. Influenced by the Cambridge School and Malinowski.

Frye, Northrop. *Fables of Identity: Studies in Poetic Mythology*. New York: Harcourt, 1963. Essays based on the view that myth is literature's basic structural principle.

Hamburger, Käte. *From Sophocles to Sartre: Figures from Greek Tragedy, Classical and Modern*. Trans. Helen Sebba. New York: Ungar, 1969. A study of recurring character figurations from classical to modern drama.

Hays, Peter L. *The Limping Hero: Grotesques in Literature*. New York: New York Univ. Press. 1971. A study of the maimed character as a mythic archetype in literature.

Hoffman, Daniel G. *Form and Fable in American Fiction*. New York: Oxford Univ. Press, 1961. Treats mythic sources and forms in classical American novels and short stories.

Jung, Carl G., and Karl Kerényi. *Essays on a Science of Mythology: The Myth of the Divine Child and the Mysteries of Eleusis*. Trans. R. F. C. Hull. Princeton: Princeton Univ. Press, 1949. Depth psychology and the classics brought to bear on selected mythic patterns.

Kirk, G. S. *Myth: Its Meaning and Functions in Ancient and Other Cultures*. Berkeley: Univ. of California Press, 1970. A critical examination of the theories of Lévi-Strauss, Cassirer, Freud, and Jung by a classicist.

Lévi-Strauss, Claude. *Mythologiques*. 4 vols. Paris: Plon, 1964–71. Detailed illustration of the structuralist method of myth analysis.

Levy, Getrude R. *The Sword from the Rock*. London: Faber, 1953. Traces the hero's development and the beginnings of epic literature.

Maranda, Pierre, ed. *Mythology: Selected Readings*. Harmondsworth, Eng.: Penguin, 1972. Essays and selections representative of current thinking, particularly in a Continental context.

McCune, Marjorie W., et al., eds. *The Binding of Proteus: Perspectives on Myth and the Literary Process*. Lewisburg, Pa.: Bucknell Univ. Press, 1980. Essays on aspects of myth and literature from the medieval to the modern period.

Murray, Henry A., ed. *Myth and Myth-Making*. New York: Braziller, 1960. Essays from the standpoint of the anthropologist, psychologist, historian, Orientalist, literary critic, and creative writer.

Richardson, Robert D., Jr. *Myth and Literature in the American Renaissance*. Bloomington: Indiana Univ. Press, 1978. Studies the deliberate use of myth by writers to resolve antithetical traditional attitudes in their works.

Righter, William. *Myth and Literature*. London: Routledge and Kegan Paul, 1975. Brief critique of current theories and practice, with some suggestions for further lines of investigation.

Rougemont, Denis de. *Love in the Western World*. Trans. Montgomery Belgion. Rev. ed. New York: Pantheon, 1956. Influential and provocative study of the Tristan legend in relation to literature.

Ruthven, K. K. *Myth*. London: Methuen, 1976. Brief introduction to the various historical attitudes toward myth, with a consideration of contemporary problems in connection with literature.

Sebeok, Thomas A., ed. *Myth: A Symposium*. 1955; rpt. Bloomington: Indiana Univ. Press, 1958. Essays by anthropologists, folklorists, philosophers, and literary critics, reflecting the views of their disciplines.

Slote, Bernice, ed. *Myth and Symbol: Critical Approaches and Applications*. Lincoln: Univ. of Nebraska Press, 1963. Essays on the interrelation of myth, literature, and symbol in various historical periods.

Vickery, John B., ed. *Myth and Literature: Contemporary Theory and Practice*. Lincoln: Univ. of Nebraska Press, 1966. Representative essays on theories of myth, their relation to literature, and specific authors and texts.

Vries, Jan de. *Heroic Song and Heroic Legend*. Trans. B. J. Timmer. London: Oxford Univ. Press, 1963. Treats the thematic relation between myth and epic and saga literature, as evidenced in a number of traditions.

Weisinger, Herbert. *The Agony and the Triumph: Papers on the Use and Abuse of Myth*. East Lansing: Michigan State Univ. Press, 1964. Essays on contemporary applications of mythic patterns to literature.

Wheelwright, Philip. *The Burning Fountain: A Study in the Language of Symbolism*. Bloomington: Indiana Univ. Press, 1954. A philosopher's approach to myth, meaning, and symbolism in literary texts from the classics to the moderns.

White, John J. *Mythology in the Modern Novel: A Study of Prefigurative Techniques*. Princeton: Princeton Univ. Press, 1971. A methodology for myth in American, German, and English fiction.

The History that Literature Makes

Richard Waswo

"POETRY," wrote W. H. Auden, "makes nothing happen." I believe that, in the long term, he was wrong. Poetry, in the large, archaic sense of any fiction, and especially that class of fictions sufficiently reiterated and reread to become legends—the meeting-grounds of history and myth—can make a great deal happen. I shall here propose that the founding legend of Western civilization—the descent from Troy—in its literary retellings from Virgil to the sixteenth century shaped the actual behavior of Europeans and Americans in their subsequent contact with other, newly "discovered" cultures. By *shape*, I mean *constitute one cause of*. I wish to insist that fictional imaginings, themselves a response to past events, can themselves become a cause of future ones. It is customary for canny academics to be more diffident and guarded in assessing the intricate commerce between fiction and fact, to imply some kind of causation without actually asserting it. For example: "The relationship between literature and history is clearly an intimate one. Literature is particularly important in spreading ideas and images about things which are unfamiliar to the general reading public, thus helping to shape opinion and through it policy."[1] Quite another reason for careful circumspection is provided by recent examination of history as a discursive practice, a narrative that forms the objects of its own interpretation.[2] We are aware that history, like nature, is not an inert collection of *dingen an sich* (things in themselves) merely awaiting accurate representation by a transparent language. My argument presumes this awareness of the constitutive power of any discourse, whether called science, myth, fiction, or history. But I am concerned here simply with one of the things that discourse may constitute: *history* in the obvious, popular sense of *what happened*. As the languages we speak determine how we know the world, so the stories those languages tell determine how we act in it.

Such determination is not produced on the venerable model of mimesis as the individual's imitation of timeless moral exempla. It is rather a determination of our consciousness, a control of perception. The process is collective, cognitive, and historically contingent. It is analogous to the way in which a contemporary anthropologist has

307

demonstrated that myth determines history. The event in this case is the well-documented murder of Captain Cook by the Hawaiians, which is shown to be the result of his literally sailing into their mythology and being unable, because of a chance accident, to sail out of it.[3] Accepted and treated as the god Lono, Cook unwittingly followed the fictional scenario of his annual celebration, right up to sailing off at the moment when the god was to be ritually killed by casting his image out to sea. Unfortunately, one of his vessels lost a mast, and Cook put back into the harbor he had left. There, his real death completed the ritual that his return had violated.

By proposing the analogy of enacted myth for the history made by literature, I am violating modernist conventions of progressive sophistication. According to the standard distinctions, myths are of course fictions unacknowledged as such; they are believed as timeless fact, concern sacred, cosmic subjects, and are ritually reenacted precisely in order to determine what happens.[4] Literature, by contrast, is conscious fiction, not articles of belief; and to enact it is to make a childish category mistake, to court madness as Don Quixote does—in short, to "regress to myth."[5] When we're all grown up, we don't act out stories anymore. "Primitive" cultures do—they have "myths"; we have Wallace Stevens. We also have Ronald Reagan and his evocation of the "evil empire" which we are enjoined to combat by means of "star wars." That myths still determine facts—and that our notion of the "primitive" could stand revision—is nowhere better illustrated than by the recent appropriation of 26 billion dollars for research and development of the Strategic Defense Initiative. But the study of serious literature, in the deific Arnoldian and disillusioned modern sense, is supposed to have little to do with all this. That literature, on the contrary, is an integral, functioning part of an entire cultural system, and that we can study it in relation to (among many other things) such gross mythic enactments in public life is one of the most useful insights of structuralism. From another angle, Northrop Frye has been pointing out for years how mythic structures are perpetuated in our most sophisticated fictions.

It is not necessary either to be a structuralist or to accept the archetypal status that Frye claims for mythic structures in order to perceive literature as one discourse that shapes our world. It *is* necessary not to scorn this function, shared by other discourses, as a "regress" to some unenlightened prior practice of either individuals or societies. We are still, in other words, acting out stories; there is no regress, for the simple reason that there has been no progress. The very idea of progress is an issue in the legend I shall shortly examine—how the West comes to see itself as "advanced" with respect to other cultures.

To disclaim this notion of progress is not, of course, to deny change. But the change is not from primitive infancy to sophisticated adulthood in our ability to recognize fictions as fictions; it is rather a change in the kind of discourse that commands the belief that determines action. Yesterday's myth is today's science. It was the appeal of science in the form of ever-advancing technologies to which the U.S. Congress was responding when it enacted the SDI. That this program had from its first announcement been identified—even if derisively—by the title of one of Lucas's archaic romances suggests the unacknowledged role that fiction plays in determining what happens to our tax dollars. It also suggests the nature of the change in the kind of discourse: myths continue to be enacted, but only by coalescing with or assuming the form of science. This is precisely what happened to the story of civilization in our founding legend: created as myth, it was elaborated as history, and finally became, in the eighteenth and nineteenth centuries, science. The story, from Virgil to the present day, has not ceased to be enacted.

Here is the bare outline of the story as told by Virgil and Geoffrey of Monmouth. Once upon a time there was a great and prosperous city called Troy, built with the help of an unkept bargain with two gods. Since gods are not, in the long term, to be mocked, a consortium among them arranged for that city to be totally destroyed, by means of a stolen wife and a ten-year siege undertaken by an unprecedented alliance of Greek attackers. The noble Trojan, Aeneas (descended from an older ruling house than that which failed to keep the bargain), leads a band of escapees from the burning city, carrying his father and his household gods. Helped and hindered by two goddesses, after many vicissitudes, Aeneas and his band arrive in Latium, the western land foretold by Jupiter to be the seat of an empire without end. There, Aeneas takes to wife the daughter of the local king, subdues the local populations in a climactic battle, builds his walls, and establishes his household gods. His descendents rule peaceably, founding more cities, until a prophecy foretells the birth of his great-grandson, Brutus, who will cause the death of his parents but will nonetheless after years of voyaging in exile be highly exalted. And so it occurs: his mother dies bearing him, and as a youth he accidentally kills his father while hunting. Sent into exile, Brutus liberates a band of Trojans enslaved in the Greek islands and there acquires a wife. He leads them through many adventures in France (founding Tours by the way) and finally arrives at the western land called Albion promised to him in a dream by the goddess Diana. Here he has only to drive away and exterminate a few giants before he can settle down for good, rename the country, and build the capital city of New Troy. Troynovant flourishes long ages before King Lud, having increased its walls and towers, calls it after himself, London—an act resented by his brother for eliminating the name of Troy.

What is remarkable about this fiction is its elaboration and acceptance as history throughout Europe from the ninth to the seventeenth centuries. Brutus, the eponymous founder both of Brittany and Britain, was only the best known (thanks to Geoffrey) of the many invented descendents of Trojan princes celebrated in prose and verse for founding cities and nations from north Germany to Italy. Holland, Belgium, Alsace, Toulouse, Neuchâtel, Pforzheim, Mainz, Venice, and numerous other places joined England and France in tracing their origins to Troy.[6] Francus, a son of Hector, who will become the hero of Ronsard's unfinished national epic, *La Franciade*, is credited as the ancestor of the Celts in the eighth century (*Liber historiae Francorum*). Brutus's first extant appearance was in the *Historia Brittonum*, compiled about 826 A.D., where his derivation from Aeneas exists alongside the much older genealogy, inherited from Jerome and Augustine, that derived the population of the three known continents from the sons of Noah: Japheth (Europe), Shem (Asia), and Ham (Africa). Both genealogies were reinforced for the Renaissance by their appearance in the fraudulent "lost" texts of Berossus the Chaldean, published in 1498 by Annius of Viterbo. By whatever confused and tortuous pathways, it was then "possible to elaborate the Trojan origin of every European people, to account for the dispersion of the arts and sciences, and to provide an etymology of illustrious antiquity for every place name."[7]

Even more remarkable was the tenacity of belief in this fiction, especially in France and England, where Wace and Lawman exfoliated from Geoffrey their poetic versions of *Brut*, in the face of repeated suspicions and denials. Contemporary dissenters to Geoffrey were William of Newburgh and Gerald of Wales. And dissent swelled rapidly in the sixteenth century, under the influence of the recognizably "modern" conception of history forged by Italian humanists and philologists. Two native Englishmen had already expressed their doubts when Polydore Vergil, the Italian appointed by the first Tudor monarchs as England's official historian, dismissed Geoffrey from serious consideration in 1534 (*Historiae Anglicae libri XXVI*). For this dismissal, Vergil incurred the wrath of many Englishmen until the end of the century, among them John Leland. Other Englishmen, however, concurred in the dismissal and added ridicule to contempt. John Selden summed up Geoffrey as a "bardic imposture."[8] Yet, in the seventeenth century people are still being rewarded for producing genealogies solemnly linking the ruling monarch to the Trojan Brut.[9] In France, the doubters were even more numerous, more prestigious, more thorough, and had as little immediate effect. The story of Trojan origins was scorned and rejected by Pasquier, Hotman, Beatus Rhenanus, and Belleforest only to return to histories produced under official patronage in the next century. As late as 1714 a writer was jailed for demonstrating that the Franks were indeed not Trojans, but Germans.[10] The story of the descent from Troy clearly had an appeal that a century of skepticism and disproof could not diminish.

In the case of any individual writer, the appeals are not far to seek, and range from the narrowly racial, political, or nationalist to the most broadly idealist and universalist. Equally apparent, at the collective level, is the dual allure of Virgil's literary reputation and his imperial theme. Scholars have not failed to observe that the initial appearances of the Trojan connection coincide roughly with the creation of Charlemagne's empire. Geoffrey's whole treatment of British history, especially the character he gives to King Arthur, is obviously, if ambiguously, related to the imperialism of his Norman overlords. That the Trojan connection was an integral part of the imperial iconography Elizabeth I borrowed from Charles V, and was similarly deployed by the French monarchy of the period, has been demonstrated by Frances Yates.[11] At a still higher collective level, the utility of the Trojan descent was to offer a unified idea of distinctively Western, or European, culture. Here was its advantage over the older derivation from Noah, which merely identified the population of the known world as sons of Adam. But only the sons of Japheth were also the sons of Troy. This localization was of increased importance to the Renaissance for two reasons. In some medieval versions, the Turks had shared the Trojan ancestry (deriving, of course, from "Teucrian") from which they were excluded once they became, in the fifteenth century, a serious military threat to the West. Second, the Trojan connection allowed Renaissance Europe to see its origins as contemporary to, and not dependent on, the imperial Rome it so ambivalently admired. Ancient Rome was but the early-maturing sibling, not the untouchably great and distant progenitor, of cultural communities on the Rhine and the Thames, the Loire and the Po.

It is at this level that I wish to interrogate the meaning of the story: as the etiology of Western civilization, the founding myth that supplies our cultural identity, distinguishing it from others. For it is surely this role and status that made the story die so hard as history, and that, as we shall see, will keep its significance alive and enactable in other forms of discourse. In its literary embodiments that I shall discuss—the *Aeneid,* the *Historia regum brittaniae,* and *The Faerie Queene*—the story is technically a legend, sharing the features of historicized myth and mythified history. It is a narrative substantially about remote but human events, which explains them by means of other narratives about divine agency. It thus shares one of the functions of myth, which is to explain a whole cultural system, accounting for current practices—"the dispersion of the arts and sciences"—and names—the "illustrious" etymologies—as Professor Denys Hay has observed.

But why *this* legend? Why did the lineal transmission of civilization from Troy become so powerful a self-image for the Occident? What kind of civilization is thus transmitted? Before giving my answers to these questions, I must observe that the Occident—that is, Rome before Virgil if not after him—had a choice of cultural ancestors. Aeneas of Troy was indeed a less obvious choice than either Hercules or Odysseus, both of whose wanderings in the Italian peninsula were commemorated in stories and cults of pre-Roman times. To fix on Troy, however, was to impose an origin that was always already destroyed, and hence required a narrative of displacement, exile, and reconstruction.

The story is therefore structured as a journey, the search for a predestined and permanent home. The story thus presents civilization as that which comes from somewhere else. Specifically, it is borne by exiles from the east to the west. There, it is imposed by force on the indigenous population, who may or may not be given the opportunity to assimilate themselves to it. In any case, should they resist, they are wiped out. The image of civilization is the city, often in the synecdochic form of walls and towers.

It is precisely this process of *transmission* that makes this picture of civilization uniquely Western—that is, Roman—and rather odd. For other civilizations do not see themselves as having required transportation to their present location. Civilization, for the Greeks and Chinese, is a home-grown product. Those outside of Greece who did not speak Greek were simply "barbarians"; the Chinese name for China means "middle" or "central" kingdom—the omphalos of the universe. We Westerners, by contrast, are migratory and peripheral; we have not produced civilization, we have been civilized. And as we have received, so shall we give.

By plotting the course of civilization as the *translatio imperii et studii,* our founding myth explains "the dispersion of the arts and sciences" by tracing them to a single source that is elsewhere than the area where they now flourish. Like most legends (including that of the fall of Troy itself), it reflects in outline the actual history of the culture.

It is, after all, the case that much of our culture—its alphabet, nu-
merals, and religion; many of its institutions and ideas—originated
in the near East and moved west by trade and by conquest. The direction of this migration is faithfully reproduced in the founding story,
as is its nature, which is straightforwardly imperialistic. The literary
versions of the myth were themselves generated by particular moments of imperialist expansion. Virgil's assigned task was to glorify
Augustus's empire; Geoffrey's self-imposed one to glorify the kind of
conquest the Normans had made of England; Spenser's gladly assumed one to glorify the reign of Elizabeth, down to the last details
(in Book V) of her foreign policy.

Having thus responded to past events, the fiction acquired definitive force and moved into other discourses current in our own time.
Its explanatory account of the "dispersion" of cultural practices from
a single source simply became the "diffusionist" theory of twentieth-
century archeology. This theory was neatly summarized by V. Gordon Childe as "the irradiation of European barbarism by Oriental
civilization." And that is the meaning, in a nutshell, of the fiction's
plot: if it's "civilized," it can't have originated *here*—and vice versa.
The strictly diffusionist theory has only in the last generation been
invalidated by the technology of radiocarbon dating, which shows
Stonehenge to be as old as some of the Pyramids. Oriental irradiation
no longer suffices to explain the remains of megalithic cultures
around the globe; nor are their producers to be regarded as "un-
couth yokels."[12] Yet even as this theoretical form of the fiction's
meaning is being discredited, another is springing up to take its
place. This is the current vogue for speculating that the culture of the
whole planet is due to extraterrestrial intervention. Thus to extrapo-
late the plot of the myth into outer space suggests the stranglehold
that the story still exercises over the Western mind. We appear unable to imagine any other conceptualization of our history than the
one it gives us: because our cultural values came from elsewhere, so
must those of the entire earth. Without interstellar "irradiation," we
remain "yokels."

As the general structure of the fictional plot thus determines our
self-consciousness, a crucial episode in its unfolding will give to this
consciousness the concrete form that will determine our behavior.
What form this was may be inferred, before examining the episode,
from the symbolic image of the transported empire—the city with its
walls and towers. Cities are not just the hallmark of our civilization;
they are part of its definition for archeologists and historians. Etymo-
logically, civilization and civility both depend on belonging to a city
(*civis, civilis*—citizen, polite; *civitas, civilitas*—citizenship, courtesy).

Cities are literally what qualify us as civilized, and they require a particular organization of food production. The historical scenario is thus described by William H. McNeill: civilization depends on the production of a large agricultural surplus of cereal grains, which permits the congregation of people in cities and their division into specialized occupations. It is the liberation of some from the labor of food production still enjoined upon the many that makes civilization happen. For this reason, it first happened where nature made it easy to produce a surplus: in the deltas and flood plains of the Nile, Tigris-Euphrates, and Indus rivers. Millennia were required to clear and bring under sufficient cultivation the forest-covered lands with capricious rainfalls of western Europe.[13] For the historian, this very gradual and lengthy development of the surplus production that gives rise to the building of cities literally requires the spread of civilization from elsewhere. Civilization, that is, in this particular form—massively producing agricultural communities settled in well-ordered and diversified cities. Nor was the link between this mode of social organization and this mode of food production lost on the ancient world. The near Eastern goddesses of vegetation in general and grain in particular—Phrygian Cybele, Greek Demeter, Roman Ceres—are typically represented in art wearing a crown shaped like a turreted city: they are the sovereigns of citizenship.

The link between agriculture and cities is what constitutes civilization in the languages we speak—those that B. L. Whorf grouped together as Standard Average European (S.A.E.)—and I shall shortly trace it in the evolution of the Trojan myth. But first I want to point out, again, its ethnocentricity. To define this mode of food production and social organization as "civilized" denies that honorific designation to other modes. For this reason, even the contemporary archeologist illuminated by radiocarbon dating must withhold the title from megalithic cultures. Whatever feats of engineering, transport, solar observation, personnel management, and piety were necessary to erect Stonehenge do not qualify. With no surviving evidence of cities or writing among megalithic peoples, the fair-minded archeologist can only describe them as "before" civilization. The crucial link between agriculture and cities also determines the marginality, indeed the "barbarism," of the other major mode of life long practiced in the West—that of nomadic and semi-nomadic pastoralism. The presence of this link in the history and literature of Rome bequeathed to the West a myth of civilization that ruled nomads (among others) out, and found any human way of relating to the earth other than by clearing and planting it to be simply primitive. To the formation of that myth I now turn.

The earliest surviving reference to the Trojan ancestry of the Romans was made by Hellicánus of Lesbos, a historian of the fifth century B.C.[14] As Rome arose to compete with and conquer other Mediterranean powers, the Trojan connection was useful to her earliest historians, Timaeus and Fabius Pictor. These founders of Roman historiography were writing in Greek in the third and possibly second centuries to legitimize for a Greek audience Rome's conquests of Carthage and possibly the eastern Mediterranean.[15] Their purpose was to provide a newly powerful nation with a glorious lineage and an ancient past, establishing Rome's claims to independent prestige in the Hellenic world. But they did not need to invent Trojan Aeneas in his role as ancestor: this had been established long before by his identification in Latium with *Sol Indiges* and his worship there since at least the fourth century in association with a panoply of other fertility gods both Greek—Vesta, the Dioscuri—and local—Ceres, Liber, and the *penates*.[16] Though actual worship of Aeneas seems to have occurred only in Latium, the story of his escape from Troy, carrying Anchises and their household gods, was also popular in southern Etruria, where its pictorial representation on vases and votive offerings occurs from the sixth century. The word for these gods, *penates*, comes from *penus*, which means storehouse or granary. Eventually these gods moved from storeroom, via food-storage chests in the home, to hearth to become familial ancestors.[17] But the power of their Latin association with harvest and grain storage continued long after Roman domination of the area. The *penates* of Lavinium, brought legendarily by Aeneas from Troy and associated with Vesta, the Dioscuri, Ceres, and Liber, were the subject of a sacrificial cult conducted annually by priests who came from Rome for the purpose. Aeneas himself continued to be worshipped in Lavinium until the second century A.D. The famous piety of Aeneas, therefore, is precisely a form of worship characteristic of a settled agricultural community, in which the production of grain and the maintenance of cattle are of supreme importance.

Etymological coincidence, other rituals, and stories reinforced the association of this agricultural cult with Troy. In Etruscan, *truia* meant labyrinth, which figured in the cult, as did what was later called the "Trojan game." Pictorial representations of both occur with those of Aeneas. The Indoeuropean word *troia* meant (as it still does in Italian and in French—*la truie*) sow. Timaeus knew the story of the white sow and thirty piglets that Virgil uses (VIII. 42–45) to prophesy the founding of Alba Longa. Timaeus also knew the story of eating the tables, employed by Virgil as a prophecy of hardship (III.255–57) with a comic end (VII.112–17), when the Trojans' first meal in Latium consists of meat on flat, consumable pieces of bread. The serving of meat on flat cakes was a feature of the Lavinian cult of the *penates*. Both stories are native, local, and predate the legend, demonstrating "the absorption by the Trojan myth of ancient Italic rites of fecundity."[18] In sum, then, the Aeneas inherited by the early historians and by Virgil appears to have been identified by the Latins with the sun and water divinity who was the founder and first king of their nation. In all respects, he is the founding father of a wall-building agricultural society.

In the later forms this society took, it is no coincidence at all that one genuine etymological triad in S.A.E. should encapsulate the relationships privileged as civilization: cult/cultivate/culture (French: *culte/cultiver/culture*; Italian: *culto/coltivare/coltura*; German: *Kult/kultivieren/Kultur*). All derived from Latin *colo* (p.p. *cultum*, which means to dwell as well as to till the soil), these words make all forms of refinement—intellectual, aesthetic, moral—as well as religious worship dependent on tillage, on the controlled nurture and growth of vegetation and human taste. Opposed to cultivation, which is civilized, is savagery, which isn't. And what is savage (*silvestris, silva*) is literally "of the forest." It is land and people that remain uncultivated. To be *incultus* is to be savage, rude, and dumb. Our languages thus encode the forms of contempt felt by a settled agricultural community for other modes of material and social organization. They determine our awareness of what is "cultured," and the founding story they all tell of the descent from Troy enacts this awareness at a crucial episode.

This episode is the arrival of the invading cultivators from the east in the western promised land. The issue is how they perceive, and what they consequently do to, the land and its local population. I call this scene the arrival of the culture-bringers; it is the moment of structural fulfillment in the narrative when the long-delayed end of the journey is reached. Though many complications follow, as many have preceded, this moment, it is the raison d'être of the story—to bring the eastern exiles to the seat of future empire.

In the *Aeneid*, this moment is complex and diffuse, occurring in two stages: the landing in Latium and the embassy to Latinus's palace (Bk. VII), and the final penetration up the Tiber to the actual site of Rome (Bk. VIII). With respect to perceiving the land and its people, no such brutal simplicities as the etymological triad and the myth will later authorize are to be found in the great and ambivalent epic of Virgil. Aeneas is not confronted on his arrival in the western promised land with a race of savage boors. Instead, King Latinus and the Latins are a society of settled hierarchy and ancient traditions like his own—and therein lies much of the pathos of the second half of the

poem. Virgil had, after all, to pay tribute to all the presumed ancestral strains of the contemporary Roman nobility—Etruscan and
Latin as well as Trojan. History—figured in the poem by the all-pow-
erful wills of the gods—had decided that the local populations were
not to be extirpated by, but assimilated to, the new order.

What can be found in the *Aeneid* is the temporal and mythic displacement of the confrontation between the invading cultivators and
the indigenous hunters and gatherers. What can also be found there
is a repeated and resonant lament for the worst consequence of war
(especially civil war): the destruction of agriculture by turning plow-
shares into swords. Explaining the Ausonian origin of the custom of
opening the gates of Janus as a declaration of war (gates within
which, we recall, *Furor* still rages though shut up by Augustus [I.
290]), Virgil describes the Latins' forging of arms:

> They hollow out safe coverings for the head,
> Bend willow frames for shields; breastplates of bronze
> Or smooth and glinting greaves they hammer out
> From ductile silver: for this, all honor
> Ceased to coulter and to scythe; for this
> All passion ended for the plow.[19]

It is surely no accident that the epic poet who gave the founding
myth the form that later writers would imitate was also the poet of
the *Georgics*. Virgil is indeed central to European civilization, as T. S.
Eliot proclaimed, not least because he responded so powerfully to its
basis in agricultural production.

Aeneas is not required to bring this latter form of culture to Italy.
We learn about its introduction there from Evander in the second
stage of the arrival scene, when the Trojans land at the site of (the
cattle market in Augustan) Rome, participate in the celebration of
Hercules (a temple to him and one to Ceres flanked the *ara maxima* in
Virgil's day), and take a tour of the not yet extant but constantly
evoked city.[20] The scene is climactic and prophetic as it contrasts (for
the reader) the wealth and glory of Rome now—its golden towers
and temples—to the poverty and rusticity of Rome then—the low
dwellings, bristling thickets, and mooing cows. It is typical of Virgil
that he should at this moment of fulfillment evoke the magnificence
of the city in a context that implies a moral criticism of it: the dignity
and simplicity of Evander and his community (who appear to be
herdsmen), and his caution to Aeneas to become worthy of a god by
daring to scorn riches (VIII.364). Aeneas, of course, knows nothing
of the present (to which this advice more strictly applies), any more

than he knows the history (for us, future for him) pictured on the shield that he receives at the end of Book VIII. But he is told about the past, the original moment of culture-bringing to the seven hills of Rome:

> These groves belonged to native Fauns and Nymphs
> And men from tree trunks born, from hardy oak,
> Who had no code of custom and no culture,
> And knew not how to yoke the ox, store goods,
> Preserving shares, but fed on branches' fruits
> And victuals of toilsome hunting.

The culture-bringer to these aborigines was the god Saturn, who "Gathered in one place this ignorant race, / Scattered through mountain heights, and gave them laws."[21]

There are three linked features in this description of the indigenous folk that will determine Western perceptions of them forever after: (1) they are identified with the landscape they inhabit; here the identification takes its strongest, most archaic form: they are autochthonous, literally "sprung from the land itself"; (2) they are totally uncivilized, have no fixed abode, no social conventions nor arts *because* they do not plow, plant, harvest, and store but instead (3) they live by gathering and hunting. All these features of course derive from various global theories of human origins and progress to civilization current in classical myth and philosophy.[22] But Evander does not present them here as a global theory. He presents them as a description of what the inhabitants of this place once were, the indigenes of these groves, their original possessors (*tenebant*).

Saturn's intervention is benevolent.[23] His lawgiving ushers in a (very brief) golden age, which is then dissipated by greed and warfare into the usual chaos of human history. For Virgil, civilization is fragile and constantly menaced, always needing to be reachieved. Much of Book VIII dramatizes its successive reachievements in this place, Rome, by cultural heroes who come from elsewhere: in the past, Saturn, Hercules, Evander; in the present, Aeneas; in the unremittingly implied future, Augustus. It is reachieved by the establishment of peace (lawgiving); but peace can usually be established only by war. Those against whom Aeneas must war are not, indeed, savage indigenes; but there are clear indications that they are on a lower cultural level than the cosmopolitan Trojans. Few Latin warriors are properly equipped: most throw lead pellets, wear wolfskin caps, and go half-barefoot (VII.685–90). In battle, these "rustic" (*agrestis*) ranks are but an hors d'oeuvre for Aeneas (X.310–11). One commentator can thus infer that the association between the Trojans and Evander's Greeks shows "the need for alliance between the cultivated nations to bring civilization to the rude Italians."[24] In the ever-evoked future, the Italians may get civilized; but in the narrative present, most of them get dead. Virgil is rather more alive than some of his commentators to the cost of achieving our particular form of civilization. And rusticity, in his presentation—especially in the humble frugality and piety of Evander and his Arcadians—has positive values that rebuke those of the achieved empire.

All the nuances, complexities, and subtly discriminated values in Virgil's treatment of the founding story will be lost as westward the course of empire takes its way. The last three chapters in the first book of Geoffrey's *History of the Kings of Britain* contain his terse account of the arrival of the culture-bringers. Having been outnumbered by the Gauls in France, the Trojans land at Totnes.

At that time the name of the island was Albion and of none was it inhabited save only a few giants. Natheless the pleasant aspect of the land, with the abundance of fish in the rivers and deer in the choice forests thereof did fill Brute and his companions with no small desire that they should dwell therein. Wherefore, after exploring certain districts of the land, they drove the giants they found to take refuge in the caverns of the mountains, and divided the country among them.... They began to till the fields, and to build them houses in such sort that after a brief space ye might have thought it had been inhabited from time immemorial. Then, at last, Brute called the island Britain ... after his own name. (I.16)[25]

A particularly "hateful" giant named Goemagog, who uprooted oak trees to use them as clubs, led an attack on the Trojans during "a high festival to the gods." All the giants were slain, except Goemagog, who was saved for a wrestling match with Corineus, who finally hurled him off a cliff into the sea. After inspecting his kingdom, Brute sought an appropriate site for his "chief city" and found it on the Thames. "He therefore founded his city there and called it New Troy, and by this name was it known for many ages thereafter, until at last, by corruption of the word, it came to be called Trinovantum" (I.17). Afterwards, when renamed by Lud, his brother "took it ill that he should be minded to do away the name of Troy in his own country." At any rate, "when the aforesaid Duke founded the said city, he granted it as of right unto the citizens that should dwell therein, and gave them a law under which they should be peacefully entreated" (I.18).

The status of the invaders as cultivators, city-builders, religion- and lawgivers is clear enough. They like the richly stocked rivers and forests; but they neither fish nor hunt. They till the land and put buildings on it. Since Geoffrey has modeled most of Brute's peregrinations throughout Book I on the *Aeneid*, it is interesting that he neglects to mention in this scene (or anywhere) that it fulfills the prophecy earlier made by Diana (I.11). Geoffrey is a long way from understanding how Virgil's subject is historical destiny and process. For him, it suffices at this moment that the Trojans simply *want* the land. So they take it. The indigenes they take it from aren't quite people, of course, but monsters.[26] The giants aren't identified with the land at the outset; they are literally driven into it, scattered into its nonarable parts, by the invaders. There need be no concern about the giants' feeding habits or their lack of *mos* and *cultus* since they're off the scale even of savagery, being subhuman. One can be briefly preserved for sport. There need be no sympathy for their extermination. The new order cultivates the land, builds its capital city, and marches toward empire. The only Virgilian concern left in the episode is for names. Only after the land is cultivated, after his tribe has altered its face, does Brute name it. And the city will finally lose its name, the trace of its illustrious descent, just as the Trojans in Virgil will lose theirs to the vanquished Latins, in Jove's final concession to Juno's wrath (XII.835).

The concern for names, again, is about all that remains from Geoffrey in Edmund Spenser's version of the episode in *The Faerie Queene*. The differences are the more remarkable because Spenser is deliberately paraphrasing Geoffrey in order to trace and honor the lineage of his "soueraine Queene" (II.x.3).[27] Since Geoffrey's emphasis was on the culture that the culture-bringers brought, he can dispose of the indigenous giants rather casually, without needing to tell us much about them. Spenser, on the contrary, tells us nothing about the culture-bringers, but a great deal about the giants. As Spenser restructures the order of Geoffrey's narrative, he begins it at the arrival scene:

> The land, which warlike Britons now possesse,
> And therein haue their mightie empire raysd,
> In antique times was saluage wildernesse,
> Vnpeopled, vnmanurd, vnprou'd, vnpraysd,
> Ne was it Island then, ne was it paysd
> Amid the *Ocean* waues, ne was it sought
> Of marchants farre, for profits therein praysd,
> But was all desolate, and of some thought
> By sea to haue bene from the *Celticke* maynland brought.

Ne did it then deserue a name to haue,
Till that the venturous Mariner that way
Learning his ship from those white rocks to saue,
Which all along the Southerne sea-coast lay,
Threatning vnheedie wrecke and rash decay,
For safeties sake that same his sea-marke made,
And namd it *Albion*. But later day
Finding in it fit ports for fishers trade,
Gan more the same frequent, and further to inuade.

But farre in land a saluage nation dwelt,
Of hideous Giants, and halfe beastly men,
That neuer tasted grace, nor goodnesse felt,
But like wild beasts lurking in loathsome den,
And flying fast as Roebucke through the fen,
All naked without shame, or care of cold,
By hunting and by spoiling liued then;
Of stature huge, and eke of courage bold,
That sonnes of men amazd their sternnesse to behold.

But whence they sprong, or how they were begot,
Vneath is to assure; vneath to wene
That monstrous error, which doth some assot,
That *Dioclesians* fiftie daughters shene
Into this land by chaunce haue driuen bene,
Where companing with feends and filthy Sprights,
Through vaine illusion of their lust vnclene,
They brought forth Giants and such dreadfull wights,
As farre exceeded men in their immeasurd mights.

They held this land, and with their filthinesse
Polluted this same gentle soyle long time:
That their owne mother loathd their beastlinesse,
And gan abhorre her broods vnkindly crime,
All were they borne of her owne natiue slime,
Vntill that *Brutus* anciently deriu'd
From royall stocke of old *Assaracs* line,
Driuen by fatall error, here arriu'd,
And them of their vniust possession depriu'd.

(II.x.5–9)

There follow two stanzas on giant-bashing (not for sport) and one on place-names, whereupon: "Thus Brute this Realme vnto his rule subdewd, / And raigned long in great felicitie" (II.x.13), and off we go into the catalogue of Britain's real and imaginary kings.

To the three essential features of the indigenous inhabitants of the place destined for empire, Spenser has, with a vengeance, added a fourth: their "filthiness," moral and sexual. His giants live by hunting (and pillaging); they are autochthonous (even their mother earth can't stand them); not only are they uncivilized noncultivators, they are bestially immoral. Such a condition might safely be assumed of those who have no *mos*; but neither Virgil nor Geoffrey saw fit to expatiate on it. Spenser must repeatedly assert it—and he can only assert it, admitting it to be but conjecture. In the absence of information about the giants' origins, the conjectures are of unspeakable practices and unnatural acts. In order the more to condemn them, the giants are quite ambiguously associated with "halfe beastly men," thus rendering them not subhuman enough to escape human moral strictures. In terms of strength, they are indeed superhuman. The intensity and gratuitousness of Spenser's denunciations in this passage are patently obsessive. Their purpose and their motive become clear only in the last line of stanza 9, where Brutus's only action is stated in negative terms: he deprived the giants of "their unjust possession."

There are literally new worlds of experience and new urgencies of history here in that single figure of speech, the transferred epithet "unjust." Logically, there can be nothing unjust about the possession of a land by its aboriginal inhabitants. The giants' possession is unjust because *they* are so; and the whole point of Spenser's version of the scene is to make them so.[28] To transfer the "injustice" from their behavior to their land-tenure renders the taking over of that land, as well as their extermination, just.

To justify *dis*possession is the new, rather desperate, and almost exclusive aim of this rewriting of the story. There is also one new implication drawn from the ancient observation of the untouched land as "savage wilderness." Unmanured and unimproved, the land is also unpraised and unsought by merchants—unprofitable. In this state, it doesn't even deserve a name. The land gets named only when it becomes a commodity (first for mariners and fishermen). It becomes an object of language and an object of exploitation at the same time.[29] To the exploitation of agriculture is added that of commerce: the blueprint for the transmission of Western civilization is now fictionally complete.

Spenser has been able to complete it because he is writing at the dawn of its enactment in modern history. He invoked this history at the beginning of Book II:

> how through hardy enterprize,
> Many great Regions are discouered,

Which to late age were neuer mentioned.
Who euer heard of th'Indian *Peru?*
Or who in venturous vessell measured
The *Amazons* huge riuer now found trew?
Or fruitfullest *Virginia* who did euer vew?

(Proem, 2)

This is the situation that gives the new emphasis to Spenser's arrival scene and the new stridency to its tone. The indigenous inhabitants of North and South America (and later, in a reversal of direction, India and Africa) are about to be perceived as they are in the whole myth, and treated as they are in Geoffrey's and Spenser's versions of it. That civilization comes from elsewhere; that it consists in dominating the land, planting fields and skyscrapers upon it, and extracting profit from it; that any nondominating human identification with uncultivated land is ipso facto primitive and savage; and that, therefore, the displacement and/or destruction of such savages in the name of all the foregoing, which is progress, is morally justified — such is the scenario of the *translatio imperii et studii* in these major literary retellings of our founding myth as the descent from Troy.

I don't think it requires demonstration that this scenario was in fact enacted as the subsequent history of European colonial expansion. That such enactment did happen is a plausible basis for my claim that literature is a cause of real events — that by determining perception, it can determine behavior. Europe's literary perception of the indigenes in its own past was reproduced as its perception of the indigenes of the new worlds in both hemispheres. These perceptions were codified in discourses other than the literary, to a brief sampling of which I now turn.

Spenser is the ideal transitional figure, for he not only brought the legend up to date, foregrounding its moral anxieties; he was also a colonial administrator who left a document defending the policies of his superiors. He made history as well as literature — not in the New World, of course, but in Ireland. This document, *A View of the Present State of Ireland* (put in final form in 1596 but not allowed to be published until 1633), is described by a historian as an elaboration and summary of all the justifications for military conquest on the basis of cultural superiority put forward by Elizabethan Englishmen.[30] In it, Spenser classifies the Irish as barbarians on the basis of the way they use and fail to use their land. Like their ancestors, the Scythians (an odd choice, until we recall that in the legend they required Noah to teach them plowing), the Irish are cattle-herders, changing their dwellings as pasture is exhausted. This encourages outlawry and

more licentious barbarism than living in towns, makes them intracta-
ble to the civility of English law, and even gives them a taste for
"freedom." The remedy, Spenser proposes, is to require by law that
anyone who has twenty cows *must* also farm, "for otherwise all men
woulde fall to pasturadge and none to husbandrye . . . loke into all
Countries that live in suche sorte by kepinge of Cattle and youe shall
finde that they are bothe verie Barbarians and uncivill, and allsoe
greatlye given to warr."[31] Spenser thus neatly inserts a middle term
(which will have a long afterlife) between the opposition of savagery
as hunting and gathering and civilization as settled cultivation: barbarism as nomadic (or even semi-nomadic) pastoralism.

   After a century and a half of European colonization of North and
South America, the legend was formalized into law by Emerich de
Vattel in *Le Droit des Gens* (1758):

The whole earth is destined to furnish sustenance for its inhabitants; but it
cannot do this unless it be cultivated. Every nation is therefore bound by the
natural law to cultivate the land which has fallen to its share, and it has no
right to extend its boundaries or to obtain help from other Nations except in
so far as the land it inhabits can not supply its needs. . . . Those who still
pursue this idle [that is, hunting] mode of life occupy more land than they
would have need of under a system of honest labor, and they may not com-
plain if other more industrious Nations, too confined at home, should come
and occupy part of their lands.

Vattel then reasons that the Spanish conquest of Peru and Mexico in
order to extract gold was usurpation, but that the English and French
colonizing of North America was "entirely lawful. The peoples of
those vast tracts of land rather roamed over them than inhabited
them."[32]

   In the later eighteenth century, the legend acquired the status of
science in the work of the Scottish social theorists. James Millar's *Observations Concerning the Distinction of Ranks in Society* (1771) ruled that
the differences between savagery, barbarism, and civilization were
the actual stages of all human progress: from hunting and gathering
to pastoralism to agriculture, commerce, and manufacture.[33]

   Such a temporal scheme both predicted and justified the doom of
the native North American and his forest. The American General
Benjamin Lincoln wrote in a letter of 1792: "Civilization directs us to
remove as far as possible that natural growth from the lands which is
absolutely essential for the food and hiding-place of those beasts of
the forests upon which the uncivilized principally depend for support." In 1851, Francis Parkman saw the consequences of this process

for the indigene and his land as simply inevitable: "he and his forest must perish together."[34]

Such inevitability, of course, is always seen as divine decree; the discourse of religion is on this point at one with that of science in the nineteenth century. Both codify the legend's diffusionist theme into justification, consolation, or obligation. In 1807, William Wilberforce, the great English abolitionist, thus argued our moral duty to colonize Africa: "And we are well warranted, by the experience of all ages, in laying it down as an incontrovertible position—that the arts and sciences, knowledge, and civilization, have never yet been found to be a native growth of any country; but that they have ever been communicated from one nation to another, from the more to the less civilized." The contemporary Evangelical mission, the Committee of the African Institution, "backed its plans for carrying European culture into Africa by pointing out the frequent appearance of a semi-divine culture-bearer in the myths of many lands."[35] Missionaries could thus see themselves as playing the roles of Noah, Saturn, Hercules, Aeneas, and so on.

And the culture they were to bear was precisely that of the legend. The only way to make Africans less "roaming and predatory," said an English colonizer in 1858 (as Spenser said of the Irish in 1596), was to make them grow grain. "No race of man, it might be safely asserted, ever acquired a respectable amount of civilization that had not some cereal for a portion of its food."[36] What this "respectable amount" (observe the telling blend of social convention and commodity quantification in that phrase: civilization can be weighed out at the corner grocery) consisted of had been specified in 1801 by Crèvecoeur, writing about the American Indian: "It is therefore only at the period when man became granivorous that he was able to feel compassion and pity, that his fierce and savage customs were replaced by gentler affections, and that his neighbors became his friends."[37]

It is ironic that the "pity" we cereal-eaters alone can feel had so often to be prevented from interfering with the march of progress. In an oration of 1830, President Andrew Jackson dispensed us from weeping over "the fate of the aborigines" with a rhetorical question: "What good man would prefer a country covered with forests and ranged by a few thousand savages to our extensive Republic, studded with cities, towns, and prosperous farms, established with all the improvements which art can devise or industry execute, occupied by more than 12,000,000 happy people, and filled with the blessings of liberty, civilization, and religion?"[38] What good man indeed could ascribe any value at all to a way of life other than his own? None— especially if he could perceive that way of life only and irrevocably *as* "other" than his own. And it was this perception that the founding myth determined. Mediated through all these discourses, its final effect was to legitimize the genocide of hunters, gatherers, and nomads.

The determining power of the fiction in all its discursive forms is seen most clearly by its exercise in defiance of the facts, by what in the irremediably "other" way of life was not perceived. The scholars who have studied the discourses sampled here reach identical conclusions on this point. That few West Africans were "predators"; that most lived in settled villages, had elaborate social codes and traditions; that shifting cultivation, far from being lazy and unproductive, was the only way to practice agriculture in a tropical rain forest—these things did not influence the European "image" of Africa even when they were being recorded by observers. The imperviousness of the image to the data makes its "most striking" feature "its variance from the African reality." It was created in Europe for European needs.[39] Americans had the same, even more urgent, needs, so that their misperception of the savages was even grosser:

The basis of their understanding had long been part of the grand rationale of westward-moving colonialism. This was the tradition of the natural and divine superiority of a farming to a hunting culture. Universally the Americans could see the Indian only as a hunter. That his culture, at least the culture of the eastern Indians whom they knew best until the second quarter of the nineteenth century, was as much agrarian as hunting, they simply could not see. They forgot, too, if they had ever known, that many of their own farming methods had been taken over directly from the Indians when they were pushing westward. One can say that their intellectual and cultural traditions, their idea of order, so informed their thoughts and their actions that they could see and conceive of nothing but the Indian who hunted.[40]

We see what we look for; our stories tell us what to look for; we find it (whether it's there or not) and then we can act out the stories. Such is the process by which our founding legend of the descent from Troy makes things happen in the world.

The process itself is not visible until twentieth-century anthropology encourages us to be less imprisoned in our own cultural assumptions so that we can see others more sympathetically.[41] And even now, the old story is being enacted in scores of tribal societies around the globe in deserts and in rain forests, where progress, in our sense of dominating the earth to make it a commodity, is making them extinct. Nor does the causal role of literature in the process become visible as long as we teach and study it in splendid aesthetic isolation from any cultural dialectic or historical consequence. To conceive it so is the more indefensible insofar as the greatest literature is always aware of itself as an active agent in a cultural system at a given moment.

As a concluding example of this awareness, I will suggest that the *Aeneid* itself presents my argument that literature is a cause of history, that fiction makes things happen. In the poem, what brings about the imperial transfer, what causes Roman history and fixes the price of its foundation, is the will of the gods. This is plural and competing, of course, but it is all-determinant. Jupiter tells us what will happen at the outset. Venus apparently is not convinced by his foreknowledge, and she and Juno struggle over the outcome until the very end. The place of human agency in the poem is as notoriously problematic as the passivity of its hero. Aeneas initiates, of his own volition, no course of action in the poem. He reacts to others; he worries, he hesitates; he never, by himself, quite knows what to do. Often under great pressure, his mind wavers, as a flickering light, reflected from a basin of agitated water, plays over the walls and ceiling of a room (VIII.21–25). He seeks and receives constant encouragement and instruction from gods, prophets, furies, and shades. He does what he is told. Aeneas is the human actor in history. The gods (and we the readers) are history; they (and we) know what has already happened. Aeneas cannot know it, even when he sees it in the form of the unborn dead or the pictures on his shield. In the poem, we share the knowledge of the gods; in life, we are Aeneas. He and we are the historical actors as famously described by Karl Marx (in the *Eighteenth Brumaire*): "Men make their own history, but they do not make it just as they please; they do not make it under circumstances chosen by themselves, but under circumstances directly encountered, given and transmitted, from the past." These circumstances include all the discourses of our culture, and we do not know where our encounter with them will lead. Yet we and Aeneas must act, so we act as the past—the gods—tells us to act. But the gods are fictions.[42] They are the stories that we tell ourselves to order the past; and they, in the poem, cause everything. In life, by enacting stories, like Aeneas, shouldering the burden of historical agency unaware, we determine the future that we cannot know.

UNIVERSITY OF GENEVA

NOTES

1   Allen J. Greenberger, *The British Image of India: A Study in the Literature of Imperialism* (Oxford, 1969), p. vii.

2   I am thinking in general of Michel Foucault, and in particular of Hayden White, *Metahistory* (Baltimore, 1973) and *Tropics of Discourse* (Baltimore, 1978).

3   See Marshall Sahlins, *Islands of History* (Chicago, 1985). The fascinating story forms part of a brilliant argument for the historicizing of structuralism. Sahlins uses myths from many sources, including ancient Rome, to show how they encode a cultural system and are enacted as history, which can then change the structure of the system. His book is an eloquent plea for causality as a two-way street and for the "indissoluble synthesis" of such presumed dichotomies "as past and present, system and event, structure and history" (p. 156).

4   A convenient table of distinctions between myths, legends, and folktales is given by William Bascom, "The Forms of Folklore: Prose Narratives," *Journal of American Folklore*, 78 (1965), 5.

5   Frank Kermode thus describes it in the course of his melancholy celebration of the modernist conviction that literature has nothing to do with life: *The Sense of An Ending: Studies in the Theory of Fiction* (New York, 1967).

6   The catalogues and stories (Venice excepted) are in Jean Lemaire de Belges, *Les Illustrations de Gaule et singularitez de Troye* (1509–1512), ed. Jean Stecher (Louvain, 1882), Vol. 2. Lemaire is analyzed by Claude-Gilbert Dubois, *Celtes et Gaulois au XVIe siècle: le développement littéraire d'un mythe nationaliste* (Paris, 1972), pp. 24–39. The origins of Venice are narrated in Giulio Strozzi's little epic, *La Venetia edificata* (Venice, 1621).

7   Denys Hay, *Europe: The Emergence of an Idea*, rev. ed. (Edinburgh, 1967), p. 108; his summary of the whole tradition is concise. Fuller accounts of the texts mentioned, and many others, may be gleaned from the following: Don Cameron Allen, *The Legend of Noah* (Urbana, 1949); Edmond Faral, *La Légende arthurienne* (Paris, 1929), Vols. 1–2; J. S. P. Tatlock, *The Legendary History of Britain* (Berkeley, 1950); Robert W. Hanning, *The Vision of History in Early Britain* (New York, 1966); and David N. Dumville, " 'Nennius' and the *Historia Brittonum*," *Studia Celtica*, 10–11 (1975–76), 78–95.

8   Arthur B. Ferguson, *Clio Unbound: Perception of the Social and Cultural Past in Renaissance England* (Durham, 1979), pp. 36–37, 106 f. On Geoffrey's contemporaries, see Nancy F. Partner, *Serious Entertainments: The Writing of History in Twelfth-Century England* (Chicago, 1977), pp. 64–71.

9   A jewel that Thomas Lyte received for performing this service for James I is displayed at the British Museum.

10   George Huppert, *The Idea of Perfect History: Historical Erudition and Historical Philosophy in Renaissance France* (Urbana, 1970), pp. 75–86.

11   Frances Yates, *Astraea: The Imperial Theme in the Sixteenth Century* (London, 1975).

12   Colin Renfrew, *Before Civilization: The Radiocarbon Revolution and Prehistoric Europe* (London, 1973), pp. 16–17.

13   William H. McNeill, *The Rise of the West* (Chicago, 1963), ch. 1–3.

14   See Geneviève Dury-Moyaers, *Enée et Lavinium: A propos des découvertes archéologiques récentes* (Brussels, 1981), p. 53. This is the most thorough survey to date of the evidence, both literary and archeological, concerning the origins of the connection between Troy and Rome, as well as of the expert disagreements about it. Earlier, but still useful, accounts are: Franz Bömer, *Rom und Troia* (Baden-Baden, 1951); Krister Hanell, "Zur Problematik der älteren römischen Geschichtschreibung," in *Histoire et historiens dans l'antiquité* (Geneva, 1956), pp. 149–84; Andras Alföldi, *Early Rome and the Latins* (Ann Arbor, 1964); G. Karl Galinsky, *Aeneas, Sicily, and Rome* (Princeton, 1969).

15   H. B. Mattingly, "Q. Fabius Pictor: Father of Roman History," *Liverpool Classical*

Monthly, 1 (1976), 3–7, argues that the historian of this name lived later (second century B.C.) than is generally assumed (third century B.C.).

16 See Dury-Moyaers, ch. 4, which is based on the discoveries made and reported in
the last quarter-century by Ferdinando Castagnoli, *Lavinium I: Topographia generale*
(Rome, 1972) and Ferdinando Castagnoli et al., *Lavinium II: Le tredici are* (Rome, 1975).

17 See Börner, pp. 54 f., and Cyril Bailey, *Phases in the Religion of Ancient Rome* (London, 1932), pp. 49–50.

18 Dury-Moyaers, p. 206.

19 *Aeneid* VII.632–36:

> tegmina tuta cavant capitum flectuntque salignas
> umbonum cratis; alii thoracas aënos
> aut levis ocreas lento ducunt argento;
> vomeris huc et falcis honos, huc omnis aratri
> cessit amor.

I quote the Latin from the Loeb edition of the *Aeneid,* tr. H. Rushton Fairclough
(Cambridge, Mass., 1974); translations, however, are my own.

20 The locations and itinerary are worked out in the commentaries. The most telling
detail appears to be that Evander's hut is located on the Palatine just where Augustus's
famously modest house then stood. I have consulted the following: John Conington
and Henry Nettleship, *The Works of Vergil* (London, 1883), Vol. 3; K. W. Gransden,
Aeneid: Book VIII (Cambridge, 1976); P. T. Eden, *A Commentary on Virgil: Aeneid VIII*
(Leiden, 1975); C. J. Fordyce, *Aeneidos libri VII–VIII,* ed. John D. Christie (Glasgow,
1977).

21 *Aeneid* VIII.314–18:

> haec nemora indigenae Fauni Nymphaeque tenebant
> gensque virum truncis et duro robore nata,
> quis neque mos neque cultus erat, nec iungere tauros
> aut componere opes norant aut parcere parto,
> sed rami atque asper victu venatus alebat.

>   321–22:

> is genus indocile ac dispersum montibus altis
> composuit legesque dedit.

22 Almost all the texts cited by the commentaries—from Hesiod to Lucretius—as
sources and analogues of this passage about autochthony and the ensuing golden age
are collected and discussed by Arthur O. Lovejoy and George Boas, *Primitivism and
Related Ideas in Antiquity* (Baltimore, 1935).

23 In the later tradition, Saturn figures as the teacher of plowing and religion. In the
syncretic riot of the Renaissance, he is often identified by these functions with Noah,
who teaches plowing as well as vine-growing. In *Les Illustrations de Gaule* (I, 33–35),
Lemaire de Belges, quoting this passage, identifies Noah with the Roman Janus, whose
nephew was Saturn.

24 Walsh, in Fordyce, p. xxvi.

25 Geoffrey of Monmouth, *History of the Kings of Britain,* rev. ed., tr. Sebastian Evans
(London, 1963), pp. 25 ff.

26   The giants are a local addition to the myth, presumably arising from the Anglo-Saxons' stupefied reaction to the megalithic and Roman remains on the island: such structures could only have been erected by giants. The latter will be very serviceable to Spenser.

27   Edmund Spenser, *The Faerie Queene*, ed. J. C. Smith (Oxford, 1912); hereafter cited in text. Spenser paraphrases virtually all of Geoffrey, out of chronological order, in Books II and III.

28   Throughout *The Faerie Queene*, of course, giants are always the emblems of unmitigated evil—moral, political, social, sexual. Their association with the Titans as impious rebels against high heaven suggests a link between the founding story and this whole complex of classical myths, into which I cannot here go.

29   The simultaneity of the two is underscored by the (clumsy and uncharacteristic) repetition of the same rhyme-word in stanza 5: "unpraysd / for profits . . . praysd."

30   Nicholas P. Canny, "The Ideology of English Colonization: From Ireland to America," *William and Mary Quarterly*, 30 (1973), 575–98. The article shows how easily exportable to the New World were the justifications of colonialism in the old, without mentioning literature as such a justification.

31   Edmund Spenser, *A View of the Present State of Ireland*, ed. W. L. Renwick (London, 1934), pp. 217, 98.

32   Emerich de Vattel, *Le Droit des Gens* (1758), translation quoted from Roy Harvey Pearce, *The Savages of America: A Study of the Indian and the Idea of Civilization* (Baltimore, 1953), pp. 70–71. Vattel's formulations were applied at the same period to the colonization of West Africa; see Philip D. Curtin, *The Image of Africa: British Ideas and Action, 1780–1850* (Madison, 1964), p. 280: nations of "predatory peoples, hunting and gathering tribes, and nomadic herdsmen" were legally ripe for occupation.

33   Curtin, p. 64. He observes that the West Africans initially profited by this scheme: having a *kind* of agriculture, they were merely "barbarous" on this scale, as Montesquieu confirmed. "No one suggested at this point [1750s–70s]," Curtin adds later, "that shifting cultivation was a form of nomadism and thus an illicit use of land, though the idea would come with time" (p. 280).

34   Quoted from Pearce, pp. 68–69, 165.

35   Quoted from Curtin, pp. 252–53.

36   J. Crawford, quoted by Curtin, p. 404.

37   Pearce, p. 142.

38   Pearce, p. 57.

39   Curtin, pp. 479–80.

40   Pearce, p. 66. He goes on: "Biblical injunction framed their belief; and on the frontier practical conditions supported it." I have tried to show that the belief owed less to the Bible than it did to an older and specifically literary tradition, and that conditions long anterior to the frontier had long been made to support it.

41   For a marvelous attempt at imagining what a wilderness-ranging culture might look and feel like, see Ursula le Guin's novel, *The Word for World Is Forest* (New York, 1983).

42   Virgil, presumably, as a neoteric and admirer of Lucretius, no more believed in the literal existence of the gods than Spenser believed in the historicity of Geoffrey.

MYTH may be defined as a story or a complex of story elements taken as expressing, and therefore as implicitly symbolizing, certain deep-lying aspects of human and transhuman existence. This definition is framed in such a way as to avoid two contrary and one-sided views of the matter. The one, represented by Cassirer, treats myth as primarily a kind of perspective, and in this vein Cassirer speaks of "transposing the Kantian principle"—that all knowledge involves, at the instant of its reception, a synthesizing activity of the mind —"into the key of myth." Evidently m. here becomes synonymous with the mythopoeic mode of consciousness; it is simply a basic way of envisaging experience, and carries no necessary connotation of storytelling. At the opposite extreme stands the view that m. is *merely* story. In its popular form this gives rise to the colloquial use of the term "m." to mean a tale that is not according to the facts, and the adjective "mythical" as a synonym for "false." A more reflective development of the same general attitude finds expression in Chase's view that "myth is literature and must be considered as an aesthetic creation of the human imagination"; in other words, that the earliest mythologizers were individual poets—which is to say "makers," or storytellers—constructing out of their especially active imaginations tall tales characterized by a peculiar complication "of brilliant excitement, of the terrific play of the forces natural and human," and eventuating in some deeply desired and socially sharable feeling of reconciliation among those forces. As distinguished from Cassirer's position our proposed definition includes the idea of narrative as an essential part of the meaning of m.; but as distinguished from Chase's position it insists that the original sources of such storytelling lie somehow below or beyond the conscious inventions of individual poets, and that the stories themselves thus serve as partly unconscious vehicles for meanings that have something to do with the inner nature of the universe and of human life.

The partial validity of each of the views mentioned, as well as the variable relationships between m. and poetry, become more evident when we distinguish between the two main senses of m.—as mythopoeia and as mythology. Friedrich Max Müller (*The Science of Religion*, II, 1864) has proposed that the adjective "mythic" be employed for the first meaning, where no clear-cut ideas of true and false have yet emerged, and "mythical" for the second, where some degree of deliberate fable-making is implied.

Giambattista Vico (*La Scienza nuova*, 1725) was the first important writer to emphasize that primitive thought is essentially poetic, in that the endowment of inanimate objects with life, will, and emotion is at once the natural tendency of primitive man and the most sublime task of poetry—a point of view carried on with various modifications by Herder (1744–1803) and by Shelley (*A Defence of Poetry*, 1821). The word "mythopoeia" has come into vogue as designating the human outlook and forms of expression most characteristic of that early stage of culture when language is still largely ritualistic and prelogical in character. Each of these two aspects of the character of primitive language has a decisive bearing upon the formation of both m. and poetry. The relation of ritual to the rhythmic and eventually the metric element in poetry needs no demonstration. The ritualistic basis of m. has been emphasized by a number of anthropologists and classical scholars during the last few decades, notably in such works as: Jane Harrison, *Themis* (1912), Francis M. Cornford, *The Origins of Attic Comedy* (1914),

A. B. Cook, *Zeus* (1914), S. H. Hooke, ed., *Myth and Ritual* (1933), Lord Raglan, *The Hero* (1937), and Theodore H. Gaster, *Thespis* (1950). Harrison cites an ancient Gr. definition of m. as "ta legomena epi tois dromenois" (the things that are spoken in ritual acts). The reason why ritual tends to engender m. becomes more evident when we consider that genuine ritual is celebrative and therefore participative. Seasonal ritual (as Gaster has shown with respect to the ancient Near East) expresses something of the worshippers' joyful sense of the coming of spring, or of the summer solstice, or of the gathering of grain, and at such times the worshippers feel themselves to be participating in the great rhythmic movement of nature. Dance and song are the natural expressions of such participation, and the words of the song tend to describe or to address or to enact the personified forces that are being celebrated. From description to address it is an easy step in a culture which does not sharply distinguish between person and thing nor between adjective and noun. When the ancient Canaanites described a storm, "Baal opens a rift in the clouds and gives forth his holy voice," they probably got as close to a naturalistic description as their language would allow them to go; the metaphors that make the description possible are such that Baal is envisaged not as an abstraction but as a superhuman operator, to be addressed and to be ritually enacted. Where a set of linguistic habits is such that virtually no distinction is made between the literal and the figurative there is likely to be just as little distinction between the descriptive and the fanciful. Such psychic and linguistic amalgams are one of the most important factors in the genesis and early growth of m.

The role of metaphor in primitive language is a second factor joining poetry and m. Our reference here must be to primary, or radical metaphor. Metaphor in the familiar sense of "the transference of a name from the thing which it properly denotes to some other thing" (Aristotle, *Poetics*) is rhetorical, not primary, for it is possible only where certain terms with fixed meanings are already available as starting-points; it is, therefore, more characteristic of the post-mythological and sophisticated than of the primitive phase of m. There is a prior semantic activity which operates, perhaps preconsciously, by fusing certain raw elements of experience—qualities, relationships, capabilities, emotional colorings, and whatever else—into a unity of reference which some symbol is taken to represent. Thus in Vedic Sanskrit the word *agni* meant fire in its various culturally important aspects: fire as lord of the sacred hearth, fire as "the spoon-mouthed one" which receives the obla-

-[539]-

tion of sanctified butter from a spoon or ladle, fire as the messenger which crackles and leaps as it bears this offering to the gods on high, fire as the dispeller of darkness and hence of evil, fire which punishes evil-doers by its burning heat, fire as the generative urge in the loins of animals, and Lord Agni as a member of the Vedic pantheon. The hymns addressed to Agni in the *Rig-Veda* are thus able to designate the god with a connotative fullness appropriate to poetry, while they also stir up mythic inquiries by suggesting relations between some of these traits and others. Again, in the ceremony of the Night Chant practiced by the Navajo Indians the giant corn plant growing at the Red Rock House and the giant squash vine growing at the Blue Water House are employed as symbols of the masculine and feminine principles respectively, as symbols of food and therefore of plenty, as magically efficacious healing devices, and hence (through the idea of regeneration implicit in each of these aspects) as symbols of man's aspiration to spiritual rebirth. Such symbols have on the one hand a richness of reference, not overexplicit, that makes them suitable materials for poetry; while on the other hand the jostling of different and sometimes incongruous meanings may stimulate the invention of mythic tales to comment upon and partly explain how those meanings are related.

In recent years, particularly through the researches of Dr. Carl G. Jung at his school, a promising line of inquiry has been developed into the collective psychology underlying primary myth-formation. Jung postulates a "collective unconscious" which consists of "primordial images" or "archetypes"—i.e., transindividual ideas with a strong feeling-tone and with a tendency to find expression in characteristic imagistic forms. The Divine Father, the Earth Mother, the World Tree, the satyr or centaur or other man–animal monster, the descent into Hell, the Purgatorial stair, the washing away of sin, the castle of attainment, the culture-hero such as Prometheus bringing fire or other basic gift to mankind, the treacherous betrayal of the hero, the sacrificial death of the god, the god in disguise or the prince under enchantment—these and many other archetypal ideas serve as persistently recurrent themes in human thought. Since they have furnished story elements to the literature of widely different cultures, Jung and Kerenyi have employed Herder's word *mythologem* to designate this aspect of them. Jung holds that they are buried deep in man's psyche, below the suppressed or inchoate memories belonging to the individual, and that the libido has recourse to them "when it becomes freed from the personal-infantile form of transference."

The epic poet's invocation of the Muse would represent, in one aspect, the poet's desire to free himself from the "personal-infantile" type of thinking through being borne along by the more deeply expressive power of archetypal thought patterns.

The emergence of a definite mythology, recognized as such, represents on the whole a later and more sophisticated stage of human thought, when the primitive mythopoeic way of envisioning the world has been largely replaced by definite conceptions and a greater reliance upon reasoning, with the result that the older mythic stories have become materials to be embellished, recontextualized, and often reinterpreted by the poet's conscious art. The *Iliad* and the *Odyssey* represent two early phases of the development of mythological out of mythopoeic thought. While they contain many traces of an earlier mythopoeic attitude and of a ritual stylization (which the practice of minstrelsy in Homer's time doubtless did much to preserve), yet the voice and genius of an individual poet are unmistakably present, selecting and regrouping and articulating the older stories according to a freshly conceived design. Aeschylus' *Oresteia*, Virgil's *Aeneid*, Dante's *Commedia*, Shakespeare's *A Midsummer Night's Dream* and *The Tempest*, and Milton's *Paradise Lost*, represent in different perspectives the zenith of literary exploitation of mythology. The mythic ideas of the emergence of divinely sanctioned Gr. law out of tribal vendetta, of the destined founding of Rome, of the faery life of the Eng. countryside, of Neoplatonic hierarchies, and of Christian eschatology are here deliberately reconceived and reformulated through the imaginatively constructed medium of the poem. Yet some degree of positive belief is still operative in each of these works, giving spiritual force to the presentation and integrating without too much apparent artifice the diverse particulars. As the attitude towards mythology becomes more overtly sophisticated—e.g., in Ovid's *Metamorphoses*, Goethe's *Faust*, and Eliot's *The Waste Land*—the problem of finding a stable unifying philosophy by which to interpret a given subject matter becomes of increasing concern to the poet (cf. PHILOSOPHY AND POETRY).

The spiritual problems of the poet in contemporary society arise in part out of the lack of myths which can be felt warmly, envisaged in concrete and contemporary imagery, and shared with a wide body of responsive readers. Consequently, since the time of Herder there has been a gradually increasing insistence upon the need of what Friedrich Schlegel (*Gespräch über die Poesie*, 1800) calls "the mother-soil of myth." Unlike Herder, who urged the revival of Teutonic mythology as a rich mine of folk imagination available to German poets, Schlegel looked toward a new and more comprehensive mythology which would combine and blend folk elements with the idealistic philosophy of Fichte and Schelling, the pantheism of Spinoza, and the sacred writings of ancient India, thus achieving a "hieroglyphical expression" of nature conceived as a system of correspondences and symbols. However, Herder was careful to warn (what every good poet knows) that the m. must be related to the poem organically, not by way of a conscious effort to plug a gap. In other words, m. in poetry is not to be conceived merely as a narrative structure, but should enter into the very life-blood of the poem—that is, into its very mode of envisaging and formulating its materials. Accordingly, Friar and Brinnin declare that "the use of metaphysical and symbolist devices has grown out of the modern poet's search for a mythology which might offer him some concrete body for metaphor and metaphysic." Thus in St.-John Perse's *Anabasis* the mythic sense of race, of rootage in the soil, of space as the area in which man moves and settles, of matter as the quarry of his building stones, of time as the cycle of seasons shot through with a firm line of communal action in the erection of cities, all conduces to an archetypal image, concretely and movingly envisaged, of the human caravan as massively operative in man's collective prehistory. Rilke's reenvisagement of the Christian mythos ("Every angel is ringed with terror"), Yeats's gradual construction of a highly individual but nonetheless powerfully expressive mythology out of the marriage of Ir. folklore with gnostic theosophy, and Eliot's synthesis of anthropology, Christian mysticism, and Gr. and Hindu metaphysics are further outstanding examples of the poetic revitalization of m. and the fresh exploration of the philosophical and religious possibilities of mythic experience through the medium of poetry in our time.

G. Vico, *The New Science* (1725; Eng. tr. 1948); T. S. Eliot, "Ulysses, Order, and M.," *The Dial*, Nov. 1923; E. Cassirer, *The Philosophy of Symbolic Forms*, II, "Mythical Thought" (1923–29; Eng. tr. 1955) and *Language and M.* (Eng. tr. 1946); F. C. Prescott, *Poetry and M.* (1927); St.-J. Perse, *Anabasis* (Eng. tr. by T. S. Eliot, 1930); H. Rosenberg, "M. and Poem," *The Symposium*, 2 (April 1931); D. Bush, *Mythology and the Renaissance Tradition in Eng. Poetry* (1932) and *Mythology and the Romantic Trad. in Eng. Poetry* (1937); M. Bodkin, *Archetypal Patterns in Poetry* (1934) and *Studies of Type-Images in Poetry, Religion, and Philosophy* (1951); Langer, ch. 7; M. Schorer, *William Blake* (1946; esp. ch. 2); P. Ure, *Towards a Mythology: Studies in the Poetry of W. B. Yeats* (1946); J. Campbell, *The Hero with a Thousand Faces* (1949); R. Chase, *Quest for M.* (1949); E. Drew, *T. S. Eliot: The Design of his Poetry* (1949); T. H. Gaster, *Thespis: Ritual, M. and Drama in the Ancient Near East* (1950); K. Friar and M. Brinnin, "M. and Metaphysics," pp. 421–443 of *Modern Poetry*, ed. by the same (1951); A. W. Watts, *M. and Ritual in Christianity* (1954); H. Weisinger, *Tragedy and the Paradox of the Fortunate Fall* (1954); Wheelwright, chs. 7–10; *M.: A Symposium*, ed. T. A. Sebeok (1955; separate issue of JAF, v. 68, no. 270); Frye; K. Burke, "Myth, Poetry and Philosophy," JAF, 73 (1960); *Myth and Mythmaking*, ed. H. A. Murray (1960); *M. and Symbol*, ed. B. Slote (1963). See also J. Campbell, *The Masks of God* (1959–); M. Eliade, *The Sacred and the Profane* (1959) and *M. and Reality* (1963); R. Y. Hathorne, *Tragedy, M. and Mystery* (1962).

P.W.

MYTHOPOEIA. See MYTH.

Myth and the Modern Novel

The Return to Myth

"The Mythical Age" was the name the German novelist Hermann Broch gave to the twentieth century.[1] It is a view which would at least seem to be corroborated by the preoccupations of many writers and critics of today. Yet although a common denominator of much modern literature, myth can assume as many shapes as Proteus himself, and the attribute "mythical" may conceal a variety of cultural phenomena. Anyone consulting the relevant critical literature on the importance of myth for recent writers or on the particular role of mythology in contemporary fiction will find himself confronted by a plethora of general statements about the survival, revival and creation of myth. The recurrent idea of a "return to myth,"[2] for example, betrays decidedly Rousseauistic overtones and needs much careful delineation if it is to be profitably applied in the modern context. In practice, one is often left uncertain whether the notion denotes a return to specific mythologies, such as Greek, Roman or Sumerian, or whether it refers to the revival of certain archaically mythical qualities in modern literature. For Broch, the return meant only "a return to myth in its ancient forms (even when they are so modern-

[1] "The Style of the Mythical Age," *Dichten und Erkennen: Essays,* I, ed. Hannah Arendt, Zürich, 1955, p. 249.

[2] Broch, *op.cit.,* p. 262. See also the works by Baisette, Fischler, Jouan and Kahler listed in the bibliography. (Abbreviated references given in footnotes are to works entered in detail in the bibliography on the subject of mythology and literature.)

3

ized as in Joyce), and so far it is not a new myth, not *the*
new myth."[3] Yet the "return to myth" is not always so precisely defined; the reader is often left wondering which kind
of myth is being reanimated.

The ambiguity of the word "myth" does not help the
reader in search of guidance. Indeed, it induces many
critics to operate with a misleadingly shifting set of ideas
or a rather private interpretation of the concept. Hence,
while Northrop Frye can state that "in literary criticism
myth means ultimately *mythos*, a structural organizing
principle of literary form"[4] and Frank Kermode rejoins that
Frye "arrives at myth through archetypes,"[5] the uninitiated
may have difficulty in tuning in to these different semantic
wavelengths: the one aesthetic, the other psychoanalytical.
In *Quest for Myth*—a work whose very title exploits this
central ambiguity—Richard Chase asserts that "an interest
in the creative literature of our century forces upon us an
interest in myth."[6] Yet he undertakes to substantiate this
point by using a blanket terminology, sometimes referring
to myths as myth and at other times as poetic images of a
different order. And to write of the survival of myth—"das
Fortleben des Mythos"—as Erich Kahler does in *Die Ver-
antwortung des Geistes*, may sound equally ambiguous. Being a particular kind of image-making, myth has always
existed as one of the categories of perception and of the
imagination. "Myth making is a permanent activity of all
men," Eliseo Vivas writes;[7] "all men can do is to abandon
one myth for the sake of another."[8] To write of its survival
as such would be to wax too dramatic. What Kahler in fact
examines, quite legitimately, is the way in which particular

[3] *op.cit.*, p. 262.   [4] *Anatomy of Criticism*, p. 341.
[5] *Puzzles and Epiphanies*, p. 72.   [6] Introduction, p. v.
[7] "Myth: Some Philosophical Problems," p. 89.
[8] *op.cit.*, p. 92.

4

myths have lived on in our literatures. By using the apparently generic word "Mythos," he implies, as Chase does, that these myths are necessarily identical with the archaic power of myth: that they survive *as myth*. Yet need a return to the use of specific myths inevitably entail a return to myth in the other sense? And have both kinds of return to myth manifested themselves jointly in modern literature? According to C. S. Lewis:

> Certain stories, which are not myths in the anthropological sense, having been invented by individuals in fully civilized periods, have what [one can] call the "mythical quality." Such are the plots of *Dr. Jekyll and Mr. Hyde*, Wells's *The Door in the Wall* or Kafka's *The Castle*.[9]

Many modern novels also leave one in little doubt that there has been a comparable return to the use of particular myths from traditional sources. Such titles as *Ulysses, Proserpina, The Centaur, The Labours of Hercules* and *Gilgamesch* all serve, in a limited sense, to show that modern novelists still use material from old mythologies in their works. So there may have been a return to myth in more ways than one.

The "return to myth" is often assumed to be a particular feature of the Modernist movement in the early part of this century. It appears in some writings on the subject as a product of the influence of depth-psychology on certain novelists. One reviewer refers to such a use of mythology as "that old wayside halt for tired novelists in our post-Freudian age."[10] An impression may be given that this method is rather a thing of the past: that any contemporary novel which still incorporates myths should be assigned as a throwback to the context of an earlier epoch. Hence the elegiac ring to many of Thomas Mann's pronouncements on

[9] "On Myth," p. 42.
[10] *TLS*, 9 September 1965, p. 769.

5

the subject, in the forties. For instance, in a letter to Karl Kerényi, he remarks:

> Um jene "Rückkehr des europäischen Geistes zu den höchsten, den mythischen Realitäten" . . . ist es wahrhaftig eine geistesgeschichtlich große und gute Sache, und ich darf mich rühmen, in meinem Werke gewissermaßen Teil daran zu haben.[11]

Although many writers of the Modernist era, including Eliot, Joyce, Kazantzakis, Pound and Yeats, were certainly preoccupied with myths, such an interest is to be found with equal richness, and at times with a far greater intricacy of expression, in much subsequent twentieth-century literature. Therefore it cannot be assumed to be a distinguishing feature primarily of earlier decades or (worse still) to be derivative of them in an eclectic sense.

A study of the preoccupation with myth in the twentieth century would be a vast undertaking. Fortunately much of the groundwork has been carried out. Studies such as Hugh Dickinson's *Myth on the Stage* and Gilbert Highet's *The Classical Tradition* have surveyed large areas. In turning my attention to another aspect of the subject, the modern predilection for mythological motifs in fiction, I am partly responding to an evident lacuna. But the choice represents more than this. Among numerous possible features characterizing the contemporary interest in myths (including the dramatization of myths, modern poems on mythological subjects, anecdotal versions and variations on myths), the novel employing motifs from traditional mythologies remains the most frequently misunderstood example of the presence and function of mythology in modern literature.

---

[11] *Gespräch in Briefen*, p. 42. "As for that 'return of the European spirit to the highest, to the mythical realities' . . . it is, from a cultural point of view, a truly great and good thing, and I may praise myself for to some extent taking part in it in my work." (Translations, unless otherwise indicated, are my own.)

6

It is as much to consider certain problems of methodology as to fill a gap in critical literature on the subject that the following study has been undertaken.

James Joyce's *Ulysses* is the best-known illustration of this type of novel with mythological motifs which, for the sake of brevity, I shall henceforth refer to as the "mythological novel."[12] The two fundamental characteristics of such works are: first, that the mythological parallel is suggested as an analogy or contrast to the contemporary world in which the main events of the novel occur; and second, that the parallel is an extended one and could be described as a motif. This characterization excludes novels such as Cesare Pavese's *Dialoghi con Leucò*, Thomas Mann's Joseph tetralogy and Jean Giono's *Naissance de l'Odyssée*; for such works remain in the world of myths, even if the narrative tone is a modern one, occasionally tinged with irony or what Mann once called the spirit of Voltaire. Whereas the role of mythological motifs is analogical, describing the modern world in the light of a readily available set of models, works that are mythical do not offer myths as analogies, but make them their principal subject-matter or structural principle.

Distinguishing Myths from Mythological Motifs

The need to differentiate mythological allusions and motifs from myth proper accounts for some of the terminology used in this study. Throughout, the phrase "mythological motifs" will be preferred to the simpler form "mythical motifs." "Mythological" here signifies no more than "embodying a scheme of references to mythology." (Usually this will be to Greek mythology, but the increase in anthropological studies has meant that a modern writer now has quantitatively more myths to choose from and qualitatively

---

[12] A list of such novels is given in the first part of the bibliography.

7

a greater understanding of them, and can turn to more recondite mythologies, when Greek images have become clichés.) By using the word "mythological," one can avoid the assumption which so readily presents itself: that a work containing substantial elements from old mythologies creates, or is even necessarily intended to generate, myth. "Mythical," the usual adjective in critical discussions, remains too indiscriminate a word for this purpose; it is commonly associated with a dynamic quality, a *mana* seldom present in works that are here described as mythological.

Any attempt at demonstrating the mythical, rather than the mythological elements in literature,[13] would draw substantially upon Romantic theory and upon such modern theoretical classics as Sir James Frazer's *The Golden Bough*, Ernst Cassirer's *Philosophy of Symbolic Forms*, Claude Lévi-Strauss's *Mythologiques* and the studies in this field by Mircea Eliade, Susanne Langer and Eliseo Vivas. We have, however, no reason to suppose that a work of literature is necessarily constructed to create or resuscitate myth, just because it includes mythological motifs.[14] Indeed, one finds that most of the writers who are generally acknowledged nowadays as successful creators of such new myths, amongst them Borges, Faulkner, Giono, Kafka and Pavese,[15] have all noticeably refrained from constructing

[13] There has already been a number of studies with this purpose; cf. the works by Andres, Frye, Kermode (1967), Mühlher and Schmidt-Henkel listed in the bibliography.

[14] This in turn does not mean that certain writers may not at times have been seeking to create a new myth out of old ones. Joyce's *Finnegans Wake* and Malcolm Lowry's *Under the Volcano* have this mythical quality. And Broch once declared the goal of his literary endeavors to be a modern counterpart to the *Epic of Gilgamesh*: "ein Mythos . . . , der es wieder mit dem Gilgamesch wird aufnehmen können" (*Briefe*, Zürich, 1957, p. 186).

[15] For representative, rather than isolated, opinions concerning the mythical quality of works by these writers, see: Carter Wheelock, *The Mythmaker: A Study of Motif and Symbol in the Short Stories of Jorge Luis Borges*, Austin and London, 1969; Oto Bihalji-Merin, "William Faulkner: Mythos der Zeit," *Sinn und Form*, xvi, 1964, pp.

8

them with bricks taken from older mythologies. E. W. Herd has even argued that in the work of Broch, Joyce and Mann "the creation of 'new myth' is frustrated . . . by the return to traditional myth-material."[16] Hence, the conclusion which suggests itself is that mythological motifs are in fact different from myths, from both old and new myths alike.

If the concept of a motif is to prove a viable one in this context, it will be helpful to exclude solitary similes and metaphors borrowed from classical mythologies and placed in isolation in modern novels. One can clearly observe the difference between isolated allusions to myths and a more organized mythological motif in Elisabeth Langgässer's *Märkische Argonautenfahrt*, a symbolic quest-novel which appeared in Germany after the Second World War.

The narrator almost works through the whole Greek pantheon before the novel has ended, yet despite numerous references to classical mythology[17]—to which a host of biblical images could be added, there is only one mythological motif in the whole of the novel: that of the Argonauts' voyage mentioned in the title. The narrator reminds readers of it towards the end of the story: "so hat seiner Fabel das alte Modell der heiligen Argo zugrunde gelegen."[18] Where-

---

752-770; Antoinette Francine, *Le Mythe de la Provence dans les premiers romans de Jean Giono*, Aix-en-Provence, 1961, esp. pp. 9-11; Wilhelm Emrich, "Die Bilderwelt Franz Kafkas," *Protest und Verheißung*, Frankfurt a.M., 1960, pp. 262f.; John Freccero, "Mythos and Logos," *Italian Quarterly*, IV, 1961, pp. 3-16.

[16] "Myth Criticism: Limitations and Possibilities," pp. 74f.

[17] Comparisons are duly made between modern characters and Proserpina (p. 19), Endymion (p. 27), Diana (p. 28), Pan and Nausicaa (p. 38), the Gorgon (p. 45), the Medusa (p. 52), Vulcan (p. 54), Orion and Andromeda (p. 57), Hera, Apollo, Hermes and Aphrodite (p. 58), Hercules (p. 65), Pan (p. 91), Tartarus (p. 126), Dionysos (p. 130), Artemis (p. 135), Eurydice (p. 141), Prometheus (p. 221), Venus (p. 222), Atreus (p. 227), Charon (p. 237), Chronos (p. 239), Achilles (p. 240), Odysseus (p. 241), Persephone (p. 247), Demeter and Kore (p. 272), Aeneas (p. 328) and Niobe (p. 339).

[18] p. 399; "and so the old model of the sacred Argo acted as foundation to the tale."

9

as the biblical references and the allusions to Greek gods appear haphazardly throughout *Märkische Argonauten-fahrt*, the Argonaut motif reveals a definite pattern in its appearances. As might be expected, the narrator stresses the importance of this mythological quest motif at the point where the main characters set out in search of the Golden Fleece: the convent at Anastasiendorf, their goal during a pilgrimage after the *tabula rasa* of the Second World War. On the second page of the novel appears the description of a photograph showing the assembled travelers. It bears the inscription: "DIE ARGONAUTEN MIT IHREN DAMEN AUF DEM WEG ZU DEM GOLDENEN VLIESS."[19] The motif signaled here once more plays an important role as the adventurers approach their goal. Their desire to compare themselves with the Argonauts allows these travelers to see their spiritual quest in very concrete, and perhaps more optimistic, terms. The title of the novel, above all, has ensured that we see the whole journey in the light of the Greek analogy. Such a calculated use of allusions for a pattern of dramatic effect and objectivization marks the main difference between references to mythology rather preciously scattered through the narrative and the motif of the quest for the Golden Fleece. It would be difficult to avoid mentioning the Argonaut motif in any interpretation of *Märkische Argonautenfahrt* (just as one could not discuss Joyce's *Ulysses* without reference to the Homeric parallels), whereas only a detailed examination of the novel's imagery would require reference to most of the other allusions.

The noticeable patterning, rather than simply the frequency, of allusions is one measure of their function within a motif-structure. Other useful criteria for assessing the relative importance of allusions include their position in the narrative and the kind of mythological figure involved. At

---

[19] "The Argonauts with their ladies *en route* to the Golden Fleece."

10

times a single word is enough to establish a motif, if it appears in a novel's title, as it does for example in *Ulysses*. Yet if it occurs in isolation elsewhere in a work, as the Greek allusions do so often in Elisabeth Langgässer's novel, one might see it as an incidental reference only and not as part of a motif. It is clear, too, that even frequent allusions to certain mythological figures and events, such as Eros, Mars or Venus, or the Odyssey, do not always produce a mythological motif. It would, for instance, be difficult to make out a case for Anthony Powell's *Venusberg* or Rachilde's *Monsieur Vénus* as mythological works. Venus is one of those mythological figures who have a general, almost allegorical connotation that does not readily lend itself to the creation of a motif linked with specific events or characters. Furthermore, it follows that if the chosen tale is not fairly straightforward, it cannot provide a clear-cut pattern. It is generally agreed, for example, that the Greek mythological figure Hermes is used as a symbol in Thomas Mann's *Felix Krull*. Yet Hermes has so many associations that one cannot really speak of a mythological motif giving any real pattern to our reading of this novel. To lend itself to creating a mythological motif, the analogy has to be well defined, clearly indicated to the reader and presented at significant points in the development of the narrative.

Myths as Literary Prefigurations

Rather than being viewed in isolation, mythological motifs will be related to the more general technique of prefiguration, a literary device which embraces both this and other kinds of patterning in the presentation of character and plot. A myth introduced by a modern novelist into his work can prefigure and hence anticipate the plot in a number of ways. Although an awareness of sources is declining, the ideal reader can still be expected to be familiar with most prefigurations beforehand, just as the novelist himself was

11

when he wrote the work. And because it is better known than the new work, the myth will offer the novelist a short-hand system of symbolic comment on modern events. "Prefiguration" is a useful word to describe this relationship, since it suggests "coming before" and hence offering a comparison with a whole configuration of actions or figures.

Although now frequent in literary criticism, the word "prefiguration" is of religious origin, a translation of the Latin technical term *figura* used to describe the scheme by which "the persons and events of the Old Testament were prefigurations of the New Testament and its history of Salvation."[20] One of the classic examples of prefiguration in this sense is the prophetic relationship between Abraham's preparation to sacrifice his son Isaac and the Crucifixion. In St. Augustine's time, the word *praefiguratio* was used instead of *figura*[21] and since then the term has been secularized and adapted to many other contexts. Obviously, when used in the secular sense, the idea of prefiguration loses its original prophetic connotation. In the literary context, Homer's *Odyssey* can hardly be interpreted as a joyous or foreboding prophecy that Joyce's *Ulysses* was to come.

One merit of the term "prefiguration" in its secularized sense is its latitude of meaning. With it, one can enlarge the scope of an investigation of such symbolic correspondences, to avoid certain misconceptions, by treating not only motifs taken from old mythologies, but also those using legends. For example, the legendary motif of Faust and the devil in John Hersey's *Too Far to Walk* is structurally very similar to many mythological motifs. A wider term also makes it possible to compare mythological motifs with literary plot-

[20] Erich Auerbach, "*Figura* in the Phenomenal Prophecy of the Church Fathers," *Scenes from the Drama of European Literature*, New York, 1959, p. 30.

[21] Auerbach, *op.cit.*, p. 39, gives the example of Noah's Ark being described as a prefiguration of the Church: "praefiguratio ecclesiae" in St. Augustine's *De civitate dei*, xiv, 27.

12

prefigurations, such as the use of Shakespeare's plays in Aldous Huxley's *Brave New World* or of Chekhov's *The Seagull* in Macdonald Harris's *Trepleff*. And prefigurations, can, of course, come from other, less dignified sources. Echoing some lines from Walt Whitman's *Song of the Exposition*,[22] Leslie Fiedler recently suggested that we "must cancel out those long overdue accounts to Greece and Rome. . . . The new mythology must come out of pop songs and comic books."[23] A recent German pop-novel, Heinz von Cramer's *Der Paralleldenker*—aptly sub-titled *Zombies Roman*—chooses its analogies from among cinema and cartoon characters.[24] These too I would see as prefigurations. For, despite the wide range of sources for literary motifs, all these patterns bear close resemblances to many mythological prefigurations usually discussed in splendid isolation. These devices need to be compared and occasionally contrasted with one another, if this type of authorial comment is really to be understood. By concentrating, nevertheless, primarily on the *mythological* motif, I hope to pinpoint certain important features of the presence of mythology in the novel and to give less treatment to other aspects, such as the use of isolated allusions, metaphors and similes— techniques which have not changed fundamentally in recent times. Interpreting the mythological motif as an in-

---

[22] Come Muse migrate from Greece and Ionia,
    Cross out please those immensely overpaid accounts,
    That matter of Troy and Achilles' wrath, and Aeneas,' Odysseus' wanderings,
    Placard "Removed" and "To Let" on the rocks of your snowy Parnassus . . .
    For know a better, fresher, busier sphere, a wide, untried domain awaits, demands you.
[23] Quoted by Ann Banks in her report, "Symposium Sidelights," *Novel*, III, 1970, pp. 208-209.
[24] Zombie, the hero of this novel published in Hamburg in 1968, is compared with Jean-Paul Belmondo (p. 23), Sean Connery (p. 24), and Batman's friend Robin (p. 212), while his mistress of the moment is prefigured by Jeanne Moreau, Brigitte Bardot and Anna Karina (pp. 23f.).

13

stance of *secularized* prefiguration serves at the same time to highlight its role as an analogical system of comment and precludes certain essentially Romantic views of myths in fiction as the prerequisite of mythical fiction.

To use the term "prefiguration" instead of "myth" entails, it is true, a mere semantic substitution, itself solving none of the problems I shall outline later. But semantic substitutions can have a heuristic value at times; they can clear away some of the misconceptions and prejudices contaminating the traditional vocabulary of the subject. And when the central word has the almost magical associations that "myth" bears, such liberation can be a useful step towards looking at the topic from a new perspective.

Historical Background

If mythology appeared in the novel in earlier times, it was not generally presented in an organized motif-pattern. There are, for instance, Virgilian overtones to Fielding's *Amelia*, but they do not pattern our reading of the novel any more than do the classical epithets of the heroic epic. It seems quite clear from surveys such as Douglas Bush's *Mythology and the Romantic Tradition in English Poetry* and Henri Peyre's *L'Influence des Littératures antiques sur la Littérature française moderne* that Romantic Hellenism in England and France found its home mainly in poetry rather than in the novel. In Germany, on the other hand, as Strich's *Die Mythologie in der deutschen Dichtung* reveals, there was both an interest in old mythologies and in the creation of a new mythology,[25] and these preoccupations did leave some mark on fiction.[26] But the German Romantics

[25] An outline of the Romantic idea of the "new mythology" can be found in the first chapter of Kenneth Negus's *E.T.A. Hoffmann's "Other World": The Romantic Author and his "New Mythology,"* Philadelphia, 1965.

[26] Hölderlin's *Hyperion*, Novalis' *Heinrich von Ofterdingen* and much of E.T.A. Hoffmann's work include mythological material.

14

tended to identify mythology with the notion of a successful poetic cosmogony and generally thought of this as the
goal of all great literature.[27] Even if traditional mythologies
were used with this end in mind, such a general interpretation of literature as the sister of mythology is not conducive,
in novel writing, to the production of strictly organized
mythological motifs. As a rule, motifs are limited to one or
two myths, whereas such a view is essentially polytheistic.
In creating his mythological motif, the twentieth-century
novelist usually borrows a single myth, or at least draws
upon a limited body of mythological material, and offers
this as comment on part of the modern plot. His aim is most
frequently to *use* myths, not to create a whole mythology,
be it new or old. In contrast, the quasi-religious Romantic
quest for all-embracing mythologies would require a whole
mythological pantheon to do justice to its aspirations. Admittedly, a number of vaguely mythical figures may still be
emphasized in relative isolation in some Romantic works.
The Titanic gods are often espoused by the Romantics
(even, for example, in the mythological Gothic of Mrs. Shelley's *Frankenstein or The Modern Prometheus*), but such
figures are largely left as unexploited, heroic embodiments
of a vague spirit of vitalism. In Hölderlin's *Hyperion*, the
eponymous hero, the one figure who might have introduced
a detailed prefiguration to modern events, is not treated in
such a way. In short, detailed prefigurations are rare in the
novel before the twentieth century.

[27] In his "Rede über die Mythologie," Friedrich Schlegel, the leading
theoretician of German Romanticism, defines mythology as a hieroglyphic expression of nature around us, transformed by the imagination and love: "ein hieroglyphischer Ausdruck der umgebenden Natur
in [der] Verklärung von Fantasie und Liebe" (*Charakteristen und
Kritiken 1 (1796-1801)*, Munich, Paderborn and Vienna, 1967, p. 318).
Modern literature, he suggests, should seek to attain this quality once
more. Similarly, Herder's "Vom Gebrauch der neuern Mythologie,"
Schelling's "Kunstphilosophie" and the theories of Creuzer, Görres and
Hülsen all equate mythology primarily with cosmogony.

15

Besides a difference in attitudes to mythology, dividing a Romantic age, either feeling the lures of Hellenism or seeking cosmogonies of a personal kind, from a later epoch of increased psychological fragmentation and introspection (where the name of a myth becomes the label for a complex), one also finds another reason for the late arrival of the mythological motif in the novel. A poetological sense of the innate appropriateness of certain themes to specific genres decreed for a long time that the place of the gods, even gods who were no longer believed in, was in drama or poetry, but not in such an unheroic, bourgeois form as the novel. In this century, when the novel—not necessarily the low-mimetic form it was in the nineteenth century—has achieved a more poetic status and is no longer considered a poor relative of the other genres, symbolic gods may enter fiction freely without any taboos being broken. Granted, however, that in this age certain changes in attitude to the novel have made it easier for mythology to play a significant role in its imagery, one still has to consider why a modern writer should ever want to include such anachronisms in his work.

One of the basic assumptions underlying the following approach is that mythological motifs, together with other prefigurative devices, form a part of what is nowadays usually known as the rhetoric of fiction. They emerged at a point in the historical development of the novel when theorists of the genre observed (and some even prescribed) a constraint upon more direct forms of authorial comment and characterization. Yet despite this striking chronological link between the device's appearance and the observable change in narrative fashions, most critical accounts of mythological literature which have successfully avoided Romantic misconceptions concerning some inherent mythogenic power in such devices, take as their Archimedean Point the findings of psychoanalysis. Freud and Jung have

16

certainly given a great impetus to the subject. In Chase's words: "the psychoanalysts make the salutary suggestion that mythology is not primarily concerned with natural phenomena [as the Romantics assumed it to be] but with human nature,"[28] a point which the novelists themselves were soon embodying in their works. Depth-psychology marks a watershed in literature; it has been argued, for instance, that "l'interprétation du mythe d'Orphée est marquée par l'optimisme avant Freud, et par le pessimisme ensuite."[29] Nevertheless, although much of our knowledge of mythological novels derives from current findings about myths themselves, it can also benefit from our changing theories of fiction. Such books as Wayne Booth's important study of *The Rhetoric of Fiction*, Herman Meyer's *The Poetics of Quotation in the European Novel*, and, more recently, Frank Kermode's account of patterns in *The Sense of an Ending*, and work on the novel by Malcolm Bradbury and David Lodge have played as decisive a role in influencing my approach to the function of mythology in the modern novel as the anthropological and psychological perspectives offered by Eliade, Freud, Jung, Kerényi and Lévi-Strauss. While previous work on the subject often stressed the impetus from depth-psychology during the first part of this century, it failed to consider other factors. Two questions have to be answered: why *mythology* should make such a striking appearance in much modern fiction, and why *the modern novel* should have recourse to mythology for much of its symbolism. Why mythology?—and why the novel?

Non-Aesthetic Theories

An underestimation of the rhetorical uses of mythology has led to an anachronistic image of many novels. This can be

[28] *Quest for Myth*, p. 94.
[29] Eva Kushner, *Le Mythe d'Orphée*, p. 24.

17

seen in the way the relationship between modern character and mythological analogy has been expressed. The modern character has sometimes been regarded as a *reincarnation* of the appropriate god, as *playing the role* of a mythological figure, or as engaging in an *imitation* of him. Yet such approaches beg a lot of questions. When told that the idea of imitation is the main structural principle underlying Mann's *Doktor Faustus*,[30] are we, for example, to assume that the hero Adrian Leverkühn is imitating Faust from the cradle— which would give him a new dimension of precociousness —and that his father is also part of the act? Furthermore, does such an interpretation imply that we can conclude with Leslie Miller that an early event like "the Leverkühn-Hetäre Esmeralda episode in *Doktor Faustus* . . . is an act of imitation on the part of Leverkühn,"[31] without wanting to modify this statement in any way? And do we assume likewise that everyone else in the novel also plays an appropriate role in conscious imitation of the well-known legend? If this were true, why should a group of fictional characters be made to behave in such a strange way?

Of course, it is deliberately perverse to pose the questions in this way, for two kinds of imitation are implied: the author's imitation of a traditional theme in a new work, and the conscious copying of some prefiguration by characters in the work (a secularized version of the *imitatio Christi*). The latter is described at some length in Mann's influential essay "Freud und die Zukunft":

Das antike Ich und sein Bewußtsein von sich war ein anderes als das unsere, weniger ausschließlich, weniger scharf umgrenzt. Es stand gleichsam nach hin-

---

[30] "die Idee der imitatio [ist] das bestimmende Gestaltprinzip des Romans" (Jürgen Plöger, *Das Hermesmotiv in der Dichtung Thomas Manns*, p. 232).

[31] "Myth and Morality: Reflections on Mann's *Doktor Faustus*," p. 206.

18

ten offen und nahm vom Gewesenen vieles mit auf, was
es gegenwärtig wiederholte, und was mit ihm "wieder
da" war. Der spanische Kulturphilosoph Ortega y Gasset drückt das so aus, daß der antike Mensch, ehe er
etwas tue, einen Schritt zurück trete, gleich dem
Torero, der zum Todesstoß aushole. Er suche in der
Vergangenheit ein Vorbild, in das er wie in eine
Taucherglocke schlüpfe, um sich so, zugleich geschützt
und entstellt, in das gegenwärtige Problem hineinzu-
stürzen. Darum sei sein Leben in gewisser Weise ein
Beleben, ein archaisierendes Verhalten.— Aber eben
dies Leben als Beleben, Wiederbeleben ist das Leben
im Mythus. Alexander ging in den Spuren des Miltiades,
und von Caesar waren seine antiken Biographen mit
Recht oder Unrecht überzeugt, er wolle den Alexander
nachahmen. Dies "Nachahmen" aber ist weit mehr, als
heut in dem Wort liegt; es ist die mythische Identifika-
tion, die der Antike besonders vertraut war, aber weit
in die neue Zeit hineinspielt *und seelisch jederzeit
möglich bleibt*. Das antike Gepräge der Gestalt Napo-
leons ist oft betont worden. Er bedauerte, daß die moderne Bewußtseinslage ihm nicht gestattete, sich für den
Sohn Jupiter-Amons auszugeben, wie Alexander. Aber
daß er sich, zur Zeit seines orientalischen Unterneh-
mens, wenigstens mit Alexander mythisch verwechselt
hat, braucht man nicht zu bezweifeln, und später, als er
sich fürs Abendland entschieden hatte, erklärte er:"Ich
bin Karl der Grosse." Wohl gemerkt—nicht etwa: "Ich
erinnere an ihn"; nicht:"Meine Stellung ist der seinen
ähnlich." Auch nicht: "Ich bin wie er"; sondern ein-
fach:"Ich *bin's*." Das ist die Formel des Mythus.

Das Leben, jedenfalls das bedeutende Leben, war
also in antiken Zeiten die Wiederherstellung des
Mythus in Fleisch und Blut; es bezog und berief sich
auf ihn; durch ihn erst, durch die Bezugnahme aufs
Vergangene wies er sich als echtes und bedeutendes
Leben aus. Der Mythus ist die Legitimation des
Lebens; erst durch ihn und in ihm findet es sein Selbst-
bewußtsein, seine Rechtfertigung und Weihe. Bis in
den Tod führte Kleopatra ihre aphroditische Charakter-
rolle weihevoll durch, — und kann man bedeutender,

19

kann man würdiger leben und sterben, als indem man
den Mythus zelebriert?[32]

This notion of imitation, which owes much to Freud, depends on the character's own self-awareness. As I shall
argue later, it seldom helps to account satisfactorily for a
mythological motif's full effect. And it is too often applied
metaphorically to novels where the protagonist is not consciously modeling his life on a forerunner's. At times, the
metaphor means little more than that the modern novelist

[32] *Adel des Geistes: Sechzehn Versuche zum Problem der Humani-
tät*, Stockholm, 1948, pp. 581f. H. T. Lowe-Porter's translation of this
passage reads: "The ego of antiquity and its consciousness of itself
were different from our own, less exclusive, less sharply defined. It
was, as it were, open behind; it received much from the past and by
repeating it gave it presentness again. The Spanish scholar Ortega y
Gasset puts it that the man of antiquity, before he did anything, took a
step backwards, like the bullfighter who leaps back to deliver the
mortal thrust. He searched the past for a pattern into which he might
slip as into a diving-bell, and being thus at once disguised and protected might rush upon his present problem. Thus his life was in a
sense a reanimation, an archaizing attitude. But it is just this life as
reanimation that is the life as myth. Alexander walked in the footsteps
of Miltiades; the ancient biographers of Caesar were convinced, rightly
or wrongly, that he took Alexander as his prototype. But such "imitation" means far more than we mean by the word today. It was a
mythical identification, peculiarly familiar to antiquity; but it is operative far into modern times, *and at all times is psychically possible.*
How often have we not been told that the figure of Napoleon was
cast in the antique mold! He regretted that the mentality of the time
forbade him to give himself out for the son of Jupiter Ammon, in
imitation of Alexander. But we need not doubt that—at least at the
period of his Eastern exploits—he mythically confounded himself with
Alexander; while after he turned his face westwards he is said to
have declared: "I am Charlemagne." Note that: not "I am like
Charlemagne" or "My situation is like Charlemagne's," but quite
simply: "I am he." That is the formulation of the myth. Life, then—at
any rate, significant life—was in ancient times the reconstitution of
the myth in flesh and blood; it referred to and appealed to the myth;
only through it, through reference to the past, could it approve itself
as genuine and significant. The myth is the legitimization of life; only
through and in it does life find self-awareness, sanction, consecration.
Cleopatra fulfilled her Aphrodite character even unto death—and
can one live and die more significantly or worthily than in the celebration of the myth?" ("Freud and the Future," *Essays of Three
Decades*, New York, 1968, pp. 424f.; my italics).

20

has based his plot on—and hence is in that sense imitating —a well-known theme.

Metaphors of imitation and reincarnation misrepresent the relationship between myths and modernity, confusing half-truths with fuller statements about the function of pre-figurative motifs. The main criticism of them is not that they are metaphors—metaphors can be very helpful for critical illumination—but that critics who use them tend to forget that they retain the essentially distorting quality of all meta-phorical utterances. Such images frequently preclude the fundamental consideration of why the aesthetic device in question is used at all. On the other hand, the alternative image of a mythological figure as a prefiguration, in the secularized sense, does not so readily discourage the neces-sary further examination of aesthetic function, since pre-figurations (in any sense) are a kind of message.

Metaphorical descriptions have a tendency—especially because of the type of metaphor used—to overstress the role of the novel's mythological "prototype,"[33] implying that the events narrated in the modern context are only compre-hensible as a version of the myth. The contention that a character is imitating a myth, or lives under the aegis of a mythological deity, makes the myth sound far more impor-tant for the novel than it usually is; the myth is simply being used in most cases to offer some kind of looser analogy. (The assumption underlying the metaphorical approach appears to be that there is only one myth per novel, which is not always the case.) In most mythological novels, the myths do not offer a scaffold upon which the modern story has been erected. Nor can one usually read the modern

[33] This term, used by Richard Ellmann in *James Joyce* (London, 1966, p. 200), has the advantage of suggesting that the myth and the work are separate entities; but the idea of a prototype puts too much stress on the myth as source. A product is usually more derivative of its prototype than the novel of its prefiguration.

21

story as a straightforward attempt at revitalizing an old myth by putting it into a modern setting. These suggestions make the novels apparently depend too deterministically on myths. They derive largely from a jejune school of comparative literature which was content to analyze works in terms of their sources. In fact, within the system of hierarchical structures implanted in such a novel, the myth is not the major component.[34]

To set the later discussion in perspective, I should like to suggest three main reasons why we find so many interpreters of modern mythological novels attributing a pre-eminent position to the mythological component.

One factor, considered in greater detail in the next chapter, is a shifting terminology which leads to a confusion of mythological elements and real myths at the purely taxonomic level. When using words which have such imprecise areas of meaning as "myth" and its cognates undoubtedly possess, the critic often becomes the unwitting victim of his own vocabulary: general and specific senses of the word can easily be elided.

A second reason, an inheritance from both Renaissance and Romantic Hellenism, is the idea that mythology, with its associations as a primitive cultic form of literature and expression, must be more significant than other elements, even when appearing in an apparently ancillary position in modern works of fiction. There is the corollary supposition, also resting on the assumption that myths are *per se* of the greatest importance: that if myth and modernity are counterpointed in fiction, the myth is bound to be set up as the norm against which our age should measure itself. For

[34] In the original religious context of prefiguration, the earlier event was subordinate to the latter, since it merely prophesied the greater thing to come. This sense of subordination—making the earlier less important than the later phenomenon, be it work of literature or coming of a Messiah—can be transferred to the secularized connotation of prefiguration.

22

example, Alexander Fischler talks of a "general myth revival" in literature which he takes to be "prompted by the
continuing search for new values founded on the old."[35]
This view, with its stress on myths as the vessels of pristine
values, seems especially suspect, since Fischler takes the
myth of Narcissus in all its ambiguity to make the point.

In many cases, this sense of value attributed to old myths
leads to the abandonment of one of the cardinal principles
of literary criticism: that context is more important than
source. As a result, a twentieth-century novel (say, Robbe-
Grillet's *Les Gommes*), set in contemporary society but
with a mythological motif running through it, can become
so distorted that the modern tale is interpreted allegorically
as a veiled myth. It would be misleading to contend that
such modern novelists as Broch, Butor, Moravia, Robbe-
Grillet and Updike are indulging in the whimsical practice
of putting classical myths into modern garb or even "returning" to myth as if to some avatar. In this sense, the back-to-
myth movement was largely curtailed after 1945. It makes
more sense and enriches our experience of these writers to
appreciate how many modern novels are inviting their
readers to *interpret* new experiences in the light of traditional sources of archetypal patterns. Rather than offer his
reader new myths or revitalized old ones, the mythological
novelist presents a modern situation and refers the reader
to a familiar analogy.

A third reason for the distorted image of mythological fiction is a procrustean desire to establish a simple identity between modern novel and myth because of the importance
attached at the present time to imagery, which is after all
the leading source of motifs. "What we often do in practice
is to exaggerate the symbolic relevance" of any pattern of
images we locate, Barbara Hardy argues. By applying our
"Jamesian standards of cross-reference and total rele-

[35] "Recent Visitors to the Fountain of Narcissus," p. 149.

23

vance"[36] to the modern psychological novel—standards which, according to her, make us over-emphasize image-patterns, we are prone to schematize and hence overrate the mythological component. As a result of this tendency, which Malcolm Bradbury sees as an attempt to transfer the New Critics' techniques from poetry criticism to that of fiction,[37] occasional parallels and scattered allusions to specific myths are forced into an exaggerated system offered to the reader as the key to the whole work rather than just a limited set of analogical comments on the plot or on a given character. Thus contrived, the pattern is elaborated to suggest a novel modeled totally on an old myth or even identical with it.

Myths in Drama and Myths in Fiction

I have already talked of myths being put into modern garb. It is an idea that sometimes occurs in discussions of mythology as an alienating device.[38] In fact, the notion of "putting into modern garb" suggests theatre; and "imitation" and "playing the role" of a god, the two metaphors most recurrently used to describe mythological fiction, are also borrowed from the stage. Criticism of mythological novels and the manner in which they function has quite often suffered from certain ideas being transferred, with insufficient modification, from our experience of mythology in drama. A comparison between the role of myths in the two genres soon shows, however, that modern fiction and modern drama are two very different contexts and that the mythological element in each of them has its own idiosyncrasies.

[36] *The Appropriate Form: An Essay on the Novel*, London, 1964, p. 13.

[37] "Towards a Poetics of Fiction: 1. An Approach through Structure," *Novel*, I, Fall 1967, pp. 45f.

[38] Hans Erich Nossack, for example, talks of myths in modern literature being used "als Kostüm für heutige Probleme" (*Die schwache Position der Literatur: Reden und Aufsätze*, Frankfurt a.M., 1966, p. 75).

24

Modern novels tend not to narrate myths straightforwardly in their traditional settings. Certainly, there are
exceptions to this generalization: Thomas Mann's *Joseph
und seine Brüder* and *Die vertauschten Köpfe,* Jean Giono's
Naissance de l'Odyssée and J. C. Powys's epics, for instance.
And contemporary readers might also cite such works as
Mary Renault's Greek novels and Michael Ayrton's recent
interpretations of the Daedalus myth in *The Testament of
Daedalus* and *The Maze-maker.* However, most people
could probably count on their fingers the works of this kind
they know. In contrast, it would take more than these digits
to enumerate even the names alone of the principal modern
playwrights who have dramatized myths. Anouilh, Claudel,
Cocteau, D'Annunzio, Gide, Giraudoux, Hauptmann, Hof-
mannsthal, Kaiser, O'Neill, Sartre, Werfel and Wilder are
but the most prominent exponents of the technique.[39] This
pattern of distribution, revealing complete myths often in
drama but seldom in fiction, is reflected in the fact that
dramatic adaptations of myths have received more attention from critics than any other aspect of mythology in
literature.[40]

In fact, the nature of the two genres partly accounts for
the distribution of motifs in fiction and drama. A myth, as
the Greek implied, is little more really than the equivalent
of a simple plot, albeit a plot traditionally related to the action of gods or heroes. Its essential quality is that of a basic
configuration of actions. For this reason, the poet Howard
Nemerov defines myth as:

> an equation, or drama, repeated cyclically until it gath-
> ers around itself in the memory of man a residuum,

[39] Another list of (somewhat different) mythological dramatists
can be found on the first page of Hugh Dickinson's *Myth on the Stage.*
[40] Cf. the general works by Aler, Asenbaum, Dietrich, Dickinson,
Hamburger, Highet, Hunger, Jouan, Maulnier and Reichert listed in
the bibliography. There are also numerous more limited studies in this
area.

25

abstracted from its various diverse repetitions, which residuum or accretion is independent of time.[41]

This approximate identification of myth with drama and hence plot, calling to mind Aristotle's contention that plot is the essence of drama, explains why myth so often appears on the stage rather than emerging as a motif to a modern plot.[42] (Such plays as *Les Mouches, Mourning Becomes Electra, Pygmalion* and Brecht's version of *Edward II*, with its motif from the Trojan War, are exceptions to this general pattern.) The modern novel, on the other hand, adheres less rigidly to the skeletal structure of plot, though it still of course maintains a "story line" in most cases. It meanders, devoting its attention more to undramatic incidentals and to the depiction of multi-faceted characters and milieux, matters independent of the direct exigencies of the plot in most cases. And—a more obvious point—it is usually much longer than a play, both in narrative and narrated time; it assumes the proportions of biography rather than being limited to a single dramatic event or plot which could easily be compared with a traditional myth. In the light of the general distribution mentioned above, it is not surprising that there have been numerous studies of myths in drama and that these have exerted a strong influence on theories about the role of mythology in fiction.

The most comprehensive surveys of the presence of ancient myths in modern literature are to be found in the 1939 edition of the *Cahiers du Sud*, dedicated "aux mythes, et surtout à leur valeur d'inspiration littéraire";[43] in Luis Díez del Corral's monograph *La función del mito clásico en la literatura contemporánea*; in a collection of essays by

[41] *The Quester Hero*, p. 3.

[42] In "Myth in Modern French Literature" (pp. 78ff.), R. G. Stone points persuasively to the element of ritual as the link between myth and drama. Ritual and plot are undoubtedly closely connected in this respect.

[43] Etienne Fuzellier, "Les Mythes," *CdS*, XLX, 1939, p. 1.

26

Dutch scholars edited by Jan Aler under the title *De Mythe in de Literatuur*; in the Spring 1959 issue of *Daedalus*; and in the University of Otago lectures on *Myth and the Modern Imagination* edited by Margaret Dalziel. With the exception of this last study, such contributions make no more than passing reference to the place of traditional mythologies in the modern novel. Admittedly, Díez del Corral's introductory chapter mentions Thomas Mann and James Joyce briefly, but the book then goes on to concentrate on poetry and drama, dealing at some length with the Symbolists, with Rilke, Eliot, Nietzsche, Anouilh and the Existentialists, a representative sample of the writers usually treated by works on this general subject. Classicists' surveys of mythology's place in literature are remarkably reticent about modern fiction: Grant's *Myths of the Greeks and Romans*, Highet's *The Classical Tradition* and Hunger's *Lexikon der griechischen und römischen Mythologie*, all, despite their stated aim of considering mythology's influence on later literatures, mention very few novels. Yet certain ways of handling mythological material are peculiar to recent fiction. Hence, any study which, either because of its date of publication or its chosen perspective, concentrates too much on drama or on novels written before 1945, inevitably gives a distorted and limited image of the subject.

Towards a Methodology: Practical Considerations

In his distinction between the adaptation of specific myths and the literary embodiment of archetypal patterns, Theodore Ziolkowski points out that archetypal patterns differ from other prefigurative motifs "inasmuch as they are not necessarily associated with a specific name or figure or concatenation of events."[44] For, more than any structural similarity between a modern plot and a classical myth, this act of naming or alluding unmistakably to a given myth is the

[44] *The Novels of Hermann Hesse*, p. 119.

27

main feature of the mythological novel. It is this, above all else, which lifts it out of a vague archetypal similarity with many myths and puts it in the referential framework of a specific mythology. (It will be necessary later to look at many of the ways in which such direct references can be made to ensure that the reader notices the analogies offered to him.) Yet an even more important factor than this wide range of techniques at the novelist's disposal is the decisive effect of presenting the appropriate analogy at a certain, carefully chosen point in the action. Patterns of expectation and innuendo can become more relevant than the simple models of cognition so often put forward by critics beholding in every mythological motif an Ariadne's thread to guide the reader through a labyrinth of fragmented modern reality. The sequence of ideas is crucial, although it is a factor to which little consideration has been given hitherto. In *The Classical Temper*,[45] S. L. Goldberg shows convincingly that one must distinguish between major and marginal references to mythology in Joyce's *Ulysses* (in a way that certain industrious allusion-hunters had signally failed to do). We can see, for example—to apply the point elsewhere —that the title of Thomas Mann's *Doktor Faustus* is a fundamental reference to the novel's main prefiguration. In contrast, the fact that a pledge between nations, which in Mann's German is talked of as a "Faustpfand," is mentioned by the narrator in the twenty-sixth chapter (i.e. immediately after the pact scene) remains an allusion of a lesser order. But what makes them different kinds of allusion, too, is their position in the work, not simply the fact that one is a direct statement of prefigurative motif whereas the other is merely a play on words. To demonstrate how important the sequence of references can be, I shall offer an approach to mythological fiction which relates the information given by allusions to the point in the work at which it is offered.

[45] Especially pp. 145-150.

28

Then, in my final chapter, other patterns of motifs will be described; with these, sequence is of less importance, the effect being largely achieved by overlapping motifs.

It would be impracticable to undertake a comprehensive survey of the modern mythological novel, nor indeed would any such *catalogue raisonné* be a feasible or worthwhile undertaking while the more fundamental questions of how the mythological elements in novels can be unmistakably recognized, how they operate and in what context they occur, remain unanswered. A certain amount of compromise is involved in striking a balance between a structural analysis and a diachronic approach to the subject. But it is a necessary compromise; for to ignore such features as the quality of a mythological novel and its historical context would be to misrepresent the subject. However, if I have felt obliged to compromise with a bias in either direction, it has certainly been in favor of the formal analysis of specific structures and to the relative detriment of historical perspectives. This has been necessary because the scales have until now been weighted too restrictively on the side of historical accounts of the metamorphosis of a given myth or the development of a particular novelist's attitude to mythology. Since the use of prefigurative motifs is to be found in all kinds of modern fiction, both good and bad, Modernist and post-war, my examples are intended to counteract the usual impression that only a small number of novelists, including Broch, Joyce, Mann and certain *nouveaux romanciers*, used the device. I have therefore examined both works by novelists who are not internationally well-known, amongst them John Bowen, Macdonald Harris and Hans Erich Nossack, as well as the more familiar exponents, and have even included novels which have proved rather infelicitous in their handling of the device. (I would put Guido Bachmann's *Gilgamesch* and Heinrich Mann's *Die Göttinnen* in the rogues' gallery.) Al-

29

though trying not to tread over-familiar paths by avoiding too many subsequent illustrations from Joyce's *Ulysses* or Thomas Mann's mythological fiction, I have at times felt compelled to fall back on such classics to make some point. In general, the selection is intended to be representative of the wide range of modern prefigurative novels in various literatures. For mythological novels do not occur in isolation in any one literature, despite the well-documented "tyranny of Greece over Germany" or the classical heritage of certain Mediterranean countries. Almost all modern literatures show an interest in mythology in the novel (although, as I have already indicated, not necessarily to the same extent). Joyce could write to his brother Stanislaus from Paris in 1920:

> *Odyssey* very much in the air here. Anatole France is writing *Le Cyclope*, G. Fauré, the musician, an opera *Pénélope*, Giraudoux has written *Elpénor* . . . Guillaume Apollinaire *Les Mamelles de Tirésias*. . . . Madame Circe advances regally toward her completion.[46]

In fact, mythology is still very much "in the air," though not specifically in the Parisian air. For this reason, I have included novels from American, English, French, German, Italian and Russian literature in order to give the topic a wider treatment than it has hitherto received.

Certainly, a study of mythology in the modern novel, no matter how confined its scope, cannot avoid considering James Joyce's *Ulysses*, the archetypal mythological novel, as it was once rightly called.[47] Above all, Joyce's *Ulysses* affords the practical advantage of being the most generally known mythological work. It also illustrates, as Goldberg has shown, a large number of devices connected with the technique of prefiguration and has been analyzed as a novel

[46] Quoted by Ellmann, *op.cit.*, p. 504.
[47] "Der Urtyp des mythischen Romans in unserer Zeit" (Gunilla Bergsten, *Thomas Manns "Doktor Faustus*," p. 195).

30

containing mythology more often than any other novel of this kind. Admittedly, a certain methodological danger nevertheless arises here, as I shall need to show later; for at times one may be tempted to transfer certain formal principles observed in Joyce's novel to the interpretation of other works on the mistaken assumption that they operate in the same way. But, this problem aside, studies of Joyce's work by such astute critics as Hugh Kenner and S. L. Goldberg have done much to increase our general understanding of the role of mythology specifically in modern novels. In contrast, French and German scholarship in this field has been variously influenced by Thomas Mann's thoughts on mythical imitation, by the ghost of neo-classicism and by the Jungian notion of a collective unconscious (if not by even more sinister ideas concerning mythology that arose in Fascist Europe during this century). Theorists are inclined to concentrate too much on myth *per se* and not enough on its role in fiction. But in general, English criticism has not been hampered by any large corpus of statements of intention (such as French and German novelists have enjoyed providing)[48] and has viewed many theories concerning mythology with a sceptical mind. And this freedom from abstract pronouncements seems to have been an asset.

[48] Apart from his remarks in "Freud und die Zukunft," Mann refers frequently to mythology in his lecture on *Joseph und seine Brüder*, in his correspondence with Karl Kerényi and in *Die Entstehung des "Doktor Faustus." Roman eines Romans*, Frankfurt a.M., 1949. As Helen Watson-Williams has shown (*André Gide and the Greek Myth*, pp. 84ff.), Gide's "Considérations sur la Mythologie grècque: Fragments du *Traité des Dioscures*" are of great importance for an appreciation of much of his work. In *Dichten und Erkennen*, Hermann Broch has three essays on the subject of myth and literature: "James Joyce und die Gegenwart," "Die mythische Erbschaft der Dichtung" and "The Style of the Mythical Age." In *Repertoire 2*, Paris, 1963, Michel Butor refers to the subject in a much-cited essay entitled "Le Roman et la Poésie."

31

mythopoesis, or poetic making; whether or not all poets make myths—some critics (such as R. Chase) regard "m." and "poetry" as largely synonymous—m. provides an essential matrix of all, or at least much, poetry. Focusing upon this mythical matrix, one may say that "literature is only a part, though a central part, of the total mythopoeic structure of concern which extends into religion, philosophy, political theory, and many aspects of history, the vision a society has of its situation, destiny, and ideals, and of reality in terms of those human factors" (N. Frye, 1967). Such a reflection takes one less far from poetry than might appear, since some of the basic elements that poetry derives from m. are recognizable in mathematics and the physical sciences (S. Buchanan, E. Schrödinger). The very development of philosophy required discrimination of *mythos* from *logos*, or thinking about m. But it is only recently that thinking about the mythical matrix of literature, and about mythical elements in it, assumed the form that has been called m. criticism. Such criticism expresses concerns felt strongly in the second half of the 20th c., but groundwork for it was laid by many writers earlier, including G. Vico, various of the German romantics, Friedrich Nietzsche, E. B. Tylor, J. G. Frazer, Sigmund Freud, and C. G. Jung. Indeed, since "m." embraces ancient and persistent human concerns, observations about its relation to literature are to be found among numerous earlier literary critics, for example, Samuel Johnson, who has much to say about the aesthetic value of myths incorporated in poetry. It may be useful to regard 20th-c. m. criticism as the outcome of a succession of overlapping cultural moments, which help to define its central concerns; a few names may roughly suggest this development. Richard Wagner saw himself, as an artist, faced by opposing claims of m. and history and consciously chose those of m.; and Friedrich Nietzsche's writings directly reflected kinds of experience that give rise to m. and prophesy, though Nietzsche's Zarathustra declared that God was dead. Writers exploring the possibilities of symbolism (q.v.) created hermetic personal poetry, which, according to some critics (including T. S. Eliot) drew upon the "primitive psyche" expressed in the collective m. of earlier times. Despite Frazer's positivistic assumptions, his massive *Golden Bough* betrayed a fascination with mythical, magical, and religious materials, which it served to retrieve from the cultural trash heap for writers reacting against positivism. James Joyce, T. S. Eliot, D. H. Lawrence, Thomas Mann, and W. B. Yeats used m. in ways that demanded explication. And the new criticism (q.v.), in demonstrating not only the strengths but also

MYTH CRITICISM. Much poetry is mythical in the sense of being about supernatural characters and events or of drawing upon them as a frame of reference. And even when poetry is not overtly mythical—when it is, say, concerned with merely human characters in a world without gods—it often has covert connections with myth (q.v.), as when 20th-c. poets describe the destruction of the world, which is an ancient and widespread mythologem or archetype (q.v.). Myth makers are poets, and m. comes into being through

-[955]-

the limits of a largely formalist approach to literature, led, as one reaction, to an emphasis upon m. in literary criticism. As a result of tendencies suggested by these names, a number of critics came to feel that literature "cannot be limited to the working out of a pattern within the framework imposed by an art form, but rather must be viewed as part of the totality of human experience. Thus the simple separation of form and content, intrinsic and extrinsic values, or the like, falls away even for the purposes of analysis—indeed, especially for such purposes. From this central assumption it is but one further step to assert that literature is part of a social situation and that literary works must be approached primarily as modes of collective belief and action. Myth and ritual, then, become essential qualities of literary expression" (H. M. Block in Vickery). And since m. and ritual also reflect the workings of the human mind, m. criticism overlaps the criticism of psychology and poetry.*

As the name of Nietzsche will suggest, much m. criticism has been directly or indirectly concerned with the origin and nature of drama. The influence of the Cambridge Anthropologists on literary criticism, heralded by G. Murray's essay on Hamlet and Orestes (1914), has been pervasive. Concern with elements of m. and ritual has led F. Fergusson, in an effective study, to see *Hamlet* as a celebration of the mystery of human life achieved through ceremonious invocations of the well-being of society, these invocations being themselves the means of securing that well-being. Though *Hamlet* is in important ways modern and skeptical, "even the most cutting ironies of Hamlet do not disavow the mystery which the rituals celebrate, or reject the purposes that inform them" (Fergusson). J.I.M. Stewart has seen Falstaff as a ritual scapegoat, and J. Holloway finds the scapegoat essential to Shakespeare's tragedies. More generally, H. Weisinger has traced the conception of tragedy back to its roots in m. and ritual in the ancient Near East. C. L. Barber has analyzed ways in which Shakespearean comedy achieves "clarification" related to that brought about by folk festivals. The early studies of C. Still (1921) and G. W. Knight (1929) initiated a continuing concern with mythical elements in Shakespeare's last plays. And various critics have studied such elements in Henrik Ibsen and more recent drama (O. Holton, K. Burkman).

Though m. criticism has been largely concerned with narrative, and especially dramatic, content rather than with details of poetic form and technique, several works of nondramatic poetry have been seen as embodying mythical motifs. Critics of *Sir Gawain and the Green Knight*, for example, have arrived at differing views of such motifs in the poem (H. Zimmer, J. Speirs, and C. Moorman). In discussing the visionary landscape of medieval allegory, P. Piehler attempts to define allegory and its relations to m. Milton's *Lycidas* has been seen as conforming to a cycle of death and rebirth, expressed in vegetation sacred to fertility gods, and in a descent into water and reemergence from it, paralleling the setting and rising of the sun (R. P. Adams in Vickery). Keats's *Endymion* has also been seen as conforming to a cyclical m., consisting of the Call to the Quest, Acceptance and Descent into the Underworld, Fulfillment of the Quest, and Return, apotheosized by a sacred marriage (R. Harrison in Vickery). Indeed, the m.-making propensities of the romantic poets—their m.-like constructions derived not so much from inherited collective belief as from the impulse to individual symbol formation (Jung)—have received much attention (Frye, 1947, H. Bloom). And indeed, Frye has pointed to Blake as one of the main inspirations behind his own critical labors.

The interests and ideas guiding the works of exegesis reviewed till now have also found expression in the critical system elaborated by Frye, principally in his *Anatomy of Crit.* This work provides an all-embracing view of literature, with special attention to modes and genres, to thematic and mythical recurrence in literature, and to the ways in which literature, like m., ultimately rests on preconscious ritual. After a "Polemical Introduction," Frye's *Anatomy* goes on to "Historical Criticism: Theory of Modes," an essay which sees the literary past as consisting of two cycles of five periods each, with each of these periods corresponding to a "mode," defined as a measure of the strength of the hero (for example, of Achilles or of Leopold Bloom) in relation to the world of the fiction in which he occurs, this fictional world, in turn, reflecting the world of the audience for which the work was written. The second essay, "Ethical Crit.: Theory of Symbols," discusses five phases of symbolism—literal, descriptive, formal, archetypal, and anagogical—paralleling the five modes of the first essay. The third essay, "Archetypal Crit.: Theory of Myths," is concerned with the ways in which myths and archetypal conventions undergo historical transformation, these elements often serving as structural principles, which may affect the audience without its awareness. The transformations of these elements parallel those of the hero and the symbol, discussed in the first essays. The fourth essay, "Rhetorical Criticism: Theory of Genres," is concerned with genre as something based on its own characteristic rhythm, which may be seen in

-[956]-

the overall, continuous flow of the epic or in minute prosodic effects. All of the elements and processes described in the *Anatomy* arise from "displacements" of m., through which m. is modified by culture so as to be logical, plausible, acceptable in accordance with prevailing stylistic and other norms. But m. remains effective even in these "displacements," since "the structural principles of literature are as closely related to mythology and comparative literature as those of painting are to geometry."

The immense appeal of Frye's critical viewpoint lies, first, in its heuristic aspect—in the way in which it invites the reader to see parallels and interconnections among forms and devices and specific literary works usually regarded as discrete, and second, in its insistence on the derivation of literature from m., not simply as "poetry" but as a fundamental way of apprehending the world. Its appeal was so great that in 1966 M. Krieger could claim that "in what approaches a decade since the publication of his masterwork, he has had an influence—indeed an absolute hold—on a generation of developing literary critics greater and more exclusive than that of any one theorist in recent critical history." Frye's work has been criticized—for being overly schematic, for neglecting style, for remaining too far from a close reading of texts, for using common literary terms in idiosyncratic ways, for surreptitiously gaining vital rhetorical effects through such emotionally colored terms as "archetype" where such plain words as "model" would do as well—and some of the criticisms of Frye shade off into criticisms that have been raised against 20th-c. m. criticism in general. One of these is that m. critics find m. a flight from the reality of history, this flight expressing certain social and political attitudes (P. Rahv). Another is that current interest in m. grants pleasant glimpses of transcendence without the bother of religious commitment and of the threat to intellectual integrity that such commitment might entail. Another is that m. criticism tends to remain on the level of coarse structure, comparing works on the basis of broad similarities, without adequately accounting for specific poetic effects. And still another is that the basic concepts and issues of m. criticism have not been adequately formulated (Weisinger in H. Murray). In general, "m. criticism" names an area of interest, rather than a specific method or viewpoint; indeed, modern criticism attributes a wide range of meanings to "m."—R. Wellek and A. Warren distinguish several—and m. critics are most often heavily indebted to one or more anthropologists, cultural historians, and philosophers for their notably various approaches. Moreover, theoretical m. critics (e.g.,

N. Frye, R. Graves, and J. Campbell) frequently aspire to a global view—for example through the assumption of a universal Monomyth or Ur-m. that brings all m. and literature into a unity. M. criticism was especially prominent in a period which may be roughly fixed between the dates of Frye's *Anatomy*, 1957, and of an excellent anthology by Vickery, 1966, which includes essays most of which were written within twenty years of that date. But the mythical matrix of poetry is sufficiently well established and sufficiently important that valuable work in this area will surely continue to be done. This sanguine view is supported by such studies as that of J. Armstrong, who regards the tree and the snake in Sumerian and Greek mythology as a single form expressing a basic imaginative polarity, and with critical sensitivity traces this form in Botticelli's *Primavera*, in three plays of Shakespeare, in Milton's *Paradise Lost*, and in Coleridge's *The Ancient Mariner* and *Kubla Khan*. As Armstrong asserts, "Myths are the most accurate means that the human mind has devised of representing its own immeasurably complex structure and content. They are essentially poetic formations, and express areas of thought and feeling where, as Blake puts it, 'ideas can only be given in their minutely appropriate words.'"

J. L. Weston, *From Ritual to Romance* (1920); C. Still, *Shakespeare's Mystery Play* (1921), *The Timeless Theme* (1936); G. Murray, *The Classical Tradition in Poetry* (1927); S. Buchanan, *Poetry and Mathematics* (1929); G. W. Knight, *M. and Miracle* (1929); N. Frye, *Fearful Symmetry* (1947), *Anatomy of Crit.* (1957), "Lit. and M." [bibliog.], in *Relations of Lit. Study*, ed. J. Thorpe (1967); R. Graves, *The White Goddess* (1948); H. Zimmer, *The King and the Corpse* (1948); J.I.M. Stewart, *Character and Motive in Shakespeare* (1949); R. Chase, *Quest for M.* (1949); F. Fergusson, *The Idea of a Theater* (1953); H. Weisinger, *Tragedy and the Paradox of the Fortunate Fall* (1953); E. Schrödinger, *Nature and the Greeks* (1954); Wellek and Warren; H. Bloom, *Shelley's Mythmaking* (1957); J. Speirs, *Medieval Eng. Poetry* (1957); C. L. Barber, *Festive Comedy in Shakespeare* (1959); C. Moorman, *Arthurian Triptych* (1960); *M. and Mythmaking*, ed. H. A. Murray (1960); J. Holloway, *The Story of the Night* (1961); *M. and Symbol*, ed. B. Slote (1963); G. Durand, *Les Structures anthropologiques de l'imaginaire* (1963); G. Bachelard, *The Poetics of Space*, tr. M. Jolas (1964), *The Psychoanalysis of Fire*, tr. A. Ross (1964); P. Rahv, *The M. and the Powerhouse* (1965); G. Hartman, "Structuralism: The Anglo American Adventure," YFS, 36–37 (1966) and *Beyond Formalism*

(1970); *M. and Lit.*, ed. J. B. Vickery (1966); *Northrop Frye in Modern Crit.*, ed. M. Krieger (1966); D. Hoffman, *Barbarous Knowledge* (1967); J. Armstrong, *The Paradise M.* (1969); W. Willeford, *The Fool and His Scepter* (1969); O. Holton, *Mythic Patterns in Ibsen's Last Plays* (1970); H. Slochower, *Mythopoesis* (1970); K. Burkman, *The Dramatic World of Harold Pinter* (1971); P. Piehler, *The Visionary Landscape* (1971); W. A. Strauss, *Descent and Return* (1971); L. Feder, *Ancient Myth in Modern Poetry* (1972).   w.w.

ACKNOWLEDGMENTS

Block, Haskell M. "Cultural Anthropology and Contemporary Literary Criticism." *Journal of Aesthetics and Art Criticism* 11 (September 1952): 46–54. Reprinted with the permission of the *Journal of Aesthetics and Art Criticism*.

Burke, Kenneth. "Myth, Poetry and Philosophy." *Journal of American Folklore* 73 (October-December 1960): 283–306. Reproduced with the permission of the American Folklore Society. Not for further reproduction.

Campbell, Joseph. "The Hero and the God." In Joseph Campbell, *The Hero with a Thousand Faces,* 2nd ed. (Princeton: Princeton University Press, 1968): 30–40. Reprinted with the permission of Princeton University Press.

Chase, Richard. "Myth as Literature." In *English Institute Essays 1947* (New York: Columbia University Press, 1948): 3–22. Reprinted with permission of the publisher. Copyright 1948 by Columbia University Press.

Douglas, Wallace W. "The Meanings of 'Myth' in Modern Criticism." *Modern Philology* 50 (May 1953): 232–42. Reprinted with the permission of the University of Chicago Press. Copyright 1953 University of Chicago.

Feder, Lillian. "Myth, Poetry, and Critical Theory." In Joseph P. Strelka, ed., *Yearbook of Comparative Criticism, Volume IX: Literary Criticism and Myth* (University Park: Pennsylvania State University Press, 1980): 51–71. Copyright 1980 by the Pennsylvania State University Press. Reproduced by permission of the publisher.

Frye, Northrop. "The Archetypes of Literature." *Kenyon Review* 13 (Winter 1951): 92–110. Reprinted with the permission of the *Kenyon Review*. Copyright by Kenyon College and Northrop Frye.

Frye, Northrop. "Myth, Fiction, and Displacement." *Daedalus* 90 (Summer 1961): 587–605. Reprinted by permission of *Daedalus*, Journal of the American Academy of Arts and Sciences.

Furst, Lilian R. "Mythology into Psychology: *Deux ex Machina* into God Within." *Comparative Literature Studies* 21 (Spring 1984): 1–15. Reprinted with the permission of the Pennsylvania State University Press.

Girard, René. "The Plague in Literature and Myth." *Texas Studies in Literature and Language* 15 (Special Classic Issue 1974): 833–50. Reprinted with the permission of University of Texas Press.

Herd, E.W. "Myth Criticism: Limitations and Possibilities." *Mosaic: A Journal of the Interdisciplinary Study of Literature* 2 (Spring 1969): 69–77. Reprinted with the permission of *Mosaic*, Vol. 2, No. 3: Bible, Myth and Literature. Spring 1969 Special issue, ed. by Kenneth McRobbie and R.P. Hoople.

Highet, Gilbert. "The Reinterpretation of the Myths." *Virginia Quarterly Review* 25 (Winter 1949): 99–115. Reprinted with the permission of the *Virginia Quarterly Review*.

Johnsen, William A. "Myth, Ritual, and Literature after Girard." In Joseph Natoli, ed., *Literary Theory's Future(s)* (Urbana: University of Illinois Press, 1989): 116–48. Copyright 1989 by the Board of Trustees of the University of Illinois. Used with the permission of the University of Illinois and the author.

Loriggio, Francesco. "Myth, Mythology and the Novel: Towards a Reappraisal." *Canadian Review of Comparative Literature* 11 (December 1984): 501–20. Reprinted with the permission of the Canadian Comparative Literature Association.

Rahv, Philip. "The Myth and the Powerhouse." *Partisan Review* 20 (November–December 1953): 635–48. Reprinted with the permission of Partisan Review, Inc.

Schorer, Mark. "Mythology (For the Study of William Blake)." *Kenyon Review* 4 (Autumn 1942): 366–80. Reprinted with the permission of the *Kenyon Review*. Copyright by Kenyon College.

Vickery, John B. "Literature and Myth." In Jean-Pierre Barricelli and Joseph Gibaldi, eds., *Interrelations of Literature* (New York: Modern Language Association, 1982): 67–89. Reprinted with the permission of the Modern Language Association of America.

Waswo, Richard. "The History that Literature Makes." *New Literary History* 19 (Spring 1988): 541–64. Reprinted with the permission of Johns Hopkins University Press.

Wheelwright, Philip. "Myth." In Alex Preminger, ed., *Princeton Encyclopedia of Poetry and Poetics* (Princeton: Princeton University Press, 1965): 538–41. Reprinted with the permission of Princeton University Press.

White, John J. "Myth and the Modern Novel." In John J. White, *Mythology in the Modern Novel* (Princeton: Princeton University Press, 1971): 3–31. Reprinted with the permission of Princeton University Press.

Willeford, William. "Myth Criticism." In Alex Preminger, ed., *Princeton Encyclopedia of Poetry and Poetics,* enlarged ed. (Princeton: Princeton University Press, 1974): 955–58. Reprinted with the permission of Princeton University Press.